PENTAGON PRESS

COMMITTED TO SERVE THE ARMED FORCES

WEST ASIA
IN TRANSITION

Volume II

WEST ASIA
IN TRANSITION

Volume II

Editor

Sanjay Singh

INSTITUTE FOR DEFENCE STUDIES & ANALYSES
NEW DELHI

PENTAGON PRESS

West Asia in Transition
Sanjay Singh (Ed.)

First Published in 2018

ISBN 978-93-86618-17-7

Published by
PENTAGON PRESS
206, Peacock Lane, Shahpur Jat
New Delhi-110049
Phones: 011-64706243, 26491568
Telefax: 011-26490600
email: rajan@pentagonpress.in
website: www.pentagonpress.in

In association with
Institute for Defence Studies and Analyses
No. 1, Development Enclave,
New Delhi-110010
Phone: +91-11-26717983
Website: www.idsa.in

Printed at Avantika Printers Private Limited.

Contents

PART 3: YEMEN

PART 4: IRAN

PART 5: ISRAEL

PART 6: EGYPT

PART 7: SYRIA-IRAQ

DPG
DELHI POLICY GROUP

Preface

The 'Arab Spring' of 2011 brought in its wake widespread instability characterized by mass protests, civil wars, widening sectarian schisms, the rise of violent extremism and deep uncertainty about the future of West Asia. The region, with which India shares civilisation ties, has a special significance for India. It is a critical strategic and economic partner and hosts over 8 million Indians. Any instability in the region also impacts the global economy and geopolitics.

In order to understand the ongoing political, social and economic transformations underway in West Asia, the Delhi Policy Group (DPG) launched a project in 2015 to study emerging trends and provide inputs to support a proactive and comprehensive Indian engagement with West Asia.

The project was also designed to provide an opportunity to young Indian scholars to engage in an exchange of ideas and contribute to the national discourse through their academic research. One of the key objectives of this project is to create a network of young Indian scholars analysing different aspects of West Asia through research covering Saudi Arabia, Yemen, Iran, Egypt, Israel, Iraq and Syria.

The project has benefited greatly from the mentoring of Senior Diplomats and Academicians who have guided the young researchers and have also provided an introduction to each section of this volume.

The research papers authored by the contributors were subjected to peer review at a three day meeting organised by the DPG in conjunction with the IDSA on December 14-15-16, 2016. DPG acknowledges the valuable partnership extended by IDSA in bringing out this joint publication.

New Delhi
June 5, 2017

Ambassador Hemant Krishan Singh
Director General, DPG

Delhi Policy Group, Core 5-A, First Floor, India Habitat Centre, Lodhi Road, New Delhi—110 003 Tel: (011)48202100, Website: www.delhipolicygroup.org, E-mail: dgoffice@dpg.org.in

Abbreviations and Acronyms

ADNOC	Abu Dhabi National Oil Company (ADNOC)
AFLPA	Armed Forces Land Projects Agency
AIPAC	American Israel Public Affairs Committee
AKP	The Justice and Development Party
AQAP	Al-Qaeda in the Arabian Peninsula
AQM	Al-Qaeda in the Maghreb
AQY	Al-Qaeda in Yemen
ASEAN	Association of Southeast Asian Nations,
ATS	Anti-Terrorist Squad
BBC	The British Broadcasting Corporation
CBI	Central Bank of Iran
CCIT	Comprehensive Convention on International Terrorism
CIA	Central Intelligence Agency
CSIS	Centre for Strategic and International Studies
E and P	Exploration and Production
EAF	Egyptian Armed forces
EIA	Energy Information Administration
EPC	Engineering, Procurement, and Construction
EU	European Union
EU3	France Britain And Germany
FFI	Foreign Financial Institutions
FMF	Foreign Military Financing
FMS	Foreign Military Sales

FSA	The Free Syrian Army
GCC	Gulf Co-operation Council
IAEA	International Atomic Energy Agency
IED	Improvised Explosive Device
ILSA	Iran Libya Sanctions Act
IMAFT	Islamic Military Alliance to Fight Terrorism
IPC	Iran Petroleum Contracts
IRGC-QF	Islamic Revolutionary Guards Corps-Quds Force
IS	Islamic State
ISA	Iran Sanctions Act
ISI	Islamic State Iraq
ISIL	Islamic State of Iraq and the Levant
ISIS	Islamic State of Iraq and Syria
ISO	Imamia Students Organization
JASTA	Justice Against Sponsors of Terrorism Act
JCPOA	Joint Comprehensive Plan of Action
JeM	Jaish-e-Mohammed
KRG	Kurdistan Regional Government
LeT	Lashkar-e-Taiba
LNG	Liquefied natural gas
MHA	Ministry of Home Affairs
MP	Military Production
NCRI	National Coalition of Resistance of Iran
NDP	National Democratic Party
NIA	National Intelligence Agency
NPC	National Petrochemical Company
NSPO	National Service Projects Organization
OAPEC	Organization of Arab Petroleum Exporting Countries
OIC	Organization of Islamic Cooperation
OPEC	Organization of the Petroleum Exporting Countries
P5+1	UN Security Council's five permanent members + European Union

PKK	Partiya Karkerên Kurdistanê (Kurdistan Workers' Party)
PLO	Palestinian Liberation Organization
POGIDC	Persia Oil and Gas Industry Development Company
PYD	Partiya Yekîtiya Demokratý
PYG	Yekîneyên Parastina Gel
QME	Qualitative Military Edge
RDS	The Royal Dutch Shell
RF	Restricted funds
SCAF	The Supreme Council of Armed Forces
SCIRI	The Islamic Supreme Council of Iraq
SDF	The Syrian Democratic Forces
SDN	Specially Designated Nationals
SNC	The Syrian National Council
UAE	United Arab Emirates
UN	United Nations
UNESCO	United Nations Educational, Scientific and Cultural Organization
UNSCOP	United Nations Special Commission on Palestine
US	United States
USA	United States America
USSR	Union of Soviet Socialist Republics
WANA	West Asia and North America
YPG	The Kurdish People's Protection Units

Acknowledgements and Disclaimer

This project and publication have been undertaken by the Delhi Policy Group (DPG) with the support of Institute of Defence Studies and Analyses (IDSA).

Founded in 1994, the Delhi Policy Group is among India's oldest independent think tanks with its primary focus on strategic issues of critical national interest. Over the past decades, it has established itself in both domestic and international circles, particularly in the areas of peace and conflict and national security.

In keeping with the growing dynamism of India's foreign and security policy, the DPG has expanded its focus areas to include India's broader regional and global role and the strategic partnerships that advance India's rise as a leading power. To support that goal, the DPG undertakes research and organises conferences and interactions across a wide canvas including strategic and geo-political issues, geo-economic issues and defence and security issues.

IDSA is a non-partisan, autonomous body, dedicated to objective research and policy relevant studies on all aspects of defence and security. Its mission is to promote national and international security through the generation and dissemination of knowledge on defence and security-related issues.

DPG and IDSA acknowledge the contribution of Dr. Preeti Singh, who copy-edited the volume, as well as the efforts of the DPG research associates, Ms. Tanzoom Ahmed and Ms. Shulagna Pal, in compiling this volume.

Introduction

Sanjay Singh

The West Asian region is in the process of profound transformation. In the wake of the 'Arab Spring' of 2010, the region has been marked by political instability arising from the forceful articulation of popular aspirations, especially by its youth, violent civil strife in some countries, widening sectarian schisms, and the rise of extremist forces in others. There is growing distrust of the existing social contract, increased stress on regional fault-lines, and uncertainty about the future. Owing to its geographic location, its centrality in the Islamic world, and its hydrocarbon resources, West Asia plays a crucial role in global affairs, particularly in the oil and gas markets and consequently the global economy. Instability in the region is of particular concern for Asia, which largely depends on oil and gas from West Asia, and will do so for the time to come.

India has civilisational ties with West Asia, a region located in India's extended neighbourhood. It hosts over 8 million Indians, and is India's largest economic and trade partner. A large number of Indians have an emotional engagement with the region, which hosts the two holy mosques and a number of holy places associated with Christianity and Islam. The Gulf's abundant hydrocarbon resources are critical for India's energy security, and the region is a major source of remittances from Indian workers employed there. India has wide-ranging institutional relations with every country in West Asia, encompassing cooperation in various fields, including counter-terrorism. India's security and wellbeing are deeply intertwined with that of West Asia. Its ongoing transformation is, therefore, of special interest for India.

It is in this context that the Delhi Policy Group (DPG) launched a project in 2016 to study the rapidly changing socio-political and economic structures as well as emerging trends in West Asia. The principal focus was on the main drivers of this transformation and on the main players. Particular attention was paid to the evolution of Islamic thought and practice in the region viz. Wahhabism, Velayat-i-Faqih, the Muslim Brotherhood, and Salafi-Jihadism, and their overarching influence in the region. The project also looked at the main regional powers—Egypt, Iran, Israel, and Saudi Arabia and their interactions with each other, as well as the areas engulfed by conflict—Iraq, Syria, and Yemen. The first part of this volume studies global Jihad, the changing energy scenario, and the consequent geopolitical implications for West Asia. It identifies the trends and forces driving these developments. The chapter on global Jihad examines how the failure of West Asian states to address the aspirations of their youth, the lack of avenues for political participation, combined with governance which is both non-transparent and unaccountable, has increased the allure of Jihad. It analyses how Jihad has become global, attracting youth in their thousands from different parts of the world, including the West, with many of them converting to Islam and being indoctrinated into extremist ideas and fundamentalist world views. It also explores how the states from the region have themselves occasionally extended support to Jihadi groups, with disastrous consequences. The second chapter examines the dependence of the region's economy and polity on the oil and gas industry which has led directly to the creation of a paternalistic social contract, which underpins regional social and political stability. This now faces a major threat from the decline in importance of hydrocarbons as a result of changes in the patterns of production and energy use as well as related technological developments.

The second part contains chapters on Saudi Arabia's role in the region, and Wahabbism. The first chapter describes the salient features of the Kingdom, its foreign policy, and its relations with other regional powers. It analyses how the Kingdom views and addresses changes in the region, the challenges it faces, and the strengths and limitations of its approach. In particular, it focuses on Saudi-Iranian rivalry, and examines the Saudi involvement in conflicts in Syria, Bahrain, and Yemen. The second chapter traces the history of the relationship between Wahhabism and the Saudi state since their birth in the early 18th century and its status today. It highlights the dynamics of the relationship, the inherent tensions and the challenges posed in the context of the ideas unleashed by the Arab Spring in the region, and the requirement for a new security architecture.

The third part comprises chapters on Yemen. The first is on the domestic and regional aspects of the civil conflict in the country, and the second on its effect on Al-Qaeda in the Arabian Peninsula (AQAP). The first describes how Yemenis demanded political and economic reforms in 2011 in line with the protests carried out in many other Arab countries at the time. This led to the overthrow of the 33-year long rule of President Ali Abdullah Saleh. The chapter examines how even though most of the existing problems were attributed to the authoritarian leader at that time, the underlying factors have proven to be far more complex and intractable. The uprisings, which sought to promote popular participation in the political process, activated a number of fault-lines along tribal and regional affiliations, and gave succour to secessionist endeavours from the south as well as to the Houthi rebels in the north. This in turn provided the justification for external armed intervention, with disastrous consequences. The second chapter describes how AQAP, an amalgam of Yemeni fighters and those driven out of Saudi Arabia, regrouped in Yemen, and managed to capitalize on the chaos prevalent there, carving out a much larger role for themselves in the process.

The part on Iran has three chapters. The first, on 'The Concept of Wilayat al-Faqih 37 Years after the Iranian Revolution', explains how this concept continues to underpin the politics in the country, and how its appeal extends beyond Iran's borders. The chapter compares the different narratives of this phenomenon, including the debates within the religious establishment. It enumerates the multiple arguments from the clergy, both inside and outside Iran, to provide a perspective on a seminal political development that has had a profound effect on regional developments. The second chapter explores how the Joint Comprehensive Plan of Action (JCPOA) was the result of an exercise in the diplomacy of exploring the art of the possible. It studies the key areas that have evolved in the post JCPOA period, including the effect on Iran-United States ties, sanctions relief, and Iran's economic situation, and how these have impacted the strategic landscape. The third chapter examines how Iran is perceived in the region, and its activities there. It also studies the changing US-Iran relationship, which is a significant factor in regional politics. It looks at how growing Saudi-Iranian tensions could be problematic for India, especially at a time when New Delhi seeks closer political and strategic partnerships with both Iran and the Gulf States.

The part on Israel explores India-Israel bilateral relations. It examines how the Indian policy of recognition-without-relations was a result of domestic imperatives and India's own ambitions within this region, and how, by 1992, the global and regional situation had evolved to produce an enabling environment for India to establish full diplomatic relations with Israel. Like much of the international community today, India supports the two-state solution even while strengthening its relations with Israel. The second chapter takes a critical look at the trajectory of US-Israel ties, the evolution of which has been non-linear and contradicts widely held perceptions about the relationship. It makes the point that these bilateral ties have not always been as smooth and robust as they appear on the surface, and are a result of the interplay of complex forces. It seeks to identify these forces and understand their effect on this relationship.

The sixth part consists of two chapters on Egypt. The first is on the growing power of the Armed Forces in Egypt and the deteriorating security situation. The second examines recent developments in state-society ties in Egypt, and analyses the imperatives and choices before President Abdel Fattah al-Sisi. These chapters examine how the leadership has become authoritarian, repressive, and intolerant of dissent, demanding absolute and unquestioning loyalty. They look at the alienation of different sections of society in Egypt as a result of the economic crisis, human rights violations, crackdowns on press freedoms, and the collapse of tourism in the face of extremist terror attacks. The chapters also study the role of the Muslim Brotherhood and its influence on Egyptian society. They examine Egypt's limitations in playing a regional role—the weakening of its institutions, the lack of an appealing economic model, and the power to extend aid. They point out that its diplomacy is constrained by internal problems, instability, and corruption, and conclude that, apart from battling terrorist groups, Egypt just does not possess the wherewithal's to focus on regional affairs.

In the part on Iraq and Syria, the first chapter examines the tragedy that has befallen Syria—the result of the incompetence of domestic governance combined with regional and international interference. It examines the legacy of the Sykes-Picot arrangement, and how Syria seems to have become a failed project—a proxy battlefield for the Saudi-Iran rivalry to play out. The second chapter carries on from the first to examine how misgovernance in Syria and Iraq created opportunities for the Islamic State to emerge, and grow to the point that it now has a presence in over 18 countries around the broader region. It goes on to study the waning influence of the Islamic State in Iraq and Syria, and its rapidly dwindling revenues as a result of concerted attacks on its infrastructure. It also points out that, today, IS is finding it difficult to finance its operations on as large a scale as it did before. It notes, however, that the digital and ideological moorings of the IS are still formidable, and that it has digitally enabled itself to expand its global outreach.

This book has been made possible through collaboration between the Delhi Policy Group (DPG) and the Institute of Defence Studies and Analysis (IDSA). It is the result of a project designed to provide an opportunity to young researchers to engage in a fruitful exchange of ideas, and contribute towards a better understanding of the current situation in West Asia through their academic research. A key objective of this project was to form a network of young Indian researchers from think-tanks and academia studying West Asia in order to build a cadre of area specialists for the future. The project has benefitted significantly from the involvement of senior diplomats and academicians who mentored the young researchers.

It is hoped that this book, drawing upon the considerable expertise of regional specialists, academics, and former civil servants will be a useful resource for policymakers in helping them to calibrate an effective, informed, and balanced strategy towards the region.

PART 1

WEST ASIA IN TRANSITION

1

Introduction

Talmiz Ahmad

Since 1979, there has hardly been a day when West Asia has not found itself in the throes of serious political and/or economic crises. The year 1979 itself, marking the 1400th year of Islam in the Hijri calendar, witnessed the Islamic Revolution in Iran; the occupation of the Haram Sharif in Mecca; and then the Soviet occupation of Afghanistan at the end of the year. These events—cataclysmic in themselves—unleashed responses from regional and global players that continue to shape West Asian politics to this day.

The Iranian Revolution was seen by the Gulf Arab monarchies as posing a doctrinal and political challenge to their interests due to the possible "export" of the revolution and the allure it could have for their own citizenry. Hence they, in alliance with the USA and Pakistan, mobilised opposition to the Soviet entry into Afghanistan on the basis of a "global jihad". This first jihad of the 20th century (after the abortive attempt of the Ottoman sultan to call a jihad at the outset of World War I) brought a hundred thousand Muslim youth from nearly all the world's Muslim countries and communities to the Pakistan-Afghanistan border, marking the first phase of transnational jihad.

Global Jihad: Al-Qaeda

Here, the recruits were indoctrinated in jihad, trained in arms and subversion, given battle experience and, in some cases, also experienced martyrdom. More importantly, the jihad tasted victory against "godless communism", marking the first major Muslim victory against a Western power. Thus, Afghanistan became the nursery of global jihad—ironically, under state sponsorship—and spawned the world's first transnational jihadi organisation, Al-Qaeda.

Under the leadership of Osama bin Laden, Al-Qaeda envisioned attacks upon the "far enemy", the USA. It started with assaults on US targets in East Africa in 1998, and the *USS Cole* off Aden in 2000. Al-Qaeda then planned and supported the 9/11 attacks on iconic US targets. Though US counter-attacks removed Al-Qaeda and its local patron, the Taliban, from Afghanistan, the shift was only temporary: it was moved to sanctuaries in Pakistan by the Pakistani intelligence service, the ISI. Thus, Al-Qaeda effectively "de-territorialised" itself and mounted attacks on local targets through its affiliated groups across West Asia and North Africa. This decade of the 2000s marks the second phase of transnational jihad.

At the end of the decade, in 2010, a new figure entered the jihadi firmament: the Iraqi national, Abu Bakr Al Baghdadi. He assumed the leadership of the Islamic State of Iraq (ISI), marking the third phase of transnational jihad. This group had earlier, in 2006, asserted its independence from Al-Qaeda and made clear its commitment to realising a "state" in West Asia, particularly after its leader re-named the organisation, the Islamic State of Iraq and Syria (ISIS) in early 2013.

The Islamic State

In June 2014, ISIS forces captured the town of Mosul, and then large swathes of territory across Iraq and Syria. Al Baghdadi proclaimed this territory to be the Islamic State (IS), which would be a "caliphate", with him as the anointed caliph. Over the next two years, the IS had a "state" the size of the UK, a population of about 6–8 million, a standing army of 100,000, a treasury with assets of about a trillion dollars, and most of the institutions of a proto-state.

ISIS has been able to allure thousands of youth from different parts of the Muslim world, from Muslim-origin migrant communities in Europe and the USA, as also from among recent converts to Islam in Western societies. While the core base of support is from Iraq and Syria, other recruits come from the Gulf Cooperation Council (GCC) countries and other Arab countries. Recruits from Europe, most of whom lead squalid and marginalised lives in their home countries, are attracted to the IS since it sharpens and gives meaning to their Muslim identity, imbues in them a sense of comradeship with their fellow-jihadis, and makes them participants in a historic enterprise in defence of their faith. The IS has also influenced several attacks on soft targets by "lone-wolf" perpetrators, who have had no direct contact with the jihadi organisation, but have been motivated by blandishments, particularly those projected on IS-sponsored social media.

The two transnational jihadi groups, Al-Qaeda and ISIS, draw their ideology and justifications for their world-view and conduct from Islamic sources, the Koran and the Hadith as well as the various commentaries of scholars over the centuries. Though the interpretations drawn by jihadi ideologues from these sources are disputed by mainstream Islamic scholars, many of whom question the scholarship of the jihadi intellectuals and their competence to represent the Muslim community at large, the fact remains that jihad does represent a major strand of contemporary political Islam.

Outlook

Recent history reveals that jihadi groups have had a peculiar relationship with state authorities: even as these groups have turned their wrath upon the regional state order, they have also, from time to time, received support from state authorities. Thus, Pakistan sponsored the Taliban, and later, the Al-Qaeda-Taliban cooperation in Afghanistan in the 1990s. From 2003, many Arab sheikdoms backed the jihadi activity in Iraq led by Abu Musab al Zarqawi, which, in time, led to the formation of ISIS. In the Syrian uprising from 2011, some GCC countries have used Salafi and even jihadi groups against the Al-Assad regime, even as the Turkish government encouraged the free-flow of jihadi youth to the battlefields of Syria, many of whom joined the ISIS.

As this chapter is being written (March 2017), government forces in Iraq and Syria, with considerable external support, have launched military attacks on ISIS strongholds in Mosul and Raqqa. But, most observers believe that military action alone will not eradicate the jihadi scourge. ISIS cadres are expected to seek refuge in various territories across West Asia which are experiencing state breakdown; from here they will continue their murderous assaults upon state authorities as well as on soft targets.

It is important to note that jihad is itself a product of the failure of West Asian states to address and fulfil the aspirations of their youth. They have been living in authoritarian regimes that are run on paternalistic, 19th century models, and find no space for participation in making political and economic choices. Moreover, West Asian state orders are not transparent or accountable regarding national accounts and national decision-making, even as the states themselves suffer economic woes due to collapsing oil prices and widespread youth unemployment. Some of these frustrated youth find a congenial sanctuary in jihadi groups, coming to believe that they are a part of a great Islamic cause, are defending their faith, and participating in a unique historical endeavour.

The Oil Factor in West Asian Affairs

West Asian economics and politics are almost entirely dependent on oil revenues. These revenues provide not only the bulk of the resources of the oil-producing countries, but also financial support to non-producers in the shape of aid and development assistance, and employment for their citizens who then send money home as remittances.

Oil revenues have kept in place a "social contract" in the oil-producing monarchies in terms of which the ruling family provides the citizenry with security and welfare (for example, employment, educational and health support, subsidies on essential goods and services, etc.); and, in turn, the citizens owe their rulers loyalty and obedience. This social contract has worked well for over the last hundred years, and has remained in place despite serious political and economic crises, domestic and regional. In fact, oil revenues provided the Gulf Sheikhdoms with the resources to confront the challenges posed by the Arab Spring by giving their restive citizens doles and other economic benefits.

This comfortable arrangement could now be facing a serious threat. First, the global energy economy is experiencing some important changes. The demand for oil is going down in developed countries due to conservation, efficiency policies, and climate change sensitivities. Second, the USA, till recently the world's largest oil importer, has itself become a major producer with shale oil. Third, the global economic slowdown, China's economic policies focusing on the quality of life rather than manufacture, and lower growth rates have significantly reduced the demand for oil imports. Finally, some Gulf Sheikhdoms led by Saudi Arabia, are embroiled in military conflicts in Syria and Yemen, and are making expensive purchases of military equipment at a time of severely declining revenues, putting even greater strain on their national exchequers.

Taken together, these developments have led to a surplus in oil markets, and a consequent precipitate fall in oil prices which plunged from a high of over US$ 100/ barrel in 2014 to a low of US$ 28/barrel in early 2016. While prices have rallied to around US$ 60/barrel from early 2017 due to a production cut agreement between OPEC and non-OPEC producers in November 2016, projections suggest that prices will remain at this level for the next few years.

Economic Reform Programmes

This fall in prices has played havoc with the budgets of oil producers, and made it difficult for them to maintain the economic and political status quo in their polities. Most Gulf producers have announced new reform policies that would effectively wean their nations away from the "addiction" to oil by developing domestic manufacturing, services capabilities, and providing new employment opportunities for youth in the private sector. However, there are no indications from official sources that these sweeping economic reforms will also be accompanied by political reforms: the rulers hope to keep the present paternalistic order in place, placating their citizens with an improved and more exciting economic landscape.

Thus, many observers remain sceptical about the Gulf Sheikhdoms' ability to put in effect successfully the ambitious reform programmes, and to do this while retaining the political status quo. For instance, about a quarter of a million Saudi youth enter the workforce annually. They have traditionally found a place for themselves in the government sector. Under the reform programme, 70 percent of them will need to join the private sector, which will raise issues of education, training, and work ethic. This will also involve a sea-change in existing employment arrangements: at present, 70 percent Saudis are in the government sector while 90 percent of employees in the private sector are foreign nationals.

These major economic changes are not likely to be implemented without significant changes in the political order. Since 1991, in every petition for reform sumbitted to the king, there has been considerable focus on political and economic reform, including the primacy of transparency and accountability, better distribution of wealth between classes and regions, and fighting corruption and nepotism.

An Indian Diplomatic Initiative

The deteriorating security scenario in West Asia—marked by the stand-off between Saudi Arabia and Iran, the on-going proxy wars between them in Syria and Yemen shaped largely in sectarian terms, and the scourge of transnational jihad—have placed India's crucial and abiding interests in jeopardy. These include India's energy security and economic interests as well as the welfare of its eight million strong community resident in the Gulf. A larger conflict in the region embracing the neighbouring Islamic giants would also endanger India's plans to develop the Chabahar port in Iran and pursue connectivity projects through Chabahar to Afghanistan, the Central Asian Republics, and on to Moscow and beyond.

This scenario poses a unique diplomatic challenge for India. How can India shape an initiative that would promote regional security and stability in West Asia? This is obviously a daunting challenge, given that India on its own has never pursued such an initiative outside the confines of South Asia. But, with the USA unable, or unwilling, to intervene in the region, and anxious that other role players (with important regional interests) shoulder some of the security responsibilities, the stage is set for India to be actively involved in peace-making in the region. This should be done preferably in tandem with other Asian powers—like China, Japan and Korea—which have similar interests in regional stability and are similarly alarmed at the deteriorating situation.

This India-led Asian initiative should first promote confidence-building measures between Iran and Saudi Arabia so that these estranged giants can begin a dialogue to address the issues that separate them. This should be followed by a more ambitious attempt to put in place a regional cooperative security arrangement that would ultimately include all the countries interested in West Asian stability.

Why is an Asian initiative likely to succeed when earlier efforts have failed? In recent years, US credibility as an effective role-player in West Asian affairs has reduced significantly. In the last days of the Obama presidency, the GCC countries were dissatisfied with the USA's accommodation of Iran on the nuclear weapons issue, while Iran remained unhappy with the USA's reluctance to lift sanctions and promote bilateral ties more enthusiastically. Iran, therefore, turned to Russia as its partner in re-shaping West Asian politics.

In its first few weeks, the Trump presidency has already generated serious uncertainties about the USA's approach to West Asia. While President Trump and his senior colleagues seem to project a visceral hostility towards Iran, the GCC countries are also not sanguine, given the President's (and his Administration's) overt Islamophobia, even as the "Justice Against Sponsors of Terrorism Act" (JASTA) remains a Damocles sword over Saudi Arabia, and restricts the growth of positive ties with the new US government.

In contrast to the USA, in pursuit of their initiative, Asian countries would be approaching West Asia with no negative baggage and no historical biases, along with a solid reputation for their non-prescriptive and non-intrusive approaches in their foreign engagements. Again, unlike the USA and other western powers, the countries concerned would be viewed as totally averse to military conflicts.

Such an initiative is likely to enjoy considerable credibility in Tehran, since the promoting countries are non-Western and attach a high value to their ties with Iran. Again, since all of them also have close ties with Saudi Arabia and the other GCC countries, the initiative will have considerable resonance in the Arab states as well.

Above all, it should be noted that this initiative would not just be confined to promoting mutual trust between the estranged Islamic giants; it will also seek to shape the framework of a new regional security order to replace the earlier US-led order. For over 30 years since 1979, the US approach to West Asia was characterised by recourse to military force, culminating in the US assault upon Iraq in 2003.

For the first time in a century, the Asian initiative will bring to the region a non-military approach to regional security that is based on the active participation of the different regional countries themselves as key role-players. Also, this initiative would not exclude other nations, including western countries, which have a stake in regional security.

2

Global Jihad by Al-Qaida and the Islamic State

Md. Muddassir Quamar

ABSTRACT

Jihadi terrorism has emerged as one of the most potent global threats and has kept the world pre-occupied, especially since the outbreak of the Arab Spring. The doctrinal idea of Jihad comes from Islamic jurisprudence where it has two meanings: one of the individual's struggles to strive for greater spirituality, and two of fighting with arms to defend the Islamic ummah. However, the use of 'Jihad' by contemporary Islamist terrorist groups has made it synonymous with terrorism. This 'modern' idea of Jihad first came into fashion during the Islamist's struggle in the 1980s against the Soviet invasion of Afghanistan. The group known as Mujahideen was funded, armed, and trained by the USA, Saudi Arabia, and Pakistan, and included Muslims from various nationalities, including Arabs. These battle hardened 'Afghan-Arab' mujahideens (fighters) went back to their respective countries after the Soviet retreat and, in 1988, formed Al-Qaida, the first global Sunni Islamist organisation committed to Jihad (armed struggle) to counter the so-called Western onslaught on Islam. They continued to receive patronage until they turned against their former benefactors during the Kuwait crisis (1990–91). Al-Qaida and its leader Osama bin Laden became the number one enemy of Saudi Arabia and the USA when it started targeting Saudi and American military installations in the Gulf. The 9/11 attacks changed the dynamics of Jihadi terror from being a localised Arab-Afghan phenomenon to a larger one that could strike at the heart of the global super power. American retaliations against Taliban-led Afghanistan and

Saddam's Iraq created breeding grounds for Jihadi groups that started mushrooming. The Arab Spring further changed the dynamics and, with weakened governments in many WANA countries, Jihadi terrorist groups started gaining ground.

The declaration of a worldwide 'Islamic caliphate' in June 2014 marks a new phase in the history of Jihadi terrorism. While Al-Qaida preferred to be a centralised coherent group with branches in strategic regions, the Islamic State (Daesh) aspires, and to an extent has succeeded in, becoming a decentralised umbrella organisation of Jihadi terrorist groups all over the world. Hence, the emergence of Daesh marks the next stage in the globalisation of Jihadi terrorism, whereby its franchises or affiliates have struck at will in the heart of Europe, Asia, and Africa, and have been able to hold ground in Iraq and Syria despite continuous military action by local, regional, and global powers. The growing reach and potency of Jihadi terrorism demand developing a wider counter-terror strategy that is based on intelligence inputs and military actions as well as de-radicalisation and social upliftment programmes.

Background

Jihadi terror has emerged as one of the most potent global threats, especially since the outbreak of the Arab Spring, and has kept the world pre-occupied. The political instabilities created due to the domino effect of events leading to the overthrow of the Zain El Abidine Ben-Ali regime in Tunisia, and the unwillingness of Arab rulers to heed the voices of the people has created fertile ground for Islamist militants to run amok in the Middle East. Iraq, Syria, Libya, and Yemen have become the hotbed for groups that are either affiliated to Al-Qaida or are its break-away. One such group, the Islamic State of Iraq (ISI), declared a world-wide Caliphate—*al-Dawlah al-Islamiyah*—on 29 June 2014, with a substantial hold over territories in Iraq and Syria under the leadership of Abu Bakr al-Baghdadi who declared himself the Caliph.[1] The group soon captured large swathes of land in Iraq, Syria and Libya, and won over smaller groups as affiliates or supporters. These include Boko Haram (Nigeria), Jundullah (Pakistan), and the Abu Sayyaf Group (Philippines). Subsequently, it has founded affiliates in Afghanistan, Libya, Yemen and Egypt and inspired 'lone wolfs' in Asia, Africa, Europe and America.

However, this is not the first time a militant Islamist group has gained such a wide, though scattered, support. Al-Qaida created affiliates in various parts of the world, including the Al-Qaida in Arabian Peninsula (AQAP), the Al-Qaida in the Maghreb (AQM), al-Shabab, etc. What distinguishes the Islamic State (IS; also known as Islamic State of Iraq and Syria [ISIS], Islamic State of Iraq and Levant [ISIL], and by the Arabic acronym Daesh) from Al-Qaida is its ability to attract fighters from various parts of the world, including from the West, and to attack targets in the heart of Europe, the USA, the Middle East, and Asia with impunity and in quick succession. Despite being a global phenomenon, the Al-Qaida is confined to smaller areas in a few troubled regions such as Iraq, Afghanistan, Pakistan, Saudi Arabia, Yemen, Somalia, and parts of Northern Africa. Before it gained global notoriety and the respect of Islamist militants because of the 11 September attacks in the USA, it was largely confined to targeting US interests in the areas of its influence. IS, on the contrary, is able to attract youths, men and women, from all over the globe to be part of a Jihad to sustain and expand the *al-Dawlah al-Islamiyah*. The ability of the IS to realise the long-held nostalgia among a section of global Muslims to revive the Caliphate (abolished in the early twentieth century with the fall of the Ottoman Empire) distinguishes it from other Islamist militant groups.

The romanticised idea of the revival of a historical politico-religious institution that once ruled over the majority of the Muslim world till its retreat and eventual decline has attracted the youth not only in conservative monarchies such as Saudi Arabia and Kuwait or in troubled areas such as Yemen and Afghanistan but also in countries with a largely secular socio-political history such as Jordan, Tunisia, Egypt, Bangladesh as well as in liberal democracies including the USA, France, Australia, and even India. It has become a major source of global concern. However, the military intervention in Syria by Russia and Iran on behalf of the Assad regime, and the intervention in Iraq by the USA and its allies to bolster the Iraqi government forces have shown some results: the IS has lost momentum as well as the control of many of its key towns and cities. It has, however, shown extraordinary resilience and expertise to withstand high-calibre military operations.

This chapter, divided into three sections, discusses the doctrinal and temporal aspects of Jihad and Jihadi terrorism; analyses the rise of the Al-Qaida and the IS; and examines the similarities and distinguishing features of the two groups. It argues that Jihadism cannot be fought only militarily; rather, it requires sustained and wider counter-terror and de-radicalisation strategies as well as the resolution of long-held socio-political grievances in Muslim societies.

Jihad and Jihadism

The doctrinal idea of Jihad comes from Islamic jurisprudence, where it is used in two meanings: the individual's struggles to strive for greater spirituality and fighting with arms to defend Islamic lands and the *ummah*. A third meaning is an aggressive 'holy war' for the conquest and expansion of Islamic rule, which devout Muslims dismiss as a misconception and an accusation made by the 'enemies' of Islam.[2] The term has relevance in both Shia and Sunni jurisprudence and, until the advent of the 'modern' concept of Jihad, it was largely understood to be a way wherein Muslims strive to strengthen their own faith and spread it to others.[3]

Nevertheless, the idea of Jihad by military means has been part of Islamic history. It is argued that it was allowed in circumstances where the faith and the *ummah* (or the land under Islamic rule) was threatened by an outside enemy. It was, however, strictly a matter of decision by the ruler to declare Jihad, and it was more often declared in consultation with the *ulema*.[4] This means that Jihad in the meaning of armed fighting was basically a concept of engaging in war with the enemy. In Islamic jurisprudence, there are well laid out rules for engagement in war, including the prohibition against the killing of non-combatants such as women, children, and the elderly.[5] There are also injunctions that prohibit damaging the habitat as well as local flora and fauna. It underscores the fact that while engaging in war for the security of the *Dar al-Islam* is mandated, certain rules are to be followed in the battle field.

Jihad as a tool for spreading Islam through offensive military campaigns is also understood as part of Islamic jurisprudence and history.[6] It is a matter of historical analysis and debate whether, in practice, Jihad is akin to a Crusade or the idea of 'holy war.' Historical evidence suggests that there were wars undertaken by Muslim rulers to expand their empires in the name of spreading Islam. Though seen as controversial by orthodox Muslims who see it as the Western labelling of Jihad, one cannot negate such occurrences. These underline the fact that Jihad as a method of defensive and offensive military campaign has been part of Islamic history and jurisprudence.

The use of Jihad by contemporary militant Islamist groups has made it synonymous with terrorism. This 'modern' idea of Jihad first came into fashion during the Islamist struggle in the 1980s against the Soviet invasion of Afghanistan.[7] It is this phenomenon of 'global jihad' that gave birth to Al-Qaida in 1988. The jihadists continued to receive state sponsorship and patronisation until they turned against their benefactors during the Kuwait crisis (1990–91). Al-Qaida, and its leader Osama Bin-Laden, became the number one enemy of Saudi Arabia and the USA when it started targeting Saudi and American military installations in the Gulf. The 11 September 2001 attacks changed the dynamics of Jihadi terror from being a localised

Arab-Afghan phenomenon to a larger phenomenon that could strike at the heart of the global super power.[8]

Before one can understand the phenomena of the Al-Qaida and the IS, it is important to understand the ideology of Jihad. 'Jihadism'—or 'militant Islamism' as it is referred to in academic literature—cannot be seen in isolation from the development of political Islam. Jihadism is a hybrid ideology of many strands of political Islam and Salafism;[9] hence it is also referred to as 'Salafi-Jihadism.' Many of the doctrinal aspects of Jihadism overlap with Wahhabism—the movement that emerged in eighteenth century Najd (central Arabia), and is considered as a puritanical strand in Islam.[10] Its emphasis on a literalist interpretation of the Quran and Hadith, and the notion of ridding the creed of any *bidah* (innovation), is one of the strongest aspects adhered to by contemporary Jihadists. However, the Wahhabi doctrine advocates a complete subservience to the ruler—if he adheres to the basic tenets of Islam—as interpreted in the Hanbali tradition[11] and hence, it is considered as a pacifist form of Salafi Islam.

It would be misleading to understand Jihadism as an extension of Wahhabism because the ideology of Jihad is more complicated than generally understood. There is no doubt that the Al-Qaida and the IS claim to be the true adherents of Salafi-Wahhabi Islam, and accuse those who do not follow them to have degenerated away from the true creed of Islam. Nonetheless, Jihadi groups go beyond the interpretations of Muhammad bin Abdul Wahhab who emphasised reforms in practiced Islam more than on launching a Jihad. In his study of the ideology of Salafi-Jihadism, Shiraz Maher writes that the roots of this thought 'are grounded in the experiences of Sunni Islam over the last century and beyond.' He adds that it emanates from 'a broad and varied ecosystem of dense Islamic jurisprudence.'[12] The idea evolved over time to reach its current stage where acts of terror have been justified by many Salafi-Jihadi ideologues, such as Abdullah Azzam, Anwar al-Awlaki and Abu Musab al-Zarqawi, as a legitimate method of engaging in war. These ideologues use existing Islamic legal concepts such as *qisas* (equal retaliation) and *tatarrus* (human shield) to justify methods of terror in the fight against the enemy.[13]

Jihadism undoubtedly takes inspiration from the Wahhabi conception of *tawhid* (oneness of God) and *al-walawal-bara* (loyalty to Islam and disavowal of un-Islamic ways), and intermixes it with Syed Qutb's ideas of Islamic sovereignty whereby it becomes the duty of all Muslims to strive for and use force to end the period of *jahiliyya* (un-Islamic rule) and establish sovereignty of Allah (*hakimiyya*) in all areas under Muslim rule.[14]

Hence, Shiraz Maher identifies *tawhid, hakimiyya, al-walawal-bara, jihad,* and *takfir* as the 'five essential and irreducible' characteristics of Salafi-Jihadism.[15] Hassan Hassan argues that Jihadi ideology is basically a "hybrid" ideology and is 'multifaceted and cannot be traced to one individual, movement, or period.'[16] It has also been argued that the ideological differences between the two major Jihadi groups, the Al-Qaida and the IS, are minor, and it is largely the differences over strategy that set the two apart.

The Globalisation of Jihadi Terror

The Al-Qaida can be considered the first global militant Islamist group that has been eclipsed by the IS, both in its ability to create mayhem and attract recruits. In fact, the IS branched out of Al-Qaida and came into its own during the height of insurgency against the 2003 US invasion in Iraq. Significantly, the two are ideologically similar; but they compete for dominance and seek attention from the same group of sympathisers. Largely, they have avoided open confrontation—except in the Syrian theatre where they fought after initial cooperation. The roots of the global Jihadist movement lies in the *mujahideen* struggle against Soviet invasion of Afghanistan.

Thomas Hegghammer argues that the seeds of global Jihad can be traced to the phenomenon of 'foreign fighters' who were initially drawn to the war in Afghanistan after Soviet occupation.[17] He writes,

> The foreign fighter phenomenon represents a violent offshoot of a qualitatively new sub-current of Islamism—populist pan-Islamism—which emerged in the 1970s as a result of strategic action by marginalised elites employed in nonviolent international Islamic organisations. Seeking political relevance and increased budgets, these activists—who were mostly based in the Hijaz region of Saudi Arabia—propagated an alarmist discourse emphasising external threats to the Muslim nation. They also established a global network of charities for the provision of inter-Muslim aid. The norms and networks established by the Hijazi pan-Islamists then enabled Arab activists in 1980s Afghanistan to recruit foreign fighters in the name of inter-Muslim solidarity.[18]

Others concur with the timeline but offer a different explanation, including the idea that Islamism that emerged in the early twentieth century had, from the beginning, resonated in various Muslim societies. In the 1970s, the leadership of militant Islamism, especially Osama Bin-Laden, was able to use modern tools to globalise his views and attract recruits from various parts of the world.[19] On the other hand, scholars argue that it was the changing global geopolitical situation that should be seen as responsible for the globalisation of Jihad.[20] Notably, there is agreement that the first global Jihadi group is Al-Qaida, established under the leadership of Bin-Laden.

Al-Qaida

The origins of Al-Qaida lie in the war in Afghanistan resulting from the 1979 Soviet attack. During the 1980s, an organised Islamist resistance movement was built in Afghanistan to fight the Soviet troops and its Afghan installed government. This was organised under the leadership of Gulbuddin Hekmatyar, a Pashtun warlord. The movement received military and financial support from the USA, Pakistan, and Saudi Arabia. One of the key phenomena during the war was that of the Arab *mujahideen*[21] which was largely orchestrated by Abdullah Azzam, a Palestinian Islamist scholar who, after obtaining a doctorate from Al-Azhar, had migrated to Saudi Arabia in 1973 to undertake a teaching position in Jeddah. In 1979, after the Soviet attack of Afghanistan, he issued a *fatwa* (religious opinion) articulating the need for Jihad against the Soviet Union for attacking a Muslim land. He argued that it is mandatory on all Muslims to defend their territories against the *kuffar* (non-believers).[22]

Azzam did not only issue this fatwa but migrated to Pakistan to undertake teaching at the International Islamic University in Peshawar in 1980. He also began organising the recruitment of Arab *mujahideen* to fight in Afghanistan. He convinced one of his former students in Saudi Arabia, Osama Bin-Laden, to come to Pakistan. This proved to be the starting point of their association which culminated in the formation of the Al-Qaida in 1988. Though the number of Arab *mujahideen* who migrated to Afghanistan to partake in Jihad was not substantial compared to the Afghan *mujahideen* who were fighting against the Soviet and Afghan troops, they had come from various parts of the Arab world. Once they returned to their native places after the Soviet retreat in late 1989, they started to proselytise their ideas in their native countries.[23]

After it was formed in 1988, the Al-Qaida soon began to strategise involvement in other Muslim areas that they considered were under occupation of non-believers. This led to the intensification of wars in Bosnia, Chechnya, and so on. They continued to receive support from their associates in Saudi Arabia and Pakistan as well as received funds from various independent individuals in the Gulf. During this early phase, they maintained relations with several like-minded Islamist groups in Egypt,

Jordan, Afghanistan, Pakistan, and the Gulf countries. Ideologically they were also inspired by the Sahwa movement that had gained substantial following in Saudi Arabia in late 1980s.[24]

The turning point in Al-Qaida's evolution came during the Kuwait crisis. It turned the newly formed Jihadi organisation against its benefactors—that is, Saudi Arabia and the USA. The Saudi response to the Kuwait crisis created a domestic political storm leading to many questions, including the ability of the al-Saud to defend the holy places—Mecca and Medina—despite their claim to be the *Khadim al-Harmain* (Servants of the two Holy Mosques) and their commitment to pan-Islamism. The need for external help from 'infidel' forces and of allowing them to be stationed in the Kingdom became a major source of embarrassment.[25] It was not just a matter of asking for American help but help from a non-Muslim force that comprised of, among others, Jews and women combatants that offended many sensibilities. It led to severe criticism of the al-Saud and its leadership, the most scathing of which came from the Sahwa movement and Al-Qaida. Bin-Laden, the Al-Qaida chief, had reportedly offered the services of the Al-Qaida to fight against the Iraqi army; but his offer was rejected by the al-Saud[26] who preferred to depend on the USA, and went on to allow the stationing of US forces in the Kingdom. This enraged Bin-Laden, who subsequently began to articulate the need to liberate the 'holy land' from 'infidel' American forces.[27]

Bin-Laden declared a war against the al-Saud, and in 1994, issued an open letter to the Grand Mufti of Saudi Arabia, Abdul Aziz Bin-Baz, articulating Al-Qaida's commitments to Islam, the Muslim *ummah* and Islamic holy lands (including in Palestine), and criticised him for his *fatwas* which justified the stationing of 'infidel' American forces in the Kingdom. He admonished him for justifying all the actions of the al-Saud that violated the sanctity of the holy places as well as his *fatwa* against the Sahwa leaders (such as Salman al-Awdah and Safar al-Hawali) who had criticised the Saudi response to the Kuwait crisis.[28] Soon, Al-Qaida declared a war on the USA. The first public pronouncement of waging Jihad against the USA came in 1996 in the form of a *fatwa* by Bin-Laden.[29] Thus, it was in the mid-1990s that Al-Qaida started to evolve into a global Jihadi organisation.

By late-1990s, the Al-Qaida had established its networks in several parts of the Middle East as well as had entered into strategic alliances with like-minded groups in Iraq, Jordan, Egypt, Sudan, Somalia, Afghanistan, and so on. Though it had orchestrated a number of low-intensity bombings in Yemen and other places targeting American interests earlier, its first major attack came in 1998. In a planned attack using truck bombs, it simultaneously struck two US embassies in Africa—in Dares Salaam and Nairobi—in which more than 200 people were killed and nearly 500 wounded. Thus began the direct confrontation between the USA and Al-Qaida. The USA launched targeted strikes at locations in Afghanistan and Sudan leading to killing of a number of Al-Qaeda operatives. By this time, Saudi Arabia had revoked Bin-Laden's citizenship (1994) and Sudan had expelled him (1996). Hereafter, facilitated by Pakistani Inter-Services Intelligence (ISI), he migrated to Taliban-controlled Afghanistan, and made his base in mountains in northern Afghanistan.[30]

Between 1998 and 2001, the Al-Qaida carried out a number of small attacks. And then, on 11 September 2001, it launched its largest attack in New York—making it one of the most defining global terrorist attacks so far. The 11 September 2001 attacks shook the world, and brought home Al-Qaida's capability of striking at the heart of the global super power. It not only changed the way the world looked at militant Islamism but also brought forth the threats posed by Al-Qaida and Jihadism.[31] The US response and the beginning of the 'War on Terror' proved to be more devastating than it was imagined.[32] The US attacks on Afghanistan (2001) and Iraq (2003) turned out to be not only less effective in rooting out militant Islamism or Jihadism but instead ended up creating further political vacuums in these countries for the breeding of militant and radical Islamist groups that then began to spread to other neighbouring countries. Iraq came under grip of devastating sectarian strife leading to a hundred thousand deaths, and Afghanistan—already in the grip of civil-war since the 1990s—deteriorated further into chaos and internal strife.[33]

The situation in Iraq after the 2003 US attack and the dismantling of the Saddam Hussein regime created fertile ground for the emergence of various smaller Sunni and Shiite insurgent groups to fight the US forces but eventually led to the beginning of a sectarian war, with various Jihadi groups establishing areas of influence in the remote areas. Tribal loyalty and sectarian hatred proved to be a devastating mixture for war-torn Iraq.[34] Gradually, many smaller Sunni Jihadi groups started to merge, leading to the emergence of what was declared to be the 'Islamic State' in 2014.

The Islamic State (IS)

The IS has its roots in the *Jama'at al-Tawhid wa al-Jihad*, a militant Islamist organisation formed by the Jordanian preacher Abu Musab al-Zarqawi, in 1999. Zarqawi was forced to flee Jordan in 2001, and took refuge in Iraq.

In 2004, he pledged allegiance to Al-Qaida and renamed his group Al-Qaida in Iraq (AQI). The AQI got involved in militancy in Iraq after the 2003 US attack, and was one of the key perpetrators of sectarian strife after the toppling of the Saddam regime with the aim of establishing Sunni Islamic rule.[35] Zarqawi was killed in an US strike in 2006, and the mantle of the group temporarily came into the hands of Abu Ayyub al-Masri after a number of Iraqi Sunni Islamist groups formed a coalition—the Mujahideen Shura Council (MSC). In October 2006, the MSC, together with a number of Sunni tribes, declared the establishment of the Islamic State of Iraq under the leadership of Abu Omar al-Baghdadi. In April 2010, the mantle of the so called Sunni Islamic State in Iraq fell on Abu Bakr al-Baghdadi after Abu Omar al-Baghdadi and Abu Ayyub al-Masri were killed in a US strike.

Between 2006 and 2011, the group remained confined to Iraq, and carried out a number of deadly bombings mainly targeting Shia shrines and congregations. This led to the intensification of the sectarian strife. It continued to focus on the Shias in Iraq, and gained significantly due to the coming together of several Sunni insurgent and tribal groups under its banner. Fawaz Gerges, a Lebanese scholar, has articulated the significance of Iraqi socio-political fault lines and the impact of the US attack on the evolution of the IS and its use of brutal methods. He writes, 'ISIS's viciousness reflects the bitter inheritance of decades of Baathist rule that tore apart Iraq's social fabric and left deep wounds that are still festering.' Gerges adds, 'In a sense, ISIS internalised the brutal tactics of the Baathist regime and Iraq's blood-drenched modern history.'[36]

A breakthrough moment for the IS came with the eruption of popular protests against the Assad regime in Syria. The unwillingness of the Syrian regime to respond to popular unrest and the use of force against the protestors (who largely comprised of Sunni Muslims) in town and cities across the country leading to hundreds of civilian deaths in May 2011 changed the direction of the popular protests into insurgency and rebellion.[37] What has ensued in Syria since has proved to be one of the bloodiest civil wars in modern history, involving various local, regional, and international actors as well as state and non-state entities, and has led to more than 500,000 casualties, and more than ten million refugees and internally displaced persons until mid-2016.[38] The Islamic State of Iraq got involved in the Syrian theatre by initially sending its fighters to confront Syrian government forces. By early 2012, it had created a franchise in Syria that came to be known as *Jabhat al-Nusra li al-Sham* or the Nusra Front, under the leadership of Abu Muhammad al-Golani, a Syrian Islamist militant.[39]

In April 2013, al-Baghdadi announced the formation of the Islamic State in Iraq and Levant (ISIL) by merging the Islamic State in Iraq and Nusra Front; in June 2014, he declared the establishment of *al-Dawlah al-Islamiyah* with substantial territorial control in western Iraq and eastern Syria, and headquartered in the city of Raqqah in Syria. What made the IS a global terrorist organisation was its ability to attract fighters from across the globe to the Syrian and Iraqi theatre, and mount lone-wolf[40] and deadly coordinated attacks across the world. Its use of social media and technology to market itself as *al-Khilafah al-Islamiyah* with political, religious as well as cultural and lifestyle appeal has been its most significant achievement.[41]

What distinguishes it from its predecessor (and now competitor) Al-Qaida is its control over large territory with, reportedly, a systematic administrative structure, bureaucracy, as well as a legal and economic system. It has been able to normalise an extraordinary situation wherein a terrorist group has been able to establish and sustain a state. The only other similar example could be the Islamic Emirate of Afghanistan (1996–2001) founded by the Taliban. However, the two are vastly different, as the Taliban were largely a fighter group drawn from within Afghanistan, did not mount attacks outside, and did not appeal to foreign fighters. More importantly, the Taliban chief Mulla Omar did not proclaim a global caliphate; rather, he was considered to be the *Amir al-Mu'mineen* (commander of the faithful), that is, the head of the Emirate.

According to reports, the IS has a huge military force and apparatus; it has more than 30,000 foreign fighters from across the Middle East, Africa, Europe, Asia and Americas on its rolls.[42] Moreover, since announcing a global caliphate, it has intensified attacks outside Iraq and Syria, with several attacks in France, Tunisia, Saudi Arabia, Egypt, Afghanistan, Bangladesh, Germany, and the USA. Its brutal use of force in territories under its control as well as killing sprees against minorities and Shias by applying most inhuman methods has invited criticism even from the Al-Qaida.[43] Its use of sex slaves and the barbaric treatment of women and homosexuals has come to light, with former captives narrating horrific instances of violence.[44] It is in the possession of sophisticated weapons, and has been able to acquire significant battle experience, thus making it a deadly force. Its ability to expand the fighting beyond its territorial control and inspire lone-wolf attacks in various parts of the world provides it extra potency.

A Comparative Analysis

The declaration of a worldwide 'Islamic Caliphate' in June 2014 marks a new phase in the history of Jihadi terrorism. While Al-Qaida preferred to be a centralised coherent group with branches in strategic regions, the IS aspires to becoming—and to an extent it has already succeeded—a decentralised umbrella organisation for Jihadi terrorist groups all over the world. Hence, the emergence of the IS marks the next stage in the globalisation of Jihadi terrorism, whereby its franchises or affiliates have struck at will in the heart of Europe, Asia and Africa, and have been able to hold ground in Iraq, Syria, Libya, and Egypt despite continuous military action by local, regional, and global powers. The Al-Qaida and IS have similar goals: to create a new world order based in Islamic *shari'a*, with the entire Muslim population living under a transnational Islamic 'Khilafah.'

Ideologically and organisationally, the two have similar roots, and take inspiration from Salafi-Wahhabi ideas intermixed with the Muslim Brotherhood's vigour to Islamise society and politicise Islam.[45] Jihadism takes inspiration from pan-Islamist ideas intermixed with militant Islamism, and is shared by both the groups. On the ideological front, there is one key difference: that is, on the establishment of a worldwide Islamic Caliphate. Al-Qaeda believes this to be the end-goal of the Islamist movement, and in that it shares its ideology with other non-violent Islamist groups who believe in the Islamisation of society before the formation of a political entity. Al-Qaida sees the USA as a global hegemonic imperial power with dominance in the Middle East, and as the main hurdle in the way of achieving this goal. Hence, it has been declared the main target of its violent resistance.[46] In contrast, the IS believes that establishing a 'truly Islamic' Caliphate is the first step towards creating a global Islamic Caliphate. It believes that the Islamisation of the society cannot be undertaken without political authority, and takes cues from Qutbism which articulates the need for political authority, the subsequent implementation of an Islamic order within its boundaries, and the constant struggle for territorial expansion of the Islamic political entity.[47]

However, ideologically, the IS is more severe and radical than the Al-Qaida. Cole Bunzel notes, "If jihadism were to be placed on a political spectrum, Al-Qaida would be its left and the Islamic State its right."[48] He further points out that, doctrinally, the IS believes in 'offensive jihad' more than the 'defensive jihad' that "traditionally jihadis ... have espoused" by focusing on the enemy within to establish a pristine Islamic society, and ridding the Islamic societies of all 'infidels' and 'apostates'. IS doctrinally believes in the idea that all Shias are apostates and deserve death, and that Muslims should maintain contacts only with 'true' Muslims.[49]

Scholars further identify a number of key features that distinguish the two, and have even set them against each other. One of the most significant differences has been the focus on the "far enemy" (that is, the West or the Jewish-Christian alliance) and the "near enemy", (that is, tyrannical Muslim rulers and a deviant Muslim populace, including Shias, non-practising Muslims, and Sufis). Notably, for Al-Qaida, the "near-enemy" is comprised mainly of tyrannical rulers who assist Western powers, especially the USA, to extend their hegemony in Muslim lands. For the IS, the "near-enemy" comprises more of deviant Muslims and non-believers living in Muslim lands rather than the rulers. While Al-Qaida is focused on fighting the "far enemy" rather than confronting the "near enemy", the IS believes in simultaneously engaging with both, and prefers to employ exemplary terrorizing punishments to subdue the "near enemy" and mount lone-wolf attacks to terrorise the "far enemy".[50]

The other difference between the two groups lies in the use of new media technology to attract supporters and new recruits. The IS has been effectively using new social media tools, especially Facebook, Twitter, and other such smart-phone based applications. However, the Al-Qaida leadership—which is a generation older than the IS leadership—continues to rely more on internet platforms and online forums that are not so popular among the youth.[51] This has been a key factor in the meteoric rise of the IS, and leaving Al-Qaida way behind in attracting the younger generation. Another key difference lies in the IS's use of brutal methods such as beheadings and the massacre of those who do not fall in line—done also as a means of infusing and spreading terror. While the Al-Qaida also shared the IS hatred of 'infidels' and 'apostates', it preferred to focus on big attacks against the USA. On the other hand, the IS is committed to the sectarian cleansing of the territory under its control. In fact, this difference has, in the past, created rifts between the leadership of the two groups.[52]

Notably, these tactical and strategic differences have escalated into a full blown war between the Al-Qaida and the IS, especially in the Syrian theatre. It has been argued that this could lead to the eventual demise of Jihadism. However, it would also be wrong to argue that their differences are too big to dismiss the possibility of their coming together in the future. The current struggle between the two is more because of competitions in terms of attracting fighters and gaining wider acceptance rather than because of their substantial ideological differences. Hence, it would be wrong to discount the possibility of the two coming together in the future to form a larger global Salafi-Jihadist entity with a wider reach and appeal.

Fighting Jihadism

In current discourse, Jihadi terror is largely seen as a security problem. Despite the debate about the futility of finding a military-only solution to jihadism, the discourse more often remains security-oriented. It is argued that military confrontation is the only solution to militant Islamism. Undoubtedly military confrontation is significant, and the recent advances and successes of the Russia-Iran-Hezbollah alliance in Syria and the US-Iraq and Kurdish successes in Iraq are indicative. However, Jihadism has shown a capability to re-emerge in a new avatar every time a Jihadi terrorist group has been defeated in any one of the war-theatres. There are numerous examples—the war in Afghanistan, the situation in Yemen, and the ongoing battle against the IS in Iraq and Syria. These show that Jihadism can re-emerge from the ashes and revive the fight. For example, the USA had declared victory in Iraq, leading President Obama to dismiss the resurgence of the Jihadist resurgence in Iraq to be only a minor threat.[53]

While finding a security solution through counter-terrorism is necessary, there is a simultaneous need to understand the ideological and socio-political roots of the problem. Jihadism as an idea emanates from the desire to find an "Islamic" solution to the socio-political churning, the lack of governance, and the foreign domination in the Middle East today. Fawaz Gerges argues that "The cause of the group's [ISIS] development and rise is located in the severe social and political conditions in Arab societies as well as in the regional and global rivalries."[54] Hence, there is need to work towards there solution of the socio-political problems looming in Arab societies through comprehensive social and political reforms.

Abdel Bari Atwan articulates the need for creating an ideological "counterbalance" to radical Islam that should rely on a "powerful Islamic figure or popular movement" since "Western organisations aiming to prevent radicalisation lack credibility."[55] Therefore, an important aspect of fighting Jihadism is developing society-oriented de-radicalisation programmes. One example of this is Algeria that has come back from being a broken society through a comprehensive de-radicalisation programme.[56] Countries like Saudi Arabia too have initiated a counter-terror and de-radicalisation programme, though its efficacy is yet to be tested.[57]

The growing reach and potency of Jihadi terrorism demands developing a wider counter-terror strategy that is based on intelligence inputs and military actions as well as de-radicalisation and social upliftment programmes. The key factors behind the global appeal of Jihadism is the ability of Jihadist groups in presenting themselves as the vanguard of Islam working against the so called "Western onslaught" on Islam, which has been furthered by the historical legacies of colonialism and imperialism in the Middle East. The desire of the people to find a solution to their socio-political grievances in Islam, and the ability of Islamist groups to stand up against tyrannical rulers have made them popular. Hence, there is a need to re-emphasise and re-invent the plurality and diversity within Islam and Islamic discourses. Undoubtedly there is immense plurality in Islam, and the debates within Islam are as diverse; but the ability of militant Islamists to present *their* interpretation as dominant and so attracting a wider following, is dangerous. Hence, above all, in confronting Jihad there is a need for a debate within Islam to counter the threats posed by radical and fundamentalist ideas.

Conclusion

Jihadism has emerged as a global threat during the past three decades—that is, since the rise of Al-Qaida in the 1990s amidst the Afghan jihad against the Soviet invasion to the emergence of the IS from within the broken society and polity of Iraq. During this period, jihadist groups received considerable state support many a time, which helped them develop resilience and appeal. Thus, Jihadism has emerged as the most potent threat to peace and stability in the Middle East as well as in the world. Though Islam is an important component of Jihadi discourse, it is mainly the skewed interpretations of Islamic doctrines by Jihadist ideologues that have legitimised the use of terrorism as a way of resistance and the fight against injustice. There are certain tactical and strategic differences among global jihadist groups, especially the Al-Qaida and the IS; but they have similar ideological roots, and their appeal lies in similar socio-political grievances. It is significant that, in the fight against Jihadism, military action is supplemented with socio-political solution. Thus, the need today is to understand the ideological roots of the problem and address it, rather than trying only to cure its symptoms.

NOTES

1. Caliph or *Khalifah* in Arabic means successor of the Prophet and the leader of the Muslim *ummah*. The title has religious and historical connotations and significance. Since the death of Prophet Muhammad in 632 AD, the institution continued to be the nominal ruler of the Muslim world. For a historical overview, see *Al-Jazeera's* three-part documentary "The Caliph", http://interactive.

aljazeera.com/aje/2016/the-caliph-islamic-history/. For a reading of the concepts and its socio-cultural significance, see Madawi al-Rasheed, Carool Kersten and Marat Shterin (eds.), *Demystifying the Caliphate: Historical Memory and Contemporary Contexts*, New York: Oxford University Press, 2015.

2. Thomas Hegghammer, "Jihadi Salafis or Revolutionaries? On Theology and Politics in the Study of Militant Islamism", in Roel Meijer (ed.), *Global Salafism: Islam's New Religious Movement*, New York: Columbia University Press, 2009, pp. 244–266.
3. For a discussion, see: Nabeel Qureshi, *Answering Jihad: A Better Way Forward*, Grand Rapids, Michigan: Zondervan, 2016. For an alternate view, see: M. A. Khan, *Islamic Jihad: A Legacy of Forced Conversion, Imperialism, and Slavery*, New York: I Universe, 2009.
4. Onder Bakircioglu, "A Socio-legal Analysis of the Concept of Jihad", in *The International and Comparative Law Quarterly*, 2010, vol. 59, no. 2, pp. 413–440.
5. Ibid.
6. Michael Bonner, *Jihad in Islamic History: Doctrines and Practices*, Princeton, NJ: Princeton University Press, 2006.
7. See, Talmiz Ahmed, *The Islamist Challenge in West Asia: Doctrinal and Political Competitions after the Arab Spring*, New Delhi: IDSA and Pentagon Press, 2013.
8. Thomas Hegghammer, *Jihad in Saudi Arabia: Violence and Pan-Islamism* (New York: Cambridge University Press, 2010).
9. Salafi Islam is a stream within the Islamist movement that calls for going back to early Islam, and following the practices of the *al-Salaf al-Saleh* (the rightly guided generation).
10. For a detailed reading on the emergence and evolution of Wahhabi Islam, see, Natana J. DeLong-Bas, *Wahhabi Islam: From Revival and Reform to Global Jihad*, New York: Oxford University Press, 2004.
11. One of the four schools of jurisprudence in Sunni Islam that was a source of inspiration for Muhammad bin Abdul Wahhab.
12. Shiraz Maher, *Salafi-Jihadism: The History of an Idea*, London: Hurst & Company, 2016, p. 6.
13. Ibid, pp. 41–68.
14. John Calvert, *Sayyid Qutb and the Origins of Radical Islam*, New York: Columbia University Press, 2010.
15. Shiraz Maher, *Salafi Jihadism*, p. 14.
16. Hassan Hassan, "The Sectarianism of the Islamic State: Ideological Roots and Political Context", Carnegie Paper, June 2016, Washington DC, Carnegie Endowment for International Peace, p. 3.
17. Thomas Hegghammer, "The Rise of Muslim Foreign Fighters: Islam and the Globalisation of Jihad", *International Security*, 2010, 35 (3): 53-94.
18. Ibid, p. 56.
19. Gilles Kepel, *Jihad: The Trail of Political Islam*, Cambridge, MS: Harvard University Press, 2002.
20. For a discussion on the causes of the globalisation of Jihad, see, Asef Mogahdam, *The Roots of Terrorism*, New York: Chelsea House, 2006.
21. These *mujahideen* received active state support to join the Afghan theatre. See, Fawaz Gerges, *The Far Enemy: Why Jihad went Global*, New York: Cambridge University Press, 2005, p. 69.

22. Abdullah Azzam, "Defence of Muslim Lands: The First Obligation after Iman", English translation of original fatwa in Arabic, retrieved from: http://www.religioscope.com/info/doc/jihad/azzam_defence_3_chap1.htm.
23. See, "Arab Veterans of Afghanistan War Lead New Islamic Holy War", *GlobalSecurity.org*, 28 October 1994, at http://www.globalsecurity.org/intell/library/news/1994/afghan_war_vetrans.html. For an academic discussion on the subject, see also, Thomas Hegghammer, "The Rise of Muslim Foreign Fighters ..." op. cit.
24. For a detailed study on the Saudi Sahwa movement, see, Stèphane Lacroix, *Awakening Islam: The Politics of Religious Dissent in Contemporary Saudi Arabia*, Cambridge, Massachusetts: Harvard University Press, 2011. For a discussion on the ideological affinity between the Sahwa movement and the Jihadism, see, Hassan Hassan, "The Sectarianism of the Islamic State ..." op. cit.
25. Richard H. Dekmejian, "The Liberal Impulse in Saudi Arabia", *Middle East Journal*, 2003, 57 (3): 400-413.
26. Douglas Jehl, "A Nation Challenged: Saudi Arabia; Holy War Lured Saudis as Rulers Looked Away", *The New York Times*, 27 December 2001, at http://www.nytimes.com/2001/12/27/world/a-nation-challenged-saudi-arabia-holy-war-lured-saudis-as-rulers-looked-away.html?pagewanted=3. Also see, Robert Lacey, *Inside the Kingdom: Kings, Clerics, Modernists, Terrorists, and the Struggle for Saudi Arabia*, New York: Viking Penguin, 2009.
27. Thomas Hegghammer, *Jihad in Saudi Arabia*... op. cit.
28. Osama Bin-Laden, "An Open Letter to Sheikh Ibn Baz from Osama Bin-Laden", original Arabic, at *Al-Arab News*, at http://alarabnews.com/alshaab/GIF/26-10-2001/Ben%20laden.htm.
29. For the text, see, "Osama Bin Laden's Declaration of Jihad against America, 1996", *Milestone Documents in World History*, at http://salempress.com/store/pdfs/bin_laden.pdf.
30. For an in-depth reading on Al-Qaida's ideology and evolution see: Christopher M. Blanchard, *Al-Qaeda: Statements and Evolving Ideology*, Congressional Research Service Report, No. RL32759, July 2007; and Abdel Bari Atwan, *The Secret History of al-Qa'ida*, London: Saqi Books, 2006.
31. Douglas Kellner, "Globalisation, Terrorism, and Democracy: 9/11 and its Aftermath", in Ino Rossi (ed.), *Frontiers of Globalisation Research: Theoretical and Methodological Approaches* (New York: Springer, 2007), pp. 243-268.
32. See: Barry Buzan, "Will the 'Global War on Terrorism' be the New Cold War", *International Affairs*, November 2006, 82 (6): 1101-1118. Also see
33. For a reading on the socio-political consequences of the war in Iraq, see, Tareq Y. Ismael and Jacqueline S. Ismael, *Iraq in the Twenty-First Century: Regime Change and the Making of a Failed State*, London and New York: Routledge, 2015. For an account of the devastation and consequences of the US attack on Afghanistan, see, Mohammd Mirwais, "Nation Building Process in Iraq and Afghanistan: A Comparative Study", Ph.D. Thesis, Jawaharlal Nehru University, New Delhi, 2016.
34. Talmiz Ahmed, *Turmoil in West Asia: The Sectarian Divide Shapes Regional Competitions*, New Delhi: IDSA, 2016.
35. Hassan Hassan, "The Sectarianism of the Islamic State ..." op.cit; see also, Joost Hilterman, "A New Sectarian Threat in the Middle East", *International Review of*

the Red Cross, December 2007, 89 (868): 795–808.

36. Fawaz Gerges, *ISIS: A History*, Princeton, NJ: Princeton University Press, 2016, p. 9.
37. For a comprehensive account of what has ensued in Syria since the outbreak of popular protests and its transformation into a civil war, see, Emile Hokayem, *Syria's Uprising and the Fracturing of the Levant*, London and New York: IISS and Routledge, 2013.
38. "Syria: Confronting Fragmentation!", Impact of Syrian Crisis Report, Syrian Centre for Policy Research, February 2016, at http://scpr-syria.org/publications/policy-reports/confronting-fragmentation/.
39. The Nusra Front parted ways with the Islamic State of Iraq and Levant in 2013, and joined hands with Al-Qaida; it entered into open fights with the Islamic State in Syria during 2013–15 and, as of July 2016, has split with Al-Qaida and renamed itself as *Jabhat al-Fatah al-Sham* (Front for the Conquest of Syria) in a bid to rid its terrorist tag.
40. Attacks committed by individuals without any material support from any group, and outside an organised command structure but motivated or inspired by an ideology or a group. The term has its origins in White supremacist attacks in USA and was popularised by individuals such as Alex Curtis and Tom Metzger. IS has appealed to its supporters globally (but especially in the West) to mount lone-wolf attacks. For a comprehensive study of the phenomenon, see, Jefferey Simon, *Lone Wolf Terrorism: Understanding the Growing Threat*, New York: Prometheus Books, 2016.
41. Thomas Hegghammer, "The Soft Power of Militant Jihad", *The New York Times*, 18 December 2015, at http://www.nytimes.com/2015/12/20/opinion/sunday/militant-jihads-softer-side.html.
42. Ashley Kirk, "Iraq and Syria: How many Foreign Fighters are Fighting for ISIL?", *The Telegraph*, 24 March 2016, at http://www.telegraph.co.uk/news/2016/03/29/iraq-and-syria-how-many-foreign-fighters-are-fighting-for-isil/.
43. Daniel Byman and Jennifer Williams, "ISIS vs. Al Qaeda: Jihadism's Global Civil War", *The National Interest*, 24 February 2015, at http://nationalinterest.org/feature/isis-vs-al-qaeda-jihadism%E2%80%99s-global-civil-war-12304.
44. Charlotte Alter, "A Yezidi Women who Escaped ISIS Slavery Tells Her Story", *Time*, 20 December 2015, at http://time.com/4152127/isis-yezidi-woman-slavery-united-nations/.
45. Hassan Hassan, "The Sectarianism of the Islamic State ..."; and Thomas Hegghammer, "The Rise of Muslim Foreign Fighters ..." op. cit.
46. Christopher M. Blanchard, *Al-Qaeda: Statements and Evolving Ideology*, op. cit; and Abdel Bari Atwan, *The Secret History of al-Qa'ida*, op. cit.
47. John Calvert, *Sayyid Qutb and the Origins of Radical Islam*, op. cit; Hassan, "The Sectarianism of the Islamic State ..." op. cit.
48. Cole Bunzel, "From Paper State to Caliphate: The Ideology of the Islamic State", Analysis Paper, No. 19, March 2015, Center for Middle East Policy, The Brookings Institution, Washington, DC, p. 9.
49. Ibid.
50. Daniel Byman and Jennifer Williams, "ISIS vs. Al Qaeda ..." op. cit.
51. Gabriel Weimann, "New Terrorism and New Media", Research Series Report, Volume 2, Woodrow Wilson International Center for Scholars, 2014, at https://

www.wilsoncenter.org/sites/default/files/STIP_140501_new_terrorism_F.pdf; see also, Charlie Winter, "The Virtual 'Caliphate': Understanding the Islamic State's Propaganda Strategy", Quilliam Foundation Report, July 2015, at https://www.quilliamfoundation.org/wp/wp-content/uploads/publications/free/the-virtual-caliphate-understanding-islamic-states-propaganda-strategy.pdf.

52. Daniel Byman and Jennifer Williams, "ISIS vs. Al Qaeda ..." op. cit.
53. David Remnick, "Going the Distance: On and Off the Road with Obama", *The New Yorker*, 27 January 2014, at http://www.newyorker.com/magazine/2014/01/27/going-the-distance-david-remnick.
54. Fawaz Gerges, *ISIS: A History*, op. cit. p. 7.
55. Abdel Bari Atwan, *Islamic State: The Digital Caliphate*, London: Saqi Books, 2015, p. 222.
56. Omar Ashour, "Islamist De-Radicalization in Algeria: Successes and Failures", The Middle East Institute Policy Brief, No. 21, November 2008, at http://www.mei.edu/content/islamist-de-radicalization-algeria-successes-and-failures.
57. Andreas Casptack, "Deradicalization Programs in Saudi Arabia: A Case Study", MEI series on Understanding Deradicalization: Pathway to Enhance Transatlantic Common Perception and Practices, 10 June 2015, at http://www.mei.edu/content/deradicalization-programs-saudi-arabia-case-study; see also, Marisa L. Porges, "The Saudi Deradicalization Experiment", Expert Brief, Council on Foreign Relations, New York, 22 January 2010, http://www.cfr.org/radicalization-and-extremism/saudi-deradicalization-experiment/p21292.

3

The Changing Energy Scenario: Geopolitical Implications for West Asia

Sameena Hameed

ABSTRACT

Energy has been the main driver of the geopolitics of the West Asian region since the discovery of oil. The oil factor has, paradoxically, promoted the stability of regimes in the Gulf through the distribution of oil rent and the Saudi-US strategic alliance, as well as caused wars to retain strategic control over the resource. The global energy scenario has profoundly changed with the US shale revolution, significant gains in energy efficiency, and renewable energy as well as increasing commitments towards environmentally friendly fuels. The declining demand for West Asian oil and gas in the USA and the simultaneous unprecedented rise in Asian demand are prompting a significant realignment in the geopolitical chessboard of the region. At the same time, the increasingly mutual discordance in US-Saudi relations is posing questions about the connection between the changing global energy scenario and the geopolitical realignment in West Asia.

As energy prices remain low in the medium term, countries dependent on oil and gas export revenue face the challenge of economic diversification, while facing political and security risks. The re-entry of Iraqi and the Iranian oil in the international market has sharpened the contestation among the Gulf countries for market share. However, the recent production cut deal between the OPEC and non-OPEC members are signalling new possibilities of a geo-economic alliance despite the existing geostrategic rivalry among the major producers. This chapter looks at changes in the global energy scenario (focusing on oil and gas), and the threats emanating there for West Asian energy producers. It also looks at the changing nature of US-Saudi relations and its geopolitical implications in the region.

The Changing Global Energy Scenario

Over the last few decades, the global energy landscape began to shift in a fundamental way. Energy demand from the developed economies of the world reduced considerably due to their efforts towards energy efficiency and using renewable energy. At the same time, the emerging Asian economies witnessed unprecedented growth in their energy consumption, as they become centres of global investment and production activities. The oil markets have essentially been demand driven primarily by the Asian countries for most of the previous decade.

The US 'shale revolution' since 2008 has become a game changer, transforming the world's largest importer of oil and gas to the largest producer. The shale gas supplies from Pennsylvania alone equal the entire natural gas export capacity of Qatar, the world's second largest natural gas exporter.[1] The increase from light tight oil production from North Dakota and Texas over the last five years is equivalent to that of Iraq's current production levels.[2]

Throughout the 2000s, as oil prices surged above US$100 a barrel, hydraulic fracturing ('fracking') and horizontal drilling to extract oil from shale formations became economically viable in the USA. Consequentially, US oil production rose from 8.5 mbpd in 2008 to 12.8 mbpd in 2014, more than offsetting the supply disruptions from West Asia and North Africa (WANA) during the period. In 2011, the USA exported refined petroleum products more than its imports for the first time in over six decades. The low US natural gas prices have provided its refineries a competitive advantage, and refined petroleum products have became its top export commodity. African and Gulf oil previously destined for the USA is now in competition for the European and Asian markets. The range of potential suppliers has transformed the oil and gas market from being that of the seller's to that of the buyers'. EIA has estimated that the USA will be a net gas exporter by 2018.[3] The terminals that were originally built to receive LNG are being repurposed for export.

Since the last few years, global oil demand growth has been unexpectedly weak for a combination of structural and cyclical factors. China has entered a new, less oil-intensive stage of development following Beijing's decision to reorient the economy away from manufacturing/ exports.[4] Reshaped by the information technology revolution, the global economy has generally become less fuel intensive. Concerns over climate change are recasting energy policies. Besides, the globalisation of the natural gas market, along with increasing cost competitiveness of renewable energy, is posing an unprecedented challenge to oil. Natural gas is the fastest growing fuel, with a rate of 1.8 per cent per annum.[5] However, in recent years, overall growth in energy demand has slowed down due to subdued growth in the major economies.

West Asian Energy Scenario: The Geopolitical Context

Energy defines the economic and political landscape of the region. West Asia holds about 52 percent of the global oil reserves and 41 percent of gas reserves; 9 out of its 13 countries are dependent on oil and gas export revenue for their government expenditure.[6] Even the countries not exporting oil, have their economies heavily influenced by the oil export revenues of their neighbours through remittances and aid flows.

Oil in exchange for security has underpinned the strategic alliance of the Gulf monarchies with the USA since the pact signed between former US President Roosevelt and Saudi King Abdul Aziz bin Saud, in 1945. Oil also provided the context to US interventions in Iran (the CIA orchestrated coup in 1953), Kuwait (to drive out Iraqi forces), and later in Iraq. The USA has protected friendly oil rich Gulf monarchies through its military bases in the region and massive weapons sales, and secured its energy supplies from the region.

Besides, oil revenues ensure domestic political stability by giving the Gulf regimes autonomous sources of income to support a cradle to grave system of patronage, and put in place a coercive security apparatus. Energy plays a key role in the determining the intactness of the 'social contract' between the regime and the people in West Asian oil exporting countries. Low energy prices has kept the cost of living affordable for the people as well as aided domestic energy intensive industries. The Gulf monarchies have doled out extensive hand-outs to appease the restive population as the Arab uprisings eventually brought down regimes in Tunisia, Egypt, and Libya. Saudi Arabia, UAE, and Kuwait followed aid diplomacy with countries like Bahrain, Jordan, Egypt, and Morocco to help contain the contagion of Arab uprisings. With dwindling oil revenues in the last two years, the socio-political buffers of the patronage system have come under pressure, and the regimes face grave internal threats. The Gulf monarchies, especially Saudi Arabia, have also been facing grave threats from Islamic extremists; many affiliated with Al Qaida or the exile groups. They interact with the larger demographic threat of a new, media savvy, unemployed educated youth who are demanding better living standards, more participation, and regime accountability.

As the West Asian region passes through a tumultuous transition, the USA and Saudi Arabia have been perceived as acting with increasing discordance with each other's interests. The US military withdrawal from Iraq, the drawdown in Afghanistan, its policy in Syria, and its rapprochement with Iran have deeply estranged Saudi Arabia over the last few years. Saudi Arabia's war in Yemen as well as its proxy wars with Iran in Syria, Lebanon, and Iraq have hurt US interests by creating instability, and have weakened the fight against the ISIS. The centrality of West Asia to the USA and its security commitments are being increasingly debated, both in the USA and the region. All this has prompted Saudi Arabia to have a more assertive foreign policy to address its security concerns. It sent its forces to Bahrain to curb the civil uprisings, and has also been waging a war on the Houthi rebels in Yemen since 2015. Saudi Arabia's regional assertiveness is influencing the behaviour of other actors in the region, and has unfolded larger geopolitical contestations for regional supremacy.

The Saudi war on Yemen has already cost an estimated US$5.3 billion, and is a huge resource drain in a period of low oil revenues. However, it has apparently served some of its vital political interests. The Saudi media has used it to build a nationalist narrative of the Kingdom as the defender of the "Sunnis" in the region; it has also bolstered a bold profile of the new king Salman and his son Mohammad bin Salman, and built the support of the Islamic cleric constituency across the ideological spectrum.[7] Besides, much of Saudi's regional assertions on Shia-Sunni antagonism have been aimed at diverting the people's attention from the failures of governance and the want of reforms.[8] The flow of oil revenues will, no doubt, eventually set the limits to their military adventurism and aid diplomacy. The war against terrorism is also providing a pretext for the authoritarian regimes to put in place more draconian security arrangements to tackle the threat of domestic instability.[9] Saudi Arabia increased the number of executions to its highest level in 20 years, and Kuwait increasingly repressed journalists and civil society activists in 2015.[10] Such a context becomes particularly useful when declining oil prices are fast eroding the capacity of the regimes to meet the rising expectations of the people; and, as they proceed with price hikes, impose taxes, and roll back state patronage, they simultaneously fail to cede more political and civil liberties.

The Re-Entry of Iran and Iraq in the Oil Market

Iraq has the fifth-largest proven crude oil reserves in the world. Post Saddam, the oil sector was opened to private and foreign investment to substantially increase oil production and export. The infrastructural bottlenecks (pipelines, port capacity, and storage facilities), security issues, and internal disputes continue to pose significant challenges. The lack of agreement between the central Iraqi government and the Kurdish Regional Government (KRG) over the sharing of oil and budget revenues for several years have inhibited investment, and has prompted the latter to export oil independently through the Turkey Ceyhan pipeline. The ability to export crude oil and collect oil revenues is central to the autonomy of Iraqi Kurdistan. However, both sides are facing fiscal constraints due to low oil prices amidst the challenge of fighting the Islamic State militants; thus recently, both the Iraqi government and the KRG have started jointly exporting Kirkuk oil after agreeing on a preliminary deal.[11] However, the future of the deal is uncertain given the disagreement and debate surrounding the 2017 budget.

Iran is estimated to have 10 per cent (158 billion barrels) of the world's proven oil reserves and 18 per cent (34 trillion cubic meters) of natural gas reserves and, thus, holds the fourth and second largest reserves of oil and gas in the world, respectively. Sanctions cost Iran significant market share: oil exports fell to 1.25 mbd in 2013, from a high of 2.6 mb/d in the pre-sanctions period. The EU tightened the US-led sanctions in 2012, which also inhibited investment in the country. Sanctions against Iran have been lifted partially following the nuclear agreement between Iran and the P5+1 countries on 14 July 2015. Since the nuclear deal, Iran has been trying to attract foreign investment in its energy sector by offering lucrative terms in exploration and development as well as in production. According to the oil ministry, the oil and gas sector needs US$100 billion in investment in the next five years. With the sanctions lifted, Iran can now commission its dormant production capacity, and swiftly market its stocks. However, the extent to which Iran is able to export to the world market is contingent on the pricing reforms in the energy sector.[12]

The Political Economy of Reforms and Diversification in West Asia

The demand for reforms in most West Asian countries gathered momentum in the 1990s during the period of low oil rent as well as discontent over deteriorating socio-economic conditions. Even in countries like Saudi Arabia—one of the most absolute monarchies in the world—

questions about the Saudi monarchy, dividing wealth, and opening the political landscape were the main issues discussed by intellectuals. After the terrorist attack of 9/11, the USA has been pressurising the Gulf regimes, especial Saudi Arabia, to adopt liberalisation reform to accommodate dissenting voices that feed into terrorism. However, the regimes have only pursued cosmetic political reforms, and tried to manage discontent through policies of economic liberalisation that have created a sophisticated form of symbiosis of the political and economic elite.

The development of the private sector constitutes a political question owing to its ability to generate income independent of the patronage system; but it was kept dependent in most of the West Asian Countries especially the Gulf by creating fragmented market structures, where State expenditure and demand are the main drivers.[13] The private sector thus created depended on the state for privileges and contracts, was mainly in low skilled sectors, and generated profit from the employment of expatriate labour.[14] It neither contributed significantly to diversification or the generation of local employment. The demographic profile is dominated by younger, more educated, and globally connected nationals. However, the lack of professional skills among the nationals as well as their unwillingness to work on market determined terms and conditions have led to huge unemployment rates, especially among the youth in the WANA region.

Oil revenues are an important fiscal source for diversification and employment generation. Many countries in the region—like Algeria and Libya—are living well beyond their budget. At the same time, highly subsidized energy prices have led to rapidly growing domestic energy consumption that bites into the exportable surplus. The political climate in these countries is generally tense, and people have been protesting for better pay and living standards. Despite experiencing relatively different pressures, Bahrain, Oman, Qatar, Saudi Arabia, UAE, and lastly Kuwait have either completely liberalised fuel prices or raised them substantially because of the sharp fall in oil income since mid-2014.[15] Bahrain and Oman have a relatively low resource base, low GDP per capita, and high fiscal deficits as compared their counterparts in the GCC. At the same time, they face more difficult political economies. Bahrain's majority Shiite population under a Sunni regime protested for political reforms during the Arab uprisings.

The Gulf States are making efforts to diversify their economies towards becoming more knowledge and skill-based and driven by Gulf nationals. Bahrain, the UAE, and Qatar announced National *Vision 2030* plans in 2008, and *Kuwait* announced its State *Vision 2030* in 2010. The recent Saudi national transformation plan aims to imbue its nationals with a sense of purpose and pride, and to boost the role of the private sector in generating skilled employment. However, a private sector that sustains itself on political patronage undermines productivity and meritocracy. The success of these projects depend on the extent to which the regimes are able to improve professional skills and productivity among nationals, replace the private sector's privileges with result-oriented incentives, and deregulate the financial markets to unleash the entrepreneurial energy in the region. However, the diversification plans would be severely limited under chronic fiscal deficits and persistently low crude prices.

OPEC and the Global Oil Deal

The increase in non-OPEC oil production by USA and Russia over the years has posed a serious challenge to OPEC, which had aimed to regulate production to influence price levels. However, amid the oil supply glut and slowing demand, OPEC members like Saudi Arabia, UAE, and Kuwait have decided, in the last two years, to defend their market share.[16] In November 2014, the OPEC, spearhead by Saudi Arabia, decided not to cut production even when oil prices continued to fall. Despite much of the speculation about the geopolitical drivers of Saudi's low oil policy, revenue maximisation through increasing market share has been the top priority.[17] However, the precipitous fall in oil prices to US$30 per barrel, and the consequent political and economic pressures have urged OPEC members to think in terms of production cuts.

The OPEC meetings at Doha in April 2016 and Algiers were embroiled in tussles between Saudi Arabia and Iran over the burden of oil production cuts, especially as the oil revenues also provide the muscle for their larger geopolitical contestations in the region. Saudi Arabia refused, at the last moment, to sign a production freeze deal in Doha that did not include the Iranians. Iran argued exemption from production cuts and for its right to increase production from 3.6 mb/d to 4.2 mb/d—its pre-sanction production level in the year 2012. In an apparently major concession, Saudi Arabia's oil minister Al-Falih had offered, before the OPEC meeting in Algeria, to reduce its output if Iran agreed to freeze production at current levels Iran again vociferously rejected the Saudi offer, thus darkening the prospects of meeting in Algeria.[18] However in Algiers, Al-Falih made a final concession, allowing Iran alongside Libya and Nigeria to "produce at the maximum levels that make sense." This enabled OPEC to agree on oil output cuts for the first time since 2008.[19] The announcement by the

Russian President Vladimir Putin in the World Energy Congress in Istanbul in October 2016 that it would join OPEC's efforts to stabilise the oil market provided incentives for the members to clinch the deal.

The OPEC meeting in Vienna on 30 November saw the trump of geo-economics over geopolitics as member countries, in dire need of higher oil price to boost their export revenues, also agreed to individual production cuts, putting aside their individual rivalry. Saudi Arabia accepted the largest cut in its oil production, while Iran was allowed a slight increase from its current production levels.[20] Iraq, which was earlier also insisting on exemptions, also agreed to production cuts. The production cut deal between the OPEC and the 12 Non-OPEC member on 9 December 2016 was hailed as the first global oil pact since the year 2001.[21] The economic stress of falling oil revenues has prompted Saudi Arabia and Russia, the two largest exporters of crude, to start their first oil cooperation talks in 15 years.[22] Russia has agreed to cut oil production by 300,000 b/d.

Russia and Gas Geopolitics in West Asia

Russia is the second-largest oil exporter, and the largest exporter of natural gas. It is dependent on oil and gas exports for nearly 40-50 percent of total budgetary income, and over 70 percent of its total export revenue. The principal drivers of the Russia's policy in West Asia are geopolitical, with strong inter-connectedness with its energy interests. It seeks to attract investment from the Gulf countries, and support energy prices by coordinating policies with major oil and gas producers.[23]

Russia depends on the EU market for about 70 percent of its exports. At the same time, the EU has long sought to reduce its dependency on Russian gas.[24] Over the years, it tried to find an alternative route through Turkey to the European markets to bypass vulnerabilities in Ukraine. Turkey imports about 58 per cent of its gas imports from Russia. Russia declared freezing the Turkish Stream Project, as the Turkish Parliament did not approve it. Its relations with Russia worsened over the downing of a Russian plane during the war in Syria. However, later, Turkey's unexpected normalisation of its relations with Russia was followed by the resumption of the stalled Turkish stream project agreement. This was indicative of its eagerness to become a transit state for Russian gas to support its energy supply for its faltering economy. Turkey has also signed a MoU with Iran in 2007 to allow the transit of Iranian gas to the European market. Iran supplies 18 per cent of its gas exports especially to parts of eastern Anatolia; however, supplies are cut off frequently which has resulted in it being deemed an unreliable exporter.[25]

At the end of 2013, Russia also signed an offshore gas deal with Syria to explore the eastern Mediterranean, which has been estimated to contain about 122 trillion cubic feet of recoverable natural gas. Its only military base in the region in Syria is strategically positioned for supporting its investments in the energy resources in the Eastern Mediterranean sea.[26] Besides, Syria has also been viewed as transit route to the European market as it possesses relatively well-developed oil and gas pipeline infrastructure in spite of its modest reserves of hydrocarbons[27] Qatar had also proposed to build a pipeline through Syria to export to European markets; however, this was rejected by Assad. Besides, with sanctions on its own gas sector, Russia's strengthened position in Syria could potentially enable it to control or stall any future pipeline supply to Europe. The July 2011 gas pipeline energy agreement signed between the governments of Syria, Iran, and Iraq—that would have consolidated the Shia axis—ignited the full-scale Saudi and Qatari assault on Assad's power.[28] Thus, along with other things, there have been strong energy geopolitical undercurrents in the war in Syria.

Besides its huge gas reserves, Iran has a unique geopolitical position and proximity to big energy importers, both along the Western-axis involving Europe and Turkey as well as along Eastern-axis involving Pakistan, India, and China. Iran also aims to use its natural gas as a foreign policy tool to obtain some strategic manoeuvring capacity in regional energy geopolitics. Despite Iran's 18 per cent share in global gas reserves, its shares in global production and trade are 5 per cent and less than 1 per cent, respectively.[29] It is also reported to be in talks with some Gulf nations, like Oman, Kuwait and UAE), to meet their shortage of gas through exports.[30] Most Gulf countries, with the exception of Qatar and Iran, are facing shortages of natural gas. The ongoing construction of the LNG terminal at Tombak (a port on Iran's Persian Gulf), is almost complete, except the liquefying terminal for want of cutting-edge technology. It is already in talks with some European countries for LNG exports. India has also evinced interest in building the Iranian LNG terminal.

Gulf Look East Policy and Asian Consumers: Towards Strategic Convergence?

The genesis of strategic economic engagement with Asia lies in the aftermath of 9/11, 2001, when the GCC countries adopted a "Look East" policy. Asia's voracious energy consumption as well as its vibrant economic growth and competitive manpower drove the growing interdependence with the WANA region through robustly growing trade, investment, and labour flows. Asia accounts for 60 per cent of GCC trade, and two third of its oil exports. India and China were tipped to overtake traditional markets for Gulf investment in Europe and USA by 2015.[31]

Gulf oil producers have been locking Asian markets by picking up stakes in the latter's downstream sectors. In Vietnam, Qatar has invested in a major petrochemicals project, and Kuwait has invested in a refinery. Saudi Arabia has joint ventures in refineries in China, Japan, and South Korea. Similarly, China and Japan have joint ventures in large integrated refining and petrochemical projects in Saudi Arabia. China has become the largest oil export market for Saudi Arabia. Asian countries like Japan and South Korea are involved in upstream energy projects in the Gulf region. Chinese companies have invested in roughly 20 per cent of Iraqi oilfield projects, and have also signed deals that more than double Iraqi exports of crude oil to China. In 2014, it became the first Asian country to conclude a joint venture agreement with Abu Dhabi's ADNOC to produce and export crude oil from its onshore and offshore fields. On a geo-economic front, President Xi's vision for a 21st-century 'Silk Road', and for the revival of the Maritime Silk Road Economic Belt (via the 'One Belt, One Road' strategy) seeks to deepen economic engagement with the Gulf region.

In recent years, leaders from the Gulf have been flocking to Asian countries for more strategic partnerships. China has been an important arms supplier to the Gulf countries and Pakistan has committed boots on the ground during wars and conflicts. While arms sale would continue to be a part of China-Gulf strategic relations, its appetite for a deeper security engagement remains limited. The top diplomatic focus of Chinese leaders will be on regions that are in geographical proximity, on maritime disputes in the East and South China seas as well as on instability in Central Asia (especially Afghanistan) and northeast Asia. In his January 2016 speech to the Arab league, the Chinese President reiterated that his country was not interested in "filling the vacuum" that may possibly arise from the scaling down of US security arrangements.[32]

The US-Saudi Alliance and West Asia: Finding a New Equilibrium

Charles Freeman, a former US ambassador to Saudi Arabia, characterised the Middle East as occupying a "pivotal geo-strategic space" between Asia, Europe, and Africa. Its enormous energy resources make it a hub for global finance and business. "What happens in the Middle East affects the world's economic, political and strategic equilibrium."[33] As energy markets shift, this helps feed a perception across the board that the West Asia's (and Saudi Arabia's, by extension) centrality to US interests is increasingly being debated, and would lead to the scaling down of its commitments in the region. The nuclear deal with Iran, particularly, has made Saudi Arabia suspicious of the long-term durability of the US-Saudi partnership as Prince Turki Al-Faisal alleges "US has pivoted to Iran". The Saudis see all this together with falling US energy imports and erstwhile President Obama's desire to untangle America from the 'Middle East's antagonisms'. To address some of these concerns, the last two years of the Obama administration re-emphasised US commitment to West Asian stability and the safety of global trade routes.[34] However, the assurances have cut not had much impact on the Kingdom, which has been asserting a more aggressive regional foreign policy.

Relations between the USA and Saudi Arabia have also turned sour over the scepticism about the Saudi regime's commitment to combating extremism, its reluctance to undertake credible liberal political reforms, and the passing of the JASTA bill that allow families of the victims of the September 11 attacks to sue the Saudi regime. To add insult to injury (in an interview to published in 'The Atlantis' in March 2016), former President Obama called the Gulf states 'free riders' of US security arrangements, at which Prince Turki Al-Faisal angrily reminded him (in an open letter to the US president published in English edition of *Asharq Al-Awsat*)[35] of the Saudi role in counter-terror operations.

However, no doubt the central issues that would shape the strategic outlook of the Trump administration are the Syrian crisis, the challenge posed by "Daesh" (the so called Islamic State), and the puzzle of US-Iran relations; all these provide renewed scope of US-GCC cooperation. Alliance with Arab friends and allies for countering "Radical Islamic Terrorism" is the top most priority for the new US President Donald Trump who has declared, "to make America safe again".[36] His strategy is of military, cyber, and financial warfare against the menace of ISIS and other jihadist networks.[37] The USA maintains multiple command headquarters in the Gulf and Saudi Arabia, which continue to be essential territory for transit by American forces to bases that are located elsewhere in the Gulf, specifically in Qatar and Kuwait, or in Iraq.[38] Hence, Saudi Arabia remains very important to American forces from a strategic point of view. However, it remains to be seen whether the USA under the Trump administration views Saudi Arabia as a strategic ally. With Trump's more mercantilist view of the international order, his idea of bringing "peace through strength",[39] as well as the strong military connect in his cabinet, the USA is likely to continue its lucrative sale of arms to the Gulf. President Trump conceives the US military role in the region more in terms of "counter-terrorism" than in terms of stabilisation or "nation-building", and has abrasively spoken of getting the Arab Gulf states to commit ground forces against ISIS in Syria as well as seek greater compensation from Saudi Arabia for US security services.[40] No less than his predecessor, President Trump refers to the Gulf's oil-rich princes with disdain. At the same time, he regards President Sisi of Egypt a stronger partner in his war against "radical Islamic Terrorism", and both are seen to be committing to mutual interests.[41]

The new US administration's stand on Iran could potentially prop up increasingly fractious US-Saudi relations. Secretary of Defence, James Mattis (a former leader of the Central Command which oversees US military operations in the Middle East and South Asia), is widely known for his views on the need to restrain Iran. Though it had renewed hope among the GCC countries of course correction in US rapprochement with Iran, it has not instilled trust and confidence in them, as the removal of the Assad regime in Syria is not on the cards.

During his election campaign, President Trump talked of breaking the oil cartels as well as energy independence for the USA. Independent oil and gas producers in the USA, who have been among Trump's strongest supporters and advisers on energy issues, have complained about dumping and the predatory pricing by OPEC earlier, and since 2014.[42] International oil companies like Exxon and Chevron have integrated production and refining operations, most of which require a blend of light and heavy crude (mostly imported) to operate efficiently.[43] Alex Tillerson, former CEO of Exxon Mobil and now US Secretary of State, played a pivotal role in expanding Exxon Mobil's activities in the Gulf region.[44] Therefore, oil and arms deals would remain the vital engagement points of the USA with the Gulf countries—especially Saudi Arabia—to suit the interest of corporate America. They serve the Gulf countries' interest as well.

Given the experience of Afghanistan, Iraq, and Syria, the interlocking and intractable nature of conflicts, and Islamic terrorism would make it difficult for the USA to militarily take on terrorist outfits without involving the larger security architecture of the region. The Gulf oil producers may be prompted to "compensate for US security" in terms of more lucrative corporate deals as well as a better oil pricing policy. The Gulf countries are also cognizant of their limitations of fully replacing their estranged strategic partner (the USA) by any other power in the near future. They are reacting with cautious optimism at the prospects of a strong Trump administration containing Iran, and while ignoring his abrasive speech and suggestive ideological antagonism, still look towards engaging the USA. While mutual disdain continues to exist, the actual disengagement is more difficult than desired. Yet, the new equilibrium in US-Gulf relations is more likely to be fashioned on a commercial underpinning than any strategic convergence.

Implications for India

India is the fourth largest energy consumer in the world, and is dependent on imports for 80 per cent of its needs. India imports two-thirds of its oil from the Gulf, mainly from Saudi Arabia, UAE, Iran, and Iraq. As an economic bloc, the GCC countries are India's largest trade partner—much ahead of the European Union and the ASEAN. India-GCC trade is about one-fifth of India's global trade, and has registered one of the highest growth rates in the last decade. About 7 million Indians work in the Gulf, remitting home more than US$35 billion annually. Though still far below its potential, there has also been a quantum growth in Gulf investment (especially from UAE) in India that is aligned to India's needs.

There is also growing synergy in energy ties. Indian companies are increasingly executing high profile EPC contracts and the manufacture of sophisticated oil field drilling equipment and platforms. UAE has offered to fill half of India's maiden strategic petroleum reserve at Mangalore, and also use it partially as its warehouse for other Asian consumers. India has high stakes in the region, and its progress and prosperity in the years ahead will be greatly influenced by the happenings in the region as well as how India-Gulf relations evolve further. Likewise, the Indian market and its technical capabilities provide immense opportunities to Gulf countries for the expansion of their trade and investment as well as for the capacity building of their human resource.

King Abdullah of Saudi Arabia's visit to India after ascending the throne in January 2006 shaped the foundational paradigm of a wide-ranging strategic partnership, which also covered security and defence cooperation. Since then, the momentum of strategic engagements have been sustained by visits by India's Presidents, Vice Presidents, and Ministers holding different important portfolios, and an equal flurry of visits of Crown Princes, Prime Ministers, and senior Ministers from the GCC countries. The extradition of the 26/11 Mumbai terror attack conspirator, Abu Jindal, and many other suspects involved in terror financing from Saudi Arabia and the UAE in the recent past are significant milestones in strategic cooperation.

The continuing disdain in Gulf-US relations will no doubt urge Gulf countries to deepen their strategic relations with India. These seem to be moving in this direction already. The 2008 India-Qatar defence cooperation pact includes a substantive Indian naval security guarantee to the offshore assets of Qatar, and also provides for a joint venture in the production of weapons and military equipment. India has cooperation agreement for defence training with most of the Gulf countries. It has been very proactive in engaging with the navies of the GCC countries in the form of joint exercises, port calls, goodwill visits to ports, and training programmes.

Since the end of the Cold War, India has shed its earlier reluctance towards multilateral maritime security, and has consistently pursued naval diplomacy with both regional and extra-regional powers (USA) in the Indian Ocean.[45] In March 2015, Prime Minister Modi unveiled a framework for the Indian Ocean, making it a foreign policy priority that emphasised deepening economic and security cooperation with maritime neighbours and island states.[46] Thus, India could actively evolve maritime security architecture for sea lanes and offshore energy assets in the Indian Ocean from the "Gulf of Aden to Malacca" in a multilateral Asian framework, along with extra-regional stakeholders. Besides, India has liberalised rules for foreign direct investment in the security sector and targets the expansion of a defence industrial base as well as arms exports. They provide vital opportunities for further strategic engagements, especially with Gulf countries, and UAE has already inked a partnership in defence and aerospace.

Conclusion

The global energy scenario has changed significantly with the shale revolution in the USA and the slowing of oil demand due to structural and cyclical factors in the last few years. Oil was central to the US-Saudi strategic alliance since decades, and oil revenues—directly or indirectly—played a crucial role in domestic stability in most West Asian countries. The West Asian region is passing through a tumultuous transition, and falling oil revenues bring further instability and regional contestation. However, setting aside geopolitical rivalries, Russia and OPEC members managed a global oil pact, indicating the triumph of geo-economics. Russia's assertion in the region also shapes the geopolitics of gas pipelines.

Mutual disdain has set in US-Saudi relations, but actual disengagement is more difficult than desired, with focal points being more on corporate interest. The new equilibrium in US-West Asia relations would, most likely, rest on the counter-terror web of alliances. The Gulf's strategic economic engagement with India and China, though long under way, has now acquired more vigour and substance. While both countries are limited in their scope of strategic engagement with the West Asian Region and cannot fully replace the US security architecture, a multilateral approach could be a way forward. India can leverage its advantageous geographical position, its experience in multilateral naval diplomacy, and its good relations with regional and extra-regional powers to put in place Asian maritime security architecture as well alliances to counter terrorism. Its economic engagement with the region contributes to domestic stability, facilitating diversification and skill generation.

NOTES

1. Ladislaw, Sarah O., Maren Leed and Molly A. Walton, "New Energy and New Geopolitics background Report 1: Balancing Strategy and Leverage", Centre for Strategic and International Studies, April 2014, at https://www.ciaonet.org/attachments/24829/uploads, accessed 15 July 2016
2. Ladislaw, Sarah O. Maren Leed and Molly A. Walton, "New Energy and New Geopolitics background Report 3: Scenario, Strategic and Pathways", Centre for Strategic and International Studies, June 2014, at https://www.ciaonet.org/attachments/24829/uploads
3. Ibid.
4. "Oil Medium Term Market Report 2015", International Energy Agency, Paris, p.19
5. *BP Energy Outlook 2016*, British Petroleum, p. 33, at https://www.bp.com/content/dam/bp/pdf/energy-economics/energy-outlook-2016/bp-energy-outlook-2016.pdf, accessed 26 September 2016
6. Ladislaw, Sarah O. Maren Leed and Molly A. Walton, "New Energy and New Geopolitics background Report 2: Geopolitical and National Security Impact, Centre for Strategic and International Studies, April 2014
7. Matthiesen, Toby, "The domestic sources of Saudi foreign policy: Islamists and the state in the wake of the Arab Uprisings", working paper, The Brookings Institution, August 2015, https://www.brookings.edu/wp-content/uploads/2016/07/Saudi-Arabia_Matthiesen_FINALv.pdf, accessed 12 August 2016
8. Ahmad, Talmiz, "Turmoil in West Asia: The Sectarian Divide Shapes Regional Competitions" IDSA Monograph Series No.50, April 2016.
9. Saudi Arabia's passed counter terrorism Law in December 2013 that defines terrorism as any activity that directly or indirectly undermines public order the state's security and stability, or endangers national unity.
10. Freedom House, 'Freedom in the World 2016: Anxious Dictators and Wavering Democracies Global Freedom Under Pressure', https://freedomhouse.org/sites/default/files/FH_FITW_Report_2016.pdf, accessed 6 August, 2016
11. Zhdannikov,Dmitry, "Iraq, Kurdistan Jointly Export Kirkuk Oil Again", Thu Sep 1, 2016, http://www.reuters.com/article/us-iraq-kurdistan-oil-idUSKCN1174Y1#, accessed 5 September, 2016
12. Subsidies on energy prices have led to inefficient domestic energy consumption.

In 2014, Iran consumed 64 per cent (1.8 mb/d) of its oil production domestically.

13. Malik, Adeel and Awadallah, Bassem, 'The Economic Roots of the Arab Spring', CSAEWorkingPaperWPS/2011–23, https://www.csae.ox.ac.uk/workingpapers/pdfs/csae-wps-2011-23.pdf, accessed 3 September 2016
14. Hertog, Steffen, 'The Private Sector and Reform in the Gulf Cooperation Council', 2013, http://www.lse.ac.uk/middleEastCentre/kuwait/documents/The-private-sector-and-reform-in-the-GCC.pdf, accessed 4 August 2016
15. France, Agence, "Kuwait Announces 'ultra' Petrol Price Rise of 83% – to 55 cents a Litre", at https://www.theguardian.com/world/2016/aug/02/kuwait-announces-petrol-price-hike-of-83-to-55-cents-a-litre
16. *The Report: Saudi Arabia 2015*, London: Oxford Business Group, p. 47
17. There has been speculation that Saudi Arabia waged a price war to push out high cost shale oil producers and reduce oil production of its political adversaries, Russia, Iran and Iraq. See Fattouh, Bassam, Poudineh, R. and Sen, Anupama, 'The Dynamics of the Revenue Maximization–Market Share Trade-Off: Saudi Arabia's Oil Policy in the 2014–2015 Price Fall', October 2015, at https://www.oxfordenergy.org/wpcms/wp-content/uploads/2015/10/WPM-61.pdf, accessed 18 December 2016
18. Boudina, Ramzi "OPEC Set for No Deal as Iran Rejects Saudi Oil Output Offer', 27 September 2016, at http://www.reuters.com/article/us-opec-meeting-saudi-idUSKCN11X0LL, accessed 28 September 2016
19. El Gamal, Rania, Alex Lawler and Vladimir Soldatkin, "OPEC agrees modest oil output curbs in first deal since 2008", 29 September 2016, at http://www.reuters.com/article/us-opec-meeting-idUSKCN11Y18K
20. 'OPEC 171st meeting Concluded', OPEC Press Release, No 24/2016, 30 Nov 2016, Vienna, at http://www.opec.org/opec_web/en/press_room/3912.htm, accessed 19 December 2016
21. For Details of the deal, see, 'OPEC and non-OPEC Ministerial Meeting', OPEC Press Release, No 25/2016,10 Dec 2016, at http://www.opec.org/opec_web/en/press_room/3944.htm, accessed 19 December 2016
22. Soldatkin, Vladimir, Gamal, Rania El and Lawler, Alex, 'OPEC, non-OPEC agree first global oil pact since 2001', 10 December 2016, at http://www.reuters.com/article/us-opec-meeting-idUSKBN13Z0J8, accessed 20 December 2016
23. Trenin, Dmitri "Russia in the Middle East: Moscow's Objectives, Priorities, and Policy Drivers", White Paper under Russia Task Force on US Policy Toward Russia, Ukraine, and Eurasia project, April 5, 2016, Carnegie Moscow Centre, at http://carnegie.ru/2016/04/05/russia-in-middle-east-moscow-s-objectives-priorities-and-policy-drivers/iwni, accessed 8 October 2016
24. The *Energy Security Strategy*released in May 2014 openly stated its aim of pushing back against Russian influence. The paper proposed, among other things, to diversify energy sources by the enlargement of the southern gas corridor through the inclusion of Iraq, Iran, and Turkmenistan. EU is still import dependent for about 90 per cent of its crude oil consumption, 66 per cent of its natural gas consumption, and 42 per cent of its solid fuel consumption.
25. Kalehsar, Omid Shokri, "Energy Factor in Iran-Turkey Relations", *Energy & Environment*, Volume 26, Issue 5, September 2015, pp.177–187.
26. Varol, Tugce, "Russia Remains Determined To Stop Israel-Turkey Pipeline Deal",

17 May 2016, at http://oilprice.com/Energy/Natural-Gas/Russia-Remains-Determined-To-Stop-Israel-Turkey-Pipeline-Deal.html, accessed 16 October 2016

27. South Front, 'The Geopolitics of Oil and Gas Pipelines in the Middle East', *Global Research*, December 2015, at http://www.globalresearch.ca/the-geopolitics-of-oil-and-gas-pipelines-in-the-middle-east/5492595, accessed 13 July 2016
28. Engdahl, F. William, 'The Secret Stupid Saudi-US Deal on Syria: Oil Gas Pipeline War', Global Research, 16 March 2016, at http://www.globalresearch.ca/the-secret-stupid-saudi-us-dealonsyria/5410130?utm_campaign=magnet&utm_source=article_page&utm_medium=related_articles,
29. Ünal, Serhan, "Post-Sanctions Iran and Regional Energy Geopolitics", February 2016, at http://www.tenva.org/wp-content/uploads/2016/02/Iran-Rapor-ENG.pdf, accessed 4 July 2016
30. Gamal, Rania El, "Oman to speed up gas import plans from Iran post-sanctions", 21 January, 2016, at http://www.reuters.com/article/us-oman-iran-gas-idUSKCN0UZ1ER, accessed 30 July 2016
31. Ehteshami, Anoushiravan and Miyagi, Yukiko, *The Emerging Middle East-East Asia Nexus*, New York: Routledge, 2015, p. 37.
32. Olimat, Mohammad S., *China and the Gulf Cooperation Council Countries: Strategic Partnership in the Changing World*, London: Lexington Books, 2016, p.47
33. Ambassador Freeman, Charles W., "Coping with Kaleidoscopic Change in the Middle East", remarks at the Arab-US Policymakers Conference, Washington, DC, 2013.
34. Ladislaw, Sarah O., Maren Leed, and Molly A. Walton, *New Energy, New Geopolitics: Background Report 3: Scenarios, Strategies, and Pathways*, Washington DC: CSIS/Roman & Little-field, 2014.
35. Prince Faisal, Turki Al, "Opinion: Mr. Obama We are not Free Riders", 14 March 2016, at http://english.aawsat.com/2016/03/article55348496/mr-obama-not-free-riders, accessed 10 August 2016
36. Trump, Donald, "Understanding the Threat: The Age of Radical Islam", Remarks at the Centre for National Interest, Youngston, August 2016, at https://assets.donaldjtrump.com/DJT_Radical_Islam_Speech.pdf, accessed 2 September 2016
37. Trump, Donald, "Donald J. Trump's Vision Foreign Policy and Defeating ISIS", https://www.donaldjtrump.com/policies/foreign-policy-and-defeating-isis, accessed 6 September 2016
38. "Shifting Sands in the US-Saudi Arabian Relationship", An interview conducted with former US Ambassador to Saudi Arabia, Charles. W. Freeman, by the Saudi-US Relations Information Service, Middle East Policy Council 2016, at http://mepc.org/articles-commentary/speeches/shifting-sands-us-saudi-arabian-relationship?print, accessed 3 November 2016
39. See, "Transcript: Donald Trump Expounds his Foreign Policy Views", The *New York Times*, 26 March 2016, at https://www.nytimes.com/2016/03/27/us/politics/donald-trump-transcript.html; see also, Politico Staff, "Full Text: Donald Trump's speech on fighting terrorism,"*Politico*, 15 August 2016, at http://www.politico.com/story/2016/08/donald-trump-terrorism-speech-227025, accessed 27 November 2016
40. See Donald Trump Remarks, at https://assets.donaldjtrump.com/

DJT_Radical_Islam_Speech.pdf; see also, Lee, Carol E. and Kholaif, Dahlia, "Donald, Trump Speaks with the Egyptian President Sisi", The *Wall Street Journal*, 23 January 2017, at http://www.wsj.com/articles/trump-to-speak-monday-with-egyptian-president-sisi-1485189876, accessed 23 January 2017.

41. John, Kemp," Trump's Empty Threat to Stop Buying Saudi oil: Kemp", *Reuters*, London, 17 November 2016, at http://www.reuters.com/article/us-usa-trump-saudi-kemp-idUSKBN13B2GN, accessed 18 December 2016
42. Even during the peak shale boom, US imported about 7 mb/d to feed its refineries.
43. This includes the liquefied natural gas business in Qatar, the joint venture partnership at the giant West Qurna oil field in Iraq, concessions at Abu Dhabi's massive offshore Upper Zakum development, and refinery upgrades in Saudi Arabia. See Munroe, Dane, "Trump Administration Set to Roil in International Oil Market", at http://www.agsiw.org/trump-administration-set/, accessed 14 January 2017
44. Mukherjee, Anit and C. Raja Mohan (eds.), *India's Naval Strategy and Asian Security*, New York: Routledge, 2016, p. 112
45. About 90 per cent of India's foreign trade by volume, and 70 per cent in value terms is seaborne, accounting for 42 per cent of its GDP. After the sea routed Mumbai terror attacks of 26–28 November 2008, the maritime threat has assumed importance.

PART 2

SAUDI ARABIA

4

Saudi Arabia: Understanding Evolving Internal and External Dynamics

Meena Singh Roy

Introduction

The Kingdom of Saudi Arabia occupies a predominant position in the West Asian region. Any narrative on the Gulf region would remain incomplete without understanding the internal and external dynamics of Saudi Arabia. In the post 'Arab Spring' period, Saudi Arabia started recalibrating its internal and external policy to manage the new security and economic challenges faced by the Kingdom. The inherent contradiction between the radical Wahhabi state ideology and the pragmatic demands of the modern government faced by the Saudi Kingdom continues to affect its internal and external policies. So far, the Kingdom has managed to maintain the balance between its Wahhabi idealism and political pragmatism. In addition, the country is confronted with economic difficulties due to the drop in the global oil prices. The attack of the Islamic State (IS) on Saudi soil, a costly quagmire in Yemen, and finally, its setbacks in Syria and increasing Iranian involvement and influence in Iraq have added to the Kingdom's problems in the region.

Given India's increasing engagement and New Delhi's growing economic, energy, and security stakes in Saudi Arabia, it is important to analyse these new developments and their impact. It is in this context that the present chapter attempts to unpack current economic challenges and changing Saudi foreign policy. It also hypothesises about future opportunities and sustainability for the India-Saudi strategic partnership.

Internal Dynamics: Addressing Economic Challenges

Saudi Arabia's economy is witnessing some difficult times given the drop in global oil prices. This situation has pushed the Kingdom into a huge budget deficit and billions of dollars in debt to private companies, mainly in the construction business. Grappling with these economic challenges, the Kingdom announced the Vision 2030 reform plan in April 2016. According to the Saudis, this is an "ambitious yet achievable" plan that aims to stimulate the country's economy and diversify its revenues. According to the vision, the plan is based on three pillars: (1) Saudi Arabia's status as the heart of the Arab and Islamic worlds; (2) its determination to become a global investment powerhouse; and (3) transform Saudi Arabia's unique strategic location into a global hub connecting three continents—Asia, Europe, and Africa. Its geographic position between key global waterways makes the Kingdom an epicentre of trade, and the gateway to the world. The Kingdom aims to transform Aramco from an oil producing company into global industrial conglomerate. The vision plans to make Saudi Arabia "a vibrant society, a thriving economy, and an ambitious nation".[2] Since 2016, the Kingdom has pursued its "Vision 2030" economic diversification effort to broaden its investment and business base, while employing more Saudi citizens in the private sector.

There has been noticeable reduction in expatriate employments in the Kingdom because of the financial problems, cost cutting, and a drive to employ more Saudis. The Saudi Binladin Group alone has left around 70,000 expats from poorer countries without a job and, at the same time, many Western expatriates are in the process of leaving the Kingdom. According to a foreign manager in the consumer electronics sector, "people are leaving because there's not enough business for their contract to be renewed". [3]

Profit margins for business people are seriously under pressure, and this is going to be complemented with more problems after the expected government plans to impose a levy on foreign workers with dependents in July. The fee is likely to start at 100 riyals a month, rising to 400 riyals monthly by 2020. In addition, the Saudi government will also raise monthly fees paid by employers who hire more foreign workers than Saudis. This is part of the government's programme to encourage the hiring of local Saudis. It is equally important to note that while there is no income tax in the Kingdom, this year the government plans to introduce taxes on some consumer items. In the current situation, expensive Western workers are being replaced by less expensive hires like the Portuguese, Greeks and, increasingly, Arab nationals. These developments are pushing many

Western workers to leave Saudi Arabia. A foreign fund manager working in the Kingdom for several years said that, "In 10 years, I don't think there will be expats, because they have to get the Saudis to work".[4]

The March 2017 data, released by the Saudi Arabian Monetary Agency (SAMA), indicate shrinking assets. Net foreign assets are reducing as the government uses savings to plug a budget deficit that reached US$79 billion in 2016, and US$107 billion if delayed payments to contractors are included. Although the country still holds foreign assets above US$ 500 billion, at the same time, the demand for imports financed by commercial lenders is also falling in the country. Now, private sector imports, financed through Saudi Arabia's commercial banks, are falling. This trend is considered to be a cautious approach adopted by the private sector.[5] Saudi inflation has also been on a downward trajectory. However, economists within and outside Saudi Arabia are of the opinion that this situation is likely to be a temporary phenomenon. Fahad Alturki, head of research at the Riyadh based Jadwa Investment, noted in his research report (23 February 2017) that

> Looking ahead, government initiatives aimed at stimulating private sector activity should have a positive impact on aggregate demand, and therefore inflation.... We expect inflation to remain subdued in the first six months of 2017, before another hike in household electricity prices pushes up inflation during the second half of 2017.[6]

The Jadwa Investment report acknowledges that the overall outlook for the Saudi economy remains poor, and projects economic growth of just 0.2 percent over the course of 2017—down from 1.4 percent in 2016 and 4.1 percent in 2015.[7] In January 2017, the International Monetary Fund (IMF) slashed its forecast for Saudi economic growth this year from 2 percent to 0.4 percent.[8] Reports about the Saudi economy from Capital Economics (CapEcon), the London based consultancy, suggest that despite serious challenges faced by the Kingdom, "things are looking up". According to CapEcon, the Saudi GDP will grow by 1 percent in 2017. It also suggests that the period of austerity in the wake of the oil-price crash is over, and there has been an upturn in new construction contract as some bills are finally being paid.[9] Thus, CapEcon's projections about the Saudi economy reflect a somewhat positive outlook for the future of the country's economy despite many limitations in implementing its Vision 2030 effectively. As the economic situation seems to be improving, the Saudi government has forecast a deficit of US$ 198 billion in 2017, and aims to eliminate the gap by 2020.

As a result of these positive developments, the Kingdom has reversed its earlier decision on the reduction of financial benefits to its public sector employees. The recent reversal of austerity measures after the public outcry is a case in point of how the Kingdom is trying to address its internal problems. In September 2016, the Saudi government sharply reduced financial perks for employees in the public sector where most of the Saudis work. It cut the salaries of ministers by 20 percent. This was one of the drastic measures taken by the government to curb a huge budget deficit due to low oil prices. On 22 April 2017, King Salman bin Abdulaziz restored "all allowances, financial benefits, and bonuses"[10] for those working in the public sector through the royal decree. In addition, a two month salary bonus for the Saudi forces fighting in Yemen was announced. This step is viewed as a tactical move, intended to help the Saudi government implement its economic reform programme with public support.[11]

The other significant internal development has been the appointment of King Salman's two sons as part of the process of bringing the next generation of Al Saud leadership in important positions, which is underway in the Kingdom. Prince Khaled bin Salman was appointed Ambassador to Washington DC, and Prince Abdulaziz bin Salman, a long time oil policy official, was appointed State Minister for Energy Affairs. In an effort to strengthen the hold of the Royal family, some of young princes of the Al Saud family were made Deputy Governors of the Kingdom's provinces.[12]

Recent initiatives by the Saudi government clearly reflect how the Kingdom has been able to address current economic challenges while maintaining the hold of the Royal family over the internal and external affairs of the country. Many experts have argued that, without political reforms, it will be difficult for the Kingdom to achieve economic development. John Edwards, a member of the Board of the Reserve Bank of Australia, has said that for Saudi vision 2030 economic plan to be successful, it will have to "profoundly change its society and politics".[13] Some other experts are of the opinion that the "Saudi Wahhabi religious doctrine is injurious to the cause of modernity".[14]

Regardless of the limitations of the Saudi Vision 2030 initiative, it can be argued that the present developmental initiatives are driven by an analysis of its own situation wherein the Kingdom is getting into a new social contract with its people. Experts, like Dennis Ross, are of the view that the national transformation and monetisation inside is one of the main priorities of the Saudi government, and this is a determined effort to produce a successful developmental model. In fact, producing a successful developmental model could have far reaching implications for the entire region.[15] How far the Saudi government would be able to successfully implement its national transformation plan is yet to be seen; but these efforts do reflects the enormous adaptability potential of the Saudi Kingdom.

Re-Adjusting External Policy

Being a 'status quo state', the Saudi Kingdom finds it very difficult to accept any fundamental change that challenges the existing internal and regional order.[16] Therefore, the main goal of the Saudi Kingdom has been not only to ensure the continuation of the monarchical, dynastic rule of the Al Saud but also to retain its influence and dominance in the Gulf, and the Islamic world in general. To achieve these goals, it has constantly adjusted and re-adjusted its internal and external policies. According to the Saudi government, its foreign policy is based on geographical, religious, historical, economic, security, and political principles and facts. Based on the priorities of the Kingdom, its foreign policy is practiced in four concentric circles: the immediate neighbouring Gulf countries; the Arab states; the larger Islamic world; and the international community.[17] Despite various geo-political, economic, and security changes in the regional and international order, the aforementioned two fundamental goals continue to guide Saudi Arabia's foreign policy.

However, in the last two years, there has been a noticeable change in Saudi Arabia's regional policy approach to address new economic and security challenges, which are reflected in the Kingdom's aggressive and assertive regional policy, and its growing cooperation with the Asian countries like India, China, and Japan as a part of its diversification policy. This is somewhat different from the past, in which the Kingdom's focus was on building strong relations with the USA and the West.

The New Regional Order

Before analysing its current policy approach, it is important to examine current regional developments, which have serious implications for Saudi Arabia. In the current context, the West Asian region is marked by a new cold war between Iran and Saudi Arabia, as manifested in Syria, Yemen, Lebanon, Iraq, and Bahrain, and seems to rule out any hope of peace and stability in the region. This war is being played by Iran and Saudi Arabia through their support for various proxies in these hot spots. In other words, a new regional order—which is still unfolding—is characterised by several new developments.

Change in US Policy Towards the Region

A rising China, and its growing economic and strategic role in Asia, is becoming far more important to Washington than West Asia, and US interest in the region is diminishing, as it is not a top priority for Washington any more. However, what is important to note that the USA will continue to be a major arms supplier to its Gulf partners, particularly, Saudi Arabia and the UAE. Washington is also still going to be viewed as an important security partner. Though the new Trump Administration's West Asia policy is still being formalised, the announcement of President Trump's visit to Saudi Arabia, Israel, and Rome is indicative of a renewed focus on this region.

The Growing Role of Russia in the Region

Russian presence in Syria and its improving relations with Turkey and Egypt are significant. The growing defence and security cooperation between Moscow and Cairo now includes the possibility of establishing a Russian airbase in Egypt. Two already acquired Mistral-class ships will now receive the originally planned Russian electronics suite, and will even carry Russian helicopters. There are also talks of MiG fighter sales to Egypt. Russia and NATO-member Turkey are now increasing their defence cooperation. They are even talking about building a long-range missile system. Turkey is also supposed to have offered Russia its military bases to fight against Da'esh in Syria.

The Growing Influence of Iran in the Region

The growing influence of Iran in the region has become the top priority for the Saudi Kingdom. Iran's influence in Iraq and Lebanon, its growing presence in Syria, Tehran's support to the Shia community in Bahrain, and its increasing role in Yemen are of serious concern to the Kingdom. Saudi-Iranian tensions have escalated since early 2016 when Saudi Arabia executed Nimr al-Nimr, a dissident Shia cleric, and the subsequent attack on the Saudi embassy in Tehran and its Consulate in Mashad. Continuing disagreements over Hajj—especially after the death of several Iranian and other pilgrim during 2015—has led to these tensions. The centrality of Iran in Saudi foreign policy is an undisputed phenomenon that gets reflected in most of the statements coming from Royal family members or other officials. Turki Al Faisal bin Abdul Aziz Al Saud, Chairman of the King Faisal Centre for Research & Islamic Studies in Riyadh, has very clearly noted that, "The first issue, without any prioritizing, is Iran". He goes on to say that "Saudi Arabia will oppose all of Iran's interference and meddling in other countries. It is Saudi Arabia's position that Iran has no right to meddle in other nations' internal affairs, especially those of Arab states."[18] This position of the Saudi regime remains unchanged, and forms a major basis of its policy in the region. The softening of the US and European approach (after the signing of the JCPOA) has pushed the Saudi regime to follow a much more aggressive regional policy in the recent past, including enhancing its military purchases and building a military "Sunni coalition".

The Civil War in Yemen

The dangerous stalemate between the Saudi-supported Hadi government and Iran-backed Houthi rebels has worsened the Civil War in Yemen. Saudi-led coalition forces have continued to bomb Houthi held areas, leading to many civilian casualties estimated at over 2,000, including about 500 children. The Houthis have also upped the ante, and have refused to recede from their advances. They have fired missiles inside the Kingdom, including one allegedly targeted at the Holy Places. Missiles from Houthi held areas have also targeted a US Naval Ship in the Red Sea, evoking a response and threatening escalation. In the meanwhile, the Al-Qaeda in Arabian Peninsula (AQAP) is taking advantage of the situation, has increased its stronghold in south eastern Yemen, and is threatening to undo the achievements of the US-led counter terrorism operation against them.

The Situation in Iraq

Despite the advances made by US-backed Iraqi forces and Kurdish militias and the reverses faced by the Islamic State (IS) throughout the year, the chances of a sectarian flare-up due to Turkish and Iranian involvement remains high. At the same time, the IS has not entirely given up its control of the strategic city of Mosul, and continues to spew its menace within and outside the region. There is also a fear that, once the international forces leave the ground, the Iraqi army will lose ground to the IS which has the ability to go underground and re-surface once the situation returns to normalcy. More importantly, the threat of Jihadist organisations—particularly the Da'esh—continues to swell, and not recede across the region. In other words, the situation in Iraq is vulnerable.

Syria

Crucial for Saudi Arabia, Syria right now appears to be engulfed in a quagmire in which Russia-Iranian-Turkish cooperation is trying to find a way out. However, this has excluded not just the USA and the West but also the Gulf Arab countries, particularly Saudi Arabia and Qatar who have been providing support to the Syrian opposition against Assad. The recent advances of Shiite, Turkish, and Kurdish forces against the Arab Sunni populace in Syria and Iraq have generated a heightened sense of insecurity among the GCC countries over the fate of their regimes in the future.

Turkey

Turkey is seeking a new role for itself, with new ambitions in the West Asian region. After President Erdogan won the controversial 16 April referendum, major changes are underway in the country. These are increasing the President's powers bringing the country close to authoritarian rule. These changes are likely to have major implications for Turkey's internal and external policy.

The Saudi Response

All these developments have led the Saudi Kingdom to re-adjust its external policy to manage these challenges, protect its predominance in the Arabian Peninsula, and retain its eminent position of leadership of the wider Muslim world as the Custodian of the Two Holy Mosques (Mecca and Medina), the birthplace of Islam. In response to these new challenges, Kingdom has bolstered its arms purchases from the USA, the UK, and France. In mid-December 2015, Prince Mohammed bin Salman announced the formation of an Islamic Military Alliance to Fight Terrorism (IMAFT). The alliance is said to share information, train, equip, and provide forces (if necessary) for the fight against IS militants. Former Pakistan army Chief, Raheel Sharif, has been appointed as the first Commander of this coalition. In the beginning, the IMAFT comprised of 34 countries—out of a total of 57 member states of the Organisation of Islamic Countries (OIC)—including Egypt, Qatar, the United Arab Emirates (UAE), Turkey, Malaysia, Pakistan, and several African nations but excluding Iran and Iraq.[19] However, this number increased to 41, with Oman joining the alliance. This is indeed an important development, given Oman's close relations with Iran.[20] Due to the exclusion of Iran and Iraq, the coalition has been viewed by many as sectarian in nature and not representing Islam as well as the "new adventure of Prince Salman".[21] More important is that, in reality, the coalition lacks an operational mechanism and a clear framework.[22] Regardless of the limitations of IMAFT, the Saudis have succeeded to bring together major Islamic countries under its security umbrella.

At another level, the Kingdom is strengthening its cooperation with key Asian partners, including China, Japan, and India. The visit of King Salman to China in March 2017 highlights the increasing role which China is seeking to play in West Asian affairs as well as Saudi's outreach to Beijing to enhance economic and energy cooperation. During this visit, both the countries signed a MoU worth US$65 billion, and included areas ranging from energy, investments, to cooperation in space. China offered Saudi Arabia participation in its Chang E-4 moon mission, and a partnership agreement for the manufacture of drones. Besides the MoU, Saudi and Chinese companies signed 21 deals to explore investments in oil and petrochemical plants, ecommerce, and cooperation in renewable energy markets. Seeking China's greater role in the region, King Salman said, "Saudi Arabia is willing to work hard with China to promote global peace, security, and prosperity". In the light of current developments, China has been seeking to play a greater role in the West Asian Region. While some experts remain sceptical, others have termed China's role as that of an "honest broker". In January 2016, Premier Xi paid visit to Saudi Arabia and Iran, striking a balance between its two key partners in the region. From the Saudi perspective, it is seeking investments from China to address its economic challenges and implementing its vision 2030 programme.[23]

Simultaneously Saudi Kingdom has approached Japan for investment and trade. During King Salman's visit in March 2017, he participated in the closing session of the Forum on the Business Vision between Saudi Arabia and Japan 2030. This Forum discussed ways to achieve the current executive programme emanating from the Saudi Vision 2030 to promote trade and investment between the two countries. A MoU on the implementation of the Japanese Saudi Vision 2030 was signed.[24]

While the Kingdom has adopted a policy to "look east", and enhance its cooperation with Asian partners, it has also been making efforts towards sustaining its cooperation with its traditional allies like the USA and Europe. These changes in Saudi Arabia's foreign policy highlight the Kingdom's ability and agility to re-adjust its foreign policy, and withstand current internal and external challenges.

Enhancing the "Strategic Partnership" with India

From India's perspective, Saudi Arabia remains a key partner in the region. The recent developments and high level visits from both sides clearly indicate the growing cooperation between the two countries. The overlapping "Look-East" policy of Saudi Arabia and the "Look-West" policy of India are indicative of a growing recognition of a mutuality of interests between the two countries. The India-Saudi partnership entered a new phase during the Congress lead UPA government (2004–2014), with high level visits from both sides. This partnership has been taken to new levels by the Modi government. The Delhi Declaration of 2006—and the subsequent signing of the Riyadh Declaration in 2010—elevated the India-Saudi bilateral relations to the level of a 'Strategic Partnership'.

King Abdullah's visit in 2006 led to the signing of the Delhi Declaration, which provided a framework of cooperation in all fields of mutual interest, including, counter-terrorism, money laundering, drugs and arms smuggling. The expanded scope of India-Saudi Arabia cooperation signalled towards Riyadh's efforts to engage with rising powers. His visit marked the beginning of a new chapter in India-Saudi relations, with a de-hyphenation of ties from Pakistan, Iran, and other external factors.

While King Abdullah's visit was a turning point in India-Saudi relations largely from the Saudi perspective, it was Indian External Affairs Minister Jaswant Singh's visit to Riyadh in 2001 that broke the Indian "mindset"[25] of viewing the Kingdom from a Pakistani prism. Singh's visit was the first high-level political contact since Indira Gandhi's visit in 1982, and focused on all aspects of bilateral ties, including energy security, regional stability, and India-Pakistan relations. An editorial in *The Hindu* ascertained that the visit

> turned the spotlight on larger issues of strategic-political stability in the southern and western parts of Asia ... [and] brought into focus a relative new notion about the connectivity between the security of West Asia (including the Gulf region) and the stability of South Asia (meaning specifically the India-Pakistan relationship).[26]

This was also the beginning of security and defence cooperation between the two countries, encompassing joint naval and military exercises, training of defence personnel, and exchange of military hardware. Subsequently, in 2012, Indian Defence Minister A.K. Antony's visit to Riyadh set the roadmap for expanding defence cooperation in the fields of training exchanges, port visits by each other's warships, and high-level military delegation visits.

This mutually beneficial relationship was further consolidated during the April 2016 visit of Prime Minister Modi to the Kingdom. This set a completely new milestone in the bilateral relations. The present strategic partnership between the two countries is based on four pillars: energy, trade and investment, diaspora, and growing security and defence cooperation. The new dimension of the partnership is reflected in the joint statement, which agrees upon

> the need to intensify bilateral defence cooperation, through the exchange of visits by military personnel and experts, the conduct of joint military exercises, the exchange of visits of ships and aircraft, and the supply of arms and ammunition and their joint development.[27]

The desire to enhance cooperation in defence and security has emerged as the key feature of the India-Saudi relations. Several visits undertaken by India's National Security Advisor, Ajit Doval, and Prime Minister's special envoy on counter-terrorism, Syed Asif Ibrahim, to Riyadh are clear signals of heightened security cooperation between the two countries. Taking the security collaboration further, the leadership of the two countries have also agreed to strengthen maritime security in the Gulf and the Indian Ocean region.

Combating terrorism and counter-radicalisation has emerged as the second important pillar of cooperation between New Delhi and Riyadh. The 2016 joint statement called on

> all states to reject the use of terrorism against other countries; dismantle terrorism infrastructures where they happen to exist and to cut off any kind of support and financing to the terrorists operating and perpetrating terrorism from their territories against other states; and bring perpetrators of acts of terrorism to justice.[28]

More importantly, the growing strategic partnership between New Delhi and Riyadh came into the limelight in April 2016, when Saudi Arabia came out as one of the first countries to condemn the terrorist attack at Uri. This was an unanticipated development, given the traditional pro-Pakistan approach of the Kingdom with regard to issues relating to Kashmir. It has been seen as a significant development as increasing Saudi focus on engaging India as its strategic partner.

Despite fruitful economic relations in the past, India was unable to capitalise on the full potential of trade and investment opportunities that the India-Saudi partnership offered. Prime Minister Modi's visit provided a renewed impetus to economic cooperation between the two countries. He requested Saudi Arabia "to be a partner in India's growth story", and invited Saudi Aramco, SABIC, and other Saudi companies to invest in the infrastructure sector, and become a part of India's mega industrial manufacturing corridors, its smart cities, and the Digital India and Start Up programmes. This offer was welcomed by the Saudis, and they expressed interest in investing in areas such as railways, roads, ports, and shipping. To attract Saudi investment, the Indian side explained the recent efforts taken by the government to improve the ease of doing business in India. For example, the joint statement noted "India's key efforts to simplify and rationalise existing rules and relax the foreign direct investment norms in key areas, including railways, defence and insurance."[29] Saudi Arabia not only acknowledges India's strong growing economy but has expressed appreciation of Prime Minister's vision for the future of the country.

Saudi Arabia is India's 4th largest trading partner, with bilateral trade accounting for US$26.7 billion in 2015–16 (see Table1).[30] Trade figures have declined slightly since 2013–14 owing to lower oil prices and overall lower international trade; but trade volume remains high.

Table 1: India-Saudi Arabia Bilateral Trade (in US$ million)

Year	*2011–12*	*2012–13*	*2013–14*	*2014–15*	*2015–16*
Exports	5,683.29	9,785.78	12,218.95	11,161.43	6,394.23
Imports	31,817.70	33,998.11	36,403.65	28,107.56	20,321.33
Total Trade	**37,500.99**	**43,783.89**	**48,622.60**	**39,268.98**	**26,715.56**

Saudi Arabia is also the 5th largest market for Indian exports. Indian companies are expected to invest US$1.6 billion in Saudi Arabia across in the IT, telecom, construction, consulting, and pharmaceutical sectors. During his visit to India in 2015, the Saudi Deputy Minister of Industries, Saleh S. Al-Solani, informed that 50 Saudi companies were already operating in India, including Saudi Aramco and SABIC, and 75 Indian companies were operating in Saudi Arabia, including Wipro, TCS, L&T, Godrej Group, and ITC.[31] Saudi investments in India have increased over the years, though it remains below the potential. Saudi companies have made a cumulative investment of US$ 75 million in the Indian market during April 2000 to December 2016. This is expected to improve, given the mutual desire on both sides to strengthen and consolidate the economic partnership in the future. Prime Minister Modi's visit has already laid the foundation for this cooperation.

The importance of Saudi Arabia as a reliable energy partner of India cannot be ignored. It is the largest supplier of crude oil to India, and 90 per cent of Indian imports from Saudi Arabia consist of petroleum. India's growing energy demands further enhance the significance of Saudi Arabia. It is estimated that India will import ninety per cent of its overall oil and gas requirements by 2040, predominantly sourced from West Asia.[32] Saudi Arabia held 15.7 per cent of the world's total proven oil reserves as of 2015—the highest in West Asia, and second only to Venezuela. In 2015, Saudi Arabia accounted for 13 per cent of total global oil production—the highest by an individual country and the same as the USA. India recorded an 8 per cent increase in oil consumption in 2014–2015.[33] Saudi Arabia has been India's highest exporter until it was edged out by Iraq in April-May 2016. While Saudi Arabia accounted for 25 per cent of Indian oil imports in 2015, the Kingdom's share fell to 18 per cent in April 2016, and Iraq's rose to 22 per cent.[34]

Nevertheless, the Saudis maintained the top position in the first three quarter of 2016–17 with US$10.7 billion worth of oil exports to India. The leadership of the two countries have agreed to transform the buyer-seller relationship in the energy sector by focusing on investment and joint ventures in petrochemical complexes, as well as cooperation in joint exploration in India, Saudi Arabia, and even in third countries. In addition, both the countries have also agreed put emphasis on areas of training and human resources development, with greater engagement in research and development in the energy sector. To further energy cooperation, the need for regular meetings—under the umbrella of India-Saudi Arabia Ministerial Energy Dialogue—has also been emphasised.

The other significant pillar of India-Saudi relations has been the presence of the Indian diaspora. Saudi Arabia is home to some 2.9 million Indians, accounting for over 30 per cent of the foreign workers employed in the Kingdom.[35] They remitted US$10.51 billion to India in 2015. The presence of the Indian community in Saudi Arabia offers both opportunities as well as challenges for New Delhi and Riyadh. During Prime Minister Modi's visit in 2016, this issue got special attention, as the Prime Minister made it point to interact with the Indian expatriate community there. Both countries signed an agreement on labour, and agreed to establish a Joint Working Group on consular issues to resolve outstanding issues.

After the Saudi government introduced Saudisation under its national transformation programme, there is a concern in India that this may adversely affect the Indian expatriate population in Saudi Arabia. In August 2016, 10,000 Indians—stranded in Saudi Arabia after being laid off by construction companies—had to be evacuated by New Delhi. The economic recession in Saudi Arabia led to over 50,000 Indians returning home in August 2015–2016.[36] Though the recent Saudi initiative to provide more jobs to its citizens may have reduced job opportunities for Indians, it is not likely to make an impact in the short and mid-term in a major way. Indeed, so far, its impact has been minimal. In this regard, New Delhi and Riyadh have managed this problem without doing any damage to its growing bilateral relations. In fact, the Saudi government, along with Qatar and Dubai, helped India in freeing its 46 nurses kidnapped by the IS in Iraq in 2014. Again, during the evacuation of the Indian citizens from Yemen, the Saudi's extended their help to India in 2015.[37]

Given the renewed focus from both sides to reinvigorate the existing strategic partnership between New Delhi and Riyadh, the scope of cooperation is likely to expand beyond the existing areas identified by both sides. Sectors like information technology, agriculture, food security pharmaceutical, medical tourism, bi-informatics, higher education, cyber and maritime security, coastal policing, and defence cooperation are promising areas for future cooperation. For pulling in more investment from Saudi Arabia, India will have to make its market more attractive and profit-oriented for private Saudi investors. As India and Saudi Arabia have stepped up cooperation in the security, defence, and economic arenas in the last few years, there is now need to sustain the current momentum of engagement by both sides.

Current analyses of Saudi Kingdom's internal and external policies indicate following trends: (a) the Kingdom is on the path of economic transformation, and forming a new social contract with its people to address its internal challenges. How far will the Kingdom be able to successfully implement the new developmental model is yet to be seen. (b) Iran forms its key priority, as the Saudis would like to prevent growing Iranian influence in the region at every cost so that it does not challenge its own domination in the Gulf region. To achieve this, it has created a Sunni military alliance. (c) The USA continues to be its significant security partner despite some differences on their priorities regarding their common interests in the region. However, under its "Look East" policy, the Kingdom is working towards building new partnerships with China, India, Japan, and Korea.

In conclusion, the Saudi Kingdom has great potential to readjust its internal and external policies, and adapt itself to new regional realities while sustaining its control within the country. It continues to protect the interests of the Saudi Royal family as well as maintain its leadership role in the Gulf region. Despite facing many challenges and limitations in the past, Saudi Arabia has been able to withstand both the storm of the "Arab Awakening" as well as the current geopolitical and economic challenges facing it within and without.

NOTES

1. The full text of "Saudi Arabia's Vision 2030", available in *Saudi Gazette*, Riyadh, 26 April 2016, at https://english.alarabiya.net/en/2016/04/26/Full-text-of-

Saudi-Arabia-s-Vision-2030.html
2. Ibid.
3. "Good times over for expats in Saudi Arabia", *The Economic Times*, 24 February 2017, at http://economictimes.indiatimes.com/nri/nris-in-news/good-times-over-for-expats-in-saudi-arabia/printarticle/57328166.cms
4. Ibid.
5. Vivian Nereim, "Saudi Data Show Economy Struggling as Lending Growth Slumps", 2 March 2017, at https://www.bloomberg.com/news/articles/2017-03-02/saudi-data-show-economy-struggling-as-lending-growth-slumps
6. Dominic Dudley, "Saudi Arabia Shrugs Off Concerns About Deflation, Despite Weak Outlook For Economy", at https://www.forbes.com/sites/dominicdudley/2017/02/23/saudi-deflation/#199d2d5a4ada
7. Ibid.
8. Vivian Nereim, "Saudi Data Show Economy Struggling as Lending Growth Slumps", 2 March 2017, at https://www.bloomberg.com/news/articles/2017-03-02/saudi-data-show-economy-struggling-as-lending-growth-slumps
9. Frank Kane, "Saudi economic growth looks set to beat pessimists' forecast", 10 March 2017, at https://www.forbes.com/sites/dominicdudley/2017/02/23/saudi-deflation/#199d2d5a4ada
10. "Saudi Arabia restores perks to state employees to fend off unrest", 24 April 2017, at https://www.theguardian.com/world/2017/apr/24/saudi-arabia-restores-perks-to-state-employees-to-fend-off-unrest
11. Ibid.
12. Ibid.
13. Hilal Khashan, "Saudi Arabia's Flawed "Vision 2030", *The Middle East Quarterly*, Winter 2017, vol. 24, no.1, at http://www.meforum.org/meq/pdfs/6397.pdf
14. Ibid.
15. Comments made by Dennis Ross, during a discussion on "America's Anxious Allies: Trip Report from Saudi Arabia, Turkey and Israel", at the Washington Institute, Washington DC, 26 September 2016, at https://www.youtube.com/watch?v=LUtG0c4ajrY
16. Saudis define their state a status quoist state. See, Awadh Albadi, "Towards Understanding Saudi Foreign Policy", *Trending Events*, No. 16, March-April, 2016, Future for Advanced Research & Studies, UAE, at http://futurecenter.ae/en/events.php?fustudy=944.
17. The Foreign Policy of the Kingdom of Saudi Arabia, at http://www.mofa.gov.sa/sites/mofaen/KingdomForeignPolicy/Pages/ForeignPolicy24605.aspx
18. "Saudi Arabia's Foreign Policy", Turki Al Faisal bin Abdul Aziz Al Saud's address to the 22nd annual Arab-US Policymakers Conference in Washington, DC, 22 October 2013, sponsored by the National Council on US-Arab Relations, at http://www.mepc.org/journal/saudi-arabias-foreign-policy
19. Ramy Aziz, "The Purpose of Saudi Arabia's Islamic Military Coalition", 16 February 2016, at http://www.jpost.com/Opinion/The-purpose-of-Saudi-Arabias-Islamic-military-coalition-445113;see also, Noah Browning and John Irish, "Saudi Arabia announces 34-state Islamic military alliance against terrorism", at http://www.reuters.com/article/us-saudi-security-idUSKBN0TX2PG20151215

20. Giorgio Cafiero, "Why did Oman join Saudi Arabia's anti-terrorism alliance?", at http://www.al-monitor.com/pulse/originals/2017/01/oman-join-saudi-arabia-anti-terror-alliance.html; also see, http://www.alhayat.com/Articles/19335576/%D8%A8%D8%A7%D9%86%D8%B6%D9%85%D8%A7%D9%85-%D8%B9%D9%85%D8%A7%D9%86——%D8%A7%D9%84%D8%AA%D8%AD%D8%A7%D9%84%D9%81-%D8%A7%D9%84%D8%A5%D8%B3%D9%84%D8%A7%D9%85%D9%8A-%D8%A5%D9%84%D9%89-41-%D8%AF%D9%88%D9%84%D8%A9-%D9%84%D9%85%D8%AD%D8%A7%D8%B1%D8%A8%D8%A9-%D8%A7%D9%84%D8%A5%D8%B1%D9%87%D8%A7%D8%A8
21. Ramy Aziz, "The Purpose of Saudi Arabia's Islamic Military Coalition", 16 February 2016, at http://www.jpost.com/Opinion/The-purpose-of-Saudi-Arabias-Islamic-military-coalition-445113;see also, Noah Browning and John Irish "Saudi Arabia announces 34-state Islamic military alliance against terrorism", at http://www.reuters.com/article/us-saudi-security-idUSKBN0TX2PG2015 1215
22. Ibid.
23. Ben Blanchard, "China, Saudi Arabia Eye $ 65 billion in deals as King Visits", 16 March 2017, at http://www.reuters.com/article/us-saudi-asia-china-idUSKBN16N0G9
24. "King Salman Visits China, his fifth Asian destination", *Al Arabiya,* English, 15 March 2017, at http://english.alarabiya.net/en/News/gulf/2017/03/15/King-Salman-visits-China-his-fifth-Asian-destination.html
25. http://www.thehindu.com/2001/01/26/stories/05262512.htm
26. http://www.thehindu.com/2001/01/26/stories/05262512.htm
27. India-Saudi Arabia Joint Statement during the visit of Prime Minister to Saudi Arabia, 3 April 2016, at http://www.mea.gov.in/bilateral-documents.htm?dtl/26595/IndiaSaudi_Arabia_Joint_Statement_during_the_visit_of_ Prime_Minister_to_Saudi_Arabia_April_03_2016
28. Ibid.
29. Ibid.
30. Ministry of Commerce and Industry, India, Export-Import DataBank, at http://commerce.gov.in/EIDB.aspx, accessed 20 April 2017
31. http://www.jantakareporter.com/business/india-saudia-business-group-33-companies-delhi-looks-beyond-energy/32131/
32. http://www.worldenergyoutlook.org/media/weowebsite/2015/IndiaEnergyOutlook_WEO2015.pdf
33. https://www.bp.com/content/dam/bp/pdf/energy-economics/statistical-review-2016/bp-statistical-review-of-world-energy-2016-full-report.pdf
34. http://oilprice.com/Latest-Energy-News/World-News/Saudi-Arabia-Loses-No-1-Spot-to-Iraq-in-Crude-Exports-to-India.html
35. Ministry of External Affairs, India, at http://mea.gov.in/images/attach/NRIs-and-PIOs_1.pdf
36. http://www.ndtv.com/india-news/centre-ensuring-protection-of-indian-workers-in-gulf-countries-sushma-swaraj-1443197
37. Ibid.

5

Saudi Arabia and the Region

Neha Kohli

ABSTRACT

The Kingdom of Saudi Arabia, a conservative Islamic monarchy, is the largest country in the Gulf region in terms of population, area, and abundant in a single natural resource: oil. It is also home to the two holiest sites of Islam, Mecca and Medina. Socially and politically conservative, the Kingdom follows a strict interpretation of Islam in the form of Wahhabism. Religious orthodoxy is particularly dominant in the domestic space; however, the country uses its political, religious, and economic clout to attempt to shape the wider Islamic world as per its conservative Wahhabi ideology.

Saudi Arabia views itself as a regional leader as well as that of the wider Islamic world. And it has not been immune to the fast-moving changes that West Asia has been witness to, over the past five years. The ideas of populism, democracy, and freedom that the Arab Spring brought to the fore in the region, spread across West Asia, fuelled in part by the access of large numbers of youth to the social media as also the consequence of immense dissatisfaction with the ruling, mostly dictatorial/monarchical regimes. The Arab Spring began in Tunisia in December 2010 with the self-immolation of a street vendor, leading to the outpouring of popular resentment against the incumbent regime, and eventually led to its downfall. This was repeated in Egypt in February 2011 when there was a popular mass uprising against Hosni Mubarak, the country's military dictator. Saudi Arabia's smaller neighbour, Shia-majority Bahrain saw a pro-democracy movement emerge in March 2011, and unrest ensued in Syria wherein the regime cracked down on popular protests for change that eventually spiralled into a civil war. More recently, Saudi Arabia has had to contend with the rise of the Islamic State (IS) in the territories of Iraq and Syria. The IS declaration of an Islamic Caliphate in 2014 affects the Kingdom as it is the site of the Two Holy Mosques (which it uses to legitimize its leadership role in the larger Islamic world). Moreover, the US-Iran rapprochement post the 2015 nuclear deal has started the process of Iran's re-integration into the global and regional orders. It is in this latter space that there arises a conflict of interest between the Islamic Republic and the Kingdom.

While the Saudi-Iran relationship has been largely confrontational since the Islamic Revolution in 1979, it tended to take the form of proxy conflicts in different arenas. This has been more so since 2011, beginning with the crushing of the pro-democracy protests in Shia-majority Bahrain—the Saudis provided financial and military aid under the aegis of the Gulf Cooperation Council (GCC) in support of the Bahraini regime to crush the movement. In Syria, the Saudis have consistently supported anti-Assad forces, ostensibly because the regime has been a long-standing ally of Iran in the Levant. Mubarak's fall in Egypt, and the coming to power of the Muslim Brotherhood was not viewed with much favour by the Kingdom; however, the re-establishment of a military regime under Abdel Fattah al-Sisi has the Saudi's tacit approval. Closer home, in Yemen, the Saudis launched a military campaign against the Houthi rebels, whom they see as an Iranian proxy. The Saudis have also pulled together a 'Sunni Coalition' of Islamic countries to undertake military action against the IS as well as for counterterrorism.

Not only are the Saudis grappling with a fast-changing—in their eyes, perhaps, worsening—regional order that allows Iran to come forward and assert itself as a regional hegemon, they are also adjusting to the American withdrawal of sorts from the region, in keeping with the latter's pivot to Asia. For half a century and more, the USA was the security guarantor for the Kingdom and the other states in the Gulf. However, post the US-Iran nuclear deal, and America's obvious interest in making Iran an ally in addressing the regional disorder, the Saudis have had to re-calibrate their foreign policy. A conservative, defensive outlook—hitherto supplemented by its religious and energy clout—has changed in the past five years. The Saudi regime is attempting a more proactive foreign policy towards the region and beyond, given the massive upheavals West Asia is witnessing. In doing so, it has not been averse to playing the sectarian card, given that it sees Iran as its main regional competitor for strategic influence—the Saudi interventions in Bahrain and Yemen, its support to anti-Assad forces in Syria are key examples of this approach. This has a domestic aspect as well, since Saudi Arabia's Eastern Province has a large Shiite population, and the regime has always been wary of Iran's perceived influence here. The foreign policy re-calibration also comes with a change in guard at home—the accession of King Salman to the throne after the death of King Abdullah in 2015, and the transition of the royal succession to the second generation leadership.

This chapter examines aspects of Saudi foreign policy, in particular how the Kingdom views and addresses the changes in the region, the challenges it faces, and the strengths and limitations of its approach. It also discusses Saudi-Iran geopolitical rivalry, and looks at the Saudi involvement in the proxy conflicts in Syria, Bahrain, and Yemen. Another aspect the paper addresses is whether there is an emerging Saudi-Egypt-Turkey-Qatar axis.

Background

Saudi Arabia is a conservative, Islamic, oil-rich monarchy that geographically dominates the Arabian Peninsula. It is also the most populous Arab country in the Gulf region, and derives a strong sense of regional and global leadership from the fact that in its territory are Mecca and Medina, two of the holiest sites in Islam and the birthplace of the religion. Modern Saudi Arabia was established in 1932, with the formal consolidation via three decades of conquest of the various provinces that make up the country, by Abd al-Aziz Ibn Abd al-Rahman Al Saud. The modern state, however, traces its lineage back to the mid-eighteenth century when a strategically significant political-religious pact was arrived at between a reformist preacher, Mohammed Ibn Abd Al Wahhab, and the emir of the small central oasis of Diriya in Najd, Mohammad Ibn Saud. It was this pact—which accorded, in agreement, political and temporal powers to Mohammad Ibn Saud and religious oversight to Mohammad Ibn Abd Al Wahhab—that enabled the former to move out of Najd and expand the borders of his domain. In modern Saudi Arabia, this alliance continues to undergird the state.

For most of its modern history, Saudi Arabia was a one-resource economy—its primary asset was oil. Demographically, militarily, historically, and even politically, Saudi Arabia lacked the heft that its larger Arab neighbours possessed (in terms of population, if not territory), both in the immediate Gulf region and in the broader West Asian region. Thus, for long, the Saudi regime depended on this oil resource to enhance its standing domestically, and remain significant for the fast growing western economies, especially the United States (USA), in the post-World War II era. Saudi Arabia firmly put itself in the Western camp during the Cold War and, over time, built a strong relationship with the USA, which guaranteed the latter with consistent energy supplies from the Kingdom in return for it providing Riyadh a security umbrella. Alongside its western leanings, regionally, and as far as the larger global Muslim world was concerned, Saudi Arabia tended to use its Islamic credentials—as the birthplace of the religion and home to its two holiest sites—in its foreign relations. This also allowed it to mitigate, to a certain extent, its lack of clout vis-à-vis other Arab states and its larger neighbour Iran. In fact, since the mid-1980s, the Saudi ruler has styled himself as the 'Custodian of the

Two Holy Mosques' in order to bolster the monarchy's Islamic identity and reach in its neighbourhood as well as in the larger Muslim world.

During the 1950s and 1960s, Saudi Arabia stood in opposition to the Nasserite version of Arab nationalism. This situation changed in the 1970s following two major occurrences: the first was the 1973 oil crisis when Saudi Arabia, along with other members of the Organisation of Petroleum Exporting Countries (OPEC), pushed for an oil embargo against western powers supporting Israel in the Yom Kippur War, which led to a significant increase in the revenue it earned from this one resource. It now had the ability, in financial and economic terms, to move towards acquiring the regional leadership role it always sought. The second was Iran, which, following the Islamic Revolution in 1979, became a cause for apprehension for Saudi Arabia given its revolutionary call for the overthrow of monarchies across the region. The presence of a large number of Shias within Saudi Arabia and its smaller Arab neighbours further added to its apprehension. Since then, Saudi foreign policy has consciously tried to hold back Iranian influence across the Gulf and the wider West Asian region, and also limit its influence domestically.

Since the 1980s, buoyed by its increasing oil wealth and antagonism towards the revolutionary regime in Tehran, Saudi Arabia has used petro-dollars to spread its own peculiar version of Wahhabi politico-religious thought beyond its borders. This is often to counter other, alternate politico-religious views as well as models of governance, specifically Iran's, which represents a revolutionary Shia theocratic state. It has also sought to increase its influence over its smaller neighbours in the Gulf region and in the wider West Asia, and is the largest member in terms of population, resources, and economic clout within the Gulf Cooperation Council (GCC), a regional security organisation. More recently, after the overthrow of Saddam Hussein in Iraq in 2003, Saudi Arabia saw itself facing newer challenges—a changed regional order, instability in Iraq, renewed threat from Iran, and asymmetrical and Islamist threats like the al-Qaeda *externally*; and calls for internal security reform *domestically*. These new realities and challenges to the state and ruling family, religious legitimacy both domestically and in the region, changing security considerations—all ultimately have impacted its foreign policy calculations.

This chapter begins by discussing the main features and foundations of Saudi foreign policy. It then examines how the Kingdom has viewed and addressed the changes in its immediate neighbourhood since 2011 in particular; the challenges it faces currently; and the strengths and limitations of its approach. Underlying its foreign policy choices and behaviour regionally is a geopolitical rivalry with Iran—one that is increasingly acquiring sectarian overtones and is being played out in proxy arenas. In effect, the Saudi approach to the region has been to continue to assert its regional standing while facing challenges to it.

The Foundations of Saudi Foreign Policy

F. Gregory Gause III defines the "fundamental goals of Saudi foreign policy" as the following: 'to protect the country from foreign domination and/or invasion and to safeguard the domestic stability of the Al Saud regime.'[1] A Saudi point of view states that the Kingdom '...is a status quo state by its very nature and therefore any radical changes that threaten [its] existing internal and regional order [are] not easily accepted.'[2] Along with ensuring the monarchical, dynastic rule of the Al Saud, the Kingdom wishes to retain its supremacy regionally in the Gulf and West Asia, and in the larger Islamic/Muslim world. These goals have remained unchanged in spite of the Kingdom having faced challenges such as Arab Nationalism/Pan-Arabism in the wider region, the Iranian Revolution and, more recently, the virtual break-up of Iraq in its near neighbourhood.

For its part, Saudi Arabia describes its foreign policy as being 'shaped within [the following] major frameworks':[3]

1. Good-neighbour policy;
2. Non-interference in the internal affairs of other countries;
3. Strengthen relations with the Gulf States and the countries of the Arabian Peninsula;
4. Strengthen relations with Arab and Islamic countries for the benefit of the common interests of these countries, as well as advocate their issues;
5. Adopt the nonalignment policy;
6. Establish cooperation [*sic*] relations with friendly countries; and
7. Play an effective role in the international and regional organisations.[4]

For Saudi Arabia, its primary areas of interest are (concentrically, as per importance) the neighbouring Gulf, the extended Arab neighbourhood in West Asia, the larger Islamic world, and the international community. Gause condenses these levels to three:

> (1) the international level, dominated by the Saudi strategic alliance with the United States and the Saudi role as an oil power; (2) the Middle East regional level, where Saudi Arabia plays a balancing game among larger and more powerful neighbors; and (3) the

Arabian Peninsula level, where Saudi Arabia asserts a hegemonic role vis-à-vis Yemen and its smaller monarchical neighbours.[5]

The Gulf Region

The Gulf region is the country's immediate neighbourhood, including the smaller monarchies of Bahrain, Kuwait, Qatar, United Arab Emirates, Oman, on the Kingdom's east and south-eastern borders, and the politically fragile and volatile state of Yemen to the south-west; it also includes Iran across the Gulf, a geographically, demographically larger neighbour that is also, in terms of religious ideology, as well as a competitor for regional dominance, at odds with Saudi Arabia. In this region, the Kingdom actually plays the role of a hegemon as it far out-ranks its Arab Gulf neighbours territorially, demographically, politically, and resource-wise. Saudi foreign policy stresses on 'blood relations, historical connections, [the] unique geographical neighbourhood that brings Arab Gulf States together, [and] the similarity of existed political and economical systems.'[6] In 1981, concerned by the revolutionary rhetoric from Tehran that was directed at the monarchical regimes of the Gulf as well as being increasingly concerned about the impact of the Iranian Revolution on their domestic constituencies, the Gulf states (except Yemen) led by Saudi Arabia formed the GCC. Key to Saudi Arabia's foreign policy goals in the Gulf are to maintain security and stability in the region; cooperate on a range of 'political, economical, security, social, cultural fields' through the GCC; and 'coordinate the policies of the GCC...especially toward the regional and international momentous issues', among others.[7]

Arab Neighbourhood

Saudi Arabia has been cognizant of its 'Arab' identity from the establishment of the modern state. This led the country, in 1945, to become one of the founding signatories of the Arab League along with Egypt, Iraq, Jordan (then Transjordan), Lebanon, and Syria. Saudi Arabia has always emphasised both its Islamic and Arab identities, and indeed sees little difference between the two. It further emphasises the 'necessity of Arab solidarity, together with coordination among the Arab countries with the aim to unify Arab stances and utilise all potentials and resources of Arab countries to serve the Arab interests.'[8] Given its location in a region that has seen persistent conflict since the end of World War II, a key feature of Saudi foreign policy has been that of mediation. While mediation might not have led to a resolution of these conflicts when it did attempt to mediate, it did help Saudi Arabia achieve its specific foreign policy objectives, along with enhancing (or maintaining) its image as well as ensuring its regional supremacy. According to Mehran Kamrava,

> Saudi Arabia views mediation as an integral tool in its foreign policy goals of maintaining an active involvement in regional issues, enhancing and deepening its influence among the different parties involved in national and cross-border disputes, and using foreign policy objectives and initiatives as a means of ensuring and perpetuating domestic political legitimacy of the state.[9]

Some examples of the Kingdom's connect to, and interest in Arab affairs, are: its stated commitment to the Palestinian issue, the 2002 Prince Abdullah Peace Initiative, the 2007 Mecca Accord, and the 1989 Taif Accord that brought the Lebanese civil war to a close.

The Islamic World

Islam has been a defining identity for the Kingdom, encompassing the political, socio-cultural and spiritual/religious realms. Saudi rule over the Kingdom's territory was legitimised by Al Saud's pact with the Wahhabis in the eighteenth century. Indeed, the two Saudi states of the eighteenth and nineteenth centuries were examples of Al Saud's expansionist aims being supported and legitimised by a Wahhabi religious sanction. In the twentieth century, leading up to the consolidation of modern Saudi Arabia, the Wahhabi conception of Islam was used by Abd Al Aziz Al Saud in the form of the *Ikhwan* (deeply religious Bedouin) who looked at the state-building project as propagating Wahhabi/Sunni orthodoxy over the conquered lands. Saudi Arabia believes in using,

> ...Her potentials and resources to serve issues of [the] Islamic World and achieve the motives of solidarity and unity based on the fact of belongingness to one belief. The Islamic symbiosis is the method to regain Muslims [*sic*] position and honour.[10]

In order to further cement its role and position in the larger Islamic/Muslim world and 'achieve Islamic solidarity', Saudi Arabia

> ...sought and initiated, together with their [*sic*] Islamic countries, to establish a system of Islamic governmental and non-governmental organizations, among which are the Muslims World League established in 1962 and the Organization of Islamic Conference established in 1969, where the Kingdom embraced the Headquarters of both organizations.[11]

Through these organisations, the Kingdom seeks to promote (and be at the forefront) of the collective security of Islamic countries, mediation efforts,[12] economic aid, relief and assistance as well as

> back up Muslims and defend their issues, and provide moral and material support to Islamic groups wherever they exist, through generous contribution in building mosques, and establishing Islamic civilized [*sic*] centres.[13]

Through its outreach in the Islamic world as a leader, the Kingdom also seeks to mitigate the effects of a 'cultural overflow and intellectual invasion' (ostensibly from the West) as also 'introduce the real and true image of Islam and its tolerance law Sharia'a, and protect Islam from all the clear accusations and slanders addressed to Islam, such as terrorism and human rights violations.'[14]

The formal adoption by King Fahd of the title, "Custodian of the Two Holy Mosques" in 1986 was another attempt at the Kingdom's assertiveness of its obvious leadership of the Islamic/Muslim world. As Mai Yamani writes, '[t]he kingdom's use of Mecca as a tool of foreign policy...[reinforces] this status; the city is a symbol unavailable to potential rivals...'[15] in the region and the Arab world.

The International Level

Since it views itself as a natural leader at the regional, Arab and Islamic levels, the Kingdom also sees itself as playing an important role internationally. It is a founding member of the United Nations (1945) and joined the Non-Aligned Movement in 1961. Furthermore, during the 1970s, it saw itself as part of the Western bloc, opposed to the Soviet Union, thus entering into an economic and security relationship with the USA. Together with pre-revolutionary Iran under Reza Shah Pehalvi, Saudi Arabia was a part of the American 'Twin Pillar' policy which was aimed at preventing the spread of Communism and also mitigating Soviet influence in the region during the height of the Cold War. Indeed, it could be said that the bedrock of Saudi foreign policy during the Cold War rested on its deep relationship with Washington.[16] What made the Kingdom key to Cold War politics was energy: Saudi Arabia accounts for almost 25 per cent of the total known oil reserves in the world. This allows it great leverage in the international arena, as it is the largest supplier of energy to many economies, especially in the Asia-Pacific region.[17] Moreover, owing to its vast reserves, it has the ability to act as a 'swing' supplier in terms of increasing or decreasing supplies as and when the need arises. As a member of the OPEC, and given its vast proven oil reserves, Saudi Arabia also has the ability to affect global oil prices in keeping with its foreign policy agenda.[18]

Moreover, since the events of 11 September 2001 (more popularly referred to as 9/11), undertaken by the Al Qaeda under the leadership of Osama Bin Laden (a Saudi national) and with the participation (and also popular support later) of many Saudis in the terror attacks, Saudi Arabia has also pushed internationally a condemnation and rejection of '...all methods and mechanisms of international terrorism, and [to] confirm that Islam is above suspicion of all terrorist activities.'[19] In doing so, it speaks of '[a]dhere[nce] to the regulations of the international law, agreements, charters, and bilateral agreements, as well as respecting them all either within the framework of international organisations or other agreements.'[20]

The Kingdom's Regional Approach since 2011

The events of the Arab Spring challenged Saudi Arabia's "status quo-ist" approach.[21] The underlying rationale of Saudi Arabia's regional approach since 2011 has been its apprehension of a resurgent Iran. More than the events in Tunisia and Egypt,[22] it was the popular uprising in neighbouring Bahrain[23] that was a great cause for concern in Riyadh. Strategically, Saudi Arabia's interest in Bahrain stems from the fact that a change in the Bahraini political situation—if the majority Bahraini Shia succeed in gaining significant concessions from the regime or, as was the apprehension in 2011, that the Shia opposition succeeds in removing the ruling regime—would have an immediate impact on Saudi Arabia's own internal stability as well.[24] Therefore, Saudi Arabia not only keeps an eye on its tiny neighbour, it also moves to influence events occurring there: thus, as the Bahraini opposition movement gained strength in the early days of the Arab Spring in 2011, the Kingdom provided financial and military aid under the aegis of the Gulf Cooperation Council (GCC) in support of the Bahraini regime to crush the movement.[25]

The Iran Factor

What drove Saudi concerns in 2011 (and does so today as well) is the fear that the 'instigator', the 'benefactor' (in the case of Bahrain and, more recently, in Yemen), as well as 'beneficiary' of the uprising is Iran. It is a reality of the geopolitical situation in the Gulf region that there are two regional giants competing for a leadership role: Saudi Arabia and Iran. Both have complex histories, and also stand on two sides of a religious divide within Islam: while Iran is overwhelmingly Shia[26] and claims leadership of Shia Muslims worldwide, the Kingdom of Saudi Arabia asserts its claims to the leadership of the larger Sunni Muslim population across the globe. Each has tried, over the past few decades, to remake the region in terms of its own political-religious state structure and primacy of national interest.

Since the Revolution in 1979, Iran's revolutionary theocratic regime sought to 'export' the revolution to the monarchies across the Gulf; indeed, it called for similar revolutions to occur in these countries. One of the targets of this revolutionary call was the Saudi regime, which now began to view Iran under Khomeini as a 'destabilizing force'. In Saudi Arabia, this became a cause for concern domestically as well, given its significant Shia population that tends to face systemic and deep-rooted discrimination. The Saudi regime has always been apprehensive of this population segment's supposed 'loyalty' to Tehran. The divergence in ideologies, policies, and with events such as the 1979 siege at the Grand Mosque in Mecca,[27] the earlier riots in Shia-dominated areas—with little to no evidence of an Iranian hand—and the constant calls for the removal of the Saudi monarchy coupled with a geopolitical contest between two large regional states, led to an estrangement and a 'bitter rivalry for power and influence in the region'. This also led to Saudi Arabia (and other Gulf regimes) supporting Iraq during the eight-year long Iran-Iraq War during the 1980s—it is estimated that Saudi Arabia contributed US$25 billion to Iraq during this period. This changed in 1990–91 with Saddam Hussein's invasion of Kuwait, which jolted the Kingdom's security perception considerably.[28]

The Iraq Context

In 2002, while the campaign against the Taliban and Osama Bin Laden in Afghanistan[29] was still on-going, the USA and Britain began laying the case for a military campaign against Iraq, calling for the removal of Saddam Hussein and the Ba'thist regime in Baghdad, ostensibly on the grounds that there were weapons of mass destruction (WMD) being harboured by his regime. Saudi-US relations had already been under considerable strain since 9/11, and the regime's response to the proposed US-led war against Saddam Hussein was apprehensive and cautious. Simply put, the Saudis were against the war in 2003, which was a complete turnabout from their position during the Kuwait crisis of 1990–91. In 2003, the Al Saud regime was not only grappling with the reality of the Saudi militants' involvement in the 9/11 attacks on the USA, but was also facing increasingly vocal criticism from within the country, especially from amongst the Islamist forces. Many were contemplating the regime's downfall. Furthermore, the George W. Bush administration's intense focus on terrorism, Osama Bin

Laden and Al Qaeda as well as Saddam Hussein meant an increasing and interventionist role of the USA in the region. The Saudis were wary of this intense focus on their own practices and, thus, did not give the same level of support to the US-led War on Iraq as they did to the 1991 campaign.

While attempts were made to link the US invasion of Iraq in March 2003 with the larger 'War on Terror' still being carried out in Afghanistan, Saddam's fall resulted in a dramatic change in the political situation in Iraq. It set in motion a battle for the control of Iraqi territory between various factions within the country. Emboldened with the removal of the dictator, the Iraqi Shia, the largest segment of Iraq's population (comprising 65 percent of the total population) suddenly found an avenue to gain power. The removal of Saddam Hussein and the US-led creation of a Shia majority state on its northern border created a great sense of unease in the Kingdom (as well as in other Arab capitals). This sense of unease was best encapsulated by the concept of the 'Shia Crescent', first articulated by King Abdullah of Jordan, that hinted at Iran as the power centre of a new regional order stretching from the Gulf to the Levant, dominated by what is essentially a minority sect in Islam. This new regional order, in Saudi eyes, would see an empowered Hezbollah in Lebanon, and the continued control of the Alawites in Syria, a Shia-dominated Iraq, and the ripple effect in Bahrain, with its Shia majority.[30] With large numbers of Saudi Shias in its Eastern Al Hasa Province, Saudi Arabia perceived this as a growing (and perennial) security problem within its borders.

Proxy Conflicts

The long-standing geopolitical rivalry between Iran and Saudi Arabia provides the context for understanding how the latter has approached its immediate region since 2011. Interestingly, Saudi-Iran rivalry has not resulted in direct confrontation; rather it has manifested itself in proxy arenas, involving both state allies and non-state actors. In the aftermath of the Iranian Revolution,

> ...the Saudis stitched together an alliance of Gulf monarchies to strengthen their regional standing [that is, the GCC]...unlike the Saudi model of a coalition of nation states, [Iran] was focused on non-state actors. Iran was behind the formation of the Hezbollah...and had been one of the consistent supporters of the...Hamas.[31]

Since 2003, this rivalry—in reality an attempt to shape the changed regional order to their own advantage—had intensified along sectarian lines. Both Iran and Saudi Arabia claimed the leadership of the Gulf regional order, and of the larger Muslim world; and both have tried, over the past four decades, to assert themselves to the advantage of the rival using rhetoric that is often couched in religious or sectarian terms. Unlikely to enter into a conflict directly, Saudi Arabia has used other spaces to confront Iran: for example, in Iraq, Bahrain, Syria and, most recently, Yemen—always viewing the 'other' from its peculiar politico-religious, ideological lens. In the words of Turki Al Faisal, Saudi Arabia views with great apprehension the

> Iranian leadership's meddling and destabilizing efforts in the countries with Shia majorities, Iraq and Bahrain, as well as those countries with significant minority Shia communities, such as Kuwait, Lebanon and Yemen...[and]...*will oppose any and all of Iran's interference and meddling in other countries* (emphasis mine).[32]

Most recently, it is Yemen that has become the primary arena of proxy conflict, along with Syria. In the latter,

> Saudi Arabia [has] funded and supplied the rebels fighting Iran's ally Bashar al-Assad; Iran...and showered Assad with military aid....In Yemen, Iran stepped up its financial and military aid for the Houthi rebels; after the rebels seized the capital Sanaa in early 2015 and began moving to take the rest of it, Saudi Arabia launched a bombing campaign to stop them.[33]

This was also spurred by moves by the USA to strike a deal with Iran on its nuclear programme and begin the removal of the harsh sanctions regime on it. For the Kingdom, any agreement that would begin Iran's rehabilitation into the mainstream, and allow it to come back as an actor on the regional state remains unacceptable.[34]

In 2015, Saudi Arabia stitched together a 'Sunni coalition', '[an]unprecedented coalition of Sunni states...to preserve what they consider as the legitimate Yemeni government...the start of Operation Storm of Resolve...'[35] This followed an uprising by the Houthis (a Shia sub-sect in Yemen) and the resignation of Abdrabbuh Mansour Hadi, Yemen's President since 2012. For Gulf regimes and their Sunni partners in the WANA region, the removal of Hadi and the Houthi successes were further evidence of Iran's proxy influence in Yemen as well as a '...Shia takeover...[while] Tehran and its allies...see this as an open act of aggression...'[36] The forming of the coalition also saw the coming together of Egypt, Turkey, Qatar,[37] and Saudi Arabia in opposition to Iran.

Assessing the Saudi Approach

How do we evaluate the Kingdom's foreign policy towards the region?

To do so, we must recall how the Saudis define their country—as a status quoist state for which threats to its internal order (regime security) and regional order (external threats) are unacceptable. Would we then define its foreign policy regionally as merely reactive? Or, as: measured, pragmatic, and consistent? To be fair, since its inception, the Saudi state has navigated a plethora of challenges and threats and yet managed to retain as well as increase its say in regional and global affairs. Contrary to much speculation over the past decade and a half regarding the stability of the regime, the Al Saud have weathered many challenges—these have been domestic as well as foreign—and managed to retain power. At the same time, despite its tendency to prefer the status-quo, the Kingdom has sought to increase as well as maintain its leadership role in regional issues: that is, it views with approval a regional order which it could dominate. Hence, it's discomfort with the idea of a dominant Iran in the Gulf or West Asia, as also (historically) a dominant Egypt or Syria or Iraq. Thus, in the 1950s and 1960s,

> Saudi Arabia addressed the nationalist movement led by president Gamal Abdel Nasser when his ideology was seen as a threat to the regional security and stability. It also confronted the communists in the region, supported Iraq in the Iran-Iraq war when it was evident that Iran sought to change the regional order [post 1979], and stood fast against Saddam Hussein's invasion of Kuwait [in 1990-91].

A key feature of Saudi foreign policy has been its deep relationship with the USA, which, though transactional, is based on the two axes of energy and security. During the Cold War, Saudi Arabia cast its lot with the US-led bloc; and Saudi influence in West Asia owed much to Riyadh's proximity and importance to Washington. Since the events of 9/11, this relationship has come under strain, although Saudi Arabia continues to maintain relations with the USA. The American invasion of Iraq, however, appears to have been the catalyst for the Kingdom to seek new friends. It has taken a 180-degree turn in doing so by beginning to look eastwards towards the growing economies of Asia. Since the mid-2000s, the two Asian economic giants—China and India—have become some of the largest consumers of Gulf energy. Moreover, there are increasing trade relations between these countries and the Kingdom. With specific reference to India, the Kingdom is seeking to develop a closer relationship with New Delhi. It is already India's largest energy source in the Gulf, and home to around 3 million Indian expatriates. The Indo-Saudi relationship has evolved into a 'strategic partnership' since 2010 when former Prime Minister Manmohan Singh visited Riyadh. The closeness has also been apparent since the visit of the late King Abdullah as the honoured guest at India's 57th Republic Day in 2006. The current ruler of Saudi Arabia, King Salman, is slated to visit India in 2017.

Six years after the Arab Spring took root in West Asia, we find that Saudi Arabia has weathered the storm reasonably well. Despite apprehension that the regime would be challenged by the wave of popular discontent sweeping the region, the regime has withstood and weathered the storm. Rather, the Kingdom has shown considerable manoeuvring capability and resilience in the face of new challenges. It has managed internal discontent, and has taken a bolder, exploratory approach to perceived external challenges. This was especially so in the case of Bahrain in 2011, when it provided military (as well as financial) aid, albeit under the GCC banner, to crush the uprising against the Al Khalifa regime. It has involved itself, though indirectly, in Syria when it supported forces rebelling against Bashar Al Assad's regime that is Iran's only Arab ally in the region. More recently, it has taken unprecedented charge in attempting to push back the Houthi rebels—again seen to be aided and supported by Iran—in Yemen where it has led a coalition of Sunni states in undertaking military action against the Houthis. Thus, the Kingdom takes the geopolitical rivalry with Iran very seriously and, despite its avowed status quoist image, has slowly begun to develop a more intrepid approach to the region. This intrepidity is also ascribable to a clear change of guard at the helm of the regime— for the first time a third generation of leadership is taking over the reins of the Kingdom. Thus, Prince Mohammad bin Salman, a favourite son of the current king, has been at the forefront of the Yemen campaign. There is also recognition that the revenue from energy is as finite as the resource itself, and hence there are attempts internally at economic and political reform.

To sum up, the Kingdom of Saudi Arabia sees itself as a regional leader, if not a hegemon, and focuses its regional policy to this end.

NOTES

1. F. Gregory Gause III, "The Foreign Policy of Saudi Arabia", in R. Hinnebusch and A. Ehteshami (eds.), *The Foreign Policies of Middle East States*, Boulder: Lynne Rienner, 2002.
2. Awadh Albadi, "Towards Understanding Saudi Foreign Policy", *Trending Events*, No. 16, March-April, 2016, Future for Advanced Research & Studies, UAE, at http://futurecenter.ae/en/events.php?fustudy=944.
3. See, "The Foreign Policy of the Kingdom of Saudi Arabia", at http://www.mofa.gov.sa/sites/mofaen/KingdomForeignPolicy/Pages/ForeignPolicy24605.aspx.

4. Ibid.
5. F. Gregory Gause III, "The Foreign Policy of Saudi Arabia", in R. Hinnebusch and A. Ehteshami (eds.), *The Foreign Policies of Middle East States*, Boulder: Lynne Rienner, 2002.
6. Ibid.
7. Ibid.
8. Ibid.
9. Mehran Kemrava, "Mediation and Saudi Foreign Policy", *Orbis*, Winter, 2013, p. 3.
10. See, "The Foreign Policy of the Kingdom of Saudi Arabia", at http://www.mofa.gov.sa/sites/mofaen/KingdomForeignPolicy/Pages/ForeignPolicy24605.aspx.
11. Ibid.
12. The Saudi mediation efforts in the larger Islamic/Muslim world are discussed in Mehran Kemrava, "Mediation and Saudi Foreign Policy", *Orbis*, Winter, 2013
13. See, "The Foreign Policy of the Kingdom of Saudi Arabia", at http://www.mofa.gov.sa/sites/mofaen/KingdomForeignPolicy/Pages/ForeignPolicy24605.aspx.
14. Ibid.
15. See, Mai Yamani, "The Two Faces of Saudi Arabia", *Survival*, February-March, 2008, p. 153.
16. The unravelling of this relationship, and the beginnings of a shift in Saudi foreign policy, could be traced to the aftermath of the 9/11 terror attacks on the USA, in which a number of Saudis were involved, including its mastermind, Osama Bin Laden. Furthermore, the American (mis)invasion of Iraq in 2003 put a further strain on the relationship.
17. Post World War II, US policy towards the region was also contingent on securing energy resources, and here Saudi Arabia played a significant role. However, in the past few years, the USA has declared a lessening dependence on West Asian energy on account of substantial shale oil/gas resources available domestically.
18. An example of this occurred 2015 onwards, especially after negotiations between the USA and Iran culminated in an agreement that began the dismantling (in phases) of the sanctions regime against the latter. With the dismantling of the sanctions regime underway, albeit in a phased manner over a decade-long period, Iran would gain greater heft on the regional as well as global stage. The Saudi refusal to cut down on production meant that global crude oil prices fell sharply, coming close to only US$30 per barrel, which had hitherto reached a high of $140 per barrel. This was also a result of the Saudi perception that the nuclear deal would embolden Iran's hand in Syria, where it is a long-standing ally of the embattled Bashar Al Assad regime. As the Russians had entered into the fight against the Islamic State in Syria on the side of Assad as well, the sharp decline also affected Russia as an oil producer. In 1973, in retaliation against American support to Israel in the Yom Kippur War, the Saudis as part of the OPEC were instrumental in declaring an oil embargo on the USA, the UK, Japan, Canada, and the Netherlands. Although the embargo was a collective OPEC decision, it led to a significant increase in the prices of crude internationally, from around US$3 per barrel to US$12 a barrel.

19. See "The Foreign Policy of the Kingdom of Saudi Arabia", at http://www.mofa.gov.sa/sites/mofaen/KingdomForeignPolicy/Pages/ForeignPolicy24605.aspx.
20. Ibid.
21. The Arab Spring refers to a series of popular and spontaneous uprisings in the West Asian and North African (WANA) region, beginning with the fall of Zine El Abidine Ben Ali in Tunisia followed by Hosni Mubarak in Egypt. The calls for popular government, democracy, et al., caused considerable alarm in the Gulf regimes. In the Kingdom, the regime appeared to tackle this challenge by unleashing financial sops for its citizenry as well as undertaking a series of political and social reforms.
22. While Egypt is a far more populous country as compared to the Kingdom, its president Hosni Mubarak was an ally. More importantly, Egypt is a Sunni majority country.
23. A tiny archipelagic nation off Saudi Arabia's eastern coast on the Gulf, Bahrain is linked to the mainland by a causeway. The Bahraini ruling family, like the al-Saud, is Sunni and has familial ties with the latter; however, what makes Bahrain unique is that it has a Shia majority—around 75 per cent—in the total native population of 500,000 in Bahrain. Like their Saudi counterparts (and until 2003, their Iraqi counterparts), the Bahraini Shia are discriminated against considerably, and are viewed as possessing a dual loyalty to Iran.
24. The Kingdom's Eastern Province is home to the majority of its 15 per cent (estimated) Shia population. In the Wahhabi view, the Shia are seen as non-Muslims, and there is a certain level of entrenched discrimination against them in the country.
25. A few decades earlier, in the immediate aftermath of the Iranian Revolution in 1979, the Saudi (as well as Bahraini) perception was that Iranian agents fomented demonstrations and riots among the Shia population within their borders—this was in response to the spontaneous reactions/support to the revolution in Iran within both Bahrain and eastern Saudi Arabia. There was renewed alarm about Iran in December 1981 as well, when Bahraini security forces foiled an attempt to depose the Al-Khalifa regime, and announced the arrest of a 75-member group, followed by another coup attempt in 1987 that failed to attract much Shiite support.
26. The Iranian Constitution of 1979 emphasizes the predominance of the "Twelver Ja'fari school", and some 90 per cent of the country's population adheres to Shiism.
27. In November 1979, during the annual Haj pilgrimage, Islamist Sunni militants known as the neo-Ikhwan, led by Juhaiman al Utaibi, seized the Grand Mosque at Mecca. They 'denounced the Saudi regime and proclaimed the appearance of a Mahdi (redeemer)', and called for a new age of Islam, unadulterated by the corruption and deviations of the past. While this was a domestic challenge to the regime, it rattled the Saudis nonetheless as the siege occurred in the same year as the revolution in Iran.
28. In August 1990, two years after Iran and Iraq had agreed to cease hostilities ending the eight-year long Iran-Iraq War, Iraqi forces invaded and occupied Kuwait (Iraq had long claimed Kuwaiti territory as its own). While Saddam Hussein had been financially bolstered with Saudi and American (via the Kingdom) financial

support in the war, it is conjectured that he invaded Kuwait not just to settle a long-standing claim to the latter's territory but also hoped to fill Iraq's depleted coffers (owing to the eight-year long Iran-Iraq war) with oil revenue from captured Kuwaiti oil fields. At that time, the Saudis perceived Iraq's action as posing a serious threat to its immediate security, even more than a possible Iranian-supported subversion. As Madawi Al Rasheed writes: '[t]he war was an unprecedented event in that, for the first time, Saudi Arabia felt that it was under the imminent threat of invasion by a neighbouring Arab state.' See, Al Rasheed, *A History of Saudi Arabia, Second Edition*, 2002, p. 158.

29. In 1998, the Al Qaeda burst upon the global consciousness with the simultaneous bombings of the US embassies in Kenya and Tanzania. A product of the decade-long jihadi laboratory in Afghanistan, the organization was led by a Saudi: Osama Bin Laden. Three years later, on 11 September 2001, this organization would undertake a series of spectacular attacks in New York and Washington DC in the USA. That the mastermind of the attacks was a Saudi national (although his passport had been revoked by the Kingdom in the 1990s) and 15 of the 19 perpetrators were Saudi nationals caused a plethora of problems for the Kingdom. According to Madawi Al Rasheed: 'While the Bush Administration was careful not to implicate Saudi Arabia, the American press spared no opportunity to link the attacks on America to Saudi Wahhabi preaching, finance, charities, and pan-Islamic education centres. For the first time, Saudi Arabia was on the receiving end of American media accusations.' Also see, Al Rasheed, *A History of Saudi Arabia, Second Edition*, 2002, p. 222.

30. Talmiz Ahmad, 'Sectarianism and Security Implications for West Asia', paper presented at the 1st Annual West Asia Conference, 10–11 September 2014, Institute for Defence Studies and Analyses, New Delhi.

31. Stanly Johny, 'The Hot Saudi-Iran Cold War', *The Hindu*, 15 June 2015.

32. Turki Al Faisal bin Abdul Aziz Al Saud, 'Saudi Arabia's Foreign Policy', *Middle East Policy*, Vol. XX, No. 4, Winter, 2013, pp. 38–39.

33. Zach Beauchamp, "Iran and Saudi Arabia's Cold War is making the Middle East even more Dangerous", *Vox.com*, 30 March 2015, at http://www.vox.com/2015/3/30/8314513/saudi-arabia-iran.

34. In an interview to *Foreign Affairs* (also quoted elsewhere), Prince Mohammad bin Salman made the Saudi position clear. "When asked about the future of the Saudi-Iranian struggle and whether Riyadh would consider opening a direct channel of communication with Iran to de-escalate tensions and forge common ground, the Prince replied: 'There is no point in negotiating with a power that is committed to exporting its exclusivist ideology, engaging in terrorism, and violating the sovereignty of other nations....Until Tehran changes its deeply problematic outlook and behaviour, Saudi Arabia has much to lose from prematurely proposing rapprochement and cooperation,' he stated." See "Crown Prince: Iran Represents the 3 Main Ills of the Region... No Point in Negotiations", *Asharq Al-Awsat*, 8 January 2017, at http://english.aawsat.com/2017/01/article55365156/crown-prince-iran-represents-3-main-ills-region-no-point-negotiations, accessed 20 January 2017.

35. Afshin Shahi, "Middle East Prepares for Meltdown as Sunni States Bomb Yemen", *Scroll.in*, 30 March 2015, at http://scroll.in/article/717229/Middle-East-prepares-for-meltdown-as-Sunni-states-bomb-Yemen.

36. Ibid.
37. In 2014, there appeared to be a diplomatic rift within the GCC over Qatar's support to the Muslim Brotherhood. In March of that year, Saudi Arabia, Bahrain, and the UAE withdrew their ambassadors from Doha "...accusing it of breaching the organisation's security agreement and violating its principles of 'unified destiny'...of failing to commit to promises it had made to not interfere in the internal affairs of its fellow GCC states, not to support organisations and individuals jeopardising their security and stability, and not to harbour 'hostile media', referring to Qatar-based *Al Jazeera* Media Network." See, "Will the GCC Survive Qatar-Saudi rivalry?" *Al Jazeera*, 18 March 2014, at http://www.aljazeera.com/indepth/features/2014/03/will-gcc-survive-qatar-saudi-rivalry-201431864034267256.html. The Saudi view was that this dispute would not be resolved unless "Doha changed its policy".

6

Wahhabism and the Kingdom of Saudi Arabia: An Evolving Symbiosis[1]

Adil Rasheed

ABSTRACT

The birth of Wahhabism and the Saudi state took place in the early 18th century, which was followed by the two sides forging a historic pact in 1744 to aid and support each other. The alliance has remained in existence to this day, and has profoundly influenced Muslim and global history for almost three centuries.

This chapter seeks to explore the love-hate tug of this 300-year long marriage by highlighting changes in the dynamics of the relationship, the inherent tensions, and the challenges posed to it by many external and internal threats—viz. the Ottoman Empire, the Ikhwan Revolt, Juhayman Al-Otayba's Grand Mosque Seizure in 1979, the rise of Al-Qaeda and the 11 September 2001 attacks, the Sahwa's constitutional reform movement, the black swan of the 'Arab Spring', the ISIS menace, the growing Shiite ascendance in the region, and the Saudi search for a new security architecture.

The Kingdom of Saudi Arabia and Wahhabism

Like Siamese twins, Wahhabism and the Saudi state were born around two and a half centuries ago, and have since stuck together in a largely symbiotic relationship. Their combined strength and shared destiny have given them considerable geo-political heft, resilience, and longevity. However, this seemingly seamless compatibility has often concealed an underlying sense of unease and restiveness that has often spilled out violently, but has almost invariably evolved into a higher level of mutually-advantageous power dynamic. This chapter seeks to explore the complex past of this synergetic relationship that continues to shape the Arab, Muslim, and world history, even as it charts a somewhat fraught and less predictable future ahead.

It should be noted here that both the Kingdom of Saudi Arabia and Wahhabism have evolved in their political and religious orientation over the centuries, and this chapter seeks to chart the trends that shaped not only the political leadership of the House of Saud but also Wahhabism, which has either been tempered by modern Salafi movements as exemplified by the Salafi-Wahhabi constitutional reformists associated with the Sahwa in Saudi Arabia, the pragmatic descendants of Abdul Wahhab (the Al Ash-Shaikh family) who dominate the Saudi religious establishment, or have been further radicalised by modern Salafi Jihadist outfits like Al-Qaeda and the ISIS.

First and Second Saudi States of Diriyah (1727-1892)

Before discussing this Saudi-Wahhabi love-hate tug, it would be important to first understand the geographical regions of the Arabian Peninsula from which both Wahhabism and the KSA have emerged. Najd, which means 'plateau', covers the north-central area of present-day Saudi Arabia.[2] It is the place of origin for both Wahhabism and the first Saudi state that came into existence in the mid-18th century.

Along the peninsula's west coast lie Hejaz (which nestles the Islamic holy cities of Mecca and Medina) and Asir (bordering Yemen). The Eastern Province (traditionally known as Hasa) extends from Najd to the Persian Gulf, which currently has a substantial Shiite population, and is rich in petroleum reserves. The vast Rub al-Khali desert dominates the kingdom's south-central stretch. Some of these historical areas have now been reconstituted to come under 13 Regions of the Kingdom.[3]

In the 18th century, the Ottoman Empire exercised a substantial degree of suzerainty over Hejaz and Hasa, but had no formal presence or influence over Najd.[4] As the region did not produce enough agricultural surplus or livestock, it was not an attractive proposition for extending control to Najd either for the Ottomans, the Hejazi Sharifs, or the Banu Khalid rulers of Hasa. Therefore, the towns and oases of this region were ruled by their own amirs, who exercised a great degree of independence. In fact, its small merchants travelled to Basra and even India to supplement their meagre resources.

In Najd, Mani ibn Rabiah Al-Muraydi of the Mrudah clan founded the settlement of Diriyahin 1446–1447. Later, a scion of the Al-Saud landholding merchant class, Muhammad ibn Al-Saud, became Diriyah's local ruler in 1727.[5] It is believed that the nascent Saudi leadership did not have a distinguished tribal pedigree; nor did it have great wealth. Some historians attribute this limitation as a reason for its adoption of the warlike Wahhabi movement, associated with the religious reformer Muhammad ibn Abdul Wahhab (1703–92), as a means for gaining territory and prestige.

Born in a family of famous theologians, Muhammad ibn Abdul Wahhab belonged to the Banu Tamim tribe and, after his religious education in Madina, Basra, and Hasa, he returned to his place of birth, the Najdi village of Uyayna. Here, ibn Abdul Wahhab developed his uncompromising stance against Sufism and Shiite Islam. He started preaching against the prevalence of pre-Islamic customs and rites, like sorcery, superstition, solarism and idol worship that had returned to Arabia, and called on Muslims to revert to the "original" teachings of Islam.

At that time, Islamic scholarship was preoccupied with settling practical matters of the community, and thus put great emphasis on the study of 'Fiqh' (Islamic jurisprudence). However, Ibn Abdul Wahhab concentrated on reviving Muslim adherence to the fundamental articles of faith (Aqaid), particularly Tawhid [6] (belief in the existence and worship of only one God, Allah). His followers called themselves 'Muwahhidun' (Unitarians); but his following was popularly known as Wahhabi.

In spite of being welcomed initially, Muhammad ibn Abdul Wahhab's religious activism in Uyayana soon became unpopular, particularly after he and his followers levelled the grave of Zayd Ibn Al Khattab (a companion of Prophet Muhammad) that was venerated by the people, cut down trees that were held sacred by the locals, and personally stoned a woman to death for committing adultery.[7] Muhammad ibn Abdul Wahhab's actions antagonized the people of Uyaynah, and its chief had to expel him from the village. It is at this time that Muhammad bin Saud invited Muhammad ibn Abdul Wahhab to Diriyah and granted him protection. A historic pact was sealed between the two sides in 1744, along with the marriage of Abdul Wahhab's daughter with the son of Muhammad Ibn Saud. It is reported that

> Muhammad ibn Saud greeted Muhammad Ibn Abdul Wahhab and said, 'This is your oasis, do not fear your enemies. By the name of God, if all Najd was summoned to throw you out, we will never agree to expel you.' Muhammad ibn Abdul Wahhab replied, 'You are the settlement's chief and wise man. I want you to grant me an oath that you will perform jihad against the unbelievers. In return

> you will be imam, leader of the Muslim community and I will be leader in religious matters.'[8]

This historic pact[9] and power sharing agreement has remained extant for over 270 years.[10] While Wahhabism thrived under the political protection of the Saudi rulers, its emphasis on jihad provided the ideological impetus for the state of Diriya to expand its boundaries, and launch the conquest of Arabia.[11] In fact, the families of Muhammad ibn Saud and Muhammad Ibn Abdul Wahhab have intermarried many times over the years, and in today's Saudi Arabia, the minister of Islamic Affairs is always a descendent of Ibn Abdul Wahhab, popularly known as from Al Ash-Sheikh family.[12]

Following this alliance, Ibn Abdul Wahhab issued the decree of jihad against adjoining tribes whose religious practices of making pilgrimages to tombs he ruled as sacrilegious. The jihadi raids, based on the doctrine of 'Takfir', became more successful under the reign of Muhammad ibn Saud's son, Abd Al-Aziz (1765–1803). Thus, under the guise of spreading the message of Wahhabism, Saudi leadership was able to subjugate most of the chieftains in Najd. Thereafter, Saudi forces moved eastward into Hasa, and terminated the rule of Banu Khalid. The capture of Qatif in 1780 opened the road to the coast of the Persian Gulf and Oman. Qatar accepted the suzerainty of the Saudi in 1797, and Bahrain followed suit and paid 'zakat' to Diriyah.

Saudi forces then expanded to the west and, in spite of strong resistance from the Sharif of Mecca, Saud ibn Abd Al-Aziz (1803–14) temporarily held sway over Taif in 1802, Mecca in 1803, and Madina in 1804. Their raid of Taif was particularly violent, where they massacred the male population and took the women and children as slaves.[13]

The Wahhabi religious leaders ordered the destruction of the domed tombs of the Prophet and of his companions, in accordance with their belief of not building monuments on graves.[14] Saudis also marched into Asir, where local leaders embraced Wahhabism; but their ingress into Yemen was unsuccessful. However, the most brutal of their attacks was on the Shiite holy city of Karbala in 1802. There, according to a Wahhabi chronicler Uthman bin Abdallah bin Bishr, the marauding forces,

> Scaled the walls, entered the city ... and killed the majority of its people in the markets and in their homes. They destroyed the dome placed over the grave of Imam Hussein (the revered grandson of the Prophet) whatever they found inside the dome and its surroundings ... including emeralds, rubies, and other jewels ... different types of

property, weapons, clothing, carpets, gold, silver, precious copies of the Quran.[15]

The sacking and plundering of Karbala resulted in the revenge killing of Saudi ruler Abd Al-Aziz in 1803 by a Shiite in a mosque in Diriyah.[16] Eventually, the Ottoman Empire responded to the Saudi-Wahhabi challenge by sending troops of the Egyptian ruler Muhammad Ali into the Arabian Peninsula in 1811, which led many tribal confederations that had accepted the Saudi yoke to switch sides in favour of the foreign troops. After freeing the region of Hejaz, the son of Muhammad Aziz (Ibrahim Pasha) invaded Najd, ravaged the capital city of Diriyah, and massacred several Wahhabi religious scholars. The Saudis surrendered on 11 September 1818 and, thereafter, the Saudi ruler Abdallah was held prisoner, taken to Istanbul, and beheaded. Thus ended the first Saudi-Wahhabi state of Diriya.[17]

Following the obliteration of the first Saudi state, a second and much smaller Saudi state (the Emirate of Najd) gradually emerged, and lasted from 1819–1891. As it limited itself to the area of Najd, it did not draw the subsequent wrath of the Ottoman and Egyptian forces, and was protected by the region's remoteness, the paucity of natural resources, and poor communication and transportation. However in 1891, the Rasheedi rulers of Jabal Shammar successfully ended the second Saudi state in the Battle of Mulayda, and forced the House of Saud led by Abd Al-Rahman bin Faysal to Kuwait.

Wahhabism: Doctrines and Detractors

Wahhabism is considered a religious movement of Sunni Islam; but its adherents prefer to call themselves 'Ahl Al-Tawhid,' 'Al-Muwahiddun' and, in modern times, Salafis. Founded by Muhammad ibn Abdul Wahhab in the mid-18th century, most of its doctrinal beliefs are in sync with the literalist Ahl Al-Hadeeth ('people of tradition') school that arose in the second and third Islamic centuries in opposition to the 'Ahl Al-Raay' ('people of legal reasoning') Sunni scholarship, that allowed the liberal use of 'Qiyas' or interpretative reasoning for settling religious and jurisprudential issues. Over the centuries, the chief proponents of the Ahl Al-Hadeeth ('people of tradition') movement were jurists and theologians, like Ahmad Ibn Hanbal (780–855), Taqiuddin Ibn Taimiyyah (1263–1328), Muhammad Al-Qayyim Al-Jawziyya (1292–1350), and Muhammad Hayya Al Sindhi (died 1750).

Muhammad Ibn Abdul Wahhab's religious orientation focused mainly on the principal Islamic article of faith known as 'Tawhid' (the oneness of God), and emphasised the eschewing of 'Shirk' (the worship or adoration of anything other than one God, that is, Allah) as well as the rejection of 'bidaa' ('innovation' in religious matters). Thus, Wahhabism took up certain strict theological positions on matters of belief that were at variance with other schools of Sunni Islam (especially of the Ahl Al-Raay), particularly on matters related to 'tawassul' (intercession of a holy person on behalf of someone to arrive at or obtain favour of God), 'istighata' (beseeching a dead saint or holy person for evoking the help of God), the doctrine of 'wahdatul wujud' (the Oneness of all beings in God, monism), and adopted controversial approaches allegedly leading to 'takfir' (declaring a person, community infidel in order to legitimise 'qital' or slaughter) and 'tajsim' (anthropomorphism).

In fact, Ibn Abdul Wahhab (the founder of Wahhabism) believed that those Muslims who disagreed with the strict theological premise of his puritanical school, in effect violated the basic tenets of Islam and, in order to restore the religion's pristine purity, it was essential to conduct jihad against 'hypocritical' Muslims. This stance taken by Ibn Abdul Wahhab drew criticism from other Muslim theologians who believed that the Shahada (profession of Islamic faith, that is, 'There is no god but Allah, Muhammad is his messenger') was sufficient for a person to be deemed a Muslim, and that shortcomings in someone's behaviour or in the observance of mandatory rites did not turn the person into 'an unbeliever'.[18]

In addition, the Shiite were considered outside the pale of Islam by Ibn Abdul Wahhab because, he argued, that the Shiite belief in the 'infallibility of the Imams' constituted 'Shirk' (blasphemy). In his book 'Kitab Al-Tawhid',[19] Ibn Abdul Wahhab regarded the Shiite as the arch-enemies of Islam, and the Jews and Christians (who have been accorded the status of 'People of the Book' by classical Islamic scholarship) as infidels and devil worshippers.[20]

Wahhabism is also opposed to Sufi schools of mysticism and their practices. As mentioned above, Ibn Abd Al-Wahhab opposed 'Tawassul' (prayer though intercession as practised by Sufis) on the basis that a plaintiff should pray directly to God, and should not use any intermediary (living or dead, saint or a prophet) as it would be tantamount to associating partners with the Almighty, which is 'Shirk' (the unpardonable sin of apostasy, punishable by death). Again, Wahhabism which opposes 'bidaa' (innovation) in religion blamed the Sufis for introducing and inculcating various new forms of worship and meditation into Islam. Being highly literal in its reading of Islamic Scriptures, Wahhabism opposes the mystical and figurative interpretation of verses by Sufi scholars, and considers such interpretations as invalid concoctions. Thus, Wahhabism—being akin to the Athari Ahl Al-Hadeeth—emphasizes the 'zahir' (apparent or the literal) meaning of the Islamic texts as opposed to their rational or spiritual interpretation of the Ahl Al-Raay schools—like the Ashari and Maturidi theology as followed by Hanafi Muslims, including the Deobandis and Barelvis that constitute the majority Sunni community in the Indian subcontinent.

In addition, Ibn Abdul Wahhab rejected the doctrine of 'Taqlid' in Sunni jurisprudence, which means strict compliance with any of the four juristic schools of Sunni Islam (Hanafi, Shafa'i, Malaki, and Hanbali). Instead, he called on his followers to revert to the Quran (Islam's holy book), the Hadith (speeches and conduct of the Prophet), and the actions of the first three generations of Muslims (the Salaf)[21] when using 'ijtihad' (independent reasoning). Notwithstanding this claim, Wahhabism has remained closely affiliated to the Hanbali school of Sunni Islam in various juristic matters.[22]

Wahhabism also espouses the radical concept of 'Al Wala Wal Al Bara'[23] (which signifies staunch loyalty to everything Islamic, and complete dissociation with the un-Islamic). According to this concept, Abdul Wahhab made it "imperative for Muslims not to befriend, ally themselves with, or imitate non-Muslims or heretical Muslims", and that this "enmity and hostility of Muslims toward non-Muslims and heretical had to be visible and unequivocal".[24]

Many Islamic theologians have also found Wahhabi doctrines similar to those of old heterodox movements in Islam, like the 'Mujassimah' (Anthropomorphism—which is the belief that God has a body and is similar to humans). From Ibn Taimiyyah to Abdal-Aziz Abdallah bin Baz, Wahhabi theologians have been criticized by several Sunni and Shiite scholars for suggesting that Allah has a 'jism' (body), has a 'hadd' (limit), and 'harakah' (movement),[25] that He is not omnipresent but is distant and separate from creation and resides in the highest heaven.[26] Some Muslim scholars have gone to the extent of applying the well-known 'Hadith of Najd'[27] to the Wahhabis, which they claim was the Prophet's warning against their emergence.[28]

The Wahhabi style and manner of jihad has often been criticized by non-Wahhabi Islamic scholars for violating the principles of Islamic warfare. Wahhabi jihad is conducted as a typically savage and tribal raid for gaining territory and lucre rather than for a religious cause.[29] While some have questioned the scholarly credentials of Abdul Wahhab, pointing out the paucity of his ecclesiastical treatises and commentary, a large and growing number of Muslims across various sects have increasingly accepted most Wahhabi ideals and doctrines in modern times. This has been so principally in their strict adherence to Tawhid, Wahhabi emphasis on the priority of personal good deeds over saintly intercession, and the reversion to a literal understanding of the Scriptures, without blind adherence to classical Islamic scholarship, religious jurists, or self-proclaimed mystics.

Ibn Saud and Kingdom of Saudi Arabia (1902–1932)

The son of Abd Al-Rahman bin Faysal was Abd Al-Aziz, popularly known in the Western world as Ibn Saud. One night, in January 1902, he scaled the walls of Al-Rashidi city of Riyadh with a contingent of 40 men, and took control of that city after killing its governor Ajlan in front of his fortress.[30] This intrepid and successful raid made the charismatic Ibn Saud popular overnight, with many of the former supporters of the House of Saud rallying to his call to arms.

For several years hence, Ibn Saud and his forces fought and captured large portions of Najd from the Rashidi rulers. Around 1912, Wahhabi scholars associated with Ibn Saud religiously radicalised young nomad raiders into soldiers for the fledgling Saudi state. This new religious militia came to be known as 'Ikhwan' (not to be confused with Egypt's Ikhwan Al-Muslimeen, translated as Muslim Brotherhood).

In December 1915, the British entered into a treaty with Ibn Saud (The Treaty of Darin), wherein the territories of the latter became a British protectorate, and attempted to define its boundaries.[31] For his part, Ibn Saud vowed to wage war against Ibn Rashid, an ally of the Ottomans. In 1921, the Battle of Hail sounded the death knell of the Rashidi rulers, and the Jebel Shammar fell into the hands of the Saudi juggernaut.[32] This conquest was followed by a protracted conflict known as the Second Nejd-Hejaz War (1924–25), which ended successfully for Ibn Saud in December 1925 with the fall of Jeddah. In 1926, the entire territory of Nejd and Hejaz was brought under Saudi rule.

However, an even bigger challenge for the Saudi ruler now emerged from within his forces. A large section of Ikhwan militants, raised by the Saudi clergy, sought to fulfil their ideal of purifying and unifying the world of Islam, an ideal which eventually clashed with the political pragmatism displayed by Ibn Saud once he unified Nejad and Hejaz into his kingdom and forged an alliance with the British.

Soon after the Battle of Ha'il, the Ikhwan independently raided

Transjordan between 1922 and 1924. Under pressure from the British, who had treaties with territories in Transjordan, Ibn Saud forbade the Ikhwan from conducting raids against non-Wahhabi Muslims. Ibn Saud also wanted to reassure the Muslim world that his state was not opposed to other Muslim sects and that the "new Wahhabi regime would not disrupt the (Haj) pilgrimage".[33]

In 1926, Ikhwan leaders met at Al-Artawiya and accused Ibn Saud "for not upholding the sharp separation of belief and infidelity". In 1927, the Ikhwan Revolt began raiding neighbouring Iraq and Kuwait, in spite of Ibn Saud's orders against it.[34] The final decisive battle took place between the Ikhwan and Saudi forces broke out in March 1929 in the Battle of Sabilla. The Ikhwan—who fought with traditional swords and spears—could not withstand machine gun fire and modern weaponry provided by the British to Ibn Saud's forces.[35] The rebellion was completely crushed in 1930, when several Ikhwan rebel leaders surrendered to the British.

In the long and tortuous history of the Saudi-Wahhabi relationship, the Ikhwan Revolt is the first episode where Wahhabi idealism directly clashed with the political pragmatism of the Saudi state. Here, it is important to note that it was a descendant of the Ikhwan survivors, Juhayman Al Otaybi, who later led the infamous Grand Mosque seizure of 1979 against the Saudi government. However, in both instances, the will of the Saudi state prevailed over the Wahabbi uprising. Eventually, on 23 September 1932, the foundation of the Kingdom of Saudi Arabia was formally proclaimed.[36]

Oil and Faisal's Modernisation (1932-1979)

Oil was discovered in Saudi Arabia's Al-Hasa region (the Shiite dominated Eastern Province) in 1936 by the US-owned California Arab Standard Oil company (Casco), the predecessor to Arabian American Oil Company (Aramco). Commercial production began in 1938. Soon oil provided the fledgling kingdom with much needed economic and political stability as well as prosperity, along with substantial political leverage internationally.

In 1964, Faisal became the King of Saudi Arabia, and developed a reputation of being a transformative and modernising figure. He ushered in a welcome shift toward steady modernisation of a highly conservative society, with fiscal responsibility and educational reforms. Although personally religious, he decreased the power of the Wahhabi scholars and included non-Wahhabis, particularly cosmopolitan Sunni Hejazis from Mecca and Jeddah, into his administration.

Even as Prince, Faisal issued a decree for the full abolition of slavery in the country in 1961. He also introduced education for women and girls in spite of opposition by the religious conservatives, although their curriculum was written and monitored by the clergy. In 1963, he established the country's first television station which started telecasting two years later— that is, after he became king.[37]

The failure of Nasser's pan-Arabism following the defeat in the 1967 Arab-Israeli War (also known as the Six-Day War), gave opportunity to King Faisal to project Saudi Arabia as the pre-eminent Arab power. In fact, King Faisal sought to replace the unsuccessful secular pan-Arabism of Nasser with a Salafi-Wahhabi brand of pan-Islamism. As early as 1962, Saudi Arabia had established the World Muslim Organization in Mecca, which was given great impetus in King Faisal's reign.[38] Although Saudi Arabia played little role in the Israel-Arab wars of 1948 and 1967, it decided to launch an economic offensive in the Yom Kippur War of 1973 between the Arab states (particularly Egypt and Syria) and Israel.

As the USA was a supporter of Israel, King Faisal decided that Saudi Arabia will participate in the oil boycott by the Organisation of Arab Petroleum Exporting Countries (OAPEC) of Western states, namely the USA, the UK, Canada, the Netherlands, and even Japan. As oil prices soared, Saudi revenues increased substantially throughout the 1970s. King Faisal, considered to be the main strategist behind using the 'oil weapon', became a highly popular leader in the Arab and Muslim world.[39]

It was under Faisal's reign that Wahhabism shed its old, misleading appellation. It took on the Salafi tag after a leading member of Al Ash-Sheikh claimed that the scions of Abdul-Wahhab preferred to call themselves 'Al-Salafiyyun'. In fact, all Wahhabis today call themselves Salafis, and their influence on the Salafi ideology has become so pronounced that the modern rationalist ideology of the original progenitors of the Salafi movement—Jamal Al-Din Afghani and Muhammad Abduh (both Sunni Asharis)—has been effectively marginalised. Ironically, it was the modernist Salafi leader, Rashid Rida, who first called Wahhabis Salafi in creed, and Hanbali in law school, or simply 'Salafi Sunnis'.[40] However, there still exist remnants of old school non-Wahhabi Salafis in the Arab world, particularly within the Muslim Brotherhood, which calls itself 'Salafi' in the 'About Us' section of its website.

However, on 25 March 1975, King Faisal was shot dead by the son of his half-brother, Faisal bin Musaid, who had recently returned from the USA. It is a generally-held belief in the Arab world that Western powers conspired in the assassination of King Faisal in retaliation of his oil embargo. Another theory is that the plot was hatched by disgruntled religious elements as King Faisal's assassin was the brother of a religious zealot who was killed by security personnel while trying to attack Saudi television headquarters.

The Grand Mosque Seizure and After (1979–2001)

Clearly, the gradual marginalisation of the radical religious elements and the pace of modernisation played a big role in the end of King Faisal's reign. The time had come for the dissident Wahhabi elements to reassert their sway over the Saudi government. The discontent manifested in 1979, when a group of young Salafi insurgents took control of the Grand Mosque of the Kaaba (from 20 November to 4 December 1979) in the city of Mecca, during the annual Haj pilgrimage. The insurgents—led by a charismatic 43 year old militant Juhayman Al-Otaybi—claimed that one of their leaders was the mythical Mahdi himself (an end-time Muslim world conqueror in Islamic eschatology), a person by the name of Muhammad Abdallah Al-Qahtani. It took two weeks for Saudi forces to end the siege, which was followed by the execution of Otaybi and his cohorts.

The seizure of Islam's holiest site, the taking of hostages from among the pilgrims, the shooting in the holy precincts, shocked the Muslim world. Some experts call it a seminal event in the evolution of Islamic terrorism.[41] The seizure of the Grand Mosque challenged the religious legitimacy of Saudi rule, and raised questions about the conservative society's acceptance of its modernisation drive. At that time, the Saudi government was headed by King Khaled, but its affairs were run by Crown Prince Fahd, who found that the religious elite sympathised with many of Juhayman's grievances against the government.

As a consequence, Fahd had to cave in to the demands of the 'ulema' on many issues even though they went against the liberalisation drive of the government; he had to give up most of the reform programmes and measures initiated since the time of King Faisal. To begin with, photographs of women in newspapers were banned, followed by the banning of the appearance of women on television. Cinemas and music shops were closed. School curriculum was changed to provide even more religious education. Classes on subjects like non-Islamic history were removed from syllabi. Gender segregation was extended in public life, 'down to the humblest coffee shop'.[42] The power of the dreaded vice squad—'the mutawween'—to check the religious violations of the citizenry was "the seizure of the Grand Mosque sent Saudi Arabia into a 30-year time warp that cut it off from the social development trajectory it had been on". Saudi Arabia became one of the worst police states in the world.

Earlier in 1979, Saudi Arabia was also shaken by a major destabilising event in the region. It was the Iranian Revolution that ousted the Shah and brought in the rule of the Shiite clerics, under Ayatollah Khomeini. Suddenly, Saudi Arabia was contending with a rival Islamic revolutionary movement which was against dynastic rule, and which had emboldened the repressed Shiite population in the Arab world. An unprecedented civil unrest ensued in the country's Qatif and Al-Hasa regions (Eastern Province) that year, which has a majority Shiite population.[43]

The third highly significant event of the year 1979 was the Soviet invasion of Afghanistan. The embattled Saudi government immediately got the opportunity to refurbish its religious credentials, and to find a legitimate theatre for releasing the Wahhabi virulence simmering within. Thus,

> the struggle for Afghanistan gave young, religious Saudis—graduates of the Kingdom's new religious universities—an opportunity to defend Islam. A few hundred travelled to Afghanistan to join Muslim guerrilla fighters, the mujahideen. The United States, Saudi Arabia, and Pakistan assisted them financially and logistically.[44]

Many of these Saudi mujahideen—like the young Osama bin Laden (future founder of the dreaded Al-Qaeda)—returned home after their decade-long successful campaign against the Soviet Union. However, in August 1990, they were confronted by a bigger internal battle. On 2 August 1990, Iraq invaded Kuwait, and Riyadh invited the US military to protect the Kingdom from Saddam's advancing forces.

This incensed religious Saudi youth and dissident members of the Saudi religious establishment, and a movement—led by 'Al-Sahwa Al-Islamiyya', or simply the 'Sahwa' (which means the Awakening)—against the government decision spread in mosques and college campuses. Inspired by the ideals of the Egyptian Muslim Brotherhood, the Sahwa is a peaceful political reform movement in Saudi Arabia, which was led, at that time, by two academicians: Salman Al-Awda and Safar Al-Hawali.

In the wake of these protests, a few teachers at King Saud University in Riyadh had set up a human rights committee (the Committee for the Defence of the Legitimate Rights, CDLR). All of them were fired, and some of them fled to exile in London where they launched a campaign to overthrow the House of Saud. Osama Bin Laden identified with Hawali and Awda's ideas that opposed the deployment of US troops in Saudi Arabia. In April 1994, after Bin Laden had associated himself with the CDLR, the Saudi Interior Ministry stripped him of his citizenship. Then, in 1996, under pressure from Riyadh, the Sudanese government expelled him from the country where he was staying in exile. Bin Laden now found shelter in Afghanistan, protected by the Taliban, from where he built up his global terror network—the Al-Qaeda. In June that year, he claimed responsibility for conducting explosions in Dhahran, which killed 19 US servicemen. He justified them as a response to the Saudi alliance with the Zionist crusade.[45] On account of his violent, global jihad, Bin Laden was soon banished from even mainstream Saudi opposition. Shortly after the September 11 attacks, both Hawali and Awda denounced Bin Laden, and called on Saudi youngsters not to follow his path.[46]

House of Saud and Internal Opposition (2001–16)

Saudi Arabia is an absolute monarchy. The Quran and the 'Sunnah' (the speeches and actions of the Prophet) are declared to be the country's constitution. There are no political parties and national elections are not permitted. The ruling family, the House of Saud or Al-Saud, has thousands of members. The most influential member of this family is the King of Saudi Arabia, who is currently King Salman bin Abdul Aziz Al Saud. The House of Saud is composed of the members of the family of Muhammad bin Saud, founder of the emirate of Diriya and his brothers. However, the ruling faction of the family is primarily led by the descendants of Ibn Saud, the founder of the Kingdom of Saudi Arabia and the third Saudi state. By some estimates, the House of Saud has 15,000 members, and they are now too deeply entrenched for any coup to depose them. They are said to have taken control of various key institutions of the Kingdom. However, a more reasonable estimate suggests that the majority of power and wealth is in the hands of only about 2,000 members of the family.[47]

Although political parties do not exist in the Kingdom, several Islamist groups, separatist Shiite organisations, constitutional reform advocates, liberal academicians, and radical terrorist groups operate as opposition forces in the country. The predominant Sunni Islamist movement in the Kingdom is constituted by the Sahwa.[48] The Sahwa movement began in the 1970s when the ideology of the Muslim Brotherhood inspired many Saudi youth.

As mentioned earlier, Sahwa members were believers in conducting peaceful political protests. They became the mainstay of the strong protest movement against the royal family (known as the Sahwa intifada) over its decision to invite US forces during the Gulf War of 1991. The regime cracked down on protesters in 1994–95, arresting hundreds of Sahwa members including Salman Al-Awda, Safar Al-Hawali, and Nasir Al-Umar.

However, most of these leaders were released by 1999. Thereafter, some Sahwa members kept a low profile, while others began to be closely associated with the regime.

However, Sahwa's political activism was rekindled after the Arab Spring of 2011. Most of its leaders did not accept the narrative of the regime and official religious establishment which said that the demonstrations in Tunisia and Egypt were 'planned and organised by the enemies of the Umma (Muslim world)' in order to 'strike the Umma and destroy its religion, values and morals'.[49] Its leaders enthusiastically responded to the call of greater political freedom and democracy, particularly Salman Al Awda whose television show on MBC—'Life is a Word' (al-haya al-kalima)—was consequently scrapped. However, the Sahwa leaders denounced the 2011 uprising in Bahrain, and supported the brutal suppression of the protests by Saudi-Arabia led GCC forces. Some international experts have attributed this double standard of the Saudi Sahwa leaders to their deeply entrenched sectarian hatred of the Shiite community.

The roughly 2 million Shiite natives—10–15 percent of the population—are mainly centred in the Eastern Province of the Kingdom. Their noteworthy political groups that claim to be resisting longstanding Wahhabi oppression include Munazzamat Al Thawra Al-Islamiya and Hezbollah Al-Hejaz.[50] There are also about 100,000 Ismaili Shiites living in the southern Najran region, bordering Yemen.

Future Threats and Prospects

The so-called 'Arab Spring' uprisings that fanned the fires of popular unrest against authoritarian states across the Middle East in 2011 left behind a bevy of weak, failing, and failed states. They whipped up a perfect storm of radical religious extremism and sectarian tension in the region. The Kingdom of Saudi Arabia and other Gulf Cooperation Council (GCC) member states have since felt quite vulnerable as their wider Arab neighbourhood has been descending into greater political chaos and confusion. After Saudi Arabia's key security provider, the United States, entered into an agreement with the Shiite theocratic regime of Iran to limit its nuclear program in lieu of ending economic sanctions, the Kingdom feels betrayed over not being consulted by the US during the course of the negotiations. It was also upset with the Obama administration for not putting enough pressure on Iran to reduce its destabilising activities in Syria, Yemen, Iraq, Lebanon, the GCC states, and other conflict zones in the area.[51] The threat posed by the Islamic State, the Al-Qaeda, and even non-jihadi revolutionary elements like the Muslim Brotherhood to the security and stability of Saudi Arabia is also on the increase, and has made the Kingdom highly restive in finding effective solutions to an escalating crisis.

In fact, Saudi government officials have been speaking of building a 'new security architecture for the GCC states and their country', and have started flexing Saudi military muscle in the region like never before. The Kingdom led an international intervention in Yemen to put down the Houthi insurrection that deposed the elected government in the country in 2015. Iran has been accused of financially and militarily supporting the Houthi rebel forces as they belong to the Zaydi-Shiite sect. The Saudi-led intervention has not succeeded in eliminating the Houthi threat; neither has it been able to reinstate the deposed government.[52]

On 15 December 2015, Saudi Arabia's young deputy Crown Prince and Defence Minister, Mohammed bin Salman, announced the creation of the Islamic Military Alliance to Fight Terrorism (IMAFT). This is a coalition of 34 states meant to face-off the festering sore of the so-called Islamic State.[53] Most experts believe that this Sunni front is directed to face off the Iranian military threat as much as its stated aim of warding off the advance of the Islamic State's forces on the northern front. Saudi Arabia has also increased its sectarian diatribe against Iran in recent times. On 2 January 2016, the Kingdom executed renowned Saudi Shiite cleric Nimr al-Nimr for sedition, which escalated sectarian hostilities across the region. Later, Saudi Arabia severed ties with Iran, and expelled its diplomats from the Kingdom.

Meanwhile, the security threat posed by Islamist terror groups, particularly by the Islamic State, has been escalating in the country. On 4 July 2016, suicide bombers killed four Saudi security forces in an attack outside the Prophet's Mosque in Medina, during the month of Ramadan and a day before the Eidul Fitr festival. There were also bombings near the US consulate in Jeddah as well as in a mosque in the Shiite dominated city of Qatif, both on the same day. These bombings top a series of such attacks being carried out by the Islamic State in the last couple of years in the country.

In conclusion, the inherent dichotomy between radical Wahhabi state ideology and the pragmatic demands of modern governance faced by the Saudi Kingdom continues to affect its polity. Although there is no apparent sign of an upcoming political upheaval in the near future, the Kingdom of Saudi Arabia is on heightened alert, both against the groundswell of internal public disaffection in the wake of falling oil revenues as much as against external threats (posed by Shiite Iran as well as Salafi ISIS) in the immediate neighbourhood. However, the Wahhabi ideology and the scions of the House of Saud, who number in their thousands, are so well-entrenched in Saudi society that any form of revolutionary overthrow of power seems highly unlikely. The rise of Shiite ascendancy in the region has further united Saudi society behind the present Saudi-Wahhabi dispensation, which has withstood many a storm in the past.

NOTES

1. Dr. Adil Rasheed is Research Fellow at the Institute for Defence and Strategic Analyses (IDSA), New Delhi.
2. Wynbrandt, James, *A Brief History of Saudi Arabia*, Checkmark Books, 2010, p. 5.
3. Ibid.
4. Al-Rasheed, Madawi, *A History of Saudi Arabia*, Cambridge University Press, 2002, p. 14.
5. Ibid.
6. Wahhab, Muhammad Ibn Abdul, *Kitab Al-Tauhid*, Darussalam Publishers and Distributors, Saudi Arabia, 1986.
7. DeLong-Bas, Natana J., *Wahhabi Islam: From Revival and Reform to Global Jihad*, New York: Oxford University Press, USA. 20014, p. 61.
8. Al-Rasheed, Madawi, *A History of Saudi Arabia*, Cambridge University Press, 2002, p. 17.
9. Parker T. Hart, *Saudi Arabia and the United States: Birth of a Security Partnership*, Indiana University Press, 1998, p. 7.
10. *Commins, Davi, The Wahhabi Mission and Saudi Arabia*, I.B. Tauris. 2009, p. 18.
11. Sebastian Maisel; John A. Shoup, *Saudi Arabia and the Gulf Arab States Today: An Encyclopaedia of Life in the Arab States*, Greenwood: February 2009.
12. Wynbrandt,, James; Gerges, Fawaz A., *A Brief History of Saudi Arabia*, 2010, p. xvii.
13. Commins, Davi, *The Wahhabi Mission and Saudi Arabia*. I. B. Tauris, 2009, p. 31.
14. Al-Rasheed, Madawi, *A History of Saudi Arabia*, Cambridge University Press, 2002, p. 21.
15. Khatab, Sayed, *Understanding Islamic Fundamentalism: The Theological and Ideological Basis of Al-Qa'ida's Political Tactics*, Oxford University Press, p. 75.
16. Al-Rasheed, Madawi, *A History of Saudi Arabia*, Cambridge University Press, 2002, p. 22.
17. Bowen, Wayne H., *The History of Saudi Arabia*, Greenwood Press, London: 2007, p 75.
18. Commins, David, *The Wahhabi Mission and Saudi Arabia*, I. B. Tauris., 2009, p. vi.
19. Algar, Hamid, *Wahhabism: A Critical Essay*. Oneonta, NY: Islamic Publications International, 2002.
20. Jan-Erik Lane; Hamadi Redissi; *Religion and Politics: Islam and Muslim Civilization (illustrated ed.)*, Ashgate Publishing, 2009, p. 253.
21. DeLong-Bas, *Wahhabi Islam: From Revival and Reform to Global Jihad*, 2004, p. 12.
22. Glasse, Cyril, *The New Encyclopedia of Islam*, Altamira, 2001.

23. Saeed al-Qahtani, Muhammad. *Al-Wala' Wa'l-Bara' According to the 'Aqeedah of the Salaf, Part 2* (PDF).
24. Abou El Fadl, Khaled, *The Great Theft: Wrestling Islam from the Extremists,* Harper San Francisco, 2005.
25. Keller, Nun Ma Mim, Keller, Nuh. "*Who or what is a Salafi? Is their approach valid?*", 1994, at http://www.masud.co.uk/ISLAM/nuh/salafi.htm
26. Ekinci, Ekram Burga, "*Wahhabism: Pure Islam or Extremism*", *Daily Sabah,* 13 February 2015, at http://www.dailysabah.com/feature/2015/02/13/wahhabism-pure-islam-or-extremism
27. Sahih Al-Bukhari 7094, Book 92 Afflictions and the End of the World, Hadith 45: The Prophet () said, "O Allah! Bestow Your blessings on our Sham! O Allah! Bestow Your blessings on our Yemen." The People said, "And also on our Najd." He said, "O Allah! Bestow Your blessings on our Sham (north)! O Allah! Bestow Your blessings on our Yemen." The people said, "O Allah's Apostle! And also on our Najd." I think the third time the Prophet said, "There (in Najd) is the place of earthquakes and afflictions and from there comes out the side of the horn of Satan."
28. Valentine, Simon Ross, *Force and Fanaticism: Wahhabism in Saudi Arabia and Beyond,* Oxford University Press, 2014, p. 223.
29. Kepel, Gilles, *The War for Muslim Minds.* Belknap Press, Harvard University Press, 2004, p. 154.
30. Ochsenwald, William, *The Middle East: A History,* McGraw Hill, 2004, p. 697.
31. Wilkinson, John C., *Arabia's Frontiers: the Story of Britain's Boundary Drawing in the Desert,* 1993.
32. Mikaberidze, Alexander (ed.),). *Conflict and Conquest in the Islamic World: A Historical Encyclopaedia,* 2011, ABC-CLIO.
33. Ibid.
34. The Ikhwan Revolt, the Polynational War Memorial, at http://www.war-memorial.net/Ikhwan-Revolt-3.295
35. Daniel Silverfarb, "Great Britain, Iraq, and Saudi Arabia: The Revolt of the Ikhwan, 1927–1930", *The International History Review,* Vol. 4, No. 2, May, 1982
36. Ibid.
37. Riedel, Bruce, "Brezhnev in the Hejaz" (PDF). *The National Interest,* 2011.
38. Al-Rasheed, Madawi, *A History of Saudi Arabia,* Cambridge University Press
39. Hertog, Steffen. *Princes, Brokers, and Bureaucrats: Oil and the State in Saudi Arabia,*Ithaca: Cornell UP, 2010.
40. Commins, David, "From Wahhabi to Salafi", Dickinson College, Faculty and Staff Publications, Carlisle, Pennsylvania, 2015. p. 156.
41. Pierre, Tristam, *1979 Seizure of the Grand Mosque in Mecca: The Attack and the Siege That Inspired Osama bin Laden,* Terrorism: Myths and Reality, Middle East Issues, about.com at http://middleeast.about.com/od/terrorism/a/me081120b.htm
42. Burgess, John, "What effect did the Grand Mosque seizure have on Saudi Arabia?", Quora.com, at https://www.quora.com/What-effect-did-the-Grand-Mosque-seizure-have-on-Saudi-Arabia
43. Jones, Toby Craig, "Rebellion on the Saudi Periphery: Modernity, Marginalization, and the Shia Uprising of 1979", *International Journal of Middle East Studies,* Cambridge University Press, 2006.

44. Shavit, Uriya, "Al-Qaeda's Saudi Origins", The *Middle East Quarterly*, Fall 2006, at http://www.meforum.org/999/al-qaedas-saudi-origins
45. Teitelbaum, Joshua, *Holier than Thou: Saudi Arabia's Islamic Opposition*, The Washington Institute for Near East Policy, 2000.
46. Ibid.
47. Cahal, Milmo, "The Acton princess leading the fight for Saudi freedom", *The Independent*, 3 January 2012.
48. Lacroix, Stephane, *Saudi Islamists and the Arab Spring*, Kuwait Programme on Development, Governance and Globalisation in the Gulf States, Number 36, May 2014.
49. *Mufti al-mamlaka: al-muzaharatkhitat li-tafkik al-umma*, alwatan.com, http://www.alwatan.com.sa/local/news_detail.aspx?articleid=40472&categoryid=5
50. Jones, Toby, "Embattled in Arabia. Shi'is and the Politics of Confrontation in Saudi Arabia" (PDF), *Combating Terrorism*, Center at West Point, 3 June 2009
51. Hess, Bill, "Will Iran and Saudi Arabia Ever Get Along?". Brookings, 20 April 2016, at https://www.brookings.edu/2016/04/20/will-saudi-arabia-and-iran-ever-get-along/
52. Law, Bill, "Yemen war rapidly becoming as messy and complicated as the conflict in Syria". *The Independent*, 17 March 2016.
53. Payne, Ed. and Abdelaziz, Salma, *Muslim Nations form Coalition to Fight Terror, Call Islamic Extremism 'Disease'*, *CNN*, 22 December 2015, at http://edition.cnn.com/2015/12/14/middleeast/islamic-coalition-isis-saudi-arabia/index.html

SUGGESTED READING

1. Al-Rasheed, Madawi, *A History of Saudi Arabia*, Cambridge University Press, 2002.
2. Commins, David, *The Wahhabi Mission and Saudi Arabia*, I.B. Tauris, 2009.
3. De Long-Bas, Natana J., *Wahhabi Islam: From Revival and Reform to Global Jihad*, New York: Oxford University Press, 2014.
4. Hertog, Steffen, *Princes, Brokers, and Bureaucrats: Oil and the State in Saudi Arabia*, Ithaca: Cornell UP, 2010.
5. Lacey, Robert. *The Kingdom: Arabia & the House of Sa'ud*, Harcourt Brace Jovanovich, Inc., 1982.
6. Lacroix, Stephane, *Saudi Islamists and the Arab Spring*, Kuwait Programme on Development, Governance and Globalisation in the Gulf States, Number 36, May 2014.
7. Mortimer, Edward,*Faith and Power: The Politics of Islam*, Vintage Books, 1982.
8. Ochsenwald, William, *The Middle East: A History*, McGraw Hill, 2004.
9. Wahhab, Muhammad Ibn Abdul, *Kitab Al-Tawhid*, Darussalam Publishers and Distributors, Saudi Arabia.
10. Wynbrandt, James, *A Brief History of Saudi Arabia*, Checkmark Books, 2010.

PART 3

YEMEN

7

Yemen: An Introduction

Ranjit Gupta

Zaidi Shia Imam Al-Hadi ila'l-Haqq Yahya, a descendant of Imam Hasan ibn Ali, founded the Rassid state, Yemen's progenitor, at Sa'dain, in 893–7 AD. Since then, Shia Imams, in varying incarnations, have ruled Yemen till 1962, when the Shia Imamate/Kingdom was overthrown by nationalist secular-minded military officers led by Colonel Abdullah Sallal. Both Colonel Sallal and Republican Yemen's second President, Abdul Rahman Yahya Al-Iryani, were Zaydi Shias; Ali Abdullah Saleh, President from 1978–2012 for 34 years, is also a Zaydi.

Modern Yemen's major problems have been almost entirely due to the incessant interference by Saudi Arabia in Yemeni affairs since the Kingdom came into existence in 1932. This began with the Saudi invasion of Yemen in 1934 when it annexed the four northern provinces of Yemen. In a role reversal, Saudi Arabia strongly supported the Imam, militarily and financially, during the Civil War in Yemen from 1962 to 1970; Nasser also deployed Egyptian troops, at their peak about 85,000, to help the nascent Yemeni Republic to survive. Notwithstanding this enormous setback, Saudi Arabia was determined to try to influence, if not control, the political dynamics within Yemen to ensure that the shared border regions remained peaceful, and Saudi Arabia's geopolitical interests in the Arabian Peninsula and the Red Sea were not undermined by pumping in billions of dollars to various tribes, clans, groupings, and the government in Yemen.

Saudi Arabia covertly organised the setting up of the Islah party in 1990, and provided it political patronage and infusion of massive funds to spread Salafist influence throughout the country, injecting sectarianism in the internal political dynamics of Yemen in a significant manner for the first time in Yemen's history. Saudi Arabia also finally succeeded in making Ali Abdullah Saleh a pawn to protect and promote Saudi interests within Yemen, through massive personal financial incentives to Saleh, from the early 1990s till 2011.

The Houthis are a Zaidi Shia tribal clan, one amongst hundreds of clans constituting the overall Zaidi Shia population of North Yemen. The charismatic leader of the Houthi clan, Hussein Badreddine Al Houthi, established an entity named 'Ansar Allah' (Partisans of God) in the 1980s as a broad minded cultural, educational, and theological movement. With the rise of Saudi influence and Islah activism, Zaidis generally began to feel increasingly angry and frustrated due to an almost complete lack of economic development, growing political marginalisation, and the undermining of their socio-religious traditions. Therefore, Ansar Allah adopted a political agenda and platform. By now, other Zaidi Shia tribes and clans joined the Movement in large numbers. Widening protests against Saleh's autocratic rule were launched by Ansar Allah by the early 1990s. All these Zaidi Shia protesters against/opponents of Saleh's rule came to be collectively dubbed as 'Houthis' in common parlance.

Under Saudi prodding, Saleh waged a bitter military campaign against the Houthis from 2004 to 2010, at the outset of which their founder leader was killed in 2004. His brother, Abdel Malek al-Houthi, and later his nephew, took over the movement's leadership.

Yemen was among the four West Asian Arab countries convulsed by massive 'Arab Spring' related protest demonstrations from February 2011 onwards. Alarmed by protégé Ali Abdullah Saleh's inability to control the burgeoning unrest, Saudi-led mediation by the Gulf Cooperation Council (GCC) forced Saleh to step down in February 2012, and imposed Abd Rabbuh Mansour Al Hadi (Vice-President under Saleh for 17 years and a Sunni military officer from the South) through a completely manipulated and entirely undemocratic one candidate 'election' which represented a flagrant disregard for peoples' hopes and aspirations. Power was redistributed among Hadi and the other existing power holders, leaving out the Houthis even though they had participated very actively in the protest demonstrations. The Houthis participated in the subsequent National Dialogue. However, following the assassination of two of its delegates they walked out. Exceedingly angry by now, and taking advantage of continuing chaos, very weak governance, and a lack of internal cohesion within the government, the Houthis finally launched an armed revolt, and very quickly took control of 3–4 northern governorates and of Sana'a itself in September 2014. Hadi resigned and fled to Aden, and soon thereafter fled to Saudi Arabia.

With both Saleh and the Houthis shut out, the stage was set for an alliance of convenience between these two erstwhile bitter enemies. Having headed the Army for so long, Saleh enjoyed considerable support within it, and particularly among the powerful Republican Guard. The army's huge weapons inventory became a key factor that enabled the Saleh-Houthi alliance to swiftly take control of many of the country's main cities and ports, and more crucially, its administrative, energy, financial, and governmental apparatus.

Since the Houthi takeover of Sana'a, Saudi Arabia has been engaged in shrill daily rhetoric that Iran has been interfering in Yemen. This has never been the case in any meaningful sense. Using this as an excuse, Saudi Arabia abandoned its long standing traditionally cautious, deliberate, low key diplomacy, and adopted a surprisingly muscular approach at the behest of Prince Mohammad bin Salman Al Saud, the very young and completely inexperienced new Saudi Defence Minister and Deputy Crown Prince, the youngest and favourite son of the newly anointed King Salman. On 15 March 2015, Saudi Arabia launched 'Operation Decisive Storm' involving extensive air strikes against the Houthi and Saleh forces in and around Sana'a, Taiz, Hodeidah, and even Aden. Two years since then, Saudi Arabia's completely unjustified aerial onslaught, with indiscriminate bombing of Yemen and its people, has resulted in unprecedentedly large scale deaths, destruction, and devastation far worse than what has happened in Syria. There was nothing that the Yemenis, the Houthis, or Iran did to justify such a drastic reaction.

The havoc caused by the Saudi onslaught in Yemen is such that, under the personal instructions of Secretary General Ban Ki Moon, the UN was unprecedentedly constrained to blacklist the Saudi coalition for the deaths of thousands of children (later withdrawn temporarily due to Saudi financial blackmail).

Though the international community accepts Hadi as the legitimate head of the Yemeni government, the dour, completely uncharismatic Hadi has no legitimacy in the eyes of the people. He has no tribal or political support base whatsoever in northern Yemen, and even in the south; he has almost none outside Aden. To the extent that support exists, it is mainly due to Saudi Arabia's military and financial support and the spread of Salafist influence.

After the Houthis assumed control of Sana'a, Iran started supplying weapons, oil, and funds to them. Saudi claims notwithstanding, Iran could not have provided anywhere near large enough consignments of weapons to the Houthis to make a tangible difference on the ground, given the huge arsenal of state-of-the-art weaponry of Saudi Arabia and its coalition of Sunni countries as well as arms supplies by the USA and the UK. From never having had even a miniscule role within Yemen and in the geopolitics relating to Yemen in the past, Saudi actions, policies, and rhetoric have made Iran a very significant player in Yemen. Iran has now acquired credible locus standi and will, inevitably and unavoidably, be an active player in the processes to determine Yemen's future.

A Saudi military victory is unimaginable; Saudi Arabia can destroy the country but it cannot win over the people. No Saudi installed regime will be acceptable to the Yemeni people now. Yemen has to get from where it is now to a viable political dispensation under a 'national unity government' in which the Houthis and southerners, as a political bloc, must be included as active and important participants; otherwise Yemen will remain mired in instability and conflict. A semblance of peace can only be re-established through negotiations mainly between the parties directly concerned domestically as well as their external patrons—Iran and Saudi Arabia under UN auspices.

Yemen is the poorest and most backward country in West Asia. 19 million Yemenis are in dire need of urgent humanitarian assistance, with 6–8 million of them, including very large numbers of children, now facing acute famine conditions. Al least one third of over a thousand airstrikes have hit homes, schools, factories, hospitals, markets, mosques, and economic infrastructure. It will take years and huge funds for the reconstruction of housing and other basic infrastructure.

The long term political consequences of recent Saudi policies are: first, the enormous strengthening of Al Qaeda in the Arabian Peninsula (AQAP) which is the strongest Al Qaeda entity in any country, and has long been based in Yemen. This will ensure ongoing domestic instability which AQAP will cause by continuing its attacks even after Saudi Arabia can be persuaded to end its invasion of Yemen. Second, the virus of sectarianism will now be a permanent feature of the domestic political scenario in Yemen where it had not existed at all through its history.

8

Al-Qaeda in the Arabian Peninsula

Dipanwita Chakravortty

ABSTRACT

Al Qaeda in the Arabian Peninsula (AQAP) was formally formed in January 2009 as a merger between the Saudi and Yemeni branches of Al Qaeda. Its members could trace their jihadist history to the 1990s when most of them returned to Yemen after fighting the Soviet occupation of Afghanistan. They had trained under Bin Laden in Afghanistan and, on return, formed various militant groups like Islamic Jihad in Yemen (1990–94), the Army of Aden Abyan (1994–98), and al-Qaeda in Yemen, or AQY (1998–2003). Post the 2001 War on Terror, there was a severe government led crackdown in various Gulf countries, including Saudi Arabia, which compelled most of these groups to disband and its members to flee to Yemen. After the attack on the US embassy in Sana'a in 2008, the realisation of the merger was seen possible.

During the formative period, the group under the leadership of Nasir al-Wuhayshi declared its sub-ordination to Al Qaeda and its leader Osama bin Laden. They were against the Al Saud monarchy in Saudi Arabia as well as the Western presence in the region. Their main strategy, as announced by their leader in November 2010, was to "capitalize on the security phobia that is sweeping America and its allies and weaken their economy with such devastation, that it would be impossible for them to interfere in the Islamic world." Since its inception, it has carried out several terrorist activities—like the attempted bombing of Northwest Airlines Flight 253 on 25 December 2009, the crash of UPS Boeing 747 cargo plane on 3 September 2010, and attacks on various western tourists. The group has been designated as a terrorist organisation by the United Nations, Australia, Canada, Russia, Syria, Iran, Yemen, Saudi Arabia, the UAE, the European Union, and the United States.

In 2011, the Arab Spring protests spread to Yemen which led President Saleh to move troops deployed throughout the country to Sana'a in a move to secure his power. This resulted in a security/power vacuum in the southern region which was traditionally against the ruling power in Sana'a. Islamist militias affiliated to AQAP, like Ansar al-Sharia, captured various cities inthe southern province and declared it an Islamic emirate. After the ousting of President Saleh, Abd Rabbuh Mansour Hadi took the reins of the fractured country. He, along with the military backing of Western countries like America, implemented a severe crackdown on the militants who were driven out of their main territories by 2012. The US drone attacks, which started in 2010 to combat AQAP, killed several top leaders of this jihadist movement. However, these attacks also destroyed the complete infrastructure of the southern province which gave space for the militant groups to work and function as guerrilla groups, and support the secessionist movement.

In recent years, Yemen has increasingly become more fractured due to the ongoing civil war and the constant interference of external powers. AQAP continues to run a shadow government in the southern province, along with carrying out global attacks like the Charlie Hebdo attack. It has become a popular choice for radicalised youth seeking to join Islamist terror organisations overseas. This chapter traces the origins of the AQAP and the subsequent spread of the group. It analyses the recent events that have led to the 'slow collapse of Yemen and the rise of AQAP'. The chapter concludes with looking at the various future prospects of the militant group not only as a Yemeni-affair but also on the larger global scale.

Origins

AQAP was formed in January 2009 when two distinct branches of Al-Qaeda came together to form a single militant organisation. In its inaugural video, aired in early 2009, the then leader of AQAP, Nasir al-Wuhayshi, formally declared the union of the Saudi and Yemeni strands of Al-Qaeda.[1] However, the antecedents of this insurgent group can be traced back to 1990s when hundreds of mujahedeen returned from Afghanistan after years of fighting with the Soviets. Due to the collapse of the Soviet Union and the changing geo-political landscape, these former mujahideens were not allowed to resettle in their own countries, like Saudi Arabia and Iraq. They were instead repatriated to Yemen by the then Yemeni ruler, Ali Abdullah Saleh, who welcomed these mujahideens with open arms. He dispatched these militants on a 'jihad' to fight against the Soviet-backed Marxist government of South Yemen.[2] The southern secessionists were crushed by these experienced jihadists and, subsequently, Northern and Southern Yemen were unified under Saleh's rule. These militants settled in South Yemen, and started to form rudimentary terror outfits; most of them were led by Osama Bin Laden who had also settled in Yemen.

Osama Bin Laden was among the group of veteran mujahideens who had gone to Afghanistan in 1979 to fight against the Soviets. He returned to Saudi Arabia in 1989 to organise funds to set up an organisation of veteran mujahideens; but the Al Saud family revoked his passport and asked him to leave the country due to his fiery pan-Islamist rhetoric. He then left for Sudan, and then subsequently settled in Yemen. He urged his fellow militants to come together to 'wage a global jihad against western imperialism', and advocated a central role for Yemen in the same.[3] He started training and financing jihadists in the country as early as 1990s, and formed one of the first jihad outfits known as the 'Islamic Jihad in Yemen'. This lasted from 1990–1994 and was a predecessor to AQAP. Soon, other groups followed, like the Army of Aden Abyan (1994–1998) and, finally, Al-Qaeda in Yemen or AQY (1998–2003). The latter was created as an offshoot to the Saudi branch of Al-Qaeda. The first major terror activity of AQY was on 12 October 2000, when a skiff piloted by its two members detonated several hundred pounds of explosives into the hull of the USS Cole, which was moored in the port of Aden. Seventeen US servicemen were killed. It is also during this period that men who eventually formed AQAP in 2009—Nasir al-Wuhayshi, Said al-Shihri, Qasim al-Raymi, and Mohamed al-Awfi—trained under the personal supervision of Osama Bin Laden. Al-Wuhayshi served as Osama Bin Laden's personal secretary between 1998 until about late 2001, when the two were separated during the US-led Battle of Tora Bora.

AQY rose to international prominence after the September 2001 attack. Under the leadership of George W. Bush, the USA declared a global 'war against terrorism', and started compiling information and portfolios of various Al-Qaeda branches. At the same time, Osama Bin Laden urged the militia members of these outfits to fight against 'these American infidel's', and topple the 'apostate monarchy in Saudi Arabia'.[4] The Bush administration pressed the Saleh government to begin aggressive counter-terrorism operations against AQY. Yemen went out of its way to demonstrate its support for the war against Al-Qaeda. For President Saleh and others in the Yemeni government, there was a distinct desire to avoid making the same mistakes that Yemen made in 1990, when it had supported Saddam Hussein. Yemen has paid a heavy price, both politically and economically, for its failures to support the US against Iraq in the build-up to the First Gulf War.[5]

During a November 2001 visit to Washington, President Saleh emphasised his support for the US plan of action. From 2002 onwards, there was a brutal lockdown on terror activities in Yemen. Special Forces and Intelligence personnel from Washington arrived in Sana'a to aid the Yemeni forces to crack down on AQY members. A US drone strike in 2002, the first such operation in the region, killed AQY's leader, Abu Ali al-Harithi, as well as several other key members of the organisation.[6] By 2003, the number of militants reduced drastically, resulting in the almost-collapse of AQY. Most members fled to Saudi Arabia and joined the Al-Qaeda branch there. They started retaliating to the crackdown of their organisation in Yemen through various terror acts against Western forces.

Soon after, the top leader of Al-Qaeda, Khaled Ali Hajj, a Yemeni and a former bodyguard of Bin Laden, was ambushed and killed by Saudi troops. The leadership passed to a veteran Saudi militant, Abdul Aziz al-Muqrin, who revived the group through a series of intense attacks. This increased fears of political instability and pushed up the global oil price.[7] The militants realised the 'Achilles heel' of the western powers, and started strategically attacking petrochemical sites and gas pipelines, thereby increasing the oil price even further and leading to a global confusion over supply of petrochemicals. The following month, a member of Al-Qaeda abducted and beheaded a 49-year old American aerospace worker named Paul Johnson. He was an American defence contractor for Lockheed Martin. The abduction and the subsequent murder of Johnson became an international embarrassment for the US army. They deployed more soldiers and drone attacks to combat the rise of terror activities instigated by Al-Qaeda.[8] The triumph of the Muqrin-led militants was short lived. In a matter of months, security forces stormed a hideout in Riyadh and killed several jihadists, including Muqrin. Post the raid, the leadership of Al-Qaeda shifted to Salih al-Awfi who failed to consolidate the militant organisation, and found it increasingly difficult to organise operational cells inside the kingdom. The Saudi and Yemeni security services, backed by the American troops and intelligence, gained the upper hand, and succeeded in preventing any major terror attacks till 2006. Gregory D. Johnsen points out that

> the interlude of a little over two years in which it appeared as though al-Qaeda in Yemen had been largely defeated was the biggest mistake of the US in its 'war against al-Qaeda'. Instead of securing the win, both the US and Yemeni governments treated the victory as absolute. They failed to realise that in this case, a defeated enemy was not a vanquished one. In effect, al-Qaeda was crossed off the list of priorities both countries and was replaced by other, seemingly more pressing concerns. While the threat from al-Qaeda was certainly not forgotten in 2004 and 2005, I argue that it was largely ignored. This lapse of vigilance by both the US and Yemen, I believe, is largely responsible for the relative ease with which one of Osama bin Laden's former secretaries [began] rebuilding al-Qaeda in the wake of his escape from Yemen in 2006.[9]

On 3 February 2006, there was a massive prison break in Yemen, in which 23 alleged al-Qaeda militants in Yemen escaped, including Jamal al-Badawi—the alleged mastermind of the *USS Cole* bombing—Qasim al-Raymi, and Nasir al-Wuhayshi who became the leader of AQAP when it was officially formed in January 2009.[10] Most of the others were either recaptured or killed. These three militants fled to Southern Yemen, and started taking in new recruits and experienced Arab fighters who were returning from Iraq and Afghanistan. The group established several bases to launch fresh attacks, and were protected by the local tribes who had increasingly become disenchanted with the Saleh government. The group rallied on the grounds of 'resurrecting al-Qaeda from the ashes to save Yemen from the despotic rule of Saleh and destroy America which had completely crippled the country through drone attacks.'[11]

The prison break incident is instrumental in completely turning the history of Al-Qaeda. Several analysts like Gregory D. Johnsen have studied this incident, and have argued that President Saleh was an accomplice to the same. In November 2005, when President Saleh visited the USA in the hope of being rewarded for Yemen's help in the 'war against terror', he was informed that the Yemeni government was suspended from the USAID program. He was further informed by the World Bank that it was slashing aid from US$ 420 million a year to US$ 280. Johnsen points out that 'permitting a prison break in a high profile prison cell allowed Saleh to dictate his terms again to the USA'.[12] Daniel Byman concurs, and argues that 'Saleh realised that it needed terrorists on the move to continue getting aid from the USA'.[13]

Nevertheless, the escape of key militants from the prison set the course for the formation of AQAP. Soon after their escape, they were able to attempt simultaneous attacks on oil and gas facilities in Marib and Hadhramaut. In March 2007, Al-Qaeda officially announced its re-emergence, naming al-Wuhayshi as its commander. It underlined its renewed presence in the country with a suicide attack on a convoy of Spanish tourists a few days later.[14] They started carrying out several scattered suicide attacks across Saudi Arabia and Yemen. The series of suicide attacks culminated in September 2008 when the US Embassy was attacked in Riyadh, resulting in 18 deaths. The U.S. started pressurising the Saudi monarchy to renew its fight against Al-Qaeda. Subsequent raids and intense crackdown forced several Al-Qaeda militants to flee to their brethren in Southern Yemen. The time was ripe for the formation of a unified militant organisation.

Formation, Doctrine, and Leadership

The formation of AQAP was announced in a video in January 2009 made by Nasir al-Wuhayshi, Qasim al-Raymi and Said Ali al-Shihri, a Saudi national who had been recently released from Guantanamo Bay in November 2007.[15] The trio announced the merger of the Saudi branch of Al-Qaeda and AQY to form the new AQAP. Raymi and Shihri pledged allegiance to Wuhayshi, and pronounced him as the leader of the new outfit. Another former Guantanamo Bay detainee, Mohammad Aliq al-Harbi (also known as Mohammad al-Awfi) appeared as the newly appointed field commander. It became a great embarrassment for Saudi Arabia as well as the USA as both men were released from the prison into the custody of the Saudi government's 'de-radicalisation' programme for militants.[16] However, the merger was acknowledged by Osama Bin Laden's deputy, Ayman al-Zawahiri. Four days later, the group released a 19-minute video titled, "We Start from Here and We will meet at Al-Aqsa." This video outlined their goal and ideology. Johnsen points out that 'the move was designed to bring Saudi Al-Qaeda members who had fled their country as well as Yemeni militants together under one umbrella as a first step towards launching attacks throughout the region.'[17]

In its inaugural video, Wuhayshi formally declared the group's intention to avenge its enemies 'with blood and destruction' in order to establish an Islamic Caliphate on the guidelines of the Sharia Law. He urged the militants of the Yemen Soldier Brigade to join its ranks and be part of 'a global organisation.'[18] He clearly outlined the guiding ideology of AQAP in his opening prayers when he said, 'O Allah! Bring conquest over the Holy Mosque and the Haramain [highway from Mecca to Medina] by our hands! O Allah Give us the honour by establishing the Islamic State with our hands.'[19] To pursue these ends, it called for a violent 'global jihad against *kafirs*.' It urged the common Muslim men to become mujahideens and fight for the right cause of Islam. Fred Burton argues that

> the primary goals of AQAP are consistent with the principles of militant jihad, which aims to purge Muslim countries of Western influence, and replace secular 'apostate' governments with fundamentalist Islamic regimes observant of sharia. Its main objectives include overthrowing the regime in Sana'a; assassinating Western nationals and their allies, including members of the Saudi royal family; striking at related interests in the region, such as embassies and energy concerns; and attacking the US homeland.[20]

Johnsen points out that the early organisational structure of AQAP was based on the ideas and personality of its leaders, especially Nasir al-

Wuhayshi.[21] He was from the southern governorate of al-Baida wherein he began propagating AQAP'S ideology through various traditions like marriage as well as through several other socialties with the numerous tribes living there. He travelled to Afghanistan in the late 1990s where he eventually became the personal secretary of Osama Bin Laden. He fought during the battle of Tora Bora before escaping into Iran where he was eventually arrested. He was extradited to Yemen in 2003. In the Yemeni prison, he met Qasim al-Raymi who was born in Sana'a, and was a trainer at an Al-Qaeda camp in Afghanistan in the 1990s. Both these leaders were well aware of the political reality of the country as well as the growing disenchantment among the youth towards the ruling government.[22] They realised that they could turn the tide against the so called saviours—the US forces—by creating a strong favourable propaganda. They were also clear on creating AQAP as an organisation that could function despite the death of the top leadership unlike its predecessors. With these clear organisational ideas, they set about creating AQAP as the most representative organisation in Yemen. According to a 2015 report, AQAP has excelled in creating an organisation

> that transcends class, tribe and regional identity in a way that no other organisation or political party ever did. Nassir al-Wuhayshi created a propaganda narrative of events that appealed to the local audience and thus, were able to sway support for their activities and recruitment.[23]

According to a 2010 report from the think-tank New America, AQAP is

> compartmentalised and hierarchical, with a distinct division of labour. It has a political leader who provides overall direction, a military chief to plan operational details, a propaganda wing that seeks to draw in recruits, and a religious branch that tries to justify attacks from a theological perspective while offering spiritual guidance.[24]

A classified US State Department cable published by *Wikileaks* reveals that Wuhayshi's duties specifically included 'approving targets, recruiting new members, allocating resources to training and attack planning, and tasking others to carry out attacks.'[25] Under the guidance of Wuhayshi, the military branch plans all of AQAP's attacks, including bomb and suicide missions. It also organises various 'lone-wolf operations' across various countries. One of the most crucial elements in the branch is Ibrahim al-Asiri, the chief bomb maker. He is responsible for all the high-profile bombing attempts, including the Christmas day bombing in 2009 and the Times Square bombing in 2010.

Apart from the technical military branch, the propaganda branch is also one of the most important parts of AQAP. This was led by Anwar al-Awlaki who was killed by a US drone strike on 30 September 2011. It is responsible for attracting recruits and building its base of support. It operated a media channel known as 'al-Malahem' which is its main propaganda arm. It also published a bi-monthly magazine in Arabic for its Yemeni as well as Saudi audience. It also published an English-periodical called *Inspire* meant for Western countries. This magazine answers questions about AQAP and it missions. It discusses how to build home-made bombs in a kitchen, and also provides other classified information. Johnsen writes that

> *Inspire* helps AQAP reach [and] influence other like-minded individuals in the West. No Longer do these individuals need to travel to Yemen or read Arabic in order to take instructions from AQAP. Now, they can just download and read the magazine in English.[26]

The first issue of *Inspire* was published in July 2010, and the latest that can be accessed online is of December 2015.[27] Apart from regular periodicals, AQAP also published books and papers. One of the more famous article-leaflet was 'Palestine: Betrayal of the Guilty Conscience.' It was published in the midst of the Gaza-Israel War of 2014.

In 2012, AQAP released a recruitment guide called 'Expectations Full', which was written by Samir Khan. This guide was initially uploaded in various Arabic websites; later it was transmitted only through mails or social media messages. The guide discusses in great detail the need to attack home-targets rather than travelling long distances to the Middle East to be part of the global jihad. It states that "attacking the enemy in their backyard is one of the most helpful missions recruits can undertake, even more than fighting together with AQAP in Yemen."[28] Apart from the conventional media, AQAP also exploits opportunities provided by social media to entice new recruits to carry out terror activities. Initially, in 2012 and 2013, AQAP posted messages on jihadist websites and forums to attract western recruits. According to Katherine Zimmerman, one Arabic language message on the Shumukh and Al-Fidaa jihadist forum posted by an anonymous user, called on recruits to launch suicide missions in their home country. The message provided email addresses for recruits to contact various members of the military committee of AQAP. These messages were quickly brought down by various government cyber cells. Since then, AQAP has shifted its concentration to Twitter and Facebook.[29] On Twitter, for example, as soon as an AQAP account is shut down, another emerges almost immediately, typically using a new name ('handle') with one character amended. In November 2014, AQAP even launched its own 'AMA' (Ask Me Anything) Twitter account, providing official answers to questions such as 'Why haven't there been further AQAP attacks inside the US? Why don't you move the war from Yemen to US soil?'[30] The job of resolving such queries from prospective jihadists falls to Sheikh Nasser bin Ali al-Ansi, the AQAP senior official who has claimed responsibility for the Charlie Hebdo attack in January 2015.

The AQAP is largely self-funded. Its funding comes primarily from two sources: robberies and kidnappings.[31] Since 2015, their income source has also included the black marketing of petro chemicals and piracy in the Red Sea. They also run various black market trades to bolster their income.

AQAP Operations until the Arab Spring (2011)

AQAP's first official operation took place in August 2009 when they tried to attack Saudi Arabia's security chief, Prince Mohammed Nayef. The suicide bomber concealed a high explosive device inside his body, and tried to blow away the convoy of the Prince. Even though he was successful, the Prince survived.[32] On the Christmas day of the same year, a Nigerian man Umar Farouk Abdulmutallab, tried to detonate a bomb concealed in his underwear in an attempt to destroy a Northwest Airlines Airbus A330. He confessed to the CIA investigators that AQAP operatives had trained him in Yemen, and Ibrahim al-Asiri had built the bomb.[33]

In January 2010, the Yemeni government launched a major offensive against AQAP, with the support of numerous US troops. The latter not only provided intelligence but also deployed unmanned drones and fired cruise missiles. They targeted the organisation's senior leaders and training camps in the governorates of Shabwa, Abyan, and Marib. The offensive was largely considered unsuccessful as, instead of disrupting the operations of AQAP, it forced the organisation to work beyond the borders of Yemen. In February 2010, Raymi issued a statement threatening the USA: 'Today you have attacked us in the middle of our household, so wait for what will befall you in the middle of yours. We will blow up the earth beneath your feet.'[34] It can be argued that the Yemeni government under Saleh actually supported the AQAP; and thus, this is how its constant resilience and efforts to carry out operations despite strong military crackdown can be explained.

AQAP and the Arab Spring (2011-2014)

The tides again changed for AQAP when the Arab Spring reached the shores of Yemen in 2011. From then till early 2015, AQAP became embroiled in the domestic politics of Yemen. Due to popular unrest, President Ali Abdullah Saleh, who came to power in 1978, ceded his position to Abd Rabbuh Mansour Al Hadi under the proposals of a GCC initiative on 23 November 2011. Mansour Hadi became the President of Yemen on 21 February 2012 in an uncontested election. Previously, Mansour Hadi was the Vice President of Yemen in the Saleh government. The transition of power was followed by a series of uprising and protests that created a situation which swiftly deteriorated into a civil war. Protestors loyal to the Saleh family sporadically attacked several government institutions; these attacks were violently responded to by the pro-government forces. The Shia group known as the Houthis, who live in the north-western part of the country, began running a parallel government in three provinces of Yemen: Al-Jawf, Hajjah, and Sa'ada. They consolidated their power using the power vacuum created by the uprisings in 2011.

In the southern part of the country, separatist sentiment regained currency due to the political chaos at the centre. The secessionist movement boycotted the elections and demanded freedom. It stated that the ruling government has always ignored the plight of the southern Yemenis, and was only interested in the revenue garnered from the oil fields. Due to the lack of political stability as well as the complete failure of the military structure in Yemen, AQAP began to expand its territorial hold, and began running a parallel government in the Southern province in alliance with various local tribes.[35] Many of its armed members set their camps in Sana'a, and were in constant clash with the armed Houthi tribesmen who were also trying to increase their territorial expanse.

Soon after, in September 2012, Mansour Hadi announced an army offensive against AQAP in the Southern Province backed by UN forces. This was supported by a three-fold increase in the number of drone attacks authorised by US President Barack Obama. However, this did not stop them from launching major terror attacks. In May 2012, as a way of protesting against the new government—which they felt was a puppet government under the leadership of western powers—they bombed a military parade is Sana'a that killed more than 120 people.[36] It was around the same time that Wuhayshi was named as the deputy leader of Al-Qaeda by Ayman al-Zawahairi. Intercepted communications revealed that two men had planned to attack various US embassies in West Asia as well as

Africa. This prompted the US to close several embassies for a long period in 2013.[37] The move to declare Wuhayshi as the next Al-Qaeda leader also symbolised the growing power of the former. His ability to carry out operations as well as continue running the organisation despite years of state offensive against him made him an asset for the parent Al-Qaeda organisation.

The year 2014 saw an increase in terror activities by the AQAP. This was due to some major domestic developments. On 23 January 2014, the National Dialogue Conference (NDC) was completed. The NDC that began on 18 March 2013 was primarily a transitional dialogue process which was stipulated as part of the UNSC Resolution 2051 and the GCC Agreement signed on 23 November 2011. Apart from the Houthis, the Southern leaders too boycotted the NDC as they had rejected the notion of a coalition government; and instead called for a split in the country. This led to several clashes between them and the government forces, resulting in many deaths and hundreds of internally displaced people (IDP).

Constant violence also impacted the economic infrastructure in north Yemen as several of the oil pipelines were either obstructed or blown up. This led to a steady increase in fuel prices which also inflated the prices of essential consumer goods, like vegetables, pulses, and grains. To aggravate the situation, on 29 July 2014, the Yemeni government decided to cut all subsidies for fuel as a measure of reducing government expenditure. This led to an almost 65 per cent increase in the price of gasoline, and a 95 per cent increase in the price of diesel within a span of a few days.[38] Completely disillusioned by the present government and its lack of steps to improve the condition, several thousands of people came out and protested against the ruling government. They started supporting the Houthis, and demanded the reinstatement of fuel subsidies.

Re-ignited by the unrest in the north, the Southern Movement supported by AQAP renewed calls for independence. On 14 October 2014, thousands of people demonstrated in Aden in support of secession and self-determination. They issued a statement calling on the Yemeni government and all military personnel stationed in the south to withdraw by 30 March 2015.[39] Over the following weeks, pro-independence rallies continued. In December 2014, several government buildings in Aden were taken over by the members of the Southern Movement.

In the garb of independence rallies, AQAP escalated its terrorist attacks in the country, targeting Houthis and government institutions. On 13 February 2014, AQAP militants carried out an attack on the central prison in Sanaa, freeing 29 prisoners, including 19 suspected of affiliation with

AQAP. Between April and December 2014, they carried out 28 distinct terror blasts in which more than 86 soldiers and around 150 Houthi tribesmen were killed.[40] On 3 December 2014, the group threatened to kill the American journalist Luke Somers (who it was holding hostage) if its unspecified demands were not met within three days. As the deadline approached, Somers was killed, along with another hostage—the South African teacher, Pierre Korkie—during a failed rescue attempt by US Special Forces.[41] This incident showed the incapability of the Western powers to combat the growing prowess of the AQAP in Yemen.

Saudi-led Intervention in Yemen and its impact on AQAP (2015–2016)

On 7 January 2015, Said and Cherif Kouachi attacked the French office of a satirical newspaper Charlie Hebdo in Paris. They killed 11 people and injured 12 more. During the operation, they announced their allegiance to AQAP which later claimed responsibility for the attack.[42] It was one of the first attacks instigated by a European citizen on a European target on the behest of an Arabic terrorist organisation. The potential reach and influence of AQAP became a fact for the Western countries, including America. It drove home the message that the 'war on jihad' had indeed become global, and that it was no longer confined to the failed state of Yemen.

In Yemen, the domestic situation worsened drastically. The Houthis consolidated their power in Sana'a by January 2015, which compelled Mansour Hadi to flee to Aden in February. In this backdrop, AQAP managed to expand its territories in the southern part of the country and create a mini-state. Even though its leader Nasir al-Wuhayshi, was killed in an American drone strike, the organisation continued to flourish under its new leader, Raymi. A senior Yemeni government official said the war against the Houthis

> provided a suitable environment for the ... expansion of Al Qaeda. The withdrawal of government army units from their bases in the south, allowed Al Qaeda to acquire very large quantities of sophisticated and advanced weapons, including shoulder-fired missiles and armed vehicles.[43]

A week after Operation Decisive Storm headed by Saudi Arabia was announced, most of the Yemeni forces withdrew from the southern provinces—including Mukalla which is one of the main sea-ports in the Gulf of Aden—and moved towards the North. The city was left completely defenceless which allowed AQAP fighter to seize government buildings and free around 150 of their comrades from jail. They were supported by tribal leaders who aided them by looting army bases in a bid to claim independence from the North. The entire area became awash with advanced weaponry which was given by the USA to the Yemeni government to fight the AQAP in the south. They also looted Mukalla's central bank branch of an estimated US$ 100 million.[44]

With this swollen war loot, they established a quasi-state, with Mukalla as its capital. The city of Mukalla was important to the AQAP as it provided them with easy access to sea-trade as well as with a strong defence. They abolished taxes for local residents and established Sharia courts. They also gained control over the ports in Mukalla and Ash Shihr where they began to impose tax and custom tariffs on ships and traders. They started operating speedboats manned by RPG-wielding fighters to impose fees on ship traffic. They earned an estimated amount of US$ 2 million every day on these port taxes. They also began to run a black market for the smuggling of fuel. Most of the oil infrastructure came under the control of tribal leaders who were in alliance with the AQAP. According to a Reuters report, 'six white oil tanks between Mukalla and Ash Shihr are linked by pipeline to the Masila oilfields which are estimated to hold more than 80 per cent of Yemen's total reserves.'[45] This complete control over the oil pipelines has prompted major international companies like Petro Masila, Nexen Energy, and Total to shut production and exports.

Apart from running an economic empire, the AQAP has also projected itself as a benevolent ruling organisation. It also refused to pledge allegiance to the Islamic State, unlike other Al-Qaeda affiliates, as it wants to portray itself different from the Islamic Caliphate. The group regularly posts pictures of its members repairing bridges, paving streets, delivering medicines, building hospitals, etc. in Hadramout and other cities under its control. AQAP leader Batarfi said that 'so many areas fell to us after the Houthis left because we are the entity people trust.' One of the residents of Mukalla, reportedly told a Reuters journalist that 'I prefer that Al-Qaeda stay here, not for Al Mukalla to be liberated. The situation is stable, more than any 'free' part of Yemen The alternative to Al-Qaeda is much worse.' The Reuters reporter interviewed a local diplomat who said that

> If Al Qaeda manages to successfully root itself as a political and economic organisation, it could become a more resilient threat, much like al Shabaab in nearby Somalia. We may be facing a more complicated al Qaeda not just a terrorist organisation but a movement controlling territory with happy people inside it.[46]

The Way Forward

With the continuance of the Saudi-led intervention in Yemen, the prospects of AQAP do not look bleak. Despite thousands of aerial bombing by the USA and the Arab coalition, AQAP does not only continue to thrive but also grow exponentially. It must also be noted that, despite constant aerial bombardment by the Arab coalition, very few establishments of AQAP have been attacked or targeted. As the focus of the international community continues to be on Syria and on the Houthis, AQAP has been provided with an excellent opportunity to model themselves as a humanitarian ruling organisation rather than a terrorist outfit. The compliance of the locals, the alliance of the tribal leaders, and a well-established economic setup has helped AQAP achieve what its parent organisation Al-Qaeda could not do—that is, create a mini Islamic caliphate without calling it so, thus avoiding focused international attention. However, they continue to be targets of aerial raids by the US which continues to view the group as one of the prominent terror outfits in the world. Recently, President Trump, as Commander in Chief, ordered his first military raid on (29 January 2017) at a suspected Al-Qaeda camp in South Yemen which resulted in the death on 30 civilians.

NOTES

1. "Al-Qaeda in the Arabian Peninsula", Council on Foreign Relations Backgrounder, 19 June 2015, at http://www.cfr.org/yemen/al-qaeda-arabian-peninsula-aqap/p9369, accessed 1 February 2017.
2. Ibid.
3. Rolins, John, "Al Qaeda and Affiliates: Historical Perspective, Global Presence, and Implications for US Policy," Congressional Research Service, 5 February 2010.
4. Ibid.
5. Johnsen, Gregory D., *The Last Refuge: Yemen, Al-Qaeda, and America's War in Arabia*, New York: W.W. Norton, 2013, p. 59
6. "CIA 'killed al-Qaeda suspects' in Yemen", *BBC*, 5 November 2002, at http://news.bbc.co.uk/2/hi/2402479.stm, accessed on 1 February 2017.
7. Tabarani, Gabriel G., *Jihad's New Heartlands: Why the West has Failed to Contain Islamic Fundamentalism*, London: Author House, 2011, p. 184.
8. Ibid.
9. Gregory D. Johnsen, *The Last Refuge: Yemen, Al-Qaeda, and America's War in Arabia*, New York: W.W. Norton, 2013, p. 23.
10. Al-Shishani, Murad Batal, "An Assessment of the Anatomy of al-Qaeda in Yemen: Ideological and Social Factors", Jamestown Foundation, 4 March 2010, at http://www.jamestown.org/programs/gta/single/?tx_ttnews%5Btt_news%5D=36111&cHash=cda33f4c3c, accessed 1 February 2017
11. Gregory D. Johnsen, *The Last Refuge: Yemen, Al-Qaeda, and America's War in Arabia*, New York: W.W. Norton, 2013, p. 15.

12. Ibid.
13. Byman, Daniel, "Our Two-Faced Friends in Sana'a", *The Slate*, 5 January 2010, accessed 1 February 2017.
14. "Profile: Al-Qaeda in the Arabian Peninsula", BBC, 16 June 2015, at http://www.bbc.com/news/world-middle-east-11483095 Accessed on 1 February 2017.
15. "Foreign Terrorist Organisations", US State Department, 20 May 2013, at https://www.state.gov/j/ct/rls/crt/2013/224829.htm, accessed 1 February 2017
16. "Profile: Al Qaeda in the Arabian Peninsula,' *Al Jazeera*, 9 May 2012, at http://www.aljazeera.com/news/middleeast/2012/05/2012597359456359.html, accessed 1 February 2017
17. Johnsen, Gregory D., *The Last Refuge: Yemen, Al-Qaeda, and America's War in Arabia*, New York: W.W. Norton, 2013, p. 69.
18. "From Here We Begin...and at Al-Aqsa We Meet", *World Analysis*, 19 February 2009, at http://worldanalysis.net/modules/news/article.php?storyid=212, accessed 1 November 2016. It has also been cited in "Profile: Al-Qaeda in the Arabian Peninsula", *Counter Extremism Project*, 2015, at http://www.counterextremism.com/threat/al-qaeda-arabian-peninsula-aqap, accessed 1 February 2017
19. Ibid.
20. Burton, Fred, "Al Qaeda in the Arabian Peninsula: Desperation or New Life?" *Stratfor Global Intelligence*, 28 January 2009, at http://www.stratfor.com/weekly/20090128_al_qaeda_arabian_peninsula_desperation_or_new_life, accessed 1 February 2017.
21. Johnsen, Gregory D., *The Last Refuge: Yemen, Al-Qaeda, and America's War in Arabia*', New York: W.W. Norton, 2013, pp. 131–132
22. Ibid. pp. 132, 208, 251
23. "Al Qaeda in Yemen: Mapping Militant Organisations", Stanford University, 8 July 2015, at http://web.stanford.edu/group/mappingmilitants/cgi-bin/groups/view/19, accessed 1 February 2017
24. Barfi, Barak, "Yemen on the Brink?: The Resurgence of Al Qaeda in Yemen", *New America Foundation*, 2 January 2010, at http://www.newamerica.net/sites/newamerica.net/files/policydocs/Barfi.pdf, accessed 1 February 2017
25. "Public Library of US Diplomacy: Instruction for USUN to Request UN 1267, Listing of Al Qaida in the Arabian Peninsula and Top Leaders", *Wikileaks*, 12 January 2010, at https://wikileaks.org/plusd/cables/10STATE2607_a.html, accessed 10 November 2016.
26. "Profile: Al-Qaeda in the Arabian Peninsula", *Counter Extremism Project*, 2015, at http://www.counterextremism.com/threat/al-qaeda-arabian-peninsula-aqap, accessed 1 February 2017.
27. *Inspire*'s first issue in July 2010 included an article titled, "Make a Bomb in the Kitchen of Your Mom," which described how to make a bomb using everyday items. The August 2014 issue contained a nine-page guide on how to make car bombs, and suggested terror targets in the UK and the USA. Its December 2014 issue featured instructions on how to make a bomb that could evade airport security.
28. Zimmerman, Katherine, "Expanding the Campaign of Violence: Al Qaeda in the Arabian Peninsula's English-Language Magazine", *Critical Threats*, 13 July 2010, at http://www.criticalthreats.org/yemen/expanding-campaign-violence-al-

qaeda-arabian-peninsulas-english-language-magazine-july-13-2010, accessed 1 February 2017.

29. Ibid.
30. "Profile: Al-Qaeda in the Arabian Peninsula", *Counter Extremism Project*, 2015, at http://www.counterextremism.com/threat/al-qaeda-arabian-peninsula-aqap, accessed 1 February 2017
31. "Al Qaeda group is operating on ransom money from the West", *LA Times*, 21 October 2013, at http://articles.latimes.com/2013/oct/21/world/la-fg-yemen-ransom-20131021, accessed 1 February 2017.
32. Coker, Margaret, "Assassination Attempt Targets Saudi Prince", *The Wall Street Journal*, 29 August 2009, at http://online.wsj.com/article/SB125144774691366169.html, accessed 1 February 2017
33. "Underwear bomber Abdulmutallab sentenced to life", BBC, 16 February 2012, at http://www.bbc.com/news/world-us-canada-17065130, accessed 1 February 2017
34. "Profile: Al Qaeda in the Arabian Peninsula", BBC, 16 June 2015, at http://www.bbc.com/news/world-middle-east-11483095, accessed 1 February 2017
35. Kasinof, Laura, "Yemen: From the Arab Spring to a Leaderless Nation", *Defence One*, 15 January 2015, at http://www.defenseone.com/threats/2015/01/yemen-arab-spring-leaderless-nation/103692/, accessed 1 February 2017
36. "Al-Qaeda claims bombing that killed nearly 100 Yemeni soldiers", *Al Arabiya*, 21 May 2012, at http://english.alarabiya.net/articles/2012/05/21/215434.html, accessed 1 February 2017
37. "Intercepted Al-Qaeda message led to shuttering embassies, consulates", *CNN*, 5 August 2013, at http://edition.cnn.com/2013/08/04/politics/us-embassies-close/, accessed 1 February 2017.
38. Salisbury, Peter, "Yemen Rage Boils Over 'Unliveable' Price Hike", *Al Jazeera*, 1 August 2014, at http://www.aljazeera.com/news/middleeast/2014/07/yemen-rage-unliveable-price-fuel-201473163925741286.html, accessed 1 February 2017.
39. UNSC Report on Yemen, December 2014, at http://www.securitycouncilreport.org/monthly-forecast/2014-12/yemen_12.php, accessed 1 February 2017.
40. Ibid.
41. "Luke Somers killed in failed rescue attempt in Yemen", *The Telegraph*, 6 December 2014, at http://www.telegraph.co.uk/news/worldnews/al-qaeda/11277098/Luke-Somers-killed-in-failed-rescue-attempt-in-Yemen.html, accessed 1 February 2017.
42. "Kouachi brothers had weapons training in Yemen", *Al Jazeera*, 11 January 2015, at http://america.aljazeera.com/articles/2015/1/11/kouachi-france.html, accessed on 1 February 2017.
43. Miller, Greg, "'Al-Qaeda Group Is Taking Advantage of Yemen Chaos to Rebuild,' Officials Say", *Washington Post*, 5 April 2015, at http://www.washingtonpost.com/world/national-security/al-qaeda-franchise-in-yemen-exploits-chaos-to-rebuild-officials-say/2015/04/04/207208da-d88f-11e4-ba28-f2a685dc7f89_story.html, accessed 1 February 2017.
44. Bayoumy,Yara, Noah Browning, Mohammad Ghobari, "How Saudi Arabia's war in Yemen has made al Qaeda stronger – and richer", Reuters, 8 April 2016, at http://www.reuters.com/investigates/special-report/yemen-aqap/, accessed 1 February 2017.

45. Ibid.
46. Ibid.

REFERENCES

"Al Qaeda in Yemen: Mapping Militant Organisations", *Stanford University*, 8 July 2015, at http://web.stanford.edu/group/mappingmilitants/cgi-bin/groups/view/19, Accessed on 1 February 2017

"Profile: Al Qaeda in the Arabian Peninsula", *Al Jazeera*, 9 May 2012, at http://www.aljazeera.com/news/middleeast/2012/05/2012597359456359.html, accessed 1 February 2017

"Profile: Al Qaeda in the Arabian Peninsula", *BBC*, 16 June 2015, at http://www.bbc.com/news/world-middle-east-11483095, accessed 1 February 2017

"Profile: Al-Qaeda in the Arabian Peninsula", *Counter Extremism Project*, 2015, at http://www.counterextremism.com/threat/al-qaeda-arabian-peninsula-aqap, accessed 1 February 2017

Al-Shishani, Murad Batal, "An Assessment of the Anatomy of al-Qaeda in Yemen: Ideological and Social Factors", *Jamestown Foundation*, 4 March 2010, at http://www.jamestown.org/programs/gta/single/?tx_ttnews%5Btt_news%5D=36111&cHash=cda33f4c3c, accessed 1 February 2017

Bayoumy, Yara, Noah Browning, Mohammad Ghobari, "How Saudi Arabia's war in Yemen has made al Qaeda stronger – and richer", *Reuters*, 8 April 2016, at http://www.reuters.com/investigates/special-report/yemen-aqap/, accessed 1 February 2017.

Johnsen, Gregory D., *The Last Refuge: Yemen, Al-Qaeda, and America's War in Arabia*, New York: W.W. Norton, 2013.

Kasinof, Laura, "Yemen: From the Arab Spring to a Leaderless Nation", *Defence One*, 15 January 2015, at http://www.defenseone.com/threats/2015/01/yemen-arab-spring-leaderless-nation/103692/, accessed 1 February 2017

Zimmerman, Katherine, "Expanding the Campaign of Violence: Al Qaeda in the Arabian Peninsula's English-Language Magazine", *Critical Threats*, 13 July 2010, at http://www.criticalthreats.org/yemen/expanding-campaign-violence-al-qaeda-arabian-peninsulas-english-language-magazine-july-13-2010, accessed 1 February 2017

9

The Yemen Conflict: Domestic and Regional Dynamics

Ashiya Parveen

ABSTRACT

Six years after the uprising, Yemen remains deeply mired in a multi-faceted conflict. In 2011, when the Arab street revolted against their autocratic rulers, the Yemenis followed suit and demanded political and economic reforms. They called on President Ali Abdullah Saleh to step down as they largely attributed their problems to his 33-year long rule. However, as the government was overthrown, several fault-lines along tribal and regional affiliations got activated. Demands for secession from the south, and the Houthi rebels in the north undermined the popular cause of the uprising. As the situation got muddier, terrorist groups like Al-Qaeda capitalised on the chaos. But it was the rise of the Houthis that proved to be a watershed in the Yemeni crisis. The external intervention that ensued entangled Yemen into power games between Saudi Arabia and Iran. With this, the sectarian narrative of the conflict gained momentum while the primary drivers of the conflict remain deep-seated local grievances.

Introduction

Six years after the Arab uprisings, Yemen is embroiled in a convoluted conflict that has pushed the Arab world's poorest country on the edge of the abyss. The country's slide from a popular uprising into civil war is taking a heavy toll on civilians. Diplomatic and military interventions have failed to yield any concrete results. Efforts made around the Hadi-Saudi

Arabia coalition and the Houthis-Saleh alliance to end the stalemate risk ignoring other local dynamics and grievances. In addition, regional and international support for different groups involved in the conflict has been fuelling the crisis. In the meantime, non-state actors, including transnational terrorist groups like Al Qaeda and ISIS, have capitalised on the security vacuum and the anarchy of a weak government to carve out space for themselves. The volatility of the situation casts a shadow on efforts to restore peace, and holds potential threat to the security and stability of the region. This chapter seeks to analyse the trajectory of the uprising which has gradually put the country on the path of destruction and devastation. It seeks to argue that the primary triggers of the popular protests are deep-seated grudges of the people; but the interests and involvement of a myriad of other players have complicated the conflict and turned it into power games.

The ongoing Yemeni crisis began as part of the Arab uprisings in early 2011, when the Yemenis revolted against the autocratic regime of the then President Ali Abdullah Saleh. They resented the lack of socio-economic security, and demanded reforms to be initiated on the ruins of the Saleh regime as they largely attributed their problems to his 33-year long rule. During his reign, Saleh relied mainly on his patronage network[1] to sustain his centralised political system, and pushed other tribal and regional issues to the periphery. As a result, corruption, poverty, and violence came to be the hallmark of Yemeni society. Pressing socio-economic problems, especially poverty and unemployment, caused chronic sufferings for most of the 25 million population.[2] Material discontent, coupled with political repression, turned Yemen into a tinderbox prior to the uprising.

During the uprising, Yemenis stood together against what Bushra al-Maqtari, a Yemeni writer and revolutionary figure, describes as "33 years of injustice, repression, and continuous wars".[3] However, as soon as the Saleh regime was gone and a transition process began, old social contradictions, especially regional and tribal, posed a serious challenge to national reconciliation efforts. The 2011 transition deal brokered by the Gulf Cooperation Council (GCC) and backed by the United Nations (UN) and the international community was cobbled together to restore a semblance of stability. However, it did not really address the political tension and the structural problems that led to the uprising. The deal granted immunity to Saleh, and sustained the old state structure by rearranging power among the established elites from the former regime and its 'loyal' opposition. Saleh was allowed to retain the presidency of the General People's Congress (GPC), Yemen's largest parliamentary party, and maintained control over most of the armed forces. The transition deal was, thus, built on a flawed ground: it sought to initiate the reconciliation process by ignoring past injustices and mainly relied on old elites, thereby failing to win the trust of the hapless and divided populations. As a result, the youth, the Houthis, and the Hirak—the core groups behind the uprising—felt discontented and alienated.

The Houthis

The Houthi movement is an offshoot of the Zaydi revivalist movement 'Believing Youth'. The Zaydi revivalist movement emerged in reaction to the state-backed and Saudi-financed promotion of the Salafi doctrine in north Yemen in the 1990s.[4] The Houthi family is a part of Zaydism, a branch of Islam, theologically situated between Sunnism and Shiism,[5] prevalent in the Saada province in the North bordering Saudi Arabia. Zaydis make about one third of the Yemeni population. In addition to their protest against cultural repression, the Houthis upped the ante against their political and economic exploitation, which won them support of many outside their Houthis and Zaydi bases.[6]

The Houthis boycotted the transition process. They did not participate in the February 2012 referendum which formally elected Saleh's Vice President and the only candidate on the ballot, Abd Rabbo Mansour Hadi, as the new President. Hadi's inauguration set forth the second phase of the GCC initiative that envisaged a national dialogue, constitutional amendment, and a new election within two years. A National Dialogue Conference (NDC) was convened, with 565 delegates from a wide gamut of political and civil society groups. The delegates were assigned a herculean task: to produce an all-agreed draft that would determine the future shape of Yemen. Notwithstanding the presence of representatives from dissident groups on the NDC, the southern and the Houthi issues emerged as the biggest stumbling block to reconciliation efforts. As a result, after ten months of discussion, the NDC collapsed inconclusively in January 2014.[7]

Thereafter, a presidential committee established by President Hadi proposed a new federal plan dividing Yemen into six regions.[8] The plan raised the hackles of the Houthis as it sought to incorporate Saada province, the historic stronghold of the Houthis, in the landlocked and resource-poor Azaal region. The Houthis viewed the move as an intended attempt to damage their ability to develop economically, and to undermine their power.[9] In addition to the distribution of resources, the devolution of power was another sticking point that stalled the transition process. Eventually, the federal text became a source of animosity towards the Sanaa-based system. The Houthis hold strong grudges against such system, which historically denied them a fair share of government attention in infrastructural development and social welfare terms.[10] In fact, their emergence as a movement in the early 2000s was a reaction to their political and economic marginalisation alongside religious repression by the state.

The Houthis fought six wars with the Saleh regime which ended in 2010, eventually drawing in neighbouring Saudi Arabia. The Houthis-Saudi Arabia confrontation added a regional dimension to the local conflict. And, a few statements by Shia religious luminaries in Iran and Iraq accusing the Saleh regime of launching a 'sectarian campaign against the Shia minority'[11] rhetorically established the Houthis' association with Iran. Playing on this rhetoric for strategic reasons, Saudi Arabia has kept itself closely linked with Yemen's national politics by backing leaders like Saleh and patronizing some *Salafi* and tribal elements.[12] The 2011 uprising broke the fragile balance of power that Saleh had maintained among various competing forces, and raised fears of a spillover of chaos into Saudi Arabia. Therefore, Riyadh hurriedly meddled in to stitch the transition deal with elite-mediation, which apparently mirrored the old pattern of exclusion and marginalisation objected to by the Houthis and other dissident groups in the first place.

The Southern Issue

The southern forces are key stakeholders in any future structure of post-Saleh Yemen. However, due to longstanding grievances against the Saleh regime, many southerners have been suspicious of the transition deal that involved former regime elements. Since the unification of the two Yemens in 1990,[13] people from the south have been resenting their political repression and the unfair distribution of resources. The defeat of the southerners in the 1994 civil war ended up adding to their woes. Examples of injustices meted out to southerners include the sacking of twenty thousand military personnel, layoffs of large numbers of public-sector employees, and the marginalisation of southerners in state institutions.[14] More than a decade later, some old members of the Yemeni Socialist Party and the youth launched Al-Hirak, or the Southern Movement, to fight for their political rights and equitable economic opportunity.[15] The 2011 uprising came as an opportunity for the southern forces to re-ignite their movement and push for their cause.

Like the Houthis, Al-Hirak boycotted the referendum, and launched a few attacks against polling stations in the southern governorates.

Notwithstanding the fact of his being a southerner, Hadi[16] could not move a majority from the south, let alone north, to rally behind him as he led the transition process. Rather, many southerners accused him of 'strategic gamesmanship and factional politics aimed at ensuring that no rival southern group becomes more powerful than him'.[17] Therefore, mass protests and threats of armed rebellion for an autonomous or independent south went on alongside the NDC. The federal plan was immediately rejected by some southerners, who insist on a separate state. Traditional leaders of the Southern Movement—like Ali Salem al Beidh, the last president of the former south—rejected the division of South Yemen into two federal states, that is, Hadramaut (Shabwa, Hadramaut, Al-Mahra and the island of Socotra) and Aden (Lahj, Abyan, Dhale and Aden governorates).[18] While leaders like al-Beidh advocates the idea of a complete separation, his predecessors, Ali Nasir Muhammad and Haidar Abu Bakr al-Attas, supported unity with the north under a federal system—with a referendum on whether to maintain unity or secede after a few years.[19] Interestingly, answers to the southern issue are not limited to the two solutions.

The locals in the south reacted to the top-down federal text with a mix of 'criticism and suspicion'.[20] According to a 2013 survey, 99 per cent of 34,000 respondents in the Al Mahra governorate rejected merger with Hadramaut, while 86 per cent of Mahirs wanted to be ruled by a cross-tribal council, opposing both 'united Yemen' and 'South Yemen' hypotheses.[21] Above all, many civilians from Hadramout want an independent state of their own, separate from both North and South Yemen.[22] On 22 April, the Hadramout Inclusive Conference (HIC) announced Hadramout as an independent federal region.[23] Thus, the issues of representation of southerners and an all-agreed possible solution to the southern question pose a great deal of challenge to national reconciliation efforts. In this context, Adam Baron writes that, in the south, power lies with key Southern Movement figures, some of whom were incorporated in the Hadi government; but, in many cases they bypassed Hadi as they tend to act autonomously.[24] In addition, southerners' antagonism towards the people of northern origin, whom they continue to regard as occupiers, is one of the major problems preventing the success of any reconciliation efforts.

Moreover, the reactions to the NDC's outcomes reflect that any attempt to provide a band-aid solution to Yemen's existential issues was bound to fail without engaging with grassroot forces other than a few organised groups. It highlights the need to broaden the remit of national dialogue and complement the top-down process with a bottom-up approach in view of the nature of Yemeni society, which is complex enough to be viewed through the perspectives of a few organised groups. It would help take ordinary Yemenis on board as they hardly felt connected with the NDC. Throughout the transition process, the Hadi government miserably failed to improve governance and ensure basic social services. The absence of governance led to clashes among tribes for control over resources. Oil and gas facilities were repeatedly attacked.[25] Amidst this, the government's decision to remove fuel subsidies irked the civilians.

The Civil War

Taking advantage of the popular disenchantment with the transitional government, the Houthis began expanding their control and took over the capital Sanaa in September 2014, which sparked the civil war. Saleh, who is adept at alternately co-opting and manipulating his political rivals, took advantage of the situation and formed an alliance with the Houthis in a bid to stage a political comeback. However, the Houthis' acceptance of Saleh as a partner, against whom they hold deep grudges and fought six wars, surprised many. Nevertheless, the Houthis benefitted from the alliance, and expanded southwards with the help of Saleh's loyalists in key army positions.[26] The alliance is said to have shared objectives: the downfall of the Hadi government, the eradication of the largest opposition party Islah,[27] and the control of the entire country. However, the age-old mistrust[28] between the two sides speaks volumes of the longevity of the alliance. While Saleh is exploiting his entrenched network, both formal and informal, to regain his lost political fortune, the Houthis' mounting campaign (according to Stacey Philbrik Yadav and Sheila Carapico), was aimed at securing its position in Yemen's future political regime in the making.[29]

Nonetheless, the Houthis' campaign stalled the transition process, which the UN tried to put back on track by brokering an agreement between the rebels and President Hadi in September. The agreement, known as Peace and National Partnership Agreement, called for an inclusive and/or non-partisan technocratic government, and mandated the withdrawal of Houthi forces from the capital.[30] However, the Houthis refused to withdraw its militias from Sanaa, citing the threat of Al Qaeda. By January 2015, the movement forced President Hadi and his cabinet to resign. The Houthis-Saleh alliance's penetration of the security forces soon after the coup informs on Hadi's failed attempt at restructuring, which is of utmost importance in a country where the military lacks professionalism and is characterised by a loose command-and-control structure. The lack of governance and the deteriorating security situation worsened further, with other dissident and terrorist groups rearing their heads to make gains by exploiting local resentments and stoking cross-tribal and regional tensions.

The local Al Qaeda affiliate, which merged with its Saudi Arabian counterpart in 2009 in a new organisation, Al Qaeda in the Arabian Peninsula (AQAP), exploited anti-northern prejudices to capture areas in Yemen's south. The security vacuum made the situation favourable for this as it stormed Mukalla, a port city and the capital of Yemen's largest Hadramaut province in April 2015. In the absence of strong resistance, the group consolidated its position in the city through tactics that should cause serious concern in national and international players. They made many Hadramis party to their occupation by forming a local council, and providing welfare services to people.[31] The situation highlights the importance of political stability and economic improvement to win over the Yemenis. In fact, it won't be an exaggeration to say that the lived reality of a deteriorating economic situation did not allow ordinary Yemenis to connect with the transitional government. And, the Houthi takeover left many exposed to mounting security threats.

The Yemenis accused the Houthis-Saleh alliance of shelling civilian residential areas, medical facilities, schools, and other civilian infrastructure.[32] Sniper attacks along with heavy shelling of civilian neighbourhoods prevented civilians from access to food and key survival needs such as water and health services.[33] Gradually, areas under Houthi control slipped into borderline famine.[34] Apart from infrastructural destruction and economic hardship, the deep polarisation of society has been one of the most damaging effects of the civil war.[35] Local unaddressed grievances, common hostility towards a faction, and the loss of trust drove tribal groups to forge alliances with different warring parties. The situation has caused the destruction of Yemen's social fabric and undermined its tribal structure, which might emerge as one of the biggest losses during the post-conflict reconstruction of society.

External Intervention

In the months following their takeover of Sanaa, the Houthis-Saleh forces stormed President Hadi's home and placed him under house arrest, prompting the resignation of the entire cabinet in January 2015.[36] Two weeks later, Hadi managed to escape from Houthi captivity and fled to the southern city of Aden. He rescinded his resignation and announced

Aden as the temporary capital of the country. From the temporary capital, Hadi declared war on the Houthis and formally asked the GCC states to intervene militarily.[37] In late March 2015, Hadi was forced to flee the country. Saudi Arabia, which saw the Houthi rise as a threat to its historic control of Yemen in view of its Shi'ite-affiliation, announced the formation of a coalition of 10 countries[38] to support the internationally recognised government.[39]

In March 2015, the coalition launched an intensive aerial campaign targeting Houthi and Saleh forces in and around Sanaa, Saada, Taiz, Al-Hudaydah, and Aden. The USA assisted with intelligence, targeting, and logistics as warplanes bombed Houthi arms depots and military camps. The coalition made significant territorial gains, and within two months, forced the Houthis to retreat from Aden—a highly strategic province as it controls the Bab al-Mandeb, the chokepoint between the Arabian and Red Seas through which 4.7 million barrels of oil transit everyday. However, after more than two years of the campaign, the coalition could not achieve its objective of reinstating the Hadi government in Sanaa. On the other hand, mounting civilian casualties and the destruction of basic infrastructure, including schools, hospitals, bridges, roads, and power plants, made life more miserable for the Yemenis. In October 2016, UN agencies estimated that since March 2015, more than 44,000 people have been killed or injured. Of Yemen's 27.4 million people, about 18.8 million need humanitarian assistance—including 10.3 million who are in acute need.[40]

It is worth noting here that the international community's involvement in the Saudi-led operation, especially of the USA and the UK, is largely driven by security concerns as a failed Yemeni state might become a safe haven for terrorist groups like AQAP and ISIS. In fact, the US policy in Yemen has been shaped largely by Al Qaeda's 2000 attack against the *USS Cole* and the Christmas Day bombing of 2009. But international support for the Saudi-led brutal campaign, which is primarily focused on the Houthis' containment, strengthened the AQAP as it gained from the resulting security vacuum, and rebounded in areas on southern coast.[41] Moreover, the USA also became subject to war crimes allegations. It faced pressure from Congress for its extensive military assistance noting it 'may amount to war crimes'.[42] At the same time, the heavy export and supply of arms by the UK to Saudi Arabia has been seen by rights groups and other bodies as central to the destruction of Yemen.[43] On the other hand, the Saudi-led coalition was held responsible for 60 percent of child deaths, and was added by the UN to the blacklist of countries accused of violating children rights.[44] Above all, after months of operations, the coalition forces could not weaken the Houthis-Saleh alliance, let alone see them rolling back from Sanaa.

The Saudi-led airstrikes not only worsened the conflict but also led to instability and chaos by destroying basic infrastructure and government institutions. Areas liberated from the Houthis' control on behalf of the Hadi government, which largely remains in exile in Saudi Arabia, remained plagued by chaos.[45] In fact, the Hadi government hardly seems to be functioning or ensuring basic security and services for stricken civilians who describe it as the 'runaway government'.[46] As a result, Yemenis continue to suffer from both Saudi-led bombings as well as from the Houthis-Saleh aggression, which has been equally responsible for abuses of human rights and humanitarian law. Amidst this, the UN's failure to persuade the warring parties to stop the conflict or hold any of them responsible for rights abuses has disheartened Yemenis. The situation has prompted Yemeni political analyst, Hisham al-Omeisy, to tweet: "Our only sin as Yemen is we're poor. Nowhere near as rich as Saudi to buy off international community's silence or UN's carte blanche." This is reflective of the feeling of abandonment that has overtaken the Yemenis.

It is worth noting here that a few decisions taken by the new US administration have laid to rest profound concerns about Washington's policy towards Yemen. Within the first week of Donald J. Trump's Presidency, Yemenis witnessed US drone strikes targeting Al Qaeda militants in which civilians were also killed. The eight-year-old daughter of Anwar al-Awlaki, a US-born Yemeni preacher who was killed in a 2011 drone attack, was said to be among the victims.[47] At the same time, the Yemenis were banned from getting visas to the USA as part of an immigration ban imposed on seven Muslim-majority countries.[48] Moreover, during his recent visit to Saudi Arabia, President Trump signed a $110 billion arms deal with the kingdom, prompting analysts to say that it would embolden Riyadh in its devastating war in Yemen.[49] Also, the Trump administration's confrontational attitude towards Iran leaves little doubt about its renewed traditional embrace of Saudi Arabia[50], which does not appear to hold a good omen for the Yemeni conflict.

Sectarian Narrative

The ongoing crisis did not begin as a Sunni-Shia struggle as the element of sectarianism has been historically minimal in Yemen. However, rise of the Houthis, seems to have exacerbated an old fear in Saudi Arabia—that of an ascendant Iran and sectarian narratives of the conflict—seem to have gained momentum. Saudi Arabia has historically sought to maintain an upper hand in the internal politics of Yemen and pursued a policy to 'keep Yemen weak' as it fears that a strong Yemeni state in its back yard could prove a major threat to its own security.[51] In this context, the rise of the Houthis, which Saudi Arabia describes as Iran's proxy, has been understood as crossing a red line. This is evident from the Saudi's massive military campaign for not just 'pushing back the putschists or securing the border, but for fighting the "Iranian threat" represented by the Zaydi Shia movement'.[52] Saudi Arabia's labelling of the Houthis as an Iranian proxy has fed many exaggerated claims that portray the Yemeni crisis as Sunni vs. Shia struggle. Here it is immensely important to remember that the primary drivers of the conflict are local political, social, and economic grievances, and that the rise of the Houthis was facilitated by popular dissatisfaction with the transitional government.

The Houthi movement is rooted in some real grievances. They have enjoyed cross-sectarian support for raising populist policy issues, both in the pre- and post-uprising periods. It must be noted here that Zaydis' view of the imam (whom they consider a worldly figure, and subject to being replaced by a more competent rival) and their rejection of certain other Shia beliefs distance Zaydism from Twelver Shi'ism of Iran.[53] Nonetheless, scholars like Peter Salisbury, have found that the core leadership of the Houthi movement is, in many cases, genuinely committed to Islamic revolutionary principles set out by its founder Hussein Badr al-Deen al-Houthi. This leadership borrows heavily from Iran's radical revolutionary principles.[54] In this context, the vagueness of the ultimate objectives maintained by the Houthis has contributed to the speculation that they hope to restore the Zaydi Imamate that ruled much of Yemen for more than a thousand years until its demise in the 1962 revolution.[55]

In addition, the support extended to the Houthis by Iran, the Hezbollah in Lebanon, and the Shi'ite majority government in Iraq, especially after their takeover of Sanaa, has contributed to the sectarian analysis of the militias' motives.[56] Iran has provided them military and financial support. It also signed a series of Memorandum of Understandings with them, on bolstering aid, modernising the Al-Hudaydah port, and increasing the number of flights between the two countries.[57] The move recognised the Houthis as the legitimate authority against the international stance. Small numbers of Islamic Revolutionary Guard Corps officers, with assistance from Hezbollah, also set up a train and equip programme for the Houthis.[58] Moreover, commenting on the conflict, Yemeni journalist Afrah Nasser noted that it was not sectarian when it began, but it is now: "As for sectarianism, Houthis are running the areas they control in a double-motivated way: sectarian and political—arresting people who don't belong to their sect and who belong to the Islah."[59] Such acts seem to have contributed to sectarian feelings, and helped groups like AQAP and ISIS to gain by stoking sectarian tensions.[60]

Nonetheless, it is difficult to fully explain the war in Yemen in strictly sectarian terms as it is far more complex than a mere Shia-Sunni conflict. Also, as sectarian narratives keep doing the rounds, especially in view of a vicious power competition between Saudi Arabia and Iran, many analysts have warned against overstating Tehran's influence in Yemen. Iran does not exercise enough leverage to shape the convoluted political equation on the ground. It is worth noting here that Saudi Arabia's views of Iran's proximity with the Houthis are also shaped by Tehran's re-emergence on the global scenario following its successful nuclear deal in 2015. Riyadh interpreted the deal as part of the US policy of retrenchment from the region, which envisaged working with Tehran and abandoning other regional partners.[61] It believed that the move would encourage Iran to pursue its policy of expansionism, thus challenging the Kingdom's regional domination.[62] Thus, it won't be wrong to say that the sectarian narrative of the conflict is largely, if not completely, pivoted on power games between the two regional rivals.

Peace Talks

As the debilitating fight did not appear to die down, regional and international players persuaded the warring parties to enter into negotiation. Delegates representing the exiled Yemeni government based in Riyadh, and the Houthis-Saleh alliance participated in two UN-sponsored talks in Switzerland in June and December 2015, which failed to yield any substantial result. A third round of talks followed in Kuwait in April 2016. UN envoy Ismail Ould Cheikh Ahmed, who replaced Jamal Benomar in early 2015, focused on brokering a ceasefire agreement between the warring parties, believing it would prepare the ground for a lasting political solution. However, three months later, the talks reached a stalemate as mistrust between the reluctant negotiators undermined efforts to de-escalate the fights.

The implementation of the UN resolution 2216 emerged as a sticking point as the two sides refused to budge an inch from their stated positions. The resolution demanded the Houthis-Saleh forces to roll back from their occupied areas and surrender heavy arms. The alliance, on the other hand, insists on the formation of a unity government and a complete halt in airstrikes before starting a political track. Notwithstanding the intransigence of the two sides, their ability to agree to or implement a ceasefire remains questionable in view of the polarisation which the conflict has deepened to a destructive level. For instance, the alliance of many local groups with a faction was not necessarily motivated by their opposition to the other. In many cases, some local groups have fought for both Hadi and Houthi-Saleh alliance in the war.[63] Thus, the situation on the ground is complex enough to be viewed from the perspectives of the two sides. And the weak legitimacy of the Hadi government, which is like a pawn in the hands of Saudi Arabia, makes the prospects for peace grimmer.

Additionally, many local groups loathe the peace talks, saying they have, once again, denied them a say in the decision-making. Many in the south had begun to view the Houthis as part of the traditional elite following the alliance with Saleh. There are others who refused to be represented by the Hadi government. 'It is Southern local authorities and local resistance who represent the people, not Hadi's government,' said Ahmed Assaleh, Spokesperson of the Southern Youth Forum in the United States, a group which works directly with the Southern leadership in Yemen.[64] Similarly, Ahmed Ashulaif, one of the local resistance leaders in the Serwah district in Mareb, asked, "Why do they choose us as partners in war but fail to engage us in peace efforts?"[65] He was referring to the Hadi government. In this context, the formation of a Southern Transitional Council on May 11 to further the struggle toward independence of the south Yemen is telling.[66] The situation speaks volume about the need for an inclusive peace process, with enough space for multiple actors in view of the people's lack of trust in the Hadi government or the Houthis-Saleh alliance.

Following the announcement by the UN envoy of the end of the peace talks in August 2016, the Saudi-led coalition resumed airstrikes and began bombing the capital Sanaa. The war has worsened since then, as the coalition has intensified its operations against the battle-hardy Houthis to win Sanaa back. Amidst this, a renewed UN push for peace agreed to by US Secretary of State, John Kerry and the GCC at the end of August was described as the 'last chance' for Yemen to avoid an even more dangerous downward spiral by Baron.[67] But, Omeisy has rightly pointed out that "...no matter how good a proposal is, it's the various parties' commitment that will define the success rate ... So to be honest, prospects are still grim."[68]

In the following months, the conflict has turned messier and bloodier. In October 2016, the Saudi-led coalition bombed a funeral ceremony in Sanaa and prison premises in Hodeida, killing about 200 people. The month also saw an exchange of missiles between the Houthis and the USA, marking the first direct military involvement of American forces in the prolonged conflict.[69] Peace efforts in the following month met with a hardened Houthis-Saleh stance as well as the equally dismissive tone of the Hadi government as is evident form Kerry's failure to make two sides abide by ceasefires.[70] It implies that because of the continued involvement of external players as well as the absence of a commitment on the part of the warring parties, peace efforts would not yield any results. The Houthis need to understand that their intransigence will not help them rule by force for a long time. North-South antagonism and economic vulnerability are some of the impediments that they cannot overlook. At the same time, Saudi Arabia must not be ignorant of the fact that its brutal campaign has destroyed Yemen to the extent of it becoming a failed state which would be equally threatening as, in its own view, a strong Yemeni state could have been. Nonetheless, at the time of the writing, the chance for peace remains a distant dream as hapless Yemenis suffer from mindless bombings and a chronic humanitarian crisis.

Conclusion

The continuing conflict will keep wreaking havoc on the impoverished Yemenis as long as international players, especially the USA, continue to aid the Saudi-led brutal campaign. Despite carrying out months of deadly air attacks, the coalition has failed to weaken the Houthis-Saleh alliance, let alone wrest Sanaa back from it. The competition for influence between the two regional rivals has entangled Yemen into a relentless struggle. Despite providing training, arms, and ammunition to the Houthis, the scale of Iran's involvement in the conflict appears to be too limited to tilt the balance in favour of the Houthi-Saleh alliance. But now, Iran cannot be excluded from any negotiation process to bring about an end to the war and a solution for the future. Nonetheless, the conflict will continue unless key international players coerce regional powers to scale down their involvement to reduce the intensity of the conflict. This would be complementary to the peace process.

Looking Ahead

- There is a need for foreign players to realise that the peace-making efforts should not be devoid of addressing the popular causes of the uprising—that is, socio-economic resentment and political frustration.
- If the key stakeholders cannot put aside their strategic and security

concerns, a simultaneous attempt to address pressing social, economic, and political problems would help them win over the Yemenis, and deter non-state actors from exploiting their sufferings.

- The involvement of local actors and grassroots forces— like the governors and leaders of key resistance forces—would ease the tension on the ground, and help build a popular constituency to add to the peace-making efforts.
- Lastly, a deeper understanding of local dynamics and the incorporation of certain tribal values would be helpful in the peace-making efforts.

NOTES

1. Sarah Philips describes the Yemeni regime as a collection of individuals whose interests and opinions are taken into account in decision making by the President, often with regard to the receipt of government contracts, licenses for economic commons, and the allocation of smuggling rights—in other words, the bounty of the patronage system. The dominant group is a small, carefully selected circle consisting of elites from the Sanhan tribe (President Saleh's tribe) and the Hashid tribes (the dominant tribal confederation of which Sanhan is a minor member), military officers who are either connected by kinship, demonstrated loyalty, or tribal links to President Saleh, and tribal leaders who command significant independent support in their local areas. For more on this see, Phillips, S., *Yemen's Democracy Experiment in Regional Perspective, Patronage and Pluralized Authoritarianism*, Palgrave Macmillan, 2008, pp. 4, 114–135.
2. Al-Qarawi, H., "The Yemeni Revolution: replacing Ali Abdullah Saleh or replacing obsolete institutions?" Arab Centre for Research and Policy Studies, 29 May 2011, at http://english.dohainstitute.org/file/get/97f1b7ab-c402-4b62-810a-ddac47637763.pdf, accessed 25 October 2016.
3. Qaed, S., "The revolution is the pen, the revolution is the change", *Yemen Times,* 23 February 2014, at http://www.yementimes.com/en/1755/intreview/3483/%E2%80%9CThe-revolution-is-the-pen-the-revolution-is-the-change%E2%80%9D.htm, accessed 1 June 2016.
4. For more on this, see, Salmoni, B.A., Loidolt, B. and Wells, M., *Regime and Periphery in Northern Yemen: The Huthi Phenomenon*, US: RAND Corporation, 2010, pp.89–109.
5. Distinct from Sunnism, the Zaydi School of Islamic theology and jurisprudence (*madhhab*) venerates Ali and the House of the Prophet as the legitimate heirs of political rule (the Imam) in the Islamic world (umma). Yet, Zaydism is also distinct from the Shi'ism associated with Iran, Iraq, and Lebanon because it differs from them over the imamate succession in the fifth generation after Ali. For more on this, see Ibid, pp. 65–75, 285–295.
6. Phillips, S., "Tracing the cracks in the Yemeni system", in McMurray, D., Ufheil-Somers, A. (eds.) *The Arab Revolts: Dispatches on Militant Democracy in the Middle East*, Bloomington: Indiana University Press, 2013, pp.137–143.
7. Day, S.W., "The Non Conclusion of Yemen's National Dialogue", *Foreign Policy,* 27 January 2014, at http://foreignpolicy.com/2014/01/27/the-non-conclusion-

of-yemens-national-dialogue, accessed 12 July 2016.

8. "Yemen to Become Six-Region Federation", Al Jazeera, 10 February 2014, at http://www.aljazeera.com/news/middleeast/2014/02/yemen-become-six-region-federation-201421012473172 6931.html, accessed 30 September 2016.
9. Kronenfeld, S., Guzansky, Y., "Yemen: A Mirror to the Future of the Arab Spring", *Military and Strategic Affairs*, Vol. 6, No. 3, 2014, pp.79–99.
10. Salmoni, B.A., Loidolt, B. and Wells, M., *Regime and Periphery in Northern Yemen: The Huthi Phenomenon*, US: RAND Corporation, 2010, op. cit., pp.89, 113–114.
11. Phillips, S., "Tracing the cracks in the Yemeni system", in McMurray, D., Ufheil-Somers, A. (eds.) *The Arab Revolts: Dispatches on Militant Democracy in the Middle East*, Bloomington: Indiana University Press, 2013, op. cit., pp.137–143.
12. Soon after Saudi Arabia was formally established in 1932, it invaded Yemen in 1934 and absorbed the Yemeni provinces of Asir, Jizan and Najran. In the Yemen civil war of 1962–1967, Saudi Arabia supported the Zaydi Imam. Since then, Saudi Arabia has sought to influence internal political dispensations by providing billions of dollars in aid. See also, Gupta, R., "Saudi Arabia's war in Yemen", *The Hindu*, 4 May 2015, at http://www.thehindu.com/opinion/lead/saudi-arabias-war-in-yemen/article7167430.ece, accessed 24 August 2016.
13. Before 1990, Yemen was divided between the former Yemeni Arab Republic, also known as North Yemen and traditionally US- and Saudi-backed; the People's Democratic Republic of Yemen (PDRY), known as South Yemen and supported by the USSR until its collapse. Ali Abdullah Saleh ruled the Yemeni Arab Republic from 1978 to 1990 and the reunified Republic of Yemen from 1990 until his ouster in 2011. Since the unification, Yemen has been rocked by internal tensions. See, Laub, Z., "Yemen in Crisis", Council on Foreign Relations, 19 April 2016, at http://www.cfr.org/yemen/yemen-crisis/p36488, accessed 10 June 2016.
14. Fraihat, I., *Unfinished Revolutions: Yemen, Libya, and Tunisia after the Arab Spring*, New Haven and London: Yale University Press, 2016, p. 42.
15. Dahlgren, S., "The Snake with a Thousand heads: The Southern Cause in Yemen", in McMurray, D., Ufheil-Somers, A. (eds.) *The Arab Revolts: Dispatches on Militant Democracy in the Middle East*, Bloomington: Indiana University Press, 2013, pp.144–151.
16. Hadi was a leading military official in independent South Yemen. He fled north following the 1987 civil war there, and played a key role in the defeat of South Yemen's last president Ali Salim Al-Beidh's attempt to regain southern independence in 1994. Within a year of being appointed Defence Minister in 1994, President Ali Abdullah Saleh promoted Hadi to Vice President, a position he held until Saleh's fall.
17. Salisbury, P., "Yemen: Stemming the Rise of a Chaos State", Middle East and North Africa Programme, Chatham House, 25 May 2016, at https://www.chathamhouse.org/sites/files/chathamhouse/publications/research/2016-05-25-yemen-stemming-rise-of-chaos-state-salisbury.pdf, accessed 15 June 2016.
18. Fraihat, I., *Unfinished Revolutions: Yemen, Libya, and Tunisia after the Arab Spring*, New Haven and London: Yale University Press, 2016, op. cit., p. 42.
19. Ibid.
20. Ardemagni, E., "Beyond the North/South narrative: Conflict and federalism in eastern Yemen", Middle East Centre Blog, the London School of Economics and

Political Science, 16 May 2016, at http://blogs.lse.ac.uk/mec/2016/05/16/beyond-the-northsouth-narrative-conflict-and-federalism-in-eastern-yemen/, accessed 30 May 2016.

21. Ibid.
22. Al-Dawsari, N., "We Lived Days in Hell: Civilian Perspectives on the Conflict in Yemen", Centre for Civilians in Conflict, 10 January 2017, at http://civiliansinconflict.org/resources/pub/we-lived-days-in-hell-civilian-perspectives-of-the-conflict-in-yemen, accessed 12 January 2017.
23. Hadramout Inclusive Conference (HIC) is a political movement that represents most political factions including Hirak in Hadramout. On 22 April, the HIC announced Hadramout as an independent federal region in a large conference in which over 3000 Hadrami leaders participated. Cited in Al-Dawsari, N., "Breaking the Cycle of Failed Negotiations in Yemen", 4 May 2017, at http://pomed.org/pomed-publications/breaking-cycle-of-failed-negotiations-yemen, accessed 30 May 2017.
24. Baron, A., "Yemen's Forgotten War: How Europe can Lay the Foundations for Peace", European Councils on Foreign Relations, 20 December 2016, at http://www.ecfr.eu/page/-/Yemenss_forgotten_war_Final.pdf, accessed 24 December 2016.
25. Al-Moshki, A.I., "2013 Oil Pipeline Sabotage Chronology", *Yemen Times*, 28 January 2014, at http://www.yementimes.com/en/1750/report/3397/2013-Oil-pipeline-sabotage-chronology.htm, accessed 4 July 2016.
26. Abi-Habib, M., "Yemen's Ousted President Saleh Helps Propel Houthi Rebel Advance", *The Wall Street Journal*, 10 April 2015, at http://www.wsj.com/articles/yemens-ousted-president-saleh-helps-propel-houthi-rebel-advance-1428704009, accessed 19 July 2016.
27. Islah's origins are in the Islamic Front, a Muslim Brotherhood-affiliated group, populated by conservative tribal leaders, businessmen, and Islamists. The Front was created by the YAR government in 1979 to combat the Marxist PDRY-supported National Democratic Front (NDF) forces. It regrouped as a formal political party shortly after unification in 1990 when political parties were legalized, with the help of considerable financial backing from Wahhabi elements within Saudi Arabia. The party is an umbrella organization for various schools of political Islamist thought, and also contains a seemingly unlikely regional and sectarian alliance of Sunni (Shafi'i) former anti-NDF radicals from Lower Yemen, and Zaydi (Shi'ite) tribal leaders from Upper Yemen. For more on this, see, Phillips, S., *Yemen's Democracy Experiment in Regional Perspective, Patronage and Pluralized Authoritarianism*, US: Palgrave Macmillan, 2008, op. cit., pp. 138–166.
28. Saleh, who himself is a Zaydi Shia, sought to justify his regime's armed conflict with the Houthis between 2004 and 2010 as a battle with the Iranian proxies "intent on creating an undefined hybrid of the pre-revolutionary Imamate and the Iranian revolutionary model in Yemen". See, Salisbury, P., "Yemen: Stemming the Rise of a Chaos State", Middle East and North Africa Programme, Chatham House, 25 May 2016,
29. Yadav, S.P., and Carapico, S., "The Breakdown of the GCC Initiative", Middle East Research and Information Project, 21 September 2014, at http://www.merip.org/mer/mer273/breakdown-gcc-initiative,accessed 22 July 2016.
30. Ibid.

31. Salisbury, P., "Yemen: Stemming the Rise of a Chaos State", Middle East and North Africa Programme, Chatham House, 25 May 2016.
32. Al-Dawsari, N., "We Lived Days in Hell: Civilian Perspectives on the Conflict in Yemen", Centre for Civilians in Conflict, 10 January 2017.
33. Ibid.
34. The Saudi-led coalition took a complex series of initiatives that are best described as 'economic warfare' against the Houthis-Saleh forces. These measures include attempts to cut areas under the control of the Sanaa government out of the international banking sector, and to limit their capacity to receive imports. These efforts have been especially effective because Yemen imports 90 per cent of its food. See also, Baron, A., "Yemen's Forgotten War: How Europe can Lay the Foundations for Peace", European Councils on Foreign Relations, 20 December 2016.
35. Al-Hamdani, S., Baron, A. and Al-Madhaji, M., "The Role of Local Actors in Yemen's Current War", July 2015, at file:///C:/Users/HP/Downloads/the_role_of_local_actors_in_yemens_current-war_en.pdf, accessed 26 August 2016.
36. Ghobari M, Bayoumy, Y. "How the Houthis drove Yemen into a political vacuum", Reuters, 11 February 2015, at http://www.reuters.com/article/us-yemen-security-hadi-idUSKBN0LF0AD20150211, accessed 20 October 2015.
37. "Yemen asks GCC for military action against Houthis", *Al Arabiya English*, 23 March 2015, at http://english.alarabiya.net/en/News/middle-east/2015/03/23/Yemen-s-Hadi-calls-for-GCC-military-intervention.html, accessed 28 July 2016.
38. The coalition includes the Kingdom of Saudi Arabia, the United Arab Emirates, Bahrain, Kuwait, Egypt, Morocco, Jordan, Sudan, Senegal, and Qatar.
39. "Saudi and Arab allies bomb Houthi positions in Yemen", *Al-Jazeera*, 26 March 2015, at http://www.aljazeera.com/news/middleeast/2015/03/saudi-ambassador-announces-military-operation-yemen-150325234138956.html, accessed 30 July 2016.
40. "Yemen: Humanitarian Needs 2017", Organization for the Coordination of Humanitarian Affairs, 28 November 2016, available at https://docs.unocha.org/sites/dms/Yemen/YEMEN%202017%20HNO_Final.pdf, accessed 17 January 2017.
41. Bayoumy, Y., Browning, N. and Ghobari, M., "How Saudi Arabia's war in Yemen has made al Qaeda stronger – and richer", 8 April 2016, at http://www.reuters.com/investigates/special-report/yemen-aqap/, accessed 20 August 2016.
42. Peterson, S., "In Yemen War, could surge in violence rekindle diplomacy", *The Christian Science Monitor*, 2 September 2016, available at http://www.csmonitor.com/World/Middle-East/2016/0902/In-Yemen-s-war-could-surge-in-violence-rekindle-diplomacy, accessed 12 September 2016.
43. Doward, J., "UK accused of blocking UN enquiry into claim of war crimes in Yemen", *The Guardian*, 25 September 2016, at https://www.theguardian.com/world/2016/sep/24/yemen-britain-human-rights-inquiry, accessed 28 September 2016.
44. However, later, the UN removed Saudi Arabia from the blacklist of countries and groups accused of violating children's rights. See also, "Rights groups condemn

removal of Saudi Arabia from UN blacklist", *The Guardian*, 7 June 2016, at https://www.theguardian.com/world/2016/jun/07/rights-groups-condemn-removal-of-saudi-arabia-from-un-blacklist, accessed 20 July 2016.

45. Baron, A., "Yemen's Forgotten War: How Europe can Lay the Foundations for Peace", European Councils on Foreign Relations, 20 December 2016.
46. Al-Dawsari, N., "We Lived Days in Hell: Civilian Perspectives on the Conflict in Yemen", Centre for Civilians in Conflict, 10 January 2017.
47. "Yemeni civilians killed in first US raid under Trump", *Al-Jazeera*, 30 January 2017, at http://www.aljazeera.com/news/2017/01/yemen-170129101045539.html, accessed 1 February 2017.
48. Mohdin, Aamna, "The sinister possible reason why Trump's 'Muslim ban' targeted seven particular countries", *Quartz*, 31 January 2017, at https://qz.com/899066/the-sinister-possible-reason-why-trumps-muslim-ban-targeted-iran-iraq-libya-somalia-sudan-syria-and-yemen/, accessed 1 February 2017.
49. Peterson, S., "With huge arms deal, US pivots back to Saudis. How does it affect the region?", *The Christian Science Monitor*, 22 May 2017, at https://www.csmonitor.com/World/Middle-East/2017/0522/With-huge-arms-deal-US-pivots-back-to-Saudis.-How-does-it-affect-the-region, accessed 30 May 2017.
50. Ibid.
51. Salisbury, P., "Yemen and the Saudi-Iranian Cold War", Middle East and North Africa Programme, Chatham House, 18 February 2015, at https://www.chathamhouse.org/sites/files/chathamhouse/field/field_document/20150218YemenIranSaudi.pdf, accessed 20 November 2016.
52. Baron, A., "Yemen's Forgotten War: How Europe can Lay the Foundations for Peace", European Councils on Foreign Relations, 20 December 2016.
53. Salmoni, B.A., Loidolt, and B., Wells, M., *Regime and Periphery in Northern Yemen: The Huthi Phenomenon*, US: RAND Corporation, 2010, op. cit., pp.285–295.
54. Salisbury, P., "Yemen and the Saudi-Iranian Cold War", Middle East and North Africa Programme, Chatham House, 18 February 2015.
55. Riedel, B., "Yemen Falls Apart", *Al-Monitor*, 22 January 2015, at http://www.al-monitor.com/pulse/originals/2015/01/yemen-hadi-resignation-houthi-al-qaeda-us-saudi.html, accessed 20 December 2015; see also, Fraihat, I., *Unfinished Revolutions: Yemen, Libya, and Tunisia after the Arab Spring*, 2016, New Haven and London: Yale University Press, 2016, op. cit., pp. 46–47.
56. Fraihat, I., *Unfinished Revolutions: Yemen, Libya, and Tunisia after the Arab Spring*, New Haven and London: Yale University Press, 2016, op. cit., p.54.
57. Esfandiari, D., Tabatabi, A., 'Yemen: An Opportunity for Iran-Saudi Dialogue', *The Washington Quarterly*, Vol.39, No.2, pp.155–174.
58. Juneau, T., "No, Yemen's Houthis actually aren't Iranian Puppets", *The Washington Post*, 16 May 2016, at https://www.washingtonpost.com/news/monkey-cage/wp/2016/05/16/contrary-to-popular-belief-houthis-arent-iranian-proxies/?utm_term=.1e1ea5acfc5a, accessed 25 December 2016.
59. Friedland, E. "Afrah Nasser: We're in the First Five Minutes of This Revolution", The Clarion Project, 15 June 2015, at http://www.clarionproject.org/analysis/afrah-nasser, accessed 14 September 2016.
60. Knutsen, A., "Ramadan Bombings in Yemen: Part of ISIS's Global Strategy?" *Critical Threats*, 17 June 2015, at http://www.criticalthreats.org/yemen/knutsen-ramadan-bombings-part-isis-global-strategy-june-17-2015, accessed 20 July 2016.

61. Esfandiari, D., Tabatabi, A., "Yemen: An Opportunity for Iran-Saudi Dialogue", *The Washington Quarterly*, Vol.39, No.2, pp.155–174.
62. However, the Trump administration through various measures help Saudi Arabia shed such fears. See, Peterson, S., "With huge arms deal, US pivots back to Saudis. How does it affect the region?", *The Christian Science Monitor*, 22 May 2017.
63. Salisbury, P., "Yemen: Stemming the Rise of a Chaos State", Middle East and North Africa Programme, Chatham House, 25 May 2016.
64. Cited in Al-Dawsari, N., "Finding a New Approach to Yemen's Peace Talks", *Atlantic Council*, 3 May 2016, at http://www.atlanticcouncil.org/blogs/menasource/finding-a-new-approach-to-yemen-s-peace-talks, accessed 4 July 2016.
65. Ibid.
66. President Hadi's recent decision to dismiss governor of Aden Aidarous al-Zubaidi, who is a prominent Hirak leader, created backlash and mass rallies in Aden in support of Hirak. On 11 May, Al-Zubaidi announced that he and other southern political leaders were forming an autonomous body to govern southern Yemen and represent it internationally. See, "Southern Yemen leaders launch body seeking split from north", 11 May 2017, at http://www.reuters.com/article/us-yemen-security-south-idUSKBN18724T, accessed 30 May 2017.
67. Peterson, S., "In Yemen War, could surge in violence rekindle diplomacy", *The Christian Science Monitor*, 2 September 2016, at http://www.csmonitor.com/World/Middle-East/2016/0902/In-Yemen-s-war-could-surge-in-violence-rekindle-diplomacy, accessed 6 October 2016.
68. Quoted in Ibid.
69. "Yemen war: US ship faces new round of Houthi missiles", *Al-Jazeera*, 16 October 2016, at http://www.aljazeera.com/news/2016/10/yemen-war-ship-faces-houthi-missiles-161016034018318.html, accessed 20 November 2016.
70. "Saudi-led coalition won't renew broken Yemen ceasefire", *Al-Jazeera*, 21 November 2016, at http://www.aljazeera.com/news/2016/11/saudi-led-coalition-won-renew-broken-yemen-ceasefire-161121140618377.html, accessed 26 November 2016.

PART 4

IRAN

10

Iran and the Region: An Introduction

Javed Ahmad Khan and Sanjay Singh

The Islamic Revolution in Iran in 1979 was a seminal event that brought to centre-stage the clergy as the ruling institution in the country. The doctrine of *Wilayat al-Faqih*, which underpins this revolutionary change, is not just a theory, but a working model of politics being currently practiced in Iran a modern nation-state, with a transcendental appeal beyond its borders. The first chapter in this section is an enquiry into the phenomenon and explores diverse aspects related to it. In view of Iran's rise as a regional power, the significance of studying the institutions of Iran and the basis of their legitimacy increases manifold. This chapter is a contribution in that direction.

In the introductory part of this chapter, the author has discussed the jurisprudential origin of the doctrine, with its historical evolution based on the distinct interpretation of the Shiite School of Islam. In the next section, the practical implementation of the doctrine is discussed, and the consequence of it is carefully investigated with particular focus on the nuances of Ayatollah Khomeini's interpretation. The discussion goes further into the challenges the doctrine of *Wilayat al-Faqih* faces as a concept and as a political doctrine. From the different competing narratives of political formation in parallel to the doctrine, to the debates within the religious domain, the arguments are examined, and their manifestation in setting up and challenging the *Wilayat al-Faqih* discourse is investigated. The chapter brings in some important arguments from the clergy, both inside and outside Iran, to put the challenges to the doctrine in a proper perspective.

One of the significant areas covered in this chapter is concerned with the appeal of the doctrine beyond Iranian borders. Here, the author provides an exclusive section to explore the doctrine's influence in countries like Lebanon, Iraq, and Pakistan. Readers can also note the important remarks made in the context of India. The chapter concludes with a discussion on developments in the practical interpretation and implementation of the doctrine, and the succession issue of Iran's Supreme Leader in the future. There is a detailed analysis of the role of Ayatollah Ali Khamenei in consolidating the rule of juris consult and the challenges of the succession issue. In the conclusion, some observations are made based on the whole thesis of the chapter.

The change in regime in Iran in 1979 transformed it from being a pillar supporting the dominant US position in the region into becoming one of its most implacable foes. The differences between the two grew with the passage of years, and were made nearly unbridgeable by the stand-off over the nuclear issue. The Joint Comprehensive Plan of Action (JCPOA) was the result of an exercise in the diplomacy of exploring the art of the possible.

The second chapter examines developments pertaining to three key areas as they have evolved in the post JCPOA period. These include the status of the Iran-United States ties; issues relating to sanctions relief and Iran's economic situation; and the regional strategic situation. JCPOA was limited to the nuclear issue and not a grand bargain. Concerns pertaining to each other's regional behaviour and policy goals remain; these have prevented a further thaw in US-Iran interactions. While the monetary benefits of the deal have not yet fully materialised on the ground, the limited promise of the deal to translate into regional geo-political goodwill is yet to be realised. The attitude of the new US administration could make the situation even more difficult.

The third chapter examines how Iran is perceived in the region, and how the US-Iran relationship is an important factor in regional politics. Directly, indirectly, or through proxies, Iran has been involved, or is seen to be accentuating, many regional conflicts and tensions in the region, and its influence extends far beyond its immediate borders to Iraq, Lebanon, Syria, Bahrain, and Yemen. This has increased fears and apprehensions amongst its regional rivals and competitors, such as Egypt, Israel, Saudi Arabia, and Turkey over Iran's hegemonic intentions. These countries are increasingly uncomfortable with the Iranian influence in regions, which they consider as their own spheres of influence—that is, the Arabian Peninsula and Levant. The authors argue that the Obama administration's actions in limiting US involvement in the Middle East and concluding the nuclear deal with Iran, has created the conditions for Iranian regional ascendance, increased its staying power, and that the growing Iranian influence will have implications for the region. For India, the resultant growing Saudi-Iranian tension will be worrisome, especially when New Delhi seeks close politico-strategic partnerships with both the Gulf States.

11

The Concept of *Wilayat al-Faqih*: 37 Years after the Iranian Revolution

Shafat Yousuf

ABSTRACT

Ayatollah Khomeini's words cited above demonstrate both the source and consequence of the divine authority of Wali al-Faqih (guardian jurisconsult). Thirty seven years after the Islamic Revolution and the establishment of the Islamic Republic of Iran, this demonstration of Wilayat al-Faqih (guardianship of the jurisconsult) as a concept and as the official doctrine of the Islamic Republic, seems intended to stave off any serious challenge to it in the present as well as in the near future. The doctrine attracts enough followers both among the laity and clergy in Iran as well as outside; they continue to see it as a legitimate interpretation of Islam's socio-political domain. The rise of Iran as a regional power strengthens the concept of Wilayat al-Faqih politically as well as jurisprudentially. There are many debates among scholars among the clergy and the laity about the scope of the authority of the jurisconsult, and the doctrine's correct interpretation and implementation. This chapter analyses the status of the concept, the debates around it, and the challenges it faces 37 years after the Islamic Revolution in Iran.

I [Khomeini] should make you aware of another issue and that is if I have named him [Mehdi Bazargan] as the ruler, I did so based on the agency granted to me by the sacred canonical laws. He whom I have designated is to be made obeisance to; the nation must obey him. This government is no ordinary one; it is a canonical government. Opposition to this government is opposition to the canon laws and is tantamount to rebellion against religion.

—*Imam Khomeini*[1]

The Concept of *Wilayat al-Faqih* (Guardianship of the Jurisconsult)

Wilayat al-Faqih (guardianship of the jurisconsult)[2] in its restricted meaning is the guardianship bestowed upon the *al-faqih al-ādil* (just Islamic jurist) in the non-litigious affairs (*al-omoor al-hisbiya*[3]) of the Muslims.[4] This is known as the limited guardianship of the Islamic jurist. In its broader meaning, *Wilayat al-Faqih* is an Islamic doctrine of political arrangement by which a *faqih* (an Islamic jurist) is considered the guardian of all the affairs of Muslims, and is religiously empowered to establish and run a political system on behalf of the Twelfth Imam.[5] This is regarded as absolute guardianship (*al-wilaya al-mutlaqa*) of the Islamic jurist.

The doctrine of *Wilayat al-Faqih* originates in the Shiite School of Islam, and forms the pivot around which the contemporary Shiite political thought revolves. It derives its legitimacy from the divine authority of the Prophet of Islam and the Imams. It lays out a guardianship-based political system in the physical absence[6] of the Twelfth Imam in which the jurist takes on the Imam's guardianship (*wilaya*) of both religion and the Muslim community (*ummah*), and acts as the deputy of the Imam.[7] While Imams were specifically appointed as guardians, the jurists (*fuqaha*) are not explicitly selected by name, but rather on the basis of scholarly qualities.

Traditionally, qualified jurists used to undertake the role of the deputies of the Imam, and perform the following traditional roles/functions: making a decree (*al-ifta*);[8] to judge (*al-qada*); and guardianship over non-litigious affairs (*al-umūr hisbiya*).[9] There were other jurists—like Mulla Naraqi (d. 1829) and Sheikh Hasan Najafi (d. 1850)—who believed in the modest political role of the Islamic jurist, although Najafi particularly argued about the authority of the jurist being very broad.[10] It is in this context that Ayatollah Mirza Hassan Shirazi (d. 1895) used his authority as a jurist and issued an edict (*hukum*) against the tobacco monopoly given by the Qajar King, Nasir al-Din Shah, to the British Imperial Tobacco Corporation of Persia in 1890. Mirza Shirazi was based in Najaf in Iraq, and it was adherence to the transcendental authority of the jurist which led to the famous Tobacco Protest (1890–92) and the subsequent withdrawal of the concession. This led to an increase in the collective resentment against the Qajars which culminated in the Constitutional Revolution of 1906.[11] The leadership of the clerical class was crucial in the protest movement of the Revolution. Roy Mottahedeh argues that, without the support of clergy, the movement would have failed.[12]

The influence of the clerics was such that the newly elected parliament was inaugurated in the presence of seventeen jurists in October 1906. The influence continued in many forms after the Constitutional Revolution and, during the Pahlavi rule, culminated in the control of power by the Iranian clergy after the Islamic Revolution of 1979. The jurist who argued for the comprehensive role of Islamic jurisconsult in all affairs of the Muslims was Ayatollah Ruhollah Khomeini (1902–1989). His contribution to the concept becomes important both at the theoretical and practical levels. He not only converted *Wilayat al-Faqih* to a fully fledged political ideology in his scholarship but was also successful in implementing it in a modern nation-state.

According to Ayatollah Khomeini, there is no difference between the authority of the Prophet and the jurisconsult and, for that matter, between the First Imam's powers and those of the jurisconsult.[13] However, on the subject of virtues, he argues that the Prophet's virtues were greater than those of the rest of mankind and, after the Prophet, the First Imam and the rest of the Imams were virtuous in the world. Khomeini does not consider the increase of governmental powers with respect to the superiority of the spiritual virtues of a jurist. This observation becomes important in the context of the constitutional amendment of Iran's constitution in 1989, when the qualification of *Wali al-Faqih* (Supreme Leader of Iran as jurisconsult) was changed from being a *marja' al-taqlid* to being simply a *mujtahid*.[14] He cautions that the just jurisconsult having the same authority as the Prophet as well as the Imams does not mean that the status of the jurisconsult is identical to them. Khomeini argues that "here we are not speaking of status, but rather of function".[15]

Khomeini believed that the governance of the jurisconsult is a rational and extrinsic matter.[16] This arrangement is similar to the appointment of a guardian for a minor. As far as responsibility is concerned, there is no difference between the guardian of a nation and the guardian of a minor.[17] The ruler's mandate is the implementation of God's laws and the supervision of the executive power. So, for Khomeini, it makes no difference if the ruler is the Prophet, the Imam, or the Imam's representative or judge appointed to any city, or a jurisconsult in the present age.

Consequences of the Implementation of the Doctrine of the Wilayat al-Faqih

In the Islamic Republic of Iran, the doctrine of *Wilayat al-Faqih* manifests in the establishment of the Office of the Supreme Leader of the Revolution (*daftar-e maqām-e mo'azzam-e rahbari*).[18] The preamble of the Iranian Constitution mentions the qualified jurist's role as the leader who would ensure that state institutions adhere to their Islamic mandate.[19] The implementation of this doctrine was not smooth, and it had to face opposition from many quarters. The most significant opposition was from the secular-liberal and communist factions which did not want the clergy's role in politics.[20] From the establishment of the Islamic Republic of Iran in February 1979 to the actual adoption of the concept of *Wilayat al-Faqih* in the Iranian Constitution, there were many debates within Iran about the role of the clerical class in state administration. Some of the debates were reflected in the debates in the constituent assembly.[21] With the overwhelming support that Khomeini enjoyed, his interpretation finally made it to the consolidation of power, and defeating the other competing narratives.

There are two aspects of Khomeini's interpretation which are very significant, and have far reaching consequences. One aspect is the authority of the ruler jurisconsult over other jurists. For Khomeini, the authority that the Prophet and the Imam had in establishing a government also exists for the ruler jurisconsult. Islamic jurists do not have absolute authority in the sense of having authority over all the other jurists of their own time—the authority of being able to appoint or dismiss them.[22] Traditionally, the *marja's* authority of pronouncing a decree (*fatwa*) was not constrained by other jurists; but now, the jurisconsult can limit the authority of a *marja'* only to the personal affairs of religion without the latter's interference in the socio-political domain. Also, according to Khomeini's interpretation, the ruling of the jurisconsult in the public domain is binding on other jurists. This affected the state-clergy relation in Iran after 1979. There were jurists, like Kazem Shariatmadari,[23] who did not accept Khomeini's interpretation of *Wilayat al-Faqih*, and hence, did not agree with the view that a jurist's authority can override the authority of other jurists.[24] Shariatmadari's opposition to the constitution and the jurist's absolute authority led to his house-arrest which resulted in protests in his home province of East Azerbaijan. Later, due to his intervention, the protest demonstrations were stopped by his followers. The new government restricted the movement of other clerics who opposed the constitution and government policies. These steps were rationalised, based on the argument of the primacy of state interests of an Islamic state, which is the second aspect of Khomeini's interpretation.

This second aspect is about the jurisconsult's authority regarding the interpreting of Islamic laws. In 1988, in his letter to then President (Ali Khamenei), Khomeini argues that the Islamic government is the absolute guardianship delegated by God, and is among the most important Islamic laws, and which is pre-eminent over all other divine religious laws like fasting and *Hajj*. The authority of the Islamic government is not confined by the framework of secondary religious laws, but goes beyond it. Hence, the jurisconsult can stop any affair if he considers it against the interests of Islam, and the Islamic country.[25] For example, in the previous year (2016), Iran did not send *Hajj* pilgrims to Saudi Arabia based on the reasoning that without the materialising of the agreement with Saudi Arabia, the security of the pilgrims would not be safeguarded. This decision has its basis in the jurisconsult's view that observing an important Islamic principle like *Hajj* can be temporarily suspended if it is not in the interest of the Islamic Republic.

The above interpretation by Khomeini has led to the principle of 'regime expediency' (*maslahat-e nizâm*[26]). According to this principle, the survival of the Islamic Republic gets elevated to a supreme religious value.[27] In this context, the Expediency Discernment Council (*Majma' Tashkhi Maslahat-e Nizam*) was created in 1988 as an institution to mediate and resolve the differences between the Parliament (Majlis) and the Guardian Council. Its mandate was in matters pertaining to legislation as well as constitutional issues, and to advise the Supreme Leader on the discernment of regime expediency in accordance with Article 110 and Article 112 of the Constitution.[28] In the 1989 amendment of Iran's Constitution, the Council's authorities are outlined. The Council will play a role in case parliament passes a law that the Guardian Council considers un-Islamic or unconstitutional; then the Council advises the Supreme Leader as to whether the law is in the interest of the regime. The law would be accepted, rejected, or amended as per the Supreme Leader's decision based on regime expediency—as defined by the Leader.[29]

Challenges to Wilayat al-Faqih as a Concept and as a Political Doctrine

There has been evolution in the debate about the doctrine of *Wilayat al-Faqih*, both at the theoretical as well as at the practical levels. Various strands of politico-theological discourses are emerging in Iran, and these are not only limited to confronting the official ideology of the state but are also challenging the traditional view of religion and politics. Some scholars have documented the discourses with respect to the latter's position on religion, and categorise them into conservative, reformist, and secular-modernist narratives.[30] According to Mehran Kamrava, these discourses emerge within the theocratic political system.[31] Presently, traditionalist religious discourse has the strongest claim—as well as stake—in the intellectual paradigm of the Iranian state. Through this discourse, the policies of the state get jurisprudential justifications, and are presented in tandem with the Islamic principles.[32]

Among the religious conservatives, Ayatollah Javadi Amoli and Ayatollah Mesbah Yazdi are the prominent ones who are part of the state structure, and have put forward an intellectual defence for the present political establishment. Javadi Amoli has said that criticizing the decree of jurisconsult is forbidden (*haram*) even by jurists (*mujtahid*) and the highest religious authorities (*marja' al-taqlid*).[33] Ayatollah Mesbah Yazdi has vociferously defended and articulated the Khomeini interpretation of *Wilayat al-Faqih*. For Yazdi, the person discovered and appointed as the supreme jurisconsult by the Assembly of Experts is to be viewed as the infallible Imam's deputy. He is presented to the people only for the purpose of information, and not to obtain their consent or endorsement.[34] For Yazdi, there is no need to obtain legitimacy from the people for the jurisconsult. The jurisconsult obtains legitimacy from God by virtue of him being Twelfth Imam's deputy. Hence, it is him who will decide the validity of a presidential election, and will approve and endorse the president's election and authority. For Yazdi, obeying the President is obeying God, because when the president's election is accepted by the jurisconsult, the former receives legitimacy and benefits from the sacred authority of the latter. He has also said that obeying the president is obligatory—like offering prayers.[35] These comments were made in the context of the disputed presidential election of Mahmoud Ahmadinejad in 2009.

In comparison with the above discourse, the reformist narrative is greatly informed by the compatibility of religion with modern democratic principles of political arrangement in the contemporary nation-state model of state formation. The basis on which the reformists take this view is the scope of interpretation granted according to the principle of *ijtihad*.[36] The election of the current President of Iran, Hassan Rouhani, could be understood within this discourse. He is a cleric, and projects himself as a 'moderate' with a revolutionary background.[37] The combination of 'moderation' and 'reformism' defines what is known as the religious reformist stand, of which Ayatollah Montazeri[38] was an important example. Montazeri can be categorised so based on his revised position in the late 1980s about the religious legitimacy of an Islamic state.[39] In Montazeri's understanding, there is primacy of the rights of people in the conception of rule of the jurisconsult. His interpretation of the jurisconsult's authority is greatly limited in comparison to Khomeini.[40] According to Mehdi Khalaji, Montazeri's approach can be understood as legal, while Khomeini's demonstration of *Wilaya* (guardianship) is greatly similar to how it is understood in Islamic mysticism (*Irfan*).[41] This view of Khalaji is based on the wider acceptance of Khomeini being an acknowledged mystic (*'Arif*).

For Montazeri, popular participation and endorsement are indispensable for legitimising the rule of the jurisconsult.[42] According to him, the people's vote, the Constitution, and laws legitimise the rule of the guardian jurisconsult. He argues for the supervisory role of the jurisconsult in political affairs. Taking the juridical view, he considers that Article 107 and Article 110 of the Iranian Constitution define the status of the jurisconsult.[43] Article 107 specifies that the Supreme Leader is equal to every other citizen in the country before the law. Article 110 has specified the extent of the authority and responsibility of the jurisconsult, and that his election by the people is based on his commitment to the Constitution. The term *motlaqeh* (absolute) in Article 57 was added later to the *Wilayat al-Faqih*.[44] Montazeri considered this addition contrary to the original true spirit of the Constitution, and therefore he did not vote for it.[45]

These positions made Montazeri's personality a rallying point for the opposition Green Movement. He emerged as its ideologue, and gave it the religious inspiration and legitimacy it really needed. Leaders of the Movement, like Moussavi, collaborated with Montazeri, and tried to get the support of the people in favour of the movement. This was further demonstrated on the eve of Montazeri's death, which became a rare rallying event against the government, with supporters of the Green Movement flocking the funeral.[46]

It is important to note that the opposition to the *Wilayat al-Faqih* concept is multi-layered. For example, Ayatollah Khoie and his disciples have not agreed to its legality, as per Shiite jurisprudence, of the political power vested in the jurist through the concept of *Wilayat al-Faqih*.[47] From the clerical perspective, one section of jurists could be said to be greatly disagreeing with the interpretation of Ayatollah Khomeini about this doctrine. Ayatollah Khoei of Iraq and Ayatollah Fazullah of Lebanon are prominent jurists belonging to this section of jurists. Another section of jurists is one which accepts the concept as legally tenable, but has differences about its implementation as also have a varying interpretation of the concept. Ayatollah Montazeri could be considered to be in this category. He accepts the doctrine's legal tenability but differs with its interpretation, and gives his own version of it. Ayatollah Sistani[48] of Iraq was regarded in the category of deniers; but he seems to have formulated a more flexible position vis-à-vis *Wilayat al-Faqih*, depicting a slight variance of opinion on the position his teacher (Ayatollah Khoie) held on this doctrine. He argues that for "general affairs to which social order is linked, the *wilayah* of a *Faqih* and the enforcement of *wilayah* depend on certain conditions, one of which is the popularity of *Faqih* among the majority of the *momeneen*.[49] This position could be considered as a silent support to the rule of the jurisconsult in Iran without actually taking an explicit position in order to safeguard the Shiite constituency in Iraq whose political stakes have risen after the fall of the Saddam regime.

From the political domain in Iran, Mehdi Karroubi—a 2009 presidential candidate and an opposition Green Movement leader who is himself a cleric—remarked in 2010 about the extension of the authority of the then jurisconsult. He said,

> Why has the authority of the Vali-ye Faqih [jurisconsult] been so greatly extended? I doubt that so much authority and power were given to the Prophets themselves, or the infallible [Shi'i] Imams. I even doubt that God considers himself to have the right to deal with his servants in the same way [that the Supreme Leader does]![50]

The unwavering allegiance towards *Wilayat al-Faqih* is sought, and the betrayal or questioning of it can put even a distinguished person out of favour. Ayatollah Khamenei made this very clear in his June 2010 Friday sermon in Tehran. For Khamenei, some people with distinct service in the time of Prophet forfeited the merits of their deeds by fighting the Imam's authority, and thus, in the same way, opposing the authority of the jurisconsult would forfeit the distinction of many prominent personalities.[51] This analogy pointed at Mehdi Karroubi and Mir Hossein Mousavi, leaders of the Green Movement, who had a distinctive past record during the Islamic Revolution as well as after it. Since they challenged the validity of the election result despite the jurisconsult's endorsement of it, they are understood to have challenged the divine authority of the latter.[52]

The proponents of the third discourse—the secular-modernist one—claim that the modern world is no place for politicised religion.[53] This discourse argues that the place of religion should be private, and the domain of politics needs to be secular wherein there is a major role for civil society and the forces of globalisation are not rejected. This discourse has yet to find a firm ground in the Iranian political scenario, for Iran is a deeply religious society and has re-oriented itself in Islamic traditions after the Islamic Revolution. There is deep suspicion of Western models of political engagement, and more often than not, this secular-modernist discourse gets sidelined by the accusation of *garbzadgi* (West-toxication).

Wilayat al-Faqih beyond the Borders of Iran

The doctrine's reach, and its following beyond the borders of Iran, are closely linked with the travel of the revolutionary ideology of the Revolution of 1979. This ideology had a deep impact on the Muslim world in general, and on the Shiite Muslims in particular. It transformed the Shiite community worldwide from 'a stage of quiet passivity into a sudden and explosive activism'.[54] The doctrine of *Wilayat al-Faqih* could be seen as being both attached with and detached from the Islamic Revolution. The Revolution contributed to the consolidation of the doctrine as the official ideology in Iran, and also opened ways for its travel along with its revolutionary philosophy to different parts of the Muslim world. The export of the revolution as a principle of foreign policy after the Revolution was abandoned in the 1990s after Iran found that it increased resistance to Iranian interests in the West Asian region.[55]

In contrast to this, the *Wilayat al-Faqih* doctrine did not subject itself to the calculations of Iranian national interests. Its following also depended on the rigorous jurisprudential debates among the scholars based in both traditional seminaries and modern universities. The increase in its following depended more on the convincing jurisprudential arguments put forth by the adherents of the doctrine rather than by the continuous push of the revolutionary ideology by Iranian political elite. After the revolutionary zeal thawed somewhat, the doctrine found its adherence being largely dependent on its being a religious concept, and viewed by a major section of Shiites as the appropriate interpretation of Islamic political thought in the post-occultation period.

The doctrine of *Wilayat al-Faqih* is a transcendental concept, and does not respect any territorial limit. The best example of the doctrine's following outside Iran would be Lebanon's Hezbollah (Party of God). In its Constitution, which was published as 'The Hizballah Program, an open letter to all the Oppressed in Lebanon and the World' in 1985, it describes itself as "...sons of the *umma*—the party of God, the vanguard of which was made victorious by God in Iran...".[56] About its adherence to *Wilayat al-Faqih*, it says: "We obey the orders of one leader, wise and just, that of our tutor and *faqih* who fulfils all the necessary conditions: Ruhollah Musawi Khomeini."[57] After Khomeini's death, Khamenei replaced him as the 'Leader' for Hezbollah. Although Ayatollah Muhammad Hussein Fadlallah was regarded as the 'spiritual leader of Hezbollah,[58] he subsequently distanced himself from the organisation. He did not agree with Khomeini's interpretation of the *Wilayat al-Faqih* doctrine, and also did not approve of Hezbollah following Ayatollah Khamenei as *marja' al-*

taqlid.[59] This is the consequence of the debate within Shiite jurists about the interpretation of the doctrine and its implementation. His distancing resulted in the increased influence of Iran's Supreme Leader in the policy decisions of the Hezbollah.

As per the ideological commitment, Hezbollah's policy decisions need to be approved by Ayatollah Khamenei.[60] Its leader, Sayyed Hassan Nasrallahm has stated that "the decision of peace and war is in the hands of [the] jurisconsult, not in the hands of the intellectuals, researchers, scientists, and regular politicians, depending on the circumstances."[61] Hence, its decision to enter Syria[62] and its presence in Iraq[63] could not be without sanctification from the Supreme Leader. All the policy postures of the Hezbollah are influenced by Iran's vision of the region and, more importantly, by the Supreme Leader's leadership. In this context, many analysts have described Hezbollah as a proxy of Iran.[64]

This approach of understanding Hezbollah seems to be a reductionist one. The frame of reference for analysing the Hezbollah has to be wider, and should begin with its ideological foundation in its historical context, and the doctrine of *Wilayat al-Faqih* is its starting mark.[65] In 2014, Sheikh Naim Qassem, Hezbollah's Deputy Secretary General, said that Hezbollah is inspired by *Wilayat al-Faqih*, and that its war with Israel as well as its intervention in Syria stem from the moral view taken from this doctrine.[66] Since adherence to the *Wilayat al-Faqih* is not limited to state boundaries, so also Hezbollah's role is not bound by any border.[67]

The establishment of the Supreme Council for the Islamic Revolution in Iraq (SCIRI, now Islamic Supreme Council of Iraq) in 1982 was based on the idea of exporting the Islamic Revolution to Iraq. It was established in Iran, and was headed by Ayatollah Baqir al-Hakim of Iraq. SCIRI embraced Iran's Islamic Republic, and agreed with the Khomeini's interpretation of *Wilayat al-Faqih*.[68]*Ashaab Ahl-e Haq* (League of Righteous People) and *Kata'ib Hezbollah* (Brigades of the Party of God) are other examples from Iraq of the transcendental following of the doctrine. They are the main Iraqi militia organisations which are fighting Islamic State of Iraq and Sham (ISIS) and have allegiance to the Supreme Leader of Iran. They adhere to the doctrine of *Wilayat al-Faqih*, and consider Ayatollah Khamenei as the guardian of their actions, and thus take instructions from his office.[69]

In the South Asian context, the case of the Imamia Students Organisation (ISO) of Pakistan is a noteworthy one. It is the largest Shiite students' organisation in Pakistan. In its official page on the social media website Facebook, it describes itself being "...under the auspices of *Rahbar e Wilayat/Wali el Faqih*—Ayatullah Syed Ali Khamenei. It has a strong and deep rooted belief in Wilayat e Faqih".[70] It also mentions that Iran's Supreme Leader has said the youth of ISO "are the [the] coolness of my eyes".[71] In the Indian context, there is no significant organised movement which adheres to the *Wilayat al-Faqih* doctrine. Most Shi'ites in India believe in Ayatollah Sistani of Iraq as their *marja' al-taqlid*. They only have a religious affiliation with Iran by virtue of the religious denomination, and no explicit political posture has been observed in the recent past.

Subsequent Developments in the Concept of Wilayat al-Faqih and Expected Succession to the Present Supreme Leader

The change of criteria for the post of Supreme Leader from *marja' al-taqlid* to simply a *mujtahid* was an attempt to balance the criteria for the head of the state in a modern Islamic state, and the practical considerations of running an Islamic government. This shows the evolution in the practical implementation of the doctrine of *Wilayat al-Faqih* from its initial theoretical conception by Ayatollah Khomeini through the challenges of developing it as a workable model. In response to the question posed by Ayatollah Ali Meshkini[72] about the jurisconsult being a *marja' al-taqlid*, Khomeini said that he had not considered it a necessary condition for becoming the Supreme Leader (*Wali al-Faqih*) when the constitution was being framed. According to him, a just *mujtahid* who is recommended by the Assembly of Experts can assume the leadership of the state.[73]

There is also the dimension of personality in the development of the *Wilayat al-Faqih* doctrine in Iran. The way Ayatollah Khomeini was able to lead was due to his charismatic personality and his undisputed religious scholarship. Although the present Supreme Leader Ayatollah Khamenei does have charisma, it is no match to that of Khomeini. Also, Khamenei's religious scholarship was not regarded being highly acclaimed by many Ayatollahs when he became the Supreme Leader.[74] Khamenei has played a different role as compared to his predecessor, and thus his successor is expected to differ from him too, given the changed circumstances. Last year's (2016) election to the Assembly of Experts (*Majlis-e Khobragan*) was held in view of the future prospect of it choosing a new Supreme Leader.[75] The new leader would have to make an effort to get acceptability as the Leader, both inside and outside Iran. As Khamenei's influence and authority consolidated only gradually, so would be the case with the new Supreme Leader.

Ayatollah Khamenei's status as the *Wali al-Faqih* is the result of many years of effort.[76] There was a huge leadership vacuum after Ayatollah

Khomeini's death, and Khamenei's filling the vacuum did not have a natural reception among the Shiites worldwide who considered Khomeini as a transcendental leader not limited to Iranian borders only. But, by virtue of the principles of *Wilayat al-Faqih* and *Maslahat* (regime expediency), Khamenei was able to turn the Supreme Leader's Office into the centre of gravity of the entire political system of Iran.[77]

During Khamenei's time, the institution of *Wilayat al-Faqih* has consolidated theoretically as well as practically. At the conceptual level, Shiites from both the clergy and the laity have increasingly started viewing the doctrine as the legitimate interpretation of the political aspect of religion in the occultation period of the Twelfth Imam. At the practical level, the authority of the Supreme Leader has increased, and found allegiance in different sectors of public life. The most important role Khamenei has played was taking all the important stakeholders of the Iranian state on board. The crucial stakeholders were the regular army (known as *Artesh* in Iran) and the Islamic Revolutionary Guards Corps (IRGC) or *Pasdaran-e Inqilab Islami*. The IRGC has emerged as the most powerful institution safeguarding the institution of *Wilayat al-Faqih* in Iran.[78]

A new leader would definitely face many challenges in consolidating himself as the Supreme Leader. Fortunately, he would have some precedents in the form of Khamenei's experience which the latter did not have luxury to look up to. There would no doubt be many parallels drawn between Khamenei and his successor. In this context, what kind of changes the institution of the jurisconsult would see depends to a great extent on the person holding the status. Personalities do shape institutions in their own shape, and get shaped by them in turn.[79] Currently, the *Wilayat al-Faqih* institution has the deep stamp of Khamenei, and the new leader would have to work for some time under the long shadow of the former.

There is no clear indication about who will succeed Khamenei as the new Supreme Leader of Iran. As the Constitution was amended at the time of Khamenei's appointment as Supreme Leader, there is a possibility of such a process being repeated in one form or another. In theory, Khamenei is empowered to change the succession rules according to the required needs if there is no clear successor, or if the Assembly of Experts does not agree on any potential candidate.[80] Presently, the Constitution of Iran has a clearly mentioned procedure for succession, which is as follows.

> In the event of the death, or resignation, or dismissal of the Leader, the experts shall take steps within the shortest possible time for the appointment of the new Leader. Till the appointment of the new Leader, a council consisting of the President, head of the judicial

> power, and a faqih from the Guardian Council, upon the decision of the Nation's Exigency Council, shall temporarily take over all the duties of the Leader. In the event, during this period, if any of them is unable to fulfil his duties for whatsoever reason, another person, upon the decision of majority of fuqaha' in the Nation's Exigency Council shall be elected in his place.[81]

Legally, the Supreme Leader can order revision of the succession rules; but at the technical level that would require a referendum.[82] Given the fact that Iran's elections have been followed in the West with keen interest, this referendum has the potential to generate extraordinary focus from the international media. Since this referendum would be a crucial one—more important than a presidential election—the stakes would be high; so would be consequential dangers. The Iranian government has been very sensitive about concerns regarding legitimacy after the 2009 protests. Holding such a referendum could present political difficulties for the Iranian state; hence the amendment of the Constitution is unlikely for this purpose.

There have been some names doing rounds in the political circles of the Iranian establishment as potential successors. Hashemi Rafsanjani[83] in 2015 stated that there is a list of potential candidates prepared by the Assembly of Experts and, whenever necessary, the Assembly would choose among them.[84] Mehdi Khalaji cites names of some prominent persons who could be considered potential candidates for the succession.[85] These names are as follows.

- Khamenei's second son and favoured candidate, Mojtaba (b. 1969);
- Mahmoud Hashemi Shahroudi (b. 1948), former judiciary chief and Guardian Council member, currently on the Expediency Council and Assembly of Experts;
- Muhammad Taqi Mesbah-Yazdi (b. 1934), an extremist cleric who believes that democracy and Islam are incompatible;
- Muhammad Yazdi (b. 1931), former judiciary chief and head of the Qom seminary's Association of Professors (*Jameh-e-ye Modarresin-e Howzeh-ye Elmiyeh-ye Qom*).

In the above list, Ayatollah Mahmoud Hashemi Shahroudi is a person to be watched due to his diverse credentials and acceptability in the security establishment.[86] He declared himself a *marja'* in 2010,[87] and was Chief Justice of Iran for 10 years—from 1999 to 2009. He is of Iraqi origin; was member of Islamic Dawa Party; and is associated with the Supreme Council for the Islamic Revolution in Iraq (now Islamic Supreme Council of Iraq). He is currently member of both the Guardian Council and the Experts Council.

Conclusion

The doctrine of *Wilayat al-Faqih* (guardianship of the jurisconsult) is a transcendental concept, extracting legitimacy from the Shiite School of Islam in the post-occultation era of the Twelfth Imam. The Islamic Republic of Iran bases its legitimacy on this concept, and acknowledges the highest authority of the Supreme Leader as the deputy of the Twelfth Imam. There are no major challenges to the doctrine theoretically and practically, although there is a wide range of debate about its legitimacy as the correct interpretation of the socio-political domain of Islam. The debates range from outright rejection of Ayatollah Khomeini's interpretation of the *Wilayat al-Faqih* to differences about the scope of authority of the jurisconsult. This doctrine attracts followers both inside and outside Iran, and there are organisations which consider Iran's Supreme Leader as the guardian of their religious affairs, which also includes the political domain. There have been concerns about the current Supreme Leader, Ayatollah Khamenei's health and old age; thus the new members of the Assembly of Experts are expected to be tasked with the question of succession of the Supreme Leader. Ayatollah Khamenei has been successful in consolidating and institutionalising the *Wilayat al-Faqih* doctrine around which the political structure of Iran revolves. Thus, scholars and policy-makers need to look at the debates within the larger religio-political discourses in Iran especially since there are no major signs that political alignments would be greatly influenced by secular-modernist narratives. In the future, some reforms of the political structure are expected; but those would be moderate in nature. They are expected to remain within the larger domain of political legitimacy of the rule of jurisconsult as envisaged by Ayatollah Khomeini.

NOTES

1. Imam Khomeini, *Sahifeh-ye Imam: An Anthology of Imam Khomeini's Speeches, Messages, Interviews, Decrees, Religious Permissions, and Letters*, Vol. 6, Tehran: The Institute for Compilation and Publication of Imam Khomeini's Works, 1999, p. 54.
2. Arabic transliteration is used throughout this chapter. Persian transliterations are notified in the endnotes.
3. *Al-omoor al-hisbiya* are the set of affairs that require an authorized guardian to oversee them. They include issuing legal opinions; propagating religious rulings; establishing the Friday and congregational prayers; implementing penal provisions; supervising endowments; discretionary mandate over children, orphans, and people of unsound mind; and collecting religious taxes. See, Ahmad Vaezi, *Shia Political Thought*, London: Islamic Centre of England, 2004, pp. 25–35. Also see, Hamid Mavani, "Khomeini's concept of governance of the

jurisconsult (Wilayat al-Faqih) revisited: The aftermath of Iran's 2009 Presidential Election", *The Middle East Journal*, Volume 67, Number 2, Spring 2013, pp. 207–228.

4. See Al-Sayyid Ali Al-Husseini Al-Sistani, "Question & Answer: Governance of Jurist", The Official Website of the Office of His Eminence Al-Sayyid Ali Al-Husseini Al-Sistani, at http://www.sistani.org/english/qa/01204/, retrieved 15 January 2016
5. In the Shiite School of Islam, there is concept of Imamate (vicegerency) after Prophethood. It is regarded as a divine institution and among the fundamental principles of Islam. There are twelve Imams who are considered guardians of religion, and vicegerants of the Prophet in all affairs, including political. Starting from Ali ibn Abi Talib (the fourth caliph) as the first Imam, all other Imams are from the progeny of Ali and Fatima, the daughter of Prophet Mohammad. Muhammad Mahdi is the Twelfth Imam who is believed to have gone into major occultation in 941 AD after a brief 72 year period of minor occultation, and would return as the 'promised Mahdi' at the end of times.
6. It is important to differentiate the physical absence of the Imam from his all-time spiritual presence in the Shiite belief.
7. In the Islamic traditions of all schools, including the Shiite School, absolute guardianship is considered from God which gets transferred to the Prophet. In the Shiite School, the divine guardianship passes to Imams after the Prophet. See, Ahmad Vaezi, pp. 25–28.
8. In the Shiite School, only a *marja' al-taqlîd* (source of emulation) can issue a *fatwâ* (decree). *Marja' al-taqlid* is the highest source of religious authority. He is a senior *mujtahid* with wide endorsement by his contemporaries about his credentials for this position. It is obligatory for the laity to follow a *marja'* in religious affairs. In juridical terms, this is known as doing *taqlîd* (following) of a *marja'*. *Mujtahid* is a cleric who has attained the level of *ijtihad*. The term *ijtihâd* means "independent reasoning" or, more specifically, "personal, independent judgment of a jurist to infer precepts from authoritative sources like the Qur'an and the Sunna." See, Abdulaziz Abdulhussein Sachedina, *The Just Ruler in Shi'ite Islam: The Comprehensive Authority of the Jurist in Imamate Jurisprudence*, Oxford: Oxford University Press, 1988, p. 135.
9. Ahmad Vaezi, op. cit., p. 30.
10. For a detailed discussion, see Abdulazziz Schedina, *The Just Ruler in Shi'ite Islam: The Comprehensive Authority of the Jurist in Imamite Jurisprudence*, New York: Oxford University Press, 1998, pp. 232–236.
11. Roy Mottahedeh, *The Mantle of the Prophet: Religion and Politics in Iran*, London: Oneworld Publications, 2014, Kindle edition, location 3744
12. Ibid.
13. Imam Khomeini, *Islamic Government: Governance of the Jurist*, trans. Hamid Algar, Tehran: The Institute for Compilation and Publication of Imam Khomein's Works, 2008, p. 46
14. For definition of *marja' al-taqlîd* and *mujtahid*, see footnote 9.
15. Imam Khomeini, *Islamic Government: Governance of the Jurist*, op. cit., p. 45
16. Ibid.

17. Ibid.
18. The terms *Rahbar-e Enqelab* (leader of the revolution) and *Vali-e Faghih* (in Persian transliteration) are generally used interchangeably in Iran.
19. The Constitution of the Islamic Republic of Iran, Iran Chamber Society, at http://www.iranchamber.com/government/laws/constitution_ch01.php, retrieved 15 January 2017.
20. Ervand Abrahamian, *A History of Modern Iran*, New York: Cambridge University Press, 2008, pp. 162–169
21. For the comprehensive commentary on the debates, see Said Saffari, "The Legitimation of the Clergy's Right to Rule in the Iranian Constitution of 1979", *British Journal of Middle Eastern Studies*, Vol. 20, No. 1,1993, pp. 64–82.
22. Ibid. p. 46.
23. He was a *marja' al-taqlîd* and was one of the most respected religious leaders of Iranian Shiites.
24. Other prominent contemporaries of Khomeini who did not agree with his interpretation were Sadiq Rouhani and Mohammad Shirazi.
25. Imam Khomeini, *Sahifeh-ye Imam*, Vol. 20, p. 427.
26. This is the Persian transliteration.
27. Mehdi Khalaji, "Shiite Jurisprudence, Political Expediency, and Nuclear Weapons", in *Nuclear Fatwa: Religion and Politics in Iran's Proliferation Strategy*, (eds.) Michael Eisenstadt and Mehdi Khalaji, Washington: The Washington Institute for Near East Policy, 2011, p. ix.
28. Wilfried Butcha, *Who Rules Iran: The Structure of Power in the Islamic Republic*, Washington: The Washington Institute for Near East Policy, 2000, p. 61.
29. Mehdi Khalaji, *Shiite Jurisprudence*, op. cit., p. x.
30. Among the scholars who have analysed these discourses are Mehran Kamrava and Farhang Rajaee.
31. Mehran Kamrava, *Iran's Intellectual Revolution*, New York: Cambridge University Press, 2008, p. 6.
32. Ibid. p. 206.
33. *"Javadi-ye Amoli: Naqz-e Hokm-e Vali-ye-Faqih Hatta bar Faqihan va Mojtahedan ham Haram Ast"* [Javadi-Amoli: It is Prohibited Even for the Jurists to Reject the Legal Ruling of the Jurisconsult], Gooya News, 4 May 2011, at http://news.gooya.com/politics/archives/2011/05/121439.php, retrieved 15 January, 2017.
34. Quoted in Hamid Mavani, see Mohammad-Taqi Mesbah Yazdi, Hoquq va Siyasat dar Qur'an [Rights and Politics in the Qur'an], (ed.) M. Shahrabi (Qom: Entesharat-e Mo'assese-ye Amuzashi va Pazhuheshi-ye Emam Khomeini, 1999), p. 317.
35. "Ayatollah Mesbah: Eta'at az Ra'is Jomhur, Eta'at az Khodast" ["Ayatollah Mesbah: Obedience to the President is Obedience to God"], *FardaNews.com*, 12 August 2009, at http://www.fardanews.com/fa/pages/?cid=885899, retrieved 15 January 2017.
36. Mehran Kamrava, op. cit., p. 88. For a definition of *ijtihad;* see footnote 14.
37. Steven Ditto, *Reading Rouhani: The Promise and Peril of Iran's New President*, Washington: The Washington Institute for Near East Policy, 2013, p. 60.

38. Ayatollah Montazeri (d. 2009) was heir-designate after Khomeini. Montazeri adopted a critical position towards the functioning of state administration during the 1980s, after he had written a four-volume work titled *Dirasat fi Wilayat al-Faqih wa Fiqh al-Dawlat al-Islamiyya*, on the *Wilayat al-Faqih* concept. He was removed as heir-designate two months before Khomeini's death. He had argued about the accountability of jurisconsult before the law, its supervisory role rather than direct rule, and people being the primary source of legitimacy of the jurisconsult.
39. Josiah Marineau, "Velayat-e Faqih in Contemporary Iran", *Papers, Essays, and Reviews (PEAR)*, Vol. 2, No. 1, Spring/Summer 2010.
40. Mehdi Khalaji, *Supreme Succession: Who will lead Post-Khamenei Iran?* Washington: The Washington Institute for Near East Policy, 2012, p. 6.
41. Mehdi Khalaji, *Supreme Succession: Who will lead Post-Khamenei Iran?* Washington: The Washington Institute for Near East Policy, 2012, p. 17.
42. Geneive Abdo and Ayatollah Hossein 'Ali Montazeri, "Re-Thinking the Islamic Republic: A 'Conversation' with Ayatollah Hossein 'Ali Montazeri", *Middle East Journal*, Vol. 55, No. 1, Winter 2001, p. 19
43. Ibid. p. 23
44. It was added in 1989 in the constitutional amendment of the Iranian Constitution.
45. Geneive Abdo, op. cit., p. 23.
46. Robert Tait, "Funeral of Iranian cleric Montazeri turns into political protest", *The Guardian*, 21 December 2009, at https://www.theguardian.com/world/2009/dec/21/iran-funeral-ayatollah-montazeri-protest, retrieved 15 January 2017.
47. Abdulaziz Sachedina, "The Rule of the Religious Jurist in Iran", in *Iran at the Crossroads*, ed. John Esposito and R.K. Ramazani, New York: Palgrave, 2001, p. 126
48. Ayatollah Sistani is the prominent *marja'e taqlid* in Iraq wielding major influence among Iraqi Shiites as well as worldwide Shiites, more particularly in South Asia.
49. Al-Sayyid Ali Al-Husseini Al-Sistani, "Question & Answer: Governance of Jurist", *The Official Website of the Office of His Eminence Al-Sayyid Ali Al-Husseini Al-Sistani*, at http://www.sistani.org/english/qa/01204/, retrieved 15 January, 2017.
50. "Mahdi Karoubi: Complete Statement for the Anniversary of the Birth of the Green Movement," *Khordaad* 88, 20 June 2010, at http://khordaad88.com/?p=1696, retrieved 15 January 2017.
51. "Ayatollah Khameneh-i: Amir al-Mo'menin ba Talheh va Zobeyr ham jangid" ["Ayatollah Khamenei: The Commander of the Faithful also Fought Against Talha and Zubayr"], Radio Zamaneh, 4 June 2010, at http://zamaaneh.com/news/2010/06/post_13363.html, retrieved 15 January 2017.
52. On 10 November 2009, Mir Hossein Mousavi called for the revision of the articles of the Constitution which give jurisconsult absolute power. He asked to make the jurisconsult accountable, and said that the Constitution is not a sacred document which cannot be modified. Quoted in Hamid Mavani (2011), "Ayatullah Khomeini's Concept of Governance (wilayat al-faqih) and the Classical Shi'i Doctrine of Imamate", *Middle Eastern Studies*, 47:5, 807–824, DOI: 10.1080/00263206.2011.613208

53. Mehran Kamarva, op. cit., p. 11.
54. Daniel Brumberg and Marvin Zonis, *Khomeini, The Islamic Republic of Iran and the Arab World*, Cambridge MA: Centre for Middle Eastern Studies, Harvard University, 1987, p. 71.
55. Kenneth Katzman, *Iran's Foreign Policy*, Congressional Research Service, 24 August 2016.
56. "An Open Letter: The Hizbullah Program", *The Jerusalem Quarterly*, Number 48, Fall 1988, at http://web.archive.org/web/20060821215729/http://www.ict.org.il/Articles/Hiz_letter.htm, retrieved 15 January 2017.
57. Ibid.
58. Sayyid Muhammad Hussein Fadlallah (d. 2010) was himself a *marja' taqleed*, and many Hezbollah members emulated him in religious affairs. Hezbollah and its *majlis al-shura* (advisory council) officially follow Ali Khamenei. See, Lara Deeb, "Hizbullah: A Primer", Middle East Research and Information Project, 31 July 2006, at http://www.merip.org/mero/mero073106?ip_login_no_cache=c6b2a8220d3a0762cb59881338bb73bb, retrieved 15 January 2017.
59. Ahmad Nizar Hamzeh, *In the Path of Hizbullah*, New York: Syracuse University Press, 2004, p. 27. See also, Lara Deeb, op. cit.
60. See Hamzeh, *In the Path of Hizbullah*, p. 33.
61. Ibid. p. 33.
62. Anne Barnard, "Hezbollah Commits to an All-Out Fight to Save Assad", *New York Times*, 25 May 2013, at http://www.nytimes.com/2013/05/26/world/middleeast/syrian-army-and-hezbollah-step-up-raids-on-rebels.html?_r=0, retrieved 15 January 2017.
63. Liz Sly and Suzan Haidamous, "Lebanon's Hezbollah acknowledges battling the Islamic State in Iraq", *The Washington Post*, 16 February 2016, at https://www.washingtonpost.com/world/middle_east/lebanons-hezbollah-acknowledges-battling-the-islamic-state-in-iraq/2015/02/16/4448b21a-b619-11e4-bc30-a4e75503948a_story.html, retrieved 15 January 2017.
64. These analysts are mostly affiliated with the think tanks in the North American and European countries.
65. Many scholars have taken this view into consideration. See, Jason Wimberly, "Wilayat al-Faqih in Hezbollah's Web of Concepts: A Perspective on Ideology", *Middle Eastern Studies*, 51:5, 2015, pp. 687–710, DOI: 10.1080/00263206.2015.1012507
66. "Qassem: Hezbollah inspired by Wilayat al-Faqih", *The Daily Star*, 18 September 2014, at http://www.dailystar.com.lb/News/Lebanon-News/2014/Sep-18/271178-qassem-hezbollah-inspired-by-wilayat-al-faqih.ashx, retrieved 15 January 2017.
67. In 2015, a senior leader of Hezbollah said: "Because we have this entire vision, we must be present wherever we need to be—in Syria, to the extent necessary, in Iraq and Yemen, in multiple Arab arenas". See, Ali Hashemi, "Senior Hezbollah official speaks out", *Al-Monitor*, 22 May 2015, at http://www.al-monitor.com/pulse/originals/2015/05/hezbollah-ready-war-israel-syria-army-michel-aoun.html, retrieved 15 January 2017.
68. Mahan Abedin, "Dossier: The Supreme Council for the Islamic Revolution in

Iraq", *Middle East Intelligence Bulletin*, Vol.5, No.10, October 2003, at https://www.meforum.org/meib/articles/0310_iraqd.htm, retrieved 15 January 2017.

69. "Kata'ib Hezbollah", see Mapping Militant Organisations, Stanford University, updated 25 August 2016, at http://web.stanford.edu/group/mappingmilitants/cgi-bin/groups/view/361, retrieved 15 January, 2017.
70. Imamia Students Organisation Pakistan, at https://www.facebook.com/isopakistanofficial/, retrieved 15 January 2017.
71. Ibid.
72. He was Chairman of the Expediency Council in 1989.
73. Khomeini, *Sahifeh-ye Imam*, Vol. 21, p. 371.
74. Mehdi Khalaji, *Supreme Succession: Who will lead Post-Khamenei Iran?* Washington: The Washington Institute for Near East Policy, 2012, p. 8
75. Farzan Sabet, 'Why Iran's Assembly of Experts election is the real race to be watching', *The Washington Post*, 24 February 2016, at https://www.washingtonpost.com/news/monkey-cage/wp/2016/02/24/why-irans-assembly-of-experts-election-is-the-real-race-to-be-watching/, retrieved 15 January 2017.
76. Khalaji, op. cit., p. 17.
77. Mehdi Khalaji, *Supreme Succession: Who will lead Post-Khamenei Iran?* Washington: The Washington Institute for Near East Policy, 2012, p. 5.
78. Afshon Ostovar, *Vanguard of the Imam: Religion, Politics, and Iran's Revolutionary Guards*, New York: Oxford University Press, 2016, Google Play Book edition, p. 13.
79. This argument is based on the works of Fred Greenstein. See, Fred I. Greenstein, "The Impact of Personality on Politics: An Attempt to Clear Away Underbrush", *The American Political Science Review*, Vol. LXI, No. 3, September 1967. Also see, Fred I. Greenstein, "The Impact of Personality on the End of the Cold War: A Counterfactual Analysis", *Political Psychology*, Vol. 19, No.1, 1998
80. Mehdi Khalaji, *Supreme Succession*, p. 8.
81. "In Law", *The Office of the Supreme Leader, Grand Ayatollah Sayyid Ali Hosseini Khamenei*, 6 February 2010, at http://www.leader.ir/en/law, retrieved on 15 January 2017]. See also, The Constitution of Islamic Republic of Iran, Iran Chamber Society, at http://www.iranchamber.com/government/laws/constitution_ch08.php, retrieved 15 January 2017.
82. Mehdi Khalaji, *Supreme Succession*, op. cit., p. 8.
83. Hashemi Rafsanjani was an important figure in the Iranian political establishment. He was instrumental in suggesting Ali Khamenei's name as the successor of Khomeini in 1989. With his death on 8 January 2017, an important figure's say in the succession process has been lost. Many believed that he was involved in the process of finding suitable candidates to succeed the current Supreme Leader when the need would arise.
84. "*Goroohi Baraay-e Intikhaab-e Rahbari dar Soorat Peesamad Haadiseh Ta'een Shuda Ast* (Committee has been formed for the selection of the Supreme Leader in case of any incident)", Iranian Labour News Agency (ILNA). This news was also copied by many leading international dailies. See, "Rafsanjani breaks taboo over selection

of Iran's next supreme leader", *The Guardian*, 14 December 2015, at https://www.theguardian.com/world/2015/dec/14/rafsanjani-breaks-taboo-over-selection-of-irans-next-supreme-leader, retrieved 15 January 2017

85. Mehdi Khalaji, *Supreme Succession*, pp. 11–12
86. Behdad Bordbar, "Who will be Iran's next supreme leader?" *Al Monitor*, 25 July 2014, at http://www.al-monitor.com/pulse/en/originals/2014/07/iransupremeleaderalikhamenei.html, retrieved 15 January 2017.
87. "*A'lâm Marji'yat Ayatollah Hashemi Shahroudi* (Declaration of Marji'yat of Ayatollah Hashemi Shahroudi)", 29 Shahrivar, 1389 (20 September 2010), at http://www.fardanews.com/fa/news/121013/ retrieved 15 January 2017.

12

The Joint Comprehensive Plan of Action (JCPOA) and Its Aftermath

S. Samuel C. Rajiv[1]

ABSTRACT

This chapter examines developments pertaining to three key issues as they have evolved in the post JCPOA period. These include the status of the Iran-United States ties, issues relating to sanctions relief and Iran's economic situation, and the regional strategic situation. Due to the continuing prevalence of concerns pertaining to each other's regional behaviour and policy goals, there has not been much further thaw in US-Iran interactions. Neither have the monetary benefits of the deal been fully materialised on the ground; nor has the limited promise of the deal translating into regional geo-political goodwill been realised. The Joint Comprehensive Plan of Action (JCPOA) of 14 July 2015 was arrived at after tortuous negotiations between Iran and its P5+1 interlocutors—the UN Security Council (UNSC) permanent members and Germany. The JCPOA was achieved despite three and half decades of mutual hostility in US-Iran ties. Both the protagonists were able to hammer out a mutually acceptable agreement on a key issue of strategic concern after negotiations that stretched for nearly nine years (given that the P5+1 process began in 2006). Since then, however, both countries continue to be suspicious of each other. While Iran is in a much stronger position economically than it was prior to the negotiation of the JCPOA, the regional security deficit has widened, with Iran and the United States and its allies (ranging from Saudi Arabia to Israel) being at the opposite end of a worsening strategic divide.

Obstacles to Further Thaw in US-Iran Relations

Given that the USA and Iran have been having contentious relations since the 1979 Islamic Revolution, the JCPOA was indeed a path-breaking development. The Obama administration's "dual-track" policy of "applying pressure in pursuit of constructive engagement, and a negotiated solution" (stated by the then Secretary of State, Hillary Clinton, in June 2011) began to bear fruit only after the coming to power of President Hassan Rouhani in June 2013.[2] Having secured over 50 per cent of the popular vote in an election that witnessed over 70 per cent voter turnout, President Rouhani stressed that his administration of "prudence and hope" would strive to follow a "moderate" policy in pursuit of national objectives.[3] This was in contrast to the confrontationist approach-cum-rhetoric of the Ahmadinejad administration which vitiated rather than helped cool down tensions. It did not help that the George W. Bush administration viewed Tehran as part of the "axis of evil", along with North Korea and Libya. And, in the vocabulary of the Iranian government, the USA continued to be the "Great Satan", with the "Zionist Entity" (Israel) being the "Little Satan".

The UNSC-mandated P5+1 process to address Iranian nuclear concerns that began in mid-2006 (in the aftermath of the referral of the Iranian nuclear issue to the UNSC in February 2006) had an uneven trajectory. Contentious relations between the interlocutors harmed rather than helped the negotiations. While the most prominent contentions were between the US and Iran, Iran and the UK were also not on the same page during the negotiations phase. For instance, the Iranian Parliament downgraded relations with Britain in November 2011 in response to UK sanctions on the Central Bank of Iran (CBI). A Charge d' Affaires was representing Britain from then on (till September 2016) when a new Ambassador was appointed.

While the P5+1/EU-3+3 process was coordinated by the European Union—given that the EU-3 (France, Britain and Germany) initiated the dialogue process with Iran way back in 2003 prior to the UNSC referral)—there was not any doubt that a solution was possible only if the USA and Iran could come to a common understanding on how to resolve the long-standing concerns over the latter's nuclear programme. President Obama talked over the telephone with President Rouhani when he was in New York to attend the 2013 UNGA sessions. This represented the highest level of contact between the leaders of the two countries in over three decades.

Reports have since revealed that the Obama administration was also having secret, "back-channel" diplomacy with Iran since at least 2009, mediated by Oman. John Kerry was an active participant in these discussions, both as a Senator (and Chairman of the Senate Foreign Relations Committee) involved in securing the release of American hostages held by Iran as well as the US Secretary of State trying to forge a common understanding on the key details of a potential nuclear agreement.[4]

As the deal was being negotiated, Washington's allies (ranging from Riyadh to Tel Aviv) aired scepticism that the USA was possibly laying the foundation for eventually normalising relations with Tehran at their expense. On its part, the USA repeatedly insisted that the JCPOA was only about resolving the concerns generated by Iran's nuclear programme, and that it would continue to oppose what it considered to be Iran's destabilising actions throughout the region. Elements of Iranian foreign policy have long been deemed as being against US interests in the region. These included Iran's support to groups like the Hamas, Hezbollah, and the Islamic Jihad, all of which are characterised as "Foreign Terrorist Organisations" (FTO) by the US State Department. Iran's alleged negative human rights record has been another key arena of contention. Iran is also on the opposite end of the divide in regional hot spots like Yemen and Syria, with American allies like Saudi Arabia actively fighting Iranian "proxies" in these places.

Prior to the JCPOA, US officials like Secretary Kerry went to great lengths to convince America's regional allies that the USA was not pursuing any "grand bargain" with Iran in the nuclear negotiations. In a meeting with the Foreign Ministers of the Gulf Cooperation Council (GCC) in Riyadh in March 2015, a few months ahead of the deal, Kerry assured them that the US would not "take [its] eyes off Iran's other destabilising actions".[5] In a statement on 17 January 2016 (a day after JCPOA Implementation Day), President Obama insisted that there remain

> ...profound differences between the United States and Iran. We remain steadfast in opposing Iran's destabilising behaviour elsewhere, including its threats against Israel and our Gulf partners, and its support for violent proxies in places like Syria and Yemen. We still have sanctions on Iran for its violations of human rights, for its support of terrorism, and for its ballistic missile program. And we will continue to enforce these sanctions, vigorously.[6]

President Obama renewed the "State of Emergency" designation with respect to Iran on 19 March 2016, contending that, despite the JCPOA, "certain actions and policies of the Government of Iran continue to pose an unusual and extraordinary threat to the national security, foreign policy, and the economy of the United States".[7] The designation was first imposed by President Bill Clinton in March 1995. In the US State Department's

"Country Report on Terrorism 2015" (released in early June 2016), Iran continues to figure as one of the three "State sponsors of terrorism", along with Sudan and Syria.[8] The US accuses Iran of sponsoring and supporting terrorist activities in Lebanon, Syria, Iraq, and Bahrain. The US Director for National Intelligence, James Clapper, had earlier in February 2016, termed Iran as the "foremost state sponsor of terror".[9]

On its part, Iran did hold out the prospect of extending greater cooperation to tackle regional security issues, like the Islamic State (IS), if its interlocutors showed flexibility over the nuclear issue. This was most pertinently a few days ahead of the final deal, conveyed in a video message by Iranian Foreign Minister Javad Zarif. While Iran and the USA have been on the same page while dealing with the menace of the IS, there has been no overt efforts at cooperation. However, Iran has been invited to international conferences pertaining to hammering out a diplomatic solution to Syria in the aftermath of the deal—a courtesy not extended to it (much to its chagrin) prior to the JCPOA.

"Acting consistent with the respective roles of the President and the Congress", the Obama administration has pledged to "refrain from imposing new nuclear-related sanctions" as part of its commitments under the JCPOA. Iran has affirmed that such an imposition would constitute "grounds to cease performing its commitments under this JCPOA, in whole or in part".[10] However, the USA has identified two missile entities involved in Iran's ballistic missile tests conducted in the aftermath of JCPOA on 24 March 2016. It has warned foreign financial institutions (FFI"s) or individuals that do business with these entities with denial of access to the US financial system, and with the blocking of their property within US jurisdiction. Further, UAE and UK-based aviation companies providing services to Mahan Air were also designated on the same day. Mahan Air is alleged to have provided financial and technological support to the Islamic Revolutionary Guard Corp-Qods Force (IRGC-QF), which continues to remain under sanctions for its alleged support to terrorism-related activities.[11]

Meanwhile, in his first detailed response to the JCPOA in October 2015, Supreme Leader, Ayatollah Seyyed Ali Khamenei extended his "gratitude" to the negotiators, but cautioned Iranians to be sceptical of the "hostile" approach of the USA. He asserted that the imposition of new sanctions, even under the "fabricated pretexts of terrorism and human rights", would constitute violation of the JCPOA.[12] On 15 June 2016, Khamenei termed the talk of the possibility of the USA and Iran mending ties as "incorrect and delusional". He argued that "compromising" with America would require

Iran to step back from its "positions and principles", and added that

> There is no end to [their demand for] such retreat. As [you saw] after the nuclear issue, they have brought up the issue of missiles. After missiles, it will be the human rights" turn. After human rights, they will raise the issue of [top oversight body] Guardian Council, then the issue of *Velayat-e-Faqih* (guardianship of jurisconsult) and finally the Constitution and the sovereignty of Islam. Therefore, such imagination that the Islamic Republic can compromise with the Americans is a wrong one.[13]

Speaking to student leaders in July 2016, Ayatollah Khamenei insisted that Iran would negotiate with the USA only for "special and specified cases", and rejected the possibility of renewed ties with the USA.[14] Addressing a national gathering of the commanders of the Iranian Revolutionary Guard Corps (IRGC) on 18 September 2016, Khamenei reminded his audience of "America's hostility through the long years after the revolution and in recent issues related to the nuclear negotiations and [also] with regard to other issues".[15] The unwavering anti-US stance of the Supreme Leader, therefore, continues to condition the framework within which President Rouhani or his Foreign Minister Zarif will have to operate.

In addition to the harsh rhetoric from Iran, coupled with US actions like sanctioning of entities linked to Iranian ballistic missile tests, the naval forces of both countries were involved in acts of brinkmanship in the waters of the Persian Gulf. The US Navy (USN) accused Iranian naval vessels of indulging in "unsafe and unprofessional" manoeuvres near the vessels of the Fifth Fleet transiting the Gulf in August 2016.[16] In an embarrassing incident to the USN, ten of its personnel belonging to the Fifth Fleet operating out of Manama, Bahrain, and two of its riverine command boats were captured by the IRGC Navy on 12 January 2016 for trespassing into Iranian waters near Farsi Island. This threatened to become a major diplomatic incident as it happened a few hours ahead of President Obama's final State of the Union address.

However, the sailors and the boats were released within 24 hours of their capture, consequent upon urgent and high-level interventions from Secretary Kerry and Foreign Minister Zarif. The USN subsequently issued "Letters of Reprimand" to most of the officers and sailors involved in the incident, with reports terming the gesture as a "potentially career-ending move".[17] On the other hand, Supreme Leader Khamenei gave out-of-turn promotions and military rewards to the IRGC commanders whose units captured the American sailors.[18]

Positive developments in their bilateral ties in the aftermath of the

JCPOA included the USA agreeing to pay Iran US$ 1.7 billion (US$ 400 million of Shah-era money paid to the USA for an arms deal which was lying in an Iran FMS [Foreign Military Sales] Trust Fund, plus US$ 1.3 billion of interest accrued on the Fund).[19] The money was paid in January and February 2016. When the first instalment was delivered on January 16, it coincided with the release of four American hostages held by Iran. This generated criticism from the Republicans who said that it was a quid pro quo—a charge that was denied by the Obama administration.

Another concrete development was the agreement reached between Iran and the USA regarding the sale of Boeing and Airbus passenger jets. The US Treasury department gave its approval for the sale of 80 Boeing jets (50 737 and 30 777 jets), and 17 Airbus jets in September 2016. Reports noted that US approval was required even for the sale of Airbus planes as they used US-manufactured electronic components. Iran concluded the deals for the planes with Boeing and Airbus in January 2016. Iran is contracted to buy a further 101 Airbus planes in addition to the 17 for which approvals were given by the US Treasury Department.

Reports noted that while the financing for fifteen 777-300 ER jets (to be delivered in 2018) was finalised, the financing for the other jets was yet to be negotiated.[20] Some American analysts noted that Iran would find it difficult to finance the purchase of the planes.[21] This assumes significance in the light of the continuing efforts in the US Congress to prevent the US Exim Bank from financing the purchase of American planes. For instance, the "No US Financing for Iran Act" was passed in the House of Representatives (243–174) on 17 November 2016, and was subsequently referred to the Senate Committee on Banking, Housing, and Urban Affairs. On its part, the White House insisted that such measures "would have a chilling effect on US and non-US entities seeking to engage in permissible business with Iran".[22]

Meanwhile, in a meeting with a German delegation on 6 October 2016, senior Iranian officials, like the Governor of the CBI Dr. Valiollah Seif, charged that the US was privileging its own business interests at the expense of those of its European allies, in allowing the sale of 80 Boeing jets as against only 17 Airbus planes. He was also cited as blaming "American sabotage as one of the main obstacles on the way to normalise banking relationships between European countries and Iran".[23]

Iran: Economic Context, Sanctions Relief

When President Rouhani took over in June 2013, the GDP growth rate was a negative 6.8 per cent. In the first quarter of 2016, the Iranian economy registered a growth rate of 4.4 per cent.[24] The government is aiming for a GDP rate of 5 per cent in 2016–17. Inflation, which stood at a high of 40.4 per cent in October 2013, reduced to 15.6 per cent in March 2015.[25] Inflation was at about 12 per cent in May 2016.[26] By August 2016, it was in single digits. Iran received 22 foreign direct investment (FDI) projects in the first quarter of 2016, as against 17 during the previous two years, signifying an upturn in its economic prospects.[27] While speaking at the administrative council session of one of Iran's provinces on 15 August 2016, President Rouhani revealed that, "after JCPOA, US$ 5 billion investment has been made and this figure is mounting ..."[28]

In June 2016, Iran's oil exports stood at 1.72 million barrels per day (bpd)—the highest figure in nearly 5 years.[29] In remarks at the sidelines of a conference in Tehran (17 October 2016), Iran's Oil Minister, Bijan Zanganeh, stated that the country's oil production "almost neared the [pre-sanctions] level" of 4 million bpd.[30] Meanwhile, the Organisation of Petroleum Exporting Countries (OPEC)—which decided to cut their collective output by 1.2 million bpd by January 2017 for a six-month period in an effort to shore up falling oil prices—gave an exemption to Iran, and allowed it to raise its output to 3.8 million bpd by January 2017.[31] By 2020, Iran plans to expand its output to 5.7 million bpd, and is in need of investments to achieve this target.

New oil production contracts, termed Iran Petroleum Contracts (IPC) and approved by the government in August 2016, are being seen as a panacea for Iran's oil industry. Though specific details of the terms of the new contracts have not been revealed, reports have noted that the IPC will allow foreign firms "much longer cost recovery after first production", thus allowing them to recoup their investments over a period as long as 20 years.[32] The earlier "buy-back" contracts were of much shorter duration (about five years), and only allowed foreign firms to "buy-back" a percentage of the hydro-carbons produced in lieu of their investments.

The "buy-back" agreements were also neutral with respect to the volume of production of a particular field. They offered no incentives for firms to exceed output targets.[33] Under the IPC, the contracted firms could look forward to greater rewards if production in the field it was developing increased due to technological competence it brought to bear on the project or because the firm had correctly assessed the amount of oil that a particular field possessed.[34]

Iran inked the first IPC with a domestic firm—the Persia Oil and Gas Industry Development Company (POGIDC)—to develop the Yaran, Koupal, and Maroon fields in early October 2016, with investments estimated to be worth US$ 2.2 billion. Reports have noted that Iran would use domestic companies like the POGIDC—one of eight such firms approved for exploration and production (E and P) activities by the Ministry of Petroleum—to develop small and medium-sized fields.[35] Foreign firms would also have to necessarily tie up with one of these eight firms to pursue their activities in Iran.

One of the first contracts with a foreign oil firm in the aftermath of the JCPOA was with the Royal Dutch Shell (RDS) on 9 October 2016, when a Letter of Intent was signed with the National Petrochemical Company (NPC). A "Preliminary Heads of Agreement" was signed with Total (also involving the China National Petroleum Corporation and Petropars) to develop the South Pars gas field on 10 November 2016. Iran would no doubt like to expedite foreign investments to develop its 52 hydro carbon fields—29 oil (on shore 21; off shore 8) and 23 gas (18 on shore and 8 off shore fields), along with 18 exploration blocks.[36]

Table 1: Value of Exports (USD Million)

	2010–11	*2011–12*	*2012–13*	*2013–14*	*2014–15*
Total Export of Goods	112,788	145,806	97,271	93,125	86,471
Oil Exports	90,191	119,148	68,058	64,882	55,352
Non-oil Exports	22,596	26,658	29,213	28,243	31,119
Oil Exports as Percentage of Total Exports	79.96	81.71	69.96	69.67	64.01

Source: Central Bank of Iran, "Annual Report 2014-15", p. 24 and p. 74, at file:///C:/Users/idsa211/Downloads/Annual%20Rewiew%201393.pdf, accessed 15 October 2016.

Table 2: Iran's Oil Exports (thousand bpd)

	2011–12	*2012–13*	*2013–14*	*2014–15*
Crude Oil Exports	2,033	1,803	1,606	1,343
Percentage Change from Preceding Year	0.59	–11.31	–10.92	–16.37

Source: Central Bank of Iran, "Annual Report 2014–15", p. 53, at file:///C:/Users/idsa211/Downloads/Annual%20Rewiew%201393.pdf, accessed 15 October 2016.

US Secretary of State, John Kerry, told a Jewish advocacy group on 19 April 2016 that Iran has only received about US$ 3 billion in restricted funds (RF's) since the JCPOA began to be implemented.[37] Iran received US$ 11.9 billion of oil money owed by its key importers during the Joint Plan of Action (JPOA) Relief Period from January 2014–June 2015 (US$ 700 million every month from February 2014). US officials estimated that the total value of sanctions relief would amount to about US$ 15 billion during the JPOA Relief Period.[38] Iran regained access to its hard currency reserves of about US$ 115 billion held in foreign banks from January 2016 —especially after getting reconnected to SWIFT. However, analysts have noted that more than half of this amount was owed to creditors, such as China (nearly US$ 20 billion for about 60 projects it was executing inside Iran), or to repay non-performing loans extended to Iranian energy companies.[39]

In the aftermath of the JCPOA, Iran wanted greater American effort to ease restrictions on non-American banks that do business with it. The November 2008 ban on "U-turn" transactions, involving non-Iranian foreign banks that do transactions on behalf of Iranian banks in USD—which is still in effect and not covered by JCPOA sanctions relief—is reportedly hindering European-based banks from doing business with Iran.[40] After talks with officials of the Iranian Finance Ministry, the US Treasury Department issued revised guidelines (6 October 2016) to the effect that

> Foreign financial institutions, including foreign-incorporated subsidiaries of US financial institutions, may process transactions denominated in US dollars or maintain US dollar-denominated accounts that involve Iran or persons ordinarily resident in Iran ... provided that such transactions or account activities do not involve, directly or indirectly, the United States financial system or any United States person.[41]

Although the Governor of the Central Bank of Iran, Valiollah Seif, maintained that there was nothing new in the revised guidelines, he was cited as stating that they did remove "past ambiguities".[42] However, in a meeting with a German delegation on 9 October 2016, Governor Seif expressed consternation at the continued non-provision of correspondent banking facilities to Iranian banks. He noted that, despite "nearly 9 months of the implementation of JCPOA, the Western side has taken no effective step in fulfilling its commitments and, in some cases, major Western banks are hesitant about correspondent relations with Iran".[43] However, US Treasury Department regulations explicitly state that US would not impose secondary sanctions on FFIs for maintaining correspondent banking relations with Iranian financial institutions that have been removed from the Specially Designated Nationals (SDN) list.[44]

However, as noted earlier, transactions denominated in USD cannot enter the US financial system or be handled by US persons. However, over 200 individuals and entities are still on the SDN list (primarily for terrorism-related designations), even though over 400 were removed on JCPOA Implementation Day. Further, since November 2011, Iran continues to be designated as a "jurisdiction of primary money laundering concern" by the US Treasury Department—the only country other than Myanmar (since 2004) to be slapped with such a designation which requires US financial institutions to exercise caution while dealing with financial institutions in these countries.[45] These restrictions which are not covered by JCPOA sanctions relief could be some of the causes of the continuing "hesitation" flagged by the CBI Governor on the part of Western banks in doing business with Iran.

In a letter to President Rouhani in the aftermath of JCPOA Implementation Day, Ali Khamenei reminded him that the lifting of sanctions would not by itself help bring about an improvement in the country's economic situation. He called for "relentless and wise efforts in all sectors with a view to [strengthen] the Economy of Resistance ..."[46] According to the Supreme Leader, significant elements of such an economy included small-scale and medium-scale industries, consumption largely based only on domestic production, emphasis on knowledge-based industries, among other aspects.

Ayatollah Khamenei accused the USA of undermining the JCPOA, and preventing Iran's economic relations with other countries. In early August 2016, he charged that "six months have passed since the signing of the JCPOA, [but] no evident and tangible effect has been seen with regard to the livelihood state of [the Iranian] people".[47] Commenting on the plethora of foreign business delegations visiting Iran in the aftermath of the JCPOA, Ayatollah Khamenei wryly noted,

> [What is the use of] foreign business people [merely] coming and going without doing anything of substance ... it has been about a year that [they] continuously come and go, [and] have done nothing. [Even] if they want to do something, it is to conquer the Iranian market, which is exactly to our detriment. The benefit of exchange of these delegations must be investment, must be new production, must be [transfer] of new technology in those places where we need new technology...[48]

The Regional Strategic Situation: Security Deficit Widens

The post-JCPOA period has been marked by the increasing rift between the two regional power houses, Saudi Arabia and Iran, which has been compounded by harsh rhetoric. Both the countries are at logger heads in the region's devastating hot-spots: Syria and Yemen. In the aftermath of the bloody air strikes conducted by Saudi-led coalition jets on a funeral ceremony in the Yemeni capital Sanaa that resulted in the death of over

150 people, Iranian naval commander Adm. Habibollah Sayari charged (16 October 2016) "inhuman Saudi Arabia" of using "most modern western and eastern weapons" against the "defenceless people in Yemen".[49]

In a very critical Op-Ed in the *New York Times* earlier (13 September 2016), Foreign Minister Zarif called for the world to be rid of Wahhabism, terming it as "fanaticism from the Dark Ages sold as a bright vision for the 21st century".[50] The new Iranian Ambassador to the UK insisted that there would be "no clear prospect for security cooperation in the region so long as Saudis do not recognise Iran's role".[51] The September 2015 stampede in Mina, which according to Tehran, led to the death of nearly 500 Iranians, has further added to the combustible mix. In a series of hard-hitting speeches since then, Iranian leaders ranging from President Rouhani to Supreme Leader Khamenei have accused Saudi Arabia of incompetence, and of failing to apologise for the incident while downplaying the number of casualties.

Prior to the JCPOA, Riyadh (like Tel Aviv) contended that the nuclear deal would embolden Tehran to their strategic detriment. As noted earlier, Secretary Kerry had to assure the GCC allies at a meeting in Riyadh (March 2015) that the US would continue to oppose Iran's regional policies. In the US-GCC Camp David Joint Statement of 14 May 2015, both sides pledged to "work together to counter Iran's destabilising activities in the region ...", and agreed on an elaborate set of measures to strengthen their strategic partnership.[52]

In his first visit to the US after the JCPOA in September 2015, King Salman extended support to the agreement, "which once fully implemented, will prevent Iran from obtaining a nuclear weapon ..."[53] Saudi analysts have since then been particularly upset with the September 2016 Justice Against Sponsors of Terrorism Act (JASTA), which allows for civil claims against foreign governments for death inside the USA as a result of act of international terrorism. They affirm that this is an instance of the USA "sanctioning Saudi Arabia" (despite Riyadh throwing out Osama bin Laden five years prior to 9/11), while the JCPOA was held as an example of Washington "rewarding Iran".[54]

The worsening conflicts in Yemen and Syria have cast their long shadow on the JCPOA. Reacting to Secretary Kerry's comments to *Foreign Affairs* magazine that Iran's policies on Syria and Yemen were complicating efforts to implement the JCPOA, Deputy Foreign Minister Abbas Araqchi insisted (5 October 2016) that "regional issues have no business with the nuclear deal, and Iran can't accept (the West's) regional excuses as an obstacle for deal implementation".[55] In comments on 14 August 2016, President Rouhani charged that the "Zionists and a handful of childish neighbours [were] unhappy about [the] brave Iranian diplomats" historic victory and lift[ing] of sanctions", and were therefore obstructing the JCPOA.[56] Earlier, on 3 August 2016, President Rouhani had accused the USA of not using "the cooperation opportunity [provided by the JCPOA] in other fields", while not elucidating on the possible fields of cooperation.[57]

Israel, which was in the forefront of efforts to militarily set back the Iranian nuclear programme, has continued to remain sceptical of the efficacy of the JCPOA to address its concerns vis-à-vis Iran. Israel accuses Iran, specifically the IRGC-QF, of supporting militant organisations like the Palestinian Islamic Jihad.[58] Iran's continuing ballistic missile tests have also irked Israel, given Israel's long-expressed concerns about the growth of Iranian ballistic missile capability. Instances like, an Iranian missile test-fired in March 2016—reportedly having a message threatening Israel's destruction scribbled across it in Hebrew—only adds to Israel's perceived or real angst.[59]

The USA has, meanwhile, continued to meet the security concerns of its allies and strengthen them militarily. For instance, the USA and Israel have concluded negotiations to extend their bilateral defence cooperation agreement (set to expire in 2018) for another ten years. The USA will provide Israel US$ 3.8 billion annually for a period of 10 years, till 2028. The Obama administration has, so far, provided to Israel more than US$ 26 billion (out of the pledged US$ 30 billion for the current phase of the agreement from 2009–2018) as part of foreign military financing (FMF) as well as support to the missile defence programmes, like the Iron Dome.[60] Israel expects to continue to maintain its qualitative military edge (QME) against its regional rivals, primarily Iran, as a result of the updated agreement.

The GCC have been equally significant recipients of US military largesse in the aftermath of the JCPOA. For instance, the Obama administration has concluded arms deals worth US$ 20.5 billion with Saudi Arabia alone in the post-JCPOA period.[61] These agreements cover a wide range of cutting-edge equipment from ammunition to Patriot Advanced Capability-3 (PAC-3) missiles to surface combatant ships to main battle tanks. As against the US$ 26 billion provided to Israel by the Obama administration, it concluded arms sales agreements worth US$ 58 billion with Riyadh since 2009.[62]

Going Forward

While the JCPOA is being implemented since January 2016, Iran's ballistic missile tests (in October 2015 and March 2016) have injected a dose of brinkmanship into the matrix. The USA, along with the UK, France, and Germany called the missile tests "inconsistent" with the JCPOA (letter to the UNSC in end March 2016). It is pertinent to note the two missing names in the list above—Russia and China, the other two of Iran's P5+1 interlocutors. Russian officials were cited as stating that these tests did not violate Resolution 2231, and that no evidence has been provided to support the contention that the missiles tested could carry nuclear warheads.[63]

In a statement released on the day the JCPOA was negotiated, Iran's P5+1 interlocutors stated the following as regards the activities relating to ballistic missiles:

> Iran is called upon not to undertake any activity related to ballistic missiles designed to be capable of delivering nuclear weapons, including launches using such ballistic missile technology, until the date eight years after the JCPOA Adoption Day or until the date on which the IAEA submits a report confirming the Broader Conclusion, whichever is earlier.[64]

Analysts have, therefore, pointed out that Iran is not explicitly banned from undertaking any ballistic missile activities. The Iranian Foreign Ministry insists that the country's ballistic missile programme was "totally for peaceful purposes", and that Iran had a "legitimate and legal right to boost its defensive capabilities and [safeguard] national security".[65]

Meanwhile, Iran's European interlocutors, as indeed China, have sought to garner the "first-mover advantage" in doing business with Iran in the aftermath of the deal. Of note here is President Xi Jinping's January 2016 visit to Egypt, Saudi Arabia, and Iran, thus becoming the first ever Head of State to visit Tehran, post the JCPOA (President Putin did visit Tehran in November 2015, but it was to attend a regional conference of gas exporting countries). India-Iran relations, on their part, have acquired a momentum in the aftermath of the visit of Prime Minister Narendra Modi in May 2016. Supreme Leader Khamenei, in a meeting with Prime Minister Modi, affirmed that Iran "welcomes expansion of relations with India, which is one of the emerging and progressive economies in the world, and (Iran) is fully serious in implementing bilateral agreements and is not influenced by any policy".[66]

While the Iranian economy is definitely doing better in the aftermath of the JCPOA than it was prior to it, the monetary benefits of the deal have still not trickled down to Tehran. Iran has urged the USA to ease restrictions on banking channels to allow the free flow of RFs. Iran also has 9.3 per cent of the world's proven oil reserves, though it is badly in need of investments to not only increase production but also develop new fields. Some reports note that Iran would need US$ 130 billion to meet its goal of raising oil production capacity to 5.7 million bpd by end 2020.[67]

Meanwhile, Republican voices in the US Congress are continuing their efforts to make Iran further accountable for what they believe to be its negative actions relating to terrorism as well as support to regimes in Syria and Yemen. Further, while the Iran Sanctions Act (ISA)—which was set to expire in December 2016—was extended unanimously on 1 December 2016, measures to prevent Iran from securing US Exim Bank financing for the purchase of Boeing planes, as noted earlier, are still being pursued.

President Donald Trump campaigned vigorously against the JCPOA, which was widely seen as one of President Obama's signature foreign policy achievements—apart from establishing full diplomatic relations with Cuba. At an American Israel Public Affairs Committee (AIPAC) event in March 2016, President Trump insisted that his "number one priority is to dismantle the disastrous deal with Iran".[68] Trump's National Security Advisor-designate, Michael Flynn as well as CIA Director-designate Mike Pompeo have also expressed opposition to the JCPOA. However, in a speech at the CSIS on 22 April 2016, his Defence Secretary-designate General James Mattis, while noting that the JCPOA was an "imperfect arms control agreement" admitted that the agreement was "not completely without some merit".[69]

President Trump though increased pressure on Iran regarding its ballistic missile activities and alleged support for terrorism—both issues outside the purview of the JCPOA. The administration imposed sanctions on 25 individuals and companies connected to the IRGC-QF and the missile programme in early February 2017 in the immediate aftermath of a 1000 km range ballistic missile launch by Iran on 29 January—the first missile tested after Trump took over. An inter-agency review of the JCPOA was also launched by the administration in mid-April, despite acknowledging that Iran was complying with the terms of the deal. Analysts note that if the Trump administration/US Congress enacts measures targeting the IRGC more specifically, it will add enormously to the domestic political pressures of the Rouhani government. President Rouhani's own prospects meanwhile in the general elections in May 2017 could be hurt if the perception grows that the benefits of the nuclear deal have not yet been fully realised. The UNSC-recognised JCPOA (and approved by the US Congress and the Majlis) would, therefore, need to continue to weather opposition from domestic political constituencies in both Iran and the USA as well as from regional rivals wary of an increase in Iran's regional standing on account of its effective implementation.

NOTES

1. I am grateful to the inputs and guidance provided by Ambassador Sanjay Singh and Dr. G. Balachandran.
2. See, US State Department, 'Joint Statement on Iran Sanctions', 23 June 2011, at http://www.state.gov/r/pa/prs/ps/2011/06/166814.htm, accessed 23 January 2012.
3. See, "Rouhani pledges 'constructive interaction' with world via moderate policy", *Press TV*, 17 June 2013, at http://www.presstv.com/detail/2013/06/17/309475/rohani-vows-constructive-interaction/, accessed 24 July 2013.
4. Ignatius, David, "The Omani 'back channel' to Iran and the secrecy surrounding the nuclear deal", *Washington Post*, 7 June 2016, at https://www.washingtonpost.com/opinions/the-omani-back-channel-to-iran-and-the-secrecy-surrounding-the-nuclear-deal/2016/06/07/0b9e27d4-2ce1-11e6-b5db-e9bc84a2c8e4_story.html?utm_term=.72907efa5e21, accessed 12 October 2016.
5. "Kerry promises Arab allies: No grand bargain with Iran", *AP*, 6 March 2015, at http://www.dailystar.com.lb/News/Middle-East/2015/Mar-06/289824-kerry-promises-arab-allies-no-grand-bargain-with-iran.ashx, accessed 12 October 2016.
6. The White House, "Statement by the President on Iran", 17 January 2016, at https://www.whitehouse.gov/the-press-office/2016/01/17/statement-president-iran, accessed 12 October 2016.
7. The White House, "Notice: Continuation of the National Emergency with Respect to Iran", 9 March 2016, at https://www.whitehouse.gov/the-pressoffice/2016/03/09/notice-and-letter-continuation-national-emergencyrespect-iran, accessed 24 March 2016.
8. The report is available at https://www.state.gov/documents/organization/258249.pdf, accessed 13 October 2016.
9. Clapper, James, "Statement for the Record: Worldwide Threat Assessment of the US Intelligence Community", Senate Armed Services Committee, 9 February 2016, p. 5, at https://www.dni.gov/files/documents/SASC_Unclassified_2016_ATA_SFR_FINAL.pdf, accessed 15 October 2016.
10. See, "S/2015/544, Annex A", S/RES/2231, UNSC Resolution 2231 (2015), 10 July 2015, p. 17, at http://www.un.org/en/sc/inc/pages/pdf/pow/RES2231E.pdf, accessed 25 July 2015.
11. US Treasury Department, "Treasury Sanctions Supporters of Iran's Ballistic Missile Program and Terrorism-Designated Mahan Air", 24 March 2016, at https://www.treasury.gov/press-center/press-releases/Pages/jl0395.aspx, accessed 19 June 2016.
12. The Office of the Supreme Leader, See, "Ayatollah Khamenei sends a letter to President Hassan Rouhani about the JCPOA", 21 October 2015, at http://www.leader.ir/langs/en/index.php?p=contentShow&id=13791, accessed 25 October 2015.
13. The Office of the Supreme Leader, "Ayatollah Khamenei: If they tear up JCPOA, we will torch it", 15 June 2016, at http://www.leader.ir/en/content/15523/Ayatollah-Khamenei-meets-with-high-ranking-Iranian-officials,-warns-about-the-US-%E2%80%98tearing-up%E2%80%99-the-JCPOA, accessed 13 October 2016.
14. The Office of the Supreme Leader, "Ayatollah Khamenei: JCPOA showed US

enmity toward Iran", 3 July 2016, at http://www.leader.ir/en/content/15936/Ayatollah-Khamenei-meets-hundreds-of-students,-rapping-the-US-over-its-obligations-under-JCPOA, accessed 13 October 2016.

15. The Office of the Supreme Leader, "Distrust in America, important component of Iran's soft power", 18 September 2016, at http://www.leader.ir/en/content/16228/The-leader-meets-with-commanders-and-officials-of-the-Islamic-Revolution-Guards-Corps, accessed 13 October 2016.
16. Ryan, Missy and Thomas Gibbons-Neff, "Navy patrol ship fires warning shots amid series of confrontations with Iranian vessels", *Washington Post*, 25 August 2016, at https://www.washingtonpost.com/news/checkpoint/wp/2016/08/25/u-s-navy-calls-high-speed-approach-by-iranian-ships-dangerous-harassment/, accessed 16 October 2016.
17. Larter, David, "Four more US sailors disciplined in Iran boat seizure incident", *Navy Times*, 9 August 2016, at https://www.navytimes.com/story/military/2016/08/09/riverines-farsi-island-punishments-continue-iran-debacle/88493396/, accessed 17 October 2016.
18. "Leader confers badge of honour on IRGC Navy command for capturing US marines", *IRNA*, 31 January 2016, at http://www8.irna.ir/en/News/81943103/ accessed 17 October 2016.
19. Solomon, Jay and Carol E. Lee, "US Sent Cash to Iran as Americans Were Freed", *Wall Street Journal*, 3 August 2016, at http://www.wsj.com/articles/u-s-sent-cash-to-iran-as-americans-were-freed-1470181874, accessed 15 October 2016; See also, Katzman, Kenneth, "Iran sanctions", Congressional Research Service, 14 December 2016, pp. 1-2, at https://fas.org/sgp/crs/mideast/RS20871.pdf, accessed 1 January 2017.
20. "Iran seals $17 billion Boeing deal, Close to Airbus Order", *CNBC*, 11 December 2016, at http://www.cnbc.com/2016/12/11/iran-seals-17-billion-boeing-deal-close-to-airbus-order.html, accessed December 13, 2016.
21. Cited in "Iran reaches deal to buy 100 new Boeing planes", *Al Jazeera*, 20 June 2016, at http://www.aljazeera.com/news/2016/06/iran-100-boeing-planes-160619082804894.html, accessed 15 October 2016.
22. "US House votes to stop sales of Boeing jetliners to Iran", *Bloomberg*, 17 November 2016, at https://www.bloomberg.com/politics/articles/2016-11-17/u-s-house-votes-to-stop-sales-of-boeing-jetliners-to-iran, accessed 13 December 2016.
23. Central Bank of Iran, "Normalization of Iran–Europe banking relations", 9 October 2016, at http://www.cbi.ir/showitem/15268.aspx, accessed 15 October 2016.
24. "Iran enjoys 4.4 per cent economic growth in 1st quarter", *Mehr News*, 15 August 2016, at http://en.mehrnews.com/news/118927/Iran-enjoys-4-4-economic-growth-in-1st-quarter, accessed 2 October 2016.
25. Central Bank of Iran, "Annual Review 2014-15", p. 2, at file:///C:/Users/idsa211/Downloads/Annual%20Rewiew%201393.pdf, accessed 15 October 2016.
26. Central Bank of Iran, "IMF assists Iran to reintegrate with the global financial system, admirable economic management in Iran", 16 May 2016, at http://www.cbi.ir/showitem/14698.aspx, accessed 17 October 2016.
27. Lyttle, Cara, "FDI in Iran soars with sanctions relief", 20 June 2016, at http://www.ft.com/cms/s/3/549d0dac-36d6-11e6-9a05-82a9b15a8ee7.html#axzz4CEnhkW6u, accessed 20 June 2016.
28. Rouhani, Hassan, "Building up trust, hope a national duty", 15 August 2016, at

http://president.ir/en/94744, accessed 5 October 2016. However, President Rouhani did not give details of which sectors these investments were pledged or the source of the investments.

29. "Iran's oil exports to Asia hits 1.7mn bpd", *Mehr News*, 10 August 2016, at http://en.mehrnews.com/news/118797/Iran-s-oil-exports-to-Asia-hits-1-7mn-bpd, accessed 15 August 2016.
30. SHANA (Petro Energy Information Network), "Zanganeh: Secondary Sources Put Iran Crude Output at 4mbd", 17 October 2016, at http://www.shana.ir/en/newsagency/271098/Zanganeh-Secondary-Sources-Put-Iran-Crude-Output-at-4mbd, accessed 15 October 2016.
31. "OPEC confounds sceptics, agrees to first oil cuts in 8 years", *Bloomberg*, 30 November 2016, at https://www.bloomberg.com/news/articles/2016-11-30/opec-said-to-agree-oil-production-cuts-as-saudis-soften-on-iran, accessed 13 December 2016.
32. Gulf Intelligence, "Buyback Vs. New Iran Petroleum Contract: A Winning Model"? 17 January 2016, at http://www.thegulfintelligence.com/Docs.Viewer/bb9597f1-191e-4d75-8060-5319427d2fb9/default.aspx, accessed 16 October 2016.
33. See, National Iranian Oil Company, "IPC woos international firms", 29 November 2015, at http://ipc.nioc.ir/Portal/Home/ShowPage.aspx?Object=NEWS&ID=0c2d3620-9063-4aa8-9cd3-1914c4a88e2a&LayoutID=218a9172-c49d-4564-8819-20b14267c753&CategoryID=4d72e300-3ba4-4c7f-92af-0c6c00a4d3f8, accessed 13 December 2016.
34. SHANA, "NIOC to Consider Several Firms for Field Study", 8 October 2016, at http://www.shana.ir/en/newsagency/270674/NIOC-to-Consider-Several-Firms-for-Field-Study, accessed 16 October 2016.
35. SHANA, "MPs Positive with Contracts Just Concluded", 16 October 2016, at http://www.shana.ir/en/newsagency/270981/MPs-Positive-with-Contracts-Just-Concluded, accessed 16 October 2016.
36. See "NIOC Projects", at http://www.nioc.ir/portal/home/?generaltext/165305/165402/165360/Projects, accessed 13 December 2016.
37. "Iran has seen only US$ 3 bn returned since nuke deal: Kerry", *AFP*, 19 April 2016, at https://www.yahoo.com/news/iran-seen-only-3-bn-returned-sincenuke-023958350.html, accessed 20 April 2016.
38. Blinken, Anthony, "Perspectives on the Strategic Necessity of Iran Sanctions", Statement Before the Senate Committee on Banking, Housing, and Urban Affairs, 27 January 2015, at http://www.state.gov/s/d/2015/236784.htm, accessed 9 April 2015.
39. Katzman, *Iran Sanctions*, op. cit. n. 19, p. 56.
40. Katzman, *Iran Sanctions*, op. cit. n. 19, pp. 27–28.
41. See, US Treasury Department, "Frequently Asked Questions Relating to the Lifting of Certain US Sanctions under the Joint Comprehensive Plan of Action (JCPOA) on Implementation Day", 7 October 2016, pp. 14–15, at https://www.treasury.gov/resource-center/sanctions/Programs/Documents/jcpoa_faqs.pdf, accessed 17 October 2016.
42. "US action to ease prohibited dollar transactions with Iran not new: CBI", *IRNA*, 18 October 2016, at http://www.irna.ir/en/News/82271279/, accessed 17 October 2016.
43. CBI, "Normalization of Iran-Europe banking relations", op. cit. n. 23.

44. "Frequently Asked Questions Relating to the Lifting of Certain US Sanctions Under the Joint Comprehensive Plan of Action (JCPOA) on Implementation Day", n. 41, p. 13 and pp. 17–18.
45. President Obama though revoked the "National Emergency with respect to Myanmar", on 7 October 2016, removing most of the sanctions imposed on Burma since 1997.
46. The Office of the Supreme Leader, "The Leader thanks President Rouhani, his administration on successful nuclear talks", 19 January 2016, at http://www.leader.ir/en/content/14050/Ayatollah-Khamenei-responds-to-President-Rouhani%E2%80%99s-letter-about-the-JCPOA, accessed 13 October 2016.
47. The Office of the Supreme Leader, "The Leader's Remarks in Meeting with People from Various Walks of Life", 2 August 2016, at http://www.leader.ir/en/speech/16093/The-Leader%E2%80%99s-Remarks-in-Meeting-with-People-from-Various-Walks-of-Life, accessed 13 October 2016.
48. Ibid.
49. "Commander: Iran's navy equipped with most sophisticated weapons", *IRNA*, 19 November 2015, at http://www8.irna.ir/en/News/81845577/, accessed 17 October 2016.
50. Javad Zarif, Mohammad, "Let Us Rid the World of Wahhabism", *New York Times*, 13 September 2016, at http://www.nytimes.com/2016/09/14/opinion/mohammad-javad-zarif-let-us-rid-the-world-of-wahhabism.html?_r=0, accessed 15 September 2016.
51. "No prospect for Saudi cooperation sans accepting Iran's role", *Mehr News*, 19 October 2016, at http://en.mehrnews.com/news/120643/No-prospect-for-Saudi-coop-sans-accepting-Iran-s-role, accessed 18 October 2016.
52. The White House, "US-Gulf Cooperation Council Camp David Joint Statement", 14 May 2015, at https://www.whitehouse.gov/the-press-office/2015/05/14/us-gulf-cooperation-council-camp-david-joint-statement, accessed 16 October 2016.
53. "King Salman supports Iran nuclear deal", *Arab News*, 6 September 2015, at http://www.arabnews.com/saudi-arabia/news/802281, accessed 16 October 2016.
54. Al-Rashed, Abdulrahman, "Rewarding Iran, Sanctioning Saudi Arabia", *Arab News*, 1 October 2016, at http://www.arabnews.com/node/992106/columns, accessed 17 October 2016.
55. "US jeopardizing nuclear deal, says Tehran", *IRNA*, 18 October 2016, at http://www.irna.ir/en/News/82270601/, accessed 5 October 2016.
56. Rouhani, Hassan, "Economic growth reached 4.4 per cent in the first three months of the current year", 14 August 2016, at http://president.ir/en/94701, accessed 5 October 2016.
57. Rouhani, Hassan, "1394 [2015]: a hard economic year due to plunge in oil prices", 3 August 2016, at http://president.ir/en/94516, accessed 5 October 2016.
58. For an analysis of Israel's take on the JCPOA, see my article "Deep Disquiet: Israel and the Iran Nuclear Deal", *Contemporary Review of the Middle East*, Sage, Vol. 3, No. 1, 2016, pp. 47–61.
59. Moore, Jack, "Iran Tests Ballistic Missiles Carrying the Message 'Israel Must Be Wiped Out'", *Newsweek*, 9 March 2016, at http://www.newsweek.com/iran-firesballistic-missiles-marked-israel-must-be-wiped-out-434989, accessed 19 June 2016.
60. See Testimony by Under Secretary Shannon, Thomas A., Senate Foreign Relations

Committee, "Hearing on Iran's Recent Actions and Implementation of the JCPOA", 5 April 2016, at http://www.foreign.senate.gov/imo/media/doc/040516_Shannon_ Testimony.pdf, accessed 21 June 2016.

61. See, "Proposed major defence sales to Saudi Arabia", pp. 33–34, in Blanchard, Christopher M., "Saudi Arabia: Background and US Relations", Congressional Research Service, 20 September 2016, at https://www.fas.org/sgp/crs/mideast/RL33533.pdf, accessed 13 October 2016.
62. Blanchard, "Summary", in "Saudi Arabia: Background and US Relations", Ibid.
63. "Russia says Iran missile tests 'don't violate' UN resolution", *RT*, 30 March 2016, at https://www.rt.com/news/337753-iran-missile-tests-un/, accessed 19 June 2016.
64. The P5+1 Statement is part of Annex B of S/RES/2231, 20 July 2015, n. 10, p. 99.
65. See, "US imposes more sanctions on Iran for ballistic missile program", *Press TV*, 24 March 2016, at http://www.presstv.com/Detail/2016/03/24/457406/US-sanctions-Iran, accessed 19 June 2016.
66. The Office of the Supreme Leader, "Ayatollah Khamenei: Let Muslims lead fight on terror", 24 May 2016, at http://www.leader.ir/en/content/15109/Ayatollah-Khamenei-meeting-with-India%E2%80%99s-Prime-Minister-Narendra-Modi, accessed 3 October 2016.
67. Faucon, Benoit, "Iran Approves New Oil-Field Contracts to Woo Western Investors", *Wall Street Journal*, 3 August 2016, at http://www.wsj.com/articles/irans-cabinet-approves-new-oil-field-contracts-to-woo-western-investors-1470225766, accessed 15 October 2016.
68. See, "Donald Trump AIPAC Speech transcript", *Time*, 21 March 2016, at http://time.com/4267058/donald-trump-aipac-speech-transcript/, accessed 13 December 2016.
69. See, Jim Lobe, "Mattis on Iran: Belligerent but don't tear up nuclear deal", 25 November 2016, at http://lobelog.com/mattis-on-iran-belligerent-but-dont-tear-up-nuclear-deal/, accessed 13 December 2016.

REFERENCES

Katzman, Kenneth and Paul K. Kerr, "Iran Nuclear Agreement", Congressional Research Service, 5 December 2016, at https://fas.org/sgp/crs/nuke/R43333.pdf

Kumaraswamy, P.R. (ed.) Special Issue, "Iran Nuclear Deal: The Joint Comprehensive Plan of Action", *Contemporary Review of the Middle East*, Vol. 3, No. 1, Sage, March 2016.

Maloney, Suzanne, "Whither the Iran Deal Under Trump?" *The Atlantic*, 20 November 2016, at http://www.theatlantic.com/international/archive/2016/11/trump-iran-jcpoa-obama-tehran/508211/

Mousavian, Seyed Hussein, *The Iranian Nuclear Crisis: A Memoir*, Carnegie Endowment for International Peace, 2012.

Rajiv, S. Samuel C., "Deep Disquiet: Israel and the Iran Nuclear Deal", *Contemporary Review of the Middle East*, Vol. 3, No. 1, Sage, March 2016.

Rajiv, S. Samuel C., *Iran Sanctions and India: Navigating the Roadblocks*,IDSA, New Delhi: July 2016.

UN Security Council, "Resolution S/RES/2231", 20 July 2015, at www.un.org. The text of the JCPOA is part of the Annex to this Resolution.

13

Iran and the Region: Changing Dynamics and New Challenges

P.R. Kumaraswamy and Md. Muddassir Quamar

ABSTRACT

The geopolitical shifts in the Middle East, especially in the wake of the popular protests in the Arab world, have paved the way for Iran's regional ascendance and the resultant apprehension in many Arab capitals. Directly, indirectly, or through proxies, Iran has been involved in—or is seen to be accentuating—many regional conflicts and tensions in the region, and its influence extends far beyond its immediate borders to Iraq, Lebanon, Syria, Bahrain, and Yemen. This has increased fears and apprehensions among its regional rivals and competitors such as Egypt, Israel, Saudi Arabia, and Turkey over Iran's hegemonic intentions. These countries are increasingly uncomfortable with Iranian influence in regions that they consider as their own spheres of influence—that is, the Arabian Peninsula and the Levant. A host of international developments—such as the declining American appetite for greater involvement in the Middle East especially under the Obama Administration, and its 'pivot to Asia' policy—has unnerved many Gulf monarchies; and the nuclear deal has created the conditions for Iranian regional ascendance, if not hegemony. These now pose an important question: what are the regional implications of growing Iranian influence? It is equally important to assess as to how long, and at what cost, the situation can be sustained. For India, growing Saudi-Iranian tension could also be worrisome, especially when New Delhi seeks close politico-strategic partnership with both the Gulf States.

Iran's Regional Position

Its size, population, history, geo-strategic location, and natural resources in terms of oil and gas make Iran an important player in the Middle East. It is also the only country in the region that is endowed with all the ingredients necessary for being a regional power. Since the Islamic Revolution of 1979, Iran has faced prolonged conflict, diplomatic isolation, and prolonged economic sanctions; but it has managed to retain stability and economic growth. The American policy of isolation (1980s), dual containment (1990s), and stringent economic sanctions (post-2005) has only contributed to Iranian resilience. If the Kuwait crisis scaled down the regional threat, the US-led invasion of Iraq in March 2003 provided a strong foothold to Iran in the Arab neighbourhood. The American-led invasion removed Saddam Hussein from power; but it transformed Arab Iraq into a Shia country in the political sense of the word, and hence a staunch ally of Iran. Thus, since 1979, both Democrat and Republican administrations in Washington have been unable to pursue a cogent and effective policy vis-à-vis Tehran, and have not been able to constrain the Islamic republic.

Iranian resilience is more palpable in the regional context. Though the Islamic revolution fundamentally transformed its relations with the USA and irreversibly harmed them, it also had ominous repercussions for the neighbouring Arab monarchies along the Persian Gulf. Emboldened by the swift manner in which the Shah and his regime was overthrown through popular support, the new clerical leadership under Ayatollah Ruhollah Khomeini adopted an aggressive posture towards the pro-western Arab monarchies in the region, and even called for 'exporting' the Islamic revolution. Khomeini's calls for the overthrow of Arab monarchies led to regional tensions, and eventually culminated in the Iraqi aggression against Iran. In this endeavour, Saddam Hussein was politically backed by the USA and funded by the Gulf monarchies.[1] The Iraqi ruler misjudged the resilience of the Islamic revolution and its popular appeal and, ironically, contributed to the consolidation of clerical rule in Iran.

The Islamic revolution and the Iran-Iraq War (1980–88) brought havoc in the fragile geopolitical situation in the Gulf. Even while supporting the Iraqi war effort, Saudi Arabia was apprehensive of the intensions of the Ba'athist leadership in Baghdad, and formed the six-member Gulf Cooperation Council (GCC).[2] All the founding members are pro-western monarchies and the exclusion of the Yemens—then as two independent states—was not accidental. Oil wealth has enabled the GCC members to pursue a rentier-based welfare state model.[3] The GCC was formed primarily as a political arrangement against the Islamic republic, especially when sections of Shia population in some Arab countries felt emboldened by the events in Iran. The Shia riots in Saudi Arabia's Eastern Province in November 1979 were partly influenced by the Islamic revolution.

Seeing Saddam Hussein as a bulwark against Tehran, Saudi Arabia and Kuwait provided huge financial support, even though countries like Oman and some within the UAE preferred a more neutral position vis-à-vis the Iran-Iraq war.[4] At the height of the tanker war (1984–87), an Iraqi missile attack destroyed Iran's main oil exporting terminal in March 1984. This resulted in retaliatory Iranian attacks against Kuwaiti and Saudi tankers. To ensure free navigation of oil tankers in the Gulf, especially through the Strait of Hormuz, the USA stepped in and reflagged the Gulf oil carriers. This escalated US-Iran tensions already marred by the 444-day hostage crisis that had ended hours before the inauguration of President Ronald Reagan's administration on 20 January 1981. The eight-year long Iran-Iraq war ended in August 1988 when the former accepted the terms of the UN Security Council Resolution 598, and both sides agreed to withdraw their armed forces to recognised international borders between the two countries. Iran suffered enormous human casualties, including nearly 12,000 civilians, and was economically battered. However, its ability to sustain and survive the war without the support of any major or regional powers, and its denial of an outright victory to Iraq—backed by the USA and many oil-rich Arab countries—decisively turned the balance in favour of Iran.[5]

The Islamic revolution and its aftermath pitched Iran against Saudi Arabia, leading to an enduring rivalry and competition that continues till date. Both see themselves as legitimate leaders of the Islamic world: Iran due to the Islamic revolution and Saudi Arabia due to the presence of Islam's two holiest sites—Mecca and Medina—within the Kingdom. Though the Iranian clergy sought to present it as an Islamic, and not Shia, revolution, the Shia population around the world, including in the Arab countries, see Tehran as the leader of the Shia community. For its part, since the discovery of oil and especially after the oil crisis of 1973, the Saudi rulers present the Kingdom as the leader of Sunni world, and the prolonged anti-Shia rhetoric of the Wahhabi ulema has merely emboldened Saudi claims.

Thus, post-1979, Saudi-Iranian relations continued to deteriorate leading to a breakdown of diplomatic relations in 1988 after the escalation of tensions over the Hajj incident in July 1987. Riyadh saw revolutionary Iran as a destabilising factor that was committed to overthrowing the Al-Saud and other Arab ruling families in the Gulf.[6] On the other hand,

Khomeini's revolutionary ideas ran counter to the monarchical system of governance and saw Al-Saud to be unsuitable and unfit to protect and govern the holy places of Islam.[7] These differences often manifest in rhetorical statements from both the capitals as well as in the tension and violence often seen during annual hajj pilgrimages, as happened in 1987 and 2015–16.

Iran-Arab Rapprochement

Though Iran was able to survive the eight-year war initiated by Iraq, it emerged from this war badly battered, with its economy in shambles. The economic cost of the war for Iran was estimated at over US$500 billion. However, the death of Khomeini in June 1989 marked a new phase of political pragmatism and, under the leadership of President Hashemi Rafsanjani (1989–1997), Iran began to mend fences not only with Europe but also with neighbouring Arab countries.[8] Rafsanjani sought to minimise the tension between the two regional rivals. The rebuilding of post-war Iran depended upon the lowering of regional tensions and economic cooperation with the Arab neighbours, especially Saudi Arabia. The pragmatism of Rafsanjani was followed by his successor Mohammed Khatami (1997–2005), and both contributed to significant improvement in Iranian-Saudi relations.[9] Iran's relations with some of the European countries, especially Britain, improved in the wake Tehran's decision to be circumspect if not dilute Khomeini's fatwa against British author Salman Rushdie over *The Satanic Verses*.

The Iraqi invasion of Kuwait (2 August 1990) fundamentally changed the regional security situation. The end of the Cold War and the impending disintegration of the USSR bolstered American claims for a global hegemony. The Kuwait crisis exposed the Arab monarchies to the territorial and energy ambitions of Saddam Hussein. In Iraqi calculations, the USA offered a tacit endorsement of its military moves against Kuwait over oil production and price fall, while the Arab monarchies lacked the military capability to fight the Iraqi armed forces.[10] However, with the invasion of Kuwait, Iraq had acquired the second largest oil reserves in the world, and hence the potential of becoming a swing producer that could determine global oil prices. This posed a fundamental challenge to the USA, and hence President George H. W. Bush organised an international effort to restore status quo ante in Kuwait. Backed by a series of UN Security Council resolutions, an USA led international coalition was assembled, and through Operation Desert Storm Kuwaiti liberation was secured on 28 February 1991.[11]

During the Kuwait crisis, Iran remained largely neutral and was not prepared to take sides between its two rivals. While the tension with the USA continued to run high, it did not wish to be too critical of the US-led coalition against a ruler who had invaded the country, and inflicted human casualties and material loss.[12] When the USA continued to see the Islamic Republic as an adversary, Tehran could not have openly endorsed Operation Desert Storm, more so since American domination of the Gulf undermined Iran's interests. At the same time, it did not wish to endorse Saddam Hussein's action as it was aware of the long-term implications of a belligerent and emboldened Iraq. Thus, Tehran treaded a fine line, and was content with Iraqi military might being systematically destroyed, and its threats to the region scaled down considerably.

The USA responded to the post-Kuwait security situation in the Gulf through a policy of dual containment whereby it sought to restrict the ability of both Iran and Iraq from gaining pre-eminence in the region lest they disrupt the US policies and harm its interests.[13] While seeking the resolution of the Israeli-Palestinian conflict, the Clinton administration did not want a powerful Iran or Iraq to hamper the prospects for peace.[14] Though the tensions with the USA continued after the Kuwait crisis, Iran pursued a policy of pragmatic rapprochement with Gulf monarchies, both for economic as well as geopolitical compulsions. Hence, during much of the 1990s, Iran's relations with the Gulf monarchies, especially Saudi Arabia, were cordial.[15]

The post-Khomeini pragmatic leadership exhibited by Rafsanjani, and later by Khatami, considerably contributed to an improvement in Iranian relations with the Gulf. As a result, towards the end of the 1990s, the economic relations between the two returned to pre-revolution levels. The Iranian foreign policy establishment recognised that it was critical to improve relations with the Arab neighbours and build bridges if Iran were to rebuild its post-war economy and fight the negative consequences of falling oil prices.[16] At the height of the oil glut during the Iran-Iraq war, it had dropped to US$10 bpd in 1986. As a country heavily dependent upon oil exports, both for domestic economy and foreign trade, Iran needed high oil prices for maintaining its economic health.

However, the 11 September 2001 terror attacks in the USA radically changed not only the global approach to terrorism but also the geopolitical dynamics in the Middle East and the Persian Gulf. The pragmatism of the 1990s and dual containment paved the way to a new 'War on Terror'; and, in his State of the Union address in January 2002, President George W. Bush clubbed Iran with Iraq and North Korea as the "axis of evil."[17] The limited rapprochement between Iran and the USA transformed to a more open confrontation and acrimony.

The Iraq Invasion and its Aftermath

The American decision to invade Iraq in March 2003, and the swift fall of the Ba'athist regime in Baghdad posed challenges and opportunities for Iran. At one level, this meant that Iran was surrounded by direct and indirect American military presence. The US presence in Afghanistan and Iraq came within the context of the "War on Terror"; but the US also increased its presence in the Persian Gulf region, especially in Bahrain and Qatar. In addition, the central Asian republics of Uzbekistan and Kyrgyzstan also allowed American military presence, and facilitated operations against Al-Qaida in Afghanistan. Thus, Iran faced a US-led military encirclement.

The US presence in Iraq and the ease with which it deposed the Ba'athist regime in Baghdad particularly unnerved Iran. The invasion and democracy promotion agenda of President George W. Bush emboldened the Shia population who were marginalised and persecuted under Saddam Hussein. Though constituting about 60 percent of the Iraqi population, the Shias had suffered under him, and were even prevented from commemorating religious ceremonies like Ashura in public. Hence, the death sentence handed over to the Iraqi leader had a Shia legacy; he was convicted for the murder of over 148 Shias in Dujail in 1982, and was hanged on 30 December 2006.

The introduction of a participatory political order in 2005 paved the way for the empowerment of the majority Shias, which, in turn, led to a political backlash from the minority Sunni population which had controlled and benefitted from the erstwhile Ba'athist political order. If the Shia-Sunni tension was insufficient, the ethnic Kurdish population that resided in the north (around the oil-rich Mosul area bordering Turkey) joined the struggle. Having been deprived of their political rights since the First World War, the Kurdish population in the region has been restless, especially in Iraq and Turkey, and the sectarian violence induced them to demand—and eventually acquire—political autonomy from the central authority in Baghdad.

Amidst the uncertainty and growing instability in post-2003 Iraq, Iran sought to stabilise the situation by developing influence among the majority Shias. It revived the traditional clerical networks that, for example, had been instrumental in Khomeini seeking asylum in Iraq during 1965 to 1978.[18] By playing an active role in stabilising the situation in Iraq, and helping in the formation of a friendly and pliable government in Baghdad, Iran gained an unprecedented strategic influence in its neighbourhood. Many Arab leaders and commentators felt that Iran emerged as the principle beneficiary of the US military campaign against Iraq. Thus, the US invasion transformed Arab Iraq into Shia Iraq.

Despite their on-going differences over the "Axis of Evil" strategy of the Bush Administration, one could notice Iran-US tactical cooperation in stabilising Iraq as well as over developments in Afghanistan. For example, during the US invasion of Afghanistan in 2001, Iran opened its airspace to US forces, and shared intelligence on Taliban. Further, in Iraq, the IRGC's Qud's force was involved in training Iraqi Shiite militias and provided material support to the Sadrist group.

However, this interest convergence, tactical cooperation, and low-level coordination in Iraq and Afghanistan did not transform US-Iran relations or reduce the tensions between them. Each one was apprehensive of the long-term strategic goals of the other in the Persian Gulf region and its neighbourhood. Both differed over American commitments to the stability of various Arab regimes (especially Saudi Arabia) and Washington's willingness to be the security provider of the Arab regimes and their security concerns vis-à-vis Iran. Both sides felt it difficult to overcome the bitterness of the past and over the new political order in the Gulf region in the wake of the Islamic revolution.

If these were insufficient, in August 2002, the dissident group, the National Coalition of Resistance of Iran (NCRI), disclosed a clandestine nuclear programme pursued by Iran. This soon became a major politico-strategic controversy over Iran's nuclear ambitions.[19] Though rudimentary efforts towards nuclear power generation were initiated under the Shah, the US-Iran political tension placed Iranian ambitions in a different context. As a country with the third largest known oil reserves (after Saudi Arabia and Canada) and the second large gas reserves (after Russia), questions were raised regarding the rationale behind the nuclear option. Under such circumstances, Iran being a signatory to the Nuclear Non-Proliferation Treaty and an adherent to non-proliferation requirements became secondary. Iranian leaders often referred to Ayatollah Khamenei's fatwa issued in October 2003 regarding the production and use of weapon of mass destruction to maintain the 'peaceful' nature of their programme.[20]

At the same time, some of the actions and activities did raise doubts about the peaceful nature of Iranian nuclear ambitions. Though the NPT recognises the right to use civilian nuclear energy, the Iranian pursuit of an effective fuel cycle programme, the construction and maintenance of nuclear installations outside the purview and inspection of the International Atomic Energy Agency, and its desire to achieve weapon grade nuclear enrichment process generated international concerns and anxiety. Between 2008 and 2015, the number of centrifuges operated by Iran rose from 5000 to 15000, and intelligence assessments suggested that Iran could develop sufficient nuclear fuel for a crude nuclear device.[21] Partly to assuage international concerns, in March 2003 Iran entered into additional safeguard arrangements with the IAEA. However, these were insufficient and hence, from early 2003, Iranian nuclear ambitions became controversial.

As efforts by various regional powers to 'mediate' the controversy proved inadequate, the US introduced a series of economic sanctions against Iran.[22] Through directed against the Iranian capacity to develop non-conventional weapons, these were largely aimed at crippling the Iranian economy. Since the introduction of Iran Libya Sanctions Act (ILSA) of 1996, later modified as Iran Sanctions Act in 2006, the Islamic republic has been at the receiving end of punitive American measures. The unilateral American measures eventually paved the way for a spate of international measures and sanctions against Iran. Since the adoption of a resolution by the IAEA in 2005, there were as many as 13 resolutions by the nuclear watchdog body and seven by the UN Security Council critical of Iran. Russia, and to a lesser extent China, intervened to water down the international measures against Iran; but these resolutions also highlighted the growing international isolation of the Islamic Republic and the trust deficit. Sanctions against banking and shipping operations severely affected the Iranian economy, and the American sanctions against energy-related investment deprived Iran of critical technology and investments in its aging oil and gas industry. Some its ambitious energy programmes—such as the Iran-Pakistan-India pipeline and LNG exports—could not take off due to US-led economic sanctions. As a result of these measures, Iranian oil and gas exports, critical components of its economy, began to dwindle, and the drastic drop in prices since mid-2014 further undermined its capabilities.

These factors as well as the American desire to seek a closure to the three-decade old Iran file through a political settlement culminated in the July 2015 Joint Comprehensive Plan of Action (JCPOA), commonly known as the nuclear deal. The process began in June 2003 when EU 3 (France, Britain, and Germany) initiated a political process, later joined by the USA in March 2013. Iran eventually reached an agreement with the five permanent members of the Security Council and Germany that, among others, curtails Iran's ability to develop weapon grade uranium-enrichment and has the provision of sanctions on violation. The agreement was endorsed by the UN Security Council in October 2015, and came into force in January 2016.

Though it was hailed by much of the international community, JCPOA did not go down well in the Middle East, especially in Israel and Saudi Arabia. For long, Israel has been advocating a 'military solution' to the Iranian nuclear controversy, while Saudi Arabia was unsuccessfully trying to flag the threats emanating from Tehran. Hence, both these countries viewed the nuclear agreement as a sign of their abandonment by the USA and Washington's desire to befriend Iran at their expense. They felt betrayed by the refusal of the Obama administration to accommodate their larger strategic concerns vis-à-vis Iran, and view the agreement a precursor and facilitator to Iranian regional hegemony in the Persian Gulf region and beyond. Thus, while the nuclear agreement has averted a possible confrontation with Iran, it has spurred a regional tension, and there are suggestions that some countries—especially Saudi Arabia—are not averse to pursuing a nuclear option as a hedging strategy.

Even while being tied down over its relations with the USA and the nuclear controversy, Iran has been enhancing its engagement in regional affairs with an aim to gain strategic depth.[23] In this endeavour, its backing of Hezbollah in Lebanon and Hamas in the Palestinian territories has proved effective; and both have made Iran a de facto neighbour of Israel. Hezbollah—which emerged as a Shiite resistance movement against the Israeli occupation of Southern Lebanon in the early 1980s with Iranian political, military, ideological and financial support—achieved a major success in 2000. Six years later, the militant group withstood the 34-day Second Lebanon War launched by Israel and, in the process, attained wider popular support among many Arab countries.

Likewise, the Madrid Conference exposed the internal Palestinian tensions between the mainstream Palestine Liberation Organization and the militant group Hamas. This was accentuated when the PLO decided to sign the Oslo agreement in September 1993, and seek a negotiated political settlement with Israel based on partitioning historic Palestine. The inter-Palestinian tension intensified when Hamas pursued a militant campaign against Oslo in the form of a suicide campaign against Israel within the June 1967 borders, and contributed to the political ascendance of Hamas as the torchbearer of the Palestinian struggle.

This, in turn, enabled Iran to make serious inroads into Palestine, and emerge as a staunch supporter of Hamas and its uncompromising posture vis-à-vis a political settlement to the Palestine problem, and provided political and financial support. Indeed, in 1979, Ayatollah Khomeini announced the fourth Friday of the Islamic holy month of Ramadan as al-Quds Day (Jerusalem day) and, since then Islamic communities around the world are marking this day with various protest actions, rallies, and events to express their support. The popularity of the al-Quds day was so overwhelming that, in 1988, the Organization of Islamic Cooperation (earlier known as Organization of Islamic Conference) formally adopted this day.

Thus, by the end of 2000s, Iran had acquired considerable strategic influence through its actions and involvement in many regional theatres. This has led to what Vali Nasr has described as the rise of the 'Shia Crescent'—stretching from the northern coast of the Persian Gulf to Iraq, Syria, and Lebanon.[24] This, in turn, unnerved major regional powers in the region, especially Israel, Saudi Arabia, and Turkey.

The enhancement of its regional influence paved the way for an Iranian defiance of the USA and the ability to withstand the host of political and economic sanctions. The withdrawal of American military troops from Iraq in December 2011, and the scaling down of western military commitments in Afghanistan were a victory for Iran. These have considerably contributed to its preeminent role in both these countries and their future. The nuclear controversy, and the manner in which Iran sought to resolve it, highlighted Iran's staying power, and its determination and ability to withstand the American desire to preserve a regional order tilted in favour of the Arab monarchies in the Gulf region. Through a tactful alliance with Syria and militant groups such as Hamas and Hezbollah, Iran has managed to expose the limits of American influence in the region, especially in Iraq, Lebanon, and Palestine. As articulated by Imad Mansour, in the late 2000s, Iran "upgrade[d] its status to a dominant power by demonstrating an ability to penetrate and influence various regional theatres", and was able to impact the regional order by frustrating various US initiatives.[25]

The Arab Spring

The outbreak of popular protests in various Arab countries since December 2010 contributed to Iran's emergence as an unintended beneficiary. At one level, many Arab regimes have been pre-occupied with internal turmoil and a popular yearning for change. While many republican regimes collapsed, oil rich Arab countries sought to contain the disgruntlement and anger through economic incentives. Both the processes, however, raised doubts over the long-term stability of most of the Arab regimes and, in the process, the Islamic republic stood out as an island of stability.

Iran also benefited from internal turmoil in some of these countries, and managed to enhance its influence through events in Bahrain, Lebanon, Iraq, Syria, and Yemen. Initially, Iran welcomed the tide of unrest against the status quo in the Arab world, and sought to present its Islamic Revolution as a model. Iran openly backed the demands of the Shia population in Bahrain, especially of the various Shia groups opposed to the Al-Khalifa rule. Some of the terror acts in Bahrain since 2011 are allegedly attributed to groups linked to Iran. Likewise, Iran is accused of providing political as well as logistical support to the Houthi rebels who took control over much of Yemen by early 2015.

The Iranian support for change in the Arab world quickly changed when its long-term ally Syria faced popular demand for political reforms. Since the early days of the Islamic Revolution, Damascus has remained the only Arab ally of Iran, and the Syrian crisis provided an opportunity for Iran not only to repay its gratitude but also to consolidate its influence in the war ravaged country. Besides political support, Tehran has been bolstering the Assad regime by providing training and material support to the Syrian armed forces. The entry of Russia in support of the Assad regime in September 2015 further strengthened the Iranian position in the Syrian crisis. A number of Iranian as well as Hezbollah fighters are actively fighting with the Syrian army. While the estimates vary, the involvement of Hezbollah and Iranian forces are indicated by periodic obituary notices in the Lebanese media. Since January 2016, Assad forces have regained some of the territories it had lost to the rebel and ISIS forces, and this was possible primarily due to the Russian air campaign as well as ground support provide by Iran and Hezbollah fighters.

The ability of Iran to take advantage of the situation created due to the Arab Spring and gain a strong foothold in many countries, especially in the Levant, disrupted the regional order and unnerved some powers. For quite sometime, especially since AKP came to power in 2002, Turkey sees the Levant as its sphere of influence, and tried to shape events in Syria after 2011. It also sought to influence Iraq by seeking to limit Kurdish autonomy lest Turkish Kurds make similar demands. Likewise, Saudi Arabia sought to influence events in Iraq and Lebanon, but had to concede to the growing influence of Iran in these countries. The resurgence of Hamas and Hezbollah considerably challenged Israeli hegemony, especially in terms of its military might. Through involvement in some of the crises in the region, Iran has expanded its regional footprint, and these are more apparent in the on-going tension between two Islamic powers in the Gulf—the Islamic Republic of Iran and the Kingdom of Saudi Arabia.

Iran-Saudi Rivalry

The most significant outcome of the ascendance of Iran has been the intensification of Saudi-Iranian rivalry. Both these countries are important players in the region, and have been at loggerheads with one another since 1979. While there were occasional lowering of tensions, especially during the tenures of Rafsanjani and Khatami, competition for regional and extra-regional influence did not abate. The Iraqi crisis following the US-led invasion has radically altered the nature of the relationship: while Iran sees Iraq as its backwaters, Saudi Arabia fears the growing political influence of Iran in that Arab country.

Soon Saudi-Iranian rivalry took a sectarian dimension and, in 2009, King Abdullah expressed apprehensions about Tehran 'converting' Iraqi Sunnis into Shias.[26] Iran's ability to influence and even shape the post-Saddam political order in Iraq was accompanied by its growing influence in Lebanon, which had traditionally remained under Saudi influence. Initial Saudi condemnation of the 'adventurism' of the Hezbollah for the Second Lebanon War proved premature as the ability of the military group to withstand Israeli military might resulted in popular support for its leader, Hassan Nasrallah.[27] The same holds true for Palestine where the Saudi-led peace initiatives—such as Abdullah Plan and Mecca Accord—were not fruitful, and did not advance Saudi interest vis-à-vis the Palestinians. In both cases, increase in Iranian influence came at the cost of Saudi Arabia.[28] Moreover, during the brief tenure of President Mohammed Morsi, even Egypt was inclined towards Tehran, and both countries looked to seek closure to the old bitterness over President Anwar Sadat providing asylum to the Shah of Iran.

The Al-Saud sees Iran as the destabilising factor in the region, with hegemonic ambitions vis-à-vis its Arab neighbours. This understanding of Iranian goals resulted in the Saudi military involvement in Yemen. The war has not only proven costly but has also turned out be a conundrum with serious financial and military costs. The rivalry between the two powers is also responsible for the stalemate in Bahrain and the continuing uncertainty. What began as economic demands of a marginalised population soon became a sectarian battle between the demographically larger Shia population and the Sunni ruling family. Active Saudi intervention in Bahraini affairs is largely aimed at preventing any role for elements closer to, or identified with Iran within the island kingdom.

Saudi-Iranian rivalry is also partly responsible for the prolongation of the Syrian crisis, and the mounting human casualties and disintegration of that country. While Iran backs the Assad regime through political and military support as well as fighters, a host of rebel forces—especially the Salafi elements such as Ahraral-Sham that are a part of the Free Syrian Army (FSA)—are financially backed by Saudi Arabia as well as by countries such as Qatar. The Arab support for radical elements opposed to Assad has also partly contributed to the evolution of the ISIS.

The regional rivalry along sectarian lines has been intensified by the nuclear deal, which the Saudis see as a sign of a shift in the US Persian Gulf policy in favour of Iran. The Obama administration's desire to conclude the deal despite opposition from long-term friends such as Saudi Arabia and Israel indicated an American preference for Iran over Saudi Arabia. This reading of the nuclear deal led to growing political contacts—and perhaps tactical understanding—between the Jewish State of Israel and the Wahhabi state of Saudi Arabia.

Conclusion

Partly due to its skilful handling of regional challenges and largely due to the incorrect policies of its adversaries, especially the USA, Iran has emerged as the most important player in the Middle East, especially in the Persian Gulf region. Before the Islamic Revolution, Iran and Saudi Arabia were the dominant players in the Gulf, primarily due to their proximity with the USA and the support and patronage both enjoyed from Washington. Three decades later, Iran's regional influence is not only independent of the USA but is also in competition and rivalry to American designs in the region. Saudi Arabia, which once shared the regional domination with Iran, is now compelled to accept a growing Iranian influence in the Persian Gulf. This comes at a time, when US commitments in the Middle East remain uncertain. Moreover, being used to American political patronage and strategic support for decades, Riyadh is more vulnerable to Tehran than it has been any time since the end of the Second World War. President Trump's administration has sounded a policy change vis-à-vis Iran by articulating the need for reviewing the nuclear deal. One of his early moves to ban immigrants from seven Muslim countries, including Iran, evoked a sharp Iranian reaction, and might lead to the further escalation of tension between Iran and the USA.

NOTES

1. Efraim Karsh, *The Iran-Iraq War,* Oxford, Osprey Publishing, 2002.
2. Gulshan Dietl, *Through Two Wars and Beyond: A Study of the Gulf Cooperation Council,* New Delhi: Lancers Books, 1991.
3. Indeed, in 2011, the GCC sought to expand, and offered memberships to the two

remaining monarchies in the Middle East—namely, the Hashemite Kingdom of Jordan on the northern edge of the Gulf of Aqaba, and the far off Morocco along the Atlantic Coast.

4. A. Reza Sheikholeslami, "Saudi Arabia and the United States: Partnership in the Persian Gulf", in Farhang Rajaee (ed.), *The Iran-Iraq War: The Politics of Aggression*, Gainesville: University Press of Florida, 1993; and Ray Takeyh, "The Iran-Iraq War: A Reassessment", *Middle East Journal*, 2010, Vol. 64, no. 3, pp. 365–383.
5. Anoushiravan Ehteshami, *Dynamics of Change in the Persian Gulf: Political Economy, War and Revolution*, New York: Routledge, 2013.
6. Joseph Kechichian, "Trends in Saudi National Security", *Middle East Journal*, 1999, vol. 53, no. 2, pp. 232–253.
7. Ariel Jahner, "Saudi Arabia and Iran: The Struggle for Power and Influence in the Gulf", *International Affairs Review*, 2012, Vol. 20, no. 3, pp. 37–49.
8. Fahad M. Alsultan and Pedram Saeid, *The Development of Saudi-Iranian Relations since the 1990s: Between Conflict and Accommodation*, London: Routledge, 2016.
9. Ibid.
10. Sheikholeslami, "Saudi Arabia and the United States" op.cit; and Takeyh, "The Iran-Iraq War", op. cit.
11. Majid Khadduri and Edmund Ghareeb, *War in the Gulf, 1990-91*, New York: Oxford University Press, 1997.
12. Shireen T. Hunter, *Iran's Foreign Policy in the Post-Soviet Era: Resisting the New International Order*, Santa Barbara, California: Praeger, 2010.
13. Anthony H. Cordesman and Ahmed S. Hashim, *Iran: Dilemmas of Dual Containment*, Boulder, Colorado: Westview Press, 1997.
14. F. Gregory Gause III, "The Illogic of Dual Containment", *Foreign Affairs*, 1994, Vol. 73, no. 2, pp. 56–66; Hisham Melhem, *Dual Containment: The Demise of a Fallacy*, Occasional Paper, Centre for Contemporary Arab Studies, Georgetown University, Washington, DC.
15. Alsultan and Saeid, *The Development of Saudi-Iranian Relations*, op. cit.
16. Hunter, *Iran's Foreign Policy in the Post-Soviet Era*, op. cit.
17. Daniel Heradstveit and G. Matthew Bonham, "What the Axis of Evil Metaphor Did to Iran", *Middle East Journal*, 2007, Vol. 61, no. 3, pp. 421–440.
18. Anoushiravan Ehteshami, "Iran's International Posture after the Fall of Baghdad", *Middle East Journal*, 2004, Vol. 58, no. 2, pp. 179–194.
19. ANI, "Dissident Group Claims Iran Secretly Running 'Clandestine Nuclear Program' for Years", February 25, 2015, at http://www.aninews.in/newsdetail-ODI/MjA1MzQy/dissident-group-claims-iran-secretly-running-039-clandestine-nuclear-program-039-for-years.html
20. Michael Eisenstadt and Mehdi Khalaji, *Nuclear Fatwa: Religion and Politics in Iran's Proliferation Strategy*, Policy Focus, No. 115, September 2011, The Washington Institute for Near East Policy, Washington, DC.
21. Iran Watch, "A History of Iran's Nuclear Program", August 9, 2016, at http://www.iranwatch.org/our-publications/weapon-program-background-report/history-irans-nuclear-program
22. Kenneth Katzman, *Iran Sanctions*, CRS Report, 9 December 2009.
23. Ray Takeyh, *Hidden Iran: Paradox and Power in the Islamic Republic*, New York: Henry Holt & Co, 2006.

24. Vali Nasr, *The Shia Revival: How Conflicts within Islam will Shape the Future*, New York: W. W. Norton, 2007.
25. Imad Mansour, "Iran and Instability in the Middle East: How Preferences Influence the Regional Order", *International Journal*, 2008, Vol. 63, no. 4, pp. 941–964.
26. *Al-Jazeera*, "Iran and the Shia Legacy", February 1, 2009, at http://www.aljazeera.com/news/middleeast/2007/03/2008525184916567546.html
27. Augustus R. Norton, *Hezbollah: A Short History*, Princeton, NJ: Princeton University Press, 2007.
28. Hazem Balousha, "Why Hamas Resumed Ties with Iran", *Al-Monitor*, 29 June 2016, at http://www.al-monitor.com/pulse/originals/2016/06/gaza-hamas-resume-relations-iran.html.

PART 5

ISRAEL

14

Israel and India: An Introduction

P.R. Kumaraswamy[1]

Israel has occupied a central position in India's Middle East policy. The roots of this policy can be traced to the early 20th century when India was fighting against the British. Nationalists led by Mahatma Gandhi and Jawaharlal Nehru found a common cause with the Arabs, and viewed the emerging conflict in Palestine over Jewish aspirations for a homeland through the anti-colonial and anti-imperial prism. The emerging domestic struggle with the Muslim League over a religious-based national identity partly influenced their views concerning Jewish nationalism. These trends culminated when India was elected to the 11-member United Nations Special Committee on Palestine (UNSCOP) wherein it proposed a federal plan when the majority members advocated partition. In line with its traditional position, on 29 November 1947 India voted against the partitioning Palestine.

Israel's existence and its eventual admission into the United Nations despite India's opposition, the emerging bonhomie between Pakistan and some of the Middle Eastern countries, and its own position regarding the recognition of states resulted in India granting recognition to Israel in September 1950. There were indications that India was keen to establish formal ties; but in the wake of the Suez crisis and Israel's collaboration with the imperial powers, India's position hardened. Hence, from the mid-1950s, recognition-without-relations marked India's Israel policy; this continued until January 1992 when full diplomatic relations were established.

Following normalisation, the political, economic, cultural and, above all, military relations have flourished. Both the Indian National Congress and the Bharatiya Janata Party (BJP), the two major national parties, have been promoting bilateral ties without diluting India's traditional position towards the Palestinian cause. Unlike the past, India no longer blames Israel for the prolongation of the Arab-Israeli conflict but seeks an accommodative political solution that is honourable and acceptable to both the parties. Like much of the international community, India supports the two-state solution.

India benefitted from a number of regional developments in pursuing a friendlier policy towards Israel and Palestine. The willingness of many Arab states to accept Israel's existence and offer conditional peace (for example, the Arab Peace Initiative) has been a positive outcome. Major powers, such as China and Russia, have revisited and revised their erstwhile hostility, and have befriended the Jewish State. Due to geostrategic as well as religious considerations, countries such as Iran and Pakistan continue to be vocal in their opposition to Israel, with Iran expressing it hostility through its support to various militant groups in the region, such as Hamas and Hezbollah. At the same time, due to prevailing regional tensions over the ascendance of Iran, countries like Saudi Arabia do not hesitate to maintain a clandestine tactical understanding if not cooperation with Israel. In short, some are friendlier towards Israel, some are hostile, and others seek a limited understanding with it. India's friendlier ties with Israel have to be seen within this complex matrix.

The recent tensions in the US-Israeli relations are an ominous development, and bilateral relations during the Obama administration (2009–2017) were anything but friendly. The contours of the new Trump administration are far from clear; but going by the geostrategic trajectory of the US-Israeli relations since 1948, especially since 1967, one can suggest that relations would continue to remain the major factor in the Middle East, and Israel will continue to depend upon the US for political, economic, and strategic support. This, in turn, means India will continue to tune its relations with the Jewish state within the larger context of the US-Israeli ties.

NOTES

1. Professor P.R. Kumaraswamy teaches the contemporary Middle East in Jawaharlal Nehru University, New Delhi and is the author of *India's Israel Policy* (Columbia University Press, 2010) and the *Historical Dictionary of the Arab-Israeli conflict* (Scarecrow Press, 2015). He is also the Honorary Director of the Middle East Institute, New Delhi, www.mei.org.in

15

The Shaping of Israel-US Relations

Moinuddin Ahmad

ABSTRACT

Israel-US relations are said to be one of the stoutest bilateral associations in the world. The cooperation and commitments between the two countries include trade, diplomacy, and the security needs of Israel in the Middle East. The leaders of both states are vocal about mutual understanding and support on various issues, particularly against terrorism. Time and again, a special reference is made to a common 'Judeo-Christian' heritage to mark the history of intimacy and trust between the people of the two counties.

However, a closer look at the trajectory of ties bares a non-linear story. The bilateral ties have not always been as smooth and robust as they appear to be. One finds that the USA has not always been close to the Jewish State as generally projected, and differences on various issues have been reported and well documented.

Even the recognition of Israel by the USA had its own political nuances. The two states have gradually come closer over a period of time, and Israel's military victory in the June 1967 war is credited with having drawn the attention of the USA towards it. Barring a few diplomatic hiccups, both have not looked back since then. Their post-Cold War engagements reflect even more clarity and determination. The recent Washington tryst with Iran on the nuclear issue sent down some jitters in Israel, making observers ponder over the trajectory of the future of the Israel-US ties.

What has been the course of Israel-US relations, particularly in the post-Cold War era? Is the Judeo-Christian heritage still relevant in building and nurturing the ties? Which external and internal actors have influenced the engagement over these years? What is the possible future of their alliance? This chapter probes these and other related questions regarding Israel-US relations.

In the history of Israel-US bilateral relations, 23 December 2016 will no doubt be regarded as a milestone. The USA did not use its veto power against a Resolution condemning Jewish settlements in the Occupied Palestinian Territories, including East Jerusalem, and chose to abstain in the United Nations Security Council. As a result, the Resolution—moved by New Zealand, Malaysia, Venezuela and Senegal—was passed calling the settlements illegal. The USA abandoning Israel at the world's most important organisation was the last thing anybody expected. Although there were several apparent differences between the two countries during most of President Barack Obama's tenure, things appeared to be ending on a high note when the USA passed one of the largest amount of aid to Israel in September.[1] This, according to the Congressional Research Service, made Israel the largest cumulative recipient of US foreign assistance since the World War II.

There was another shocker in store for Israel as the Jewish state celebrated Hanukkah. The US Secretary of State, John Kerry, appeared on television and justified the US move at the UN. Reminding the Benjamin Netanyahu government and the world that the outgoing Obama administration had been the most favourable partner for Israel,[2] Kerry categorically said that the Israeli settlements are a huge hindrance to the two-state solution agreed to by the international community. Israeli leaders were quick to respond: they condemned Kerry and laid claim to Jerusalem as the "eternal capital" of the State of Israel.

"For how long you people are living in America? Jerusalem has been the capital of the Jews for 3000 years," Naftali Bennet (leader of the Israeli Right Wing party, *HaBait HaYehuda* or The Jewish Home) told a *CNN* news anchor. Only a few minutes after Kerry ended his speech, Prime Minister Netanyahu was on social media posting a 2008 photo of President Obama at Western Wall, asking: "When Obama visited Israel Western Wall as US Presidential candidate in 2008, why was he calling it a part of occupied territory." Netanyahu rebuked Kerry, saying: "Israelis do not need to be lectured about the importance of peace by foreign leaders."

What has gone wrong with the Israel-US bilateral relations? The two states, separated by continents and oceans, have always been found standing together and always there for each other. The 'all-weather' friends, said to be the carriers of Judeo-Christian tradition, seem to be at a crossroads—so much so that the USA had to part ways at the UN.

However, there is a silver lining: President Donald Trump has indicated support for Israel in the future, beginning with naming David Friedman as the next US Ambassador to Israel. President Trump seems to be very eager to work with Israel—he even took to Twitter right after the UN vote, and declared: "Things will be different after 20 January", the day he took office as the President of the USA. Only time will tell how things shape up under the Trump Presidency; but it is obvious that the bilateral relations will keep commentators and researchers busy. Prime Minister Netanyahu, who currently faces criminal charges, may not be there to lead Israel; whoever succeeds him will have to deal with the realities of international diplomacy.

Researchers take into account diplomacy, international relations, history, culture, and politics as some of the factors that guide the relations between two states. These are not static but are dynamic factors, continuously changing, and therefore impacting the relations. Israel-US relations are also the product of a variety of factors nurtured by them, and shape themselves for the future accordingly. The following is a brief account of more than six decades of association, its permutations and combinations, its highs and lows. Going back in time will demonstrate how the leadership in Israel and the US have nurtured these relations.

The Beginning: the Birth of a Nation and the Building of New Ties

The Israel-US relationship is arguably one of the stoutest bilateral associations in the world. The cooperation and commitments between the two states include the trade, diplomacy, and security needs of Israel in the Middle East.[3] The leaders of both the states are vocal about mutual understanding and support on various issues, particularly against terrorism. Time and again, a special reference to a common 'Judeo-Christian' heritage is made to mark the history of intimacy and trust between the people of the two counties.

Since the creation of Israel, many US presidents, beginning with Harry S. Truman, have rhetorically referred to the establishment of Israel as a fulfilment of a biblical prophecy. For them, as it is for the Jewish community, it is an act of return to the holy land after being forced to stay away for more than two millennia. The creation of Israel was, indeed, a remarkable event for those people who saw world history from a biblical perspective. However, the extent to which it has impacted the relations between US and Israel is not easy to assess.

In 1952, a few days before Christmas, President-elect Dwight

Eisenhower gave a speech before the Freedom Foundation in New York wherein he explicitly emphasised the Judeo-Christian tradition in these words:

> Our form of government has no sense unless it is founded in a deeply felt religious faith, and I don't care what it is. With us, of course, it is the Judeo-Christian concept; but it must be a religion that all men are created equal.[4]

As he chose to use this specific term in his official address, it can be assumed that Eisenhower had a fair idea about what would be the relation between the people of the two countries in the years to come.

One public statement coming four years after the creation of Israel is not enough. A closer look at the trajectory of ties tells a more nuanced story. The bilateral ties have not always been as smooth and robust as they appear to be. The USA has not always been close to the Jewish State as generally projected, and differences on various issues have been well documented. While there seems an effort by commentators to put the Judeo-Christian angle into the equation of US-Israel relations, several events show that, despite the so called heritage, their relations have evolved through a series of pragmatic choices and decisions.

Even the recognition of Israel by the USA had political nuances.[5] To begin with, the USA chose to watch the newly found Jewish State from a distance, perceiving it to be some sort of a burden on post-World War II America. Although President Truman wasted no time in recognising Israel, no major foreign policy figure from the US administration presented themselves on the international arena as a supporter of the Jewish State. This continued for several years. Some have even argued that the hurry in recognising Israel was due to the fact the USA, already in confrontation with the USSR, did not want the latter to become the first to do so.[6]

For the people of Israel, President Truman was a tough person to assess, especially when it came to his words and deeds. Although he is believed to have had knowledge of Jewish history and the persecution of Jews, including the Holocaust, he did not demonstrate that he had a special place for Jews in his heart. He even went on to tell Chaim Weizmann that, instead of talking about a Jewish state, he should seek a Palestinian state based on a pluralistic model, like the USA in which Jews, Muslims, and Christians would all live together in peace.[7] President Truman recognised the State of Israel and, in his words, to do so was a "[m]orally and politically correct choice...in the context of maintaining America's true national security."[8]

In the following years, as President Eisenhower's disagreements with the Jewish state during his first term were making news, things got worse when Israel attacked Egypt, in collaboration with Britain and France, during the Suez crisis in October 1956. The US President, seemingly agitated by Israel's defiance of a UN call to withdraw from Egyptian territory, warned that such a decision would cost Israel dear.[9] Quickly realising that it had to go it alone while taking certain decisions of national interest and security, Israel initially refused to withdraw; it agreed only when its vessels were guaranteed free passage through the Straits of Tiran at the mouth of the Gulf of Aqaba. Under the persistent threat by the USA to support UN sanctions, Ben-Gurion agreed to pull out under the condition that the UN would agree to place a patrolling force at the Israeli-Egyptian border in the Sinai. The conditions were met and, despite the US show of high handedness, its pledge to support Israel's access to the Gulf of Aqaba was seen as a US commitment to Israeli security. Meanwhile, Israeli tactics on the war front left the top US officials quite amazed. The Israeli pounding of Soviet-backed Egyptian troops pierced through the impervious layers of US foreign policy design, eventually making the Jewish State a prime beneficiary of the new Eisenhower Doctrine unveiled in early 1957. Washington was well aware that Cold War politics could not blind its policy makers to the other potential partners in the Middle East.

During the same period, Israel is believed to have begun its nuclear programme with the help of France. Eventually, Israel began to examine the possibility of establishing its own nuclear infrastructure, with Shimon Peres playing a key role.[10] Israel began the construction of a reactor in 1958. Two years later, French President Charles de Gaulle decided on changes in the French nuclear policy towards Israel, and asked the latter to publicly declare that it was not building a nuclear reactor.

In one of his speeches a few months before becoming the President, John F. Kennedy (President Eisenhower's successor) summed up how his predecessors have supported and honoured the "special relationship" with the Jews and their prophesised state.

> It was President Woodrow Wilson who forecast with prophetic wisdom the creation of a Jewish homeland. It was President Franklin Roosevelt who kept alive the hopes of Jewish redemption during the Nazi terror. It was President Harry Truman who first recognised the new State of Israel and gave it status in world affairs. And may I add that it would be my hope and my pledge to continue this Democratic tradition—and to be worthy of it.[11]

However, after becoming President, he too, arguably, was not able to move beyond rhetoric as he found himself occupied with the Cold War politics. Before the Lyndon B. Johnson Administration (1965–69), none of the Israeli prime ministers had met the US President in Washington. Kennedy once met with Ben-Gurion in New York.

The Six-Day War: Power Recognises Power

If the creation of a Jewish state in Israel was the fulfilment of some sort of prophecy, Israel decimating its Arab neighbours and capturing their territories—Sinai Peninsula from Egypt; Golan Heights from Syria; and, most importantly, West Bank (including East Jerusalem) from Jordan—was even more significant. When the war broke out, the USA and its forces were busy in Vietnam. The USA would have wanted to help Israel straightaway, but did not do so because of its interests in the Arab states. At that time, it only chose to play a conciliatory role. While Israel was cherishing the moment of victory and the control of the biblical sites, and the Arabs were left flabbergasted by their defeat at the hands of a small neighbour, the USA carefully examined the potential and promise Israel had for the future.

After winning the war against its Arab neighbours, Israel established itself as a force to reckon with in the Middle East. US policy makers, who saw prospects in Israel during the Suez crisis, were compelled to give a serious thought to a future alliance with the Jewish State. The victory also gave impetus to the opinion makers and sympathisers of Israel to develop a discourse of cooperation between the USA and Israel. The USA was engaged in the Cold War and also maintaining good relations with the oil-rich Arab states, and so found it difficult to keep Israel—a country that exhibited remarkable resilience and defence capability—at bay.

Israel-US relations took a leap of faith from this time onwards. Although there was sympathy in the USA for the persecuted Jews of Europe, US official policy had never before reflected an all-out support for Israel. Now the rhetoric changed, setting the tone for the decades to come. Recognising the power of Israel, the USA began to give due attention to bilateral relations and began taking out the best from the alliance in the region. With the Arab states directly or indirectly dispelled from the battle ground and mourning their loss, and dealing with the internal discontent between the regimes and the people, the USA found the best bet in Israel.

While Certain questions need to be asked: What exactly changed after 1967? Did Israel-US relations remain unchanged since then? Did it grow in leaps and bounds? Or, were there some hiccups? How did US foreign policy makers respond to the opportunities offered by Israel as a confident regional ally? Did the USA ignore its oil supplier Arab friends? How did this impact Israel-US relations?

Although Israel continued to battle it out with its neighbours after 1967, things did change slightly as the USA began its assistance and involvement. Still locking horns with the USSR in the Middle East and elsewhere, the USA made full use of Israel in its conflicts in the vicinity. Israel's efficiency in information gathering proved handy for the USA; for example, when Israel provided USA with the captured equipment belonging to the USSR during the War of Attrition (1967–70).

Encouraged by this, the USA began to move ahead in cementing a strategic relationship, taking one step at a time. The negotiating skills of the US Secretary of State, Henry Kissinger (1973–77) following the October War of 1973 brought the two governments closer than ever before. The USA started to give written promises of support for Israel's security in its conflict with its enemies, and sought Israel's flexibility in negotiations over territorial withdrawals. What followed the war was not that simple as the Arab oil embargo loomed large over the USA. However, the understanding with Israel came in handy as it agreed for disengagement accords, and accepted peace with Egypt through Kissinger's "shuttle diplomacy". Uncertainty prevailed for a short period of time in 1975, when President Gerald R. Ford conducted a "reassessment" of Israel-US relations. This remained controversial as the Ford administration was asked about the need for such an inconclusive exercise.

While Ben-Gurion was negotiating with French leaders in the late 1950s over the nuclear reactor, the USA came into picture. On 9 December 1960, Secretary of State, Christian Harter expressed the administration's concern over the revelation that Israel was building a nuclear reactor.[12] The USA put pressure on Israel to allow its scientists to inspect the reactor and its operations. Israel resisted the pressure; but, finally, in May 1961 accepted and permitted a one-time inspection of the reactor by two US scientists.

In a bid to legitimise its nuclear programme, Israel declared that it would not be the first to introduce nuclear weapons into the Middle East. However, this was not enough to ward off American pressure. Finally, upon receipt of a firmly worded memorandum from President Kennedy in May 1963, Ben-Gurion agreed to an annual inspection of the Dimona reactor. American officials visited the Dimona reactor in Spring 1964, February 1965, and again in 1967, prior to the outbreak of the June War. The improvement of Israel's relations with the USA under Prime Minister Eshkol, led to speculation about a possible agreement between the two whereby Israel would suspend its nuclear programme in return for political concessions from the USA, including arms supply arrangements.[13] The USA decided to end inspections of the Dimona reactor in the early 1970s, partly due to the suspicion that Israel had moved beyond the stage of developing a nuclear capability. Continued American surveillance of the reactor in the absence of steps to compel termination of the nuclear armament programme, was liable to be interpreted as an expression of tacit American support for the programme.[14]

It is worth noting that, throughout the discussions regarding security in general and the nuclear issue in particular, Israel demanded American formal assurances in the form of a defence treaty. This would also comprise the transfer of needed American conventional arms. The USA, on the other hand, remained concerned about the Israeli nuclear programme and, from 1968 onwards, Washington persisted in its demands that Israel sign the NPT. One example out of the many that reflected continued American concern about the Israeli nuclear effort was the discussion held between Deputy Prime Minister, Yigal Allon and Secretary of State, Dean Rusk on 10 September 1968, in the presence of Ambassador Yitzhak Rabin. In this discussion, Rusk stressed American concerns regarding nuclear developments in Israel, and also demanded that Israel sign the NPT once again.[15] Indeed, the USA increasingly preferred to avoid the difficult dilemmas of how to react to Israel's ongoing nuclear development.[16]

The American-Israeli "special relationship" also contributed to the USA refraining from pursuing a vigorous diplomatic campaign to pressurise Israel into signing the NPT, and giving up its nuclear development. Moreover, Washington's recognition that Israel indeed continuously faces existential threats added to its reluctance to apply major pressures.[17] Meanwhile, it is also argued that for the USA, the scope and direction of Israel's nuclear programme pose strategic and political problems. At the strategic level, the military and other implications of Israel's undeclared nuclear capabilities have to be addressed. And, at the domestic political level, the Congress and the administration need to devise policies that better reflect and respond to these realities.[18]

Warm Relations amid Continuing Cold War: Camp David and Beyond

After the October War, the USA had no choice but to take firm stand in policy making vis-à-vis Israel. Although taking along the Arab nations was a necessity of time, the USA could not afford to abandon Israel. President Carter did not want to alienate the Arabs, and sought peace between them and Israel in order to smoothly meet the increasing demand of crude oil from the Middle East. His administration brought about more commitments, economic and military aid, and more military cooperation for Israel (largely veiled from the eyes of both the Arabs as well as the American public). On the other hand, it also saw harsh public quarrels with Menachem Begin over the "intransigence" of withdrawing from the West Bank and Gaza. Periodic efforts were also made by the Carter Administration to mobilise American Jewish leaders against Begin's policies. Carter's diplomatic success at Camp David (1978) and the subsequent brokering of the peace treaty between Egypt and Israel in 1979 remain a remarkable chapter in the Israel-US ties. It also set up what may be an impossible standard for personal involvement by other American presidents in peacemaking.

While the USA was maintaining good relations with the Jewish state, yet—despite verbal and written assurances to Israel[19]—the USA was not quite sure in terms of its involvement in the Arab-Israeli conflict. US commitments to Israel's security and survival were becoming frequent and, as far as diplomacy was concerned, these were informal and implicit for the most part. An analysis of the subsequent events during the Cold War suggests that US policymakers treated the Arab-Israeli conflict within the broader context of the US-Soviet tussle, and never in isolation.

Irrespective of what was happening at the level of diplomacy, people in the USA admired Israel for its military prowess and self-reliance. This period also saw a heavy loss of American lives and resources in South Vietnam. These factors helped compensate for periodic strains in the relationship over how much hard-won territory Israel should yield to its Arab adversaries for less than full peace. During the same period, Israel made a request for large amounts of US military and economic aid due to the losses suffered in the 1973 war against a determined Egypt under Anwar Sadat.

What began then, continues till date, and has virtually become a permanent Israeli dependence on the USA. Even now, every year, Israel receives billions of US dollars in direct military and economic aid, and that too in a lump sum at the beginning of the fiscal year. This is quite unlike US foreign aid to other countries (for example, considerable US aid goes to Pakistan and Egypt).[20] According to Ora Coren and Nadan Feldman, till 2012, the US has provided Israel with US$ 233.7 billion in aid (after adjusting for inflation) since 1948.[21] Israel received the most aid in the 1970s between the October War and the 1979 peace agreement with Egypt. For signing the accord with Egypt, Israel received it's largest-ever aid for a single year—some US$ 15.7 billion in grants and loans after adjusting for inflation (it was US$ 4.7 billion at the time)—which was used to fund the transfer of army bases in the Sinai Peninsula back to Israel.[22]

The first US aid to Israel arrived in 1949, and was used for such basic purposes as buying food and absorbing Jewish refugees. Since the late 1970s, US aid has been about US$ 3 billion annually, of which US$ 1.8 billion is military assistance, and the rest for civilian purposes. In 1998, Benjamin Netanyahu, in his first term as Prime Minister, led a drive to convert the civilian portion to military aid, totalling US$ 2.5 billion to US$ 3 billion a year. Some 70 per cent of the aid is designated for Israeli purchases of military equipment from American companies.[23] This humongous aid had a lot to do with the Cold War politics, as the aid was linked to the policies of the bi-polar world. It was expected that things would change after the Cold War; but this was not the case.

This makes one wonder what fuels the unique relationship between the two states. The increasing interest of the USA in the region, particularly in countering the influence of the USSR, coupled with the energy requirement, made US policy makers think of Israel as an all-season partner. They found a good option in a needy Israel, which would serve its purpose to a good effect. After the disintegration of the USSR, a major concern at the back of the mind of US policymakers was put to rest. The last decade of the twentieth century saw the two states closer than ever before.

All this has not come easy for Israel though. It is worth remembering that, since the formation of the State, Israeli leadership had tried to convince US Presidents about their needs. However, various administrations took their time and much calculation to eventually extend support to Israel. US foreign policy now appears to be overwhelmingly pro-Israel when it comes to the Middle East, particularly with regard to the Arab-Israeli conflict. US support for Israel at international forums, its aid for the Jewish State, as well as cooperation in many fields make the two states the best allies in the world.[24]

However, besides Israel, the USA found it worthwhile to back Egypt and the Kingdom of Saudi Arabia as well. US policy was different with Iran (after the 1979 Revolution), Syria, and Saddam's Iraq. The US also started taking direct interest in the peace process between Israel and Palestine. So far, it has tried to broker several agreements between the two, albeit without much success.[25] The main factor that has kept US interest in Israel permanent is said to be the various groups constituting the Israeli lobby, aiming at influencing US foreign policy in favour of the Jewish State.[26] Moreover, the narrative of a Judeo-Christian heritage seeks both the states to be duty bound to work for mutual interest.[27]

End of Cold War: New Dynamics in Bilateral Bond

Have the factors described been able to achieve the results they desired? To what extent they have been able to influence the US foreign policy? The Cold War was seen as the reason behind several decisions made by the USA as far as Israel was concerned. After the collapse of the USSR, the USA became the most powerful country in the world, and Israel was one of the biggest beneficiaries of its monetary and military might. At the same time, the USA used its power to try and bring the conflicting parties to the negotiating table. When George W. Bush became the US President, he was holding quite a powerful office, with most of the Arab countries and Israel cooperating with him. Seeing this as an opportunity, he invited Egypt, Israel, Lebanon, Syria, and a joint Jordanian-Palestinian delegation to Madrid, Spain, in 1991. This led to the Oslo peace process.

Later, under the presidency of Bill Clinton, the USA continued to use its position to foster peace between Israel and the Arab States, including the Palestine. The Oslo Accords between Israel and Palestine signed at the White House, although not a treaty became guidelines for future negotiations. The last agreement of the second millennium was negotiated, once again, under the US administration, and came to be known as Camp David II. Meanwhile, the USA carefully weighed its options for engagement with the region, and kept everyone happy.

September 11 Attacks: US-Israel as allies in the 'War on Terror'

The September 11 terror attacks changed the world completely in terms of security and political alliances. The event not only shocked the world, it made almost certain that the USA was going to avenge the attacks on its soil by uprooting terrorism allegedly emanating from the Middle East; in this Israel became a reliable partner. Israel's own security concerns and its expertise in intelligence gathering during the Second Intifada (which began in 2000), could be trusted easily by the USA. However, this also became the occasion by an emotional speech by Israeli Prime Minister Ariel Sharon, in which he called upon the US to help them fight "terror attacks by the Palestinians".

> ...I turn to the Western democracies, first and foremost the leader of the free world, the United States. Do not repeat the dreadful mistake

> of 1938, when the enlightened democracies of Europe decided to sacrifice Czechoslovakia for the sake of a temporary, convenient solution. Don't try to appease the Arabs at our expense. We will not accept this. Israel will not be Czechoslovakia. Israel will fight terror. There's no difference between 'good terror' and 'bad terror,' just as there is no difference between 'good murder' and 'bad murder.' Terrorism, as we witnessed this week in Alei Sinai, is worse than murder.[28]

Although the USA took into account Israel's perspective on the situation, Sharon's blunt address did not go down well with the US administration. President George W. Bush was reportedly so furious that his administration compelled Sharon to convey to the White House a clarification-cum-apology for his radical comparison.[29] However, the September 11 attack was a crucial step in Israel gaining American approval for military incursions in the West Bank in April 2002.

The Bush administration's zeal in creating and fighting the evil of terrorism, coupled with the pressure from neoconservative thinkers in Israel, pushed US foreign policy makers further towards Israel in fighting terrorism. The US administration backed the disengagement plan by Sharon and, in return, rewarded his successor, Ehud Olmert, by remaining silent (or supporting) attacks on Lebanon's Shia Militia Hezbollah, and Palestine's Sunni Militant group Hamas. Bush's unconditional support to Israel had a lot to do with his own self proclaimed god-given duty to fight against what he called the evil.

This went on unabated till George Bush remained in office. While the US administration was busy in wars in Afghanistan and Iraq, the Right-wing governments in Israel continued the construction of Jewish settlements in the occupied territories, and support Jewish militant groups living there—all in the name of security. The Bush administration hardly ever disappointed Israel, and continued all the promised aid as well as its support in international forums. Things only changed only after the USA got a new President in 2008.

Between a Carrot and Stick: Israel and the Obama Administration

Since the creation of the Jewish State, Israel arguably had the toughest time under the Obama administration. President Obama came at a time when US forces were engaged in the Iraq, Afghanistan and, in the later part of his tenure, with engagements in the Middle East—that is, when the so called Arab Spring brought people into the streets, leaving several states with domestic turmoil, instability, and even armed conflict.

In June 2009, President Obama addressed the Muslim world from Cairo, speaking about his vision for solving the Israeli-Palestinian conflict. He reiterated his words at the United Nations General Assembly a few months later. In both speeches, President Obama expressed his wish to see an end to the occupation and an end to the building of settlements, and expressed his commitments to seeing an independent Palestinian state living side by side with Israel. "The United States does not accept the legitimacy of continued Israeli settlements". With these words, President Obama sent jitters to Israel, which was expecting support from the USA at this crucial juncture.

Since President Obama assumed office, there were several points of discord between the two countries. The USA ignored the concerns of Israel regarding the Iranian nuclear issue, and went ahead with the deal in 2016. Israel had repeatedly said that Iran was developing nuclear arsenal which would be detrimental for peace and security in the region; but the USA was convinced by the International Atomic Energy Agency (IAEA) monitoring Iran's nuclear enrichment, that it was safe. Both President Obama and Prime Minister Netanyahu never appeared to be getting along as both leaders also clashed over the issue of settlements in the Palestinian territories. President Obama did not mince words when it came to criticizing Israeli settlements in the Palestinian Territories. Thus, though promising peace in the region, President Obama ended his tenure with more chaos in the region than in 2009. The relationship between President Obama and Prime Minister Netanyahu was marked by rifts on many issues, including the two-state solution. Prime Minister Netanyahu continues to defend the occupation of the Palestinian Territories, and has categorically said that he would not consider withdrawing from the West Bank in the next twenty years.[30] While addressing a gathering at the Centre for American Progress (November 2015), Prime Minister Netanyahu rejected the notion that the Israeli settlement construction in the occupied West Bank constitutes a threat to peace. "There have been no new settlements built in the past 20 years," he said in an attempt to differentiate between building new communities and new settlement units. "The additions are in existing communities."[31]

This did not go well with the US administration. Prime Minister Netanyahu tried to frame the construction of new settlement units as necessary. The Israeli leader did not hide his anger with the Obama administration; indeed, he left many fuming when, in March 2016, he cancelled a visit to the White House which the US President got to know only through the press. The world media reacted to the event, taking it as a defining moment in the history of Israel-US relations. As *The Times of Israel* noted, there is no previous public record of an Israeli Prime Minister ever rejecting an invitation to meet a US President in the White House.[32]

Things finally hit rock bottom in the UN on 23 December 2016 when the USA chose to abstain from voting on a resolution condemning settlements. For Prime Minister Netanyahu, it was the final betrayal by a president who was supposed to be an ally, but never really was. For President Obama, it was the inevitable result of Prime Minister Netanyahu's own stubborn defiance of international concerns with his policies.[33]

Lobby, Heritage, and Diplomacy: Is there indeed a Judeo-Christian Heritage?

The very mention of the 'Judeo-Christian Heritage' sparks several debates. The biblical perspective of the history and politics of the world may be a reductive approach to interpreting events; however, it has always kept a section of analysts busy at their desks. The US-Israel relationship has been an obvious example to promote this theory. Anything said and done by the leaders from either side can be taken as an expression of imagined promises between the two sets of people. There may be several commonalities between how a section of Jews and Christians perceive their past and plan their future. Yet, claiming that there is an alliance operating beyond the common sense of international diplomacy needs a lot to establish its truth. As mentioned above, there have been several US leaders who have used the rhetoric of the 'special relationship' between the two countries. However, there are even more instances wherein expediency has prevailed over everything else. The USA, for all practical purposes, has chosen pragmatism, despite the presence of any 'special relationship' based on the Judeo-Christian heritage.

With the advent of the twenty first century, while probing the *End of History* (1992) and the *Clash of Civilizations* (1996), theories coined by Francis Fukuyama and Samuel P. Huntington respectively, a working paper by John Mearsheimer and Stephen Walt: "The Israel Lobby and U.S. Foreign Policy"[34] provoked an equally important debate. The controversial thesis in this paper opened up a Pandora's Box. While a section of academics praised the scholars for starting a new debate, others accused them of shoddy scholarship. These papers accused the American Jews of working only in the interest of Israel, and that American Jews often act on behalf of the wishes of a foreign government, and that there are forces within the US Jewish community that prevent any significant dissent from this stance. These authors probed the premises of the US support extended to Israel, and concluded that the USA is backing Israel on very flimsy ground.

Away from the game of allegations and defence, and irrespective of the comments being made about the bilateral relationship, the reality of public opinion in the US vis-à-vis Israel is quite favourable. People who support Israel and want the US administration to do so often argue that the USA should support Israel due to a moral obligation resulting from the persecution faced by the Jews in Europe.[35] Another argument that is often put forward is the fact that Israel, like the USA, is a democracy—in fact the only democracy in the Middle East. Therefore, a democracy should stand by another democracy.

One of the strongest arms of the alleged Israel (also Zionist) lobby in the USA is the American-Israeli Public Affairs Committee (AIPAC). The AIPAC is a lobbying group whose main aim is advocacy for the state of Israel and to influence US foreign policy makers to remain favourable to the Jewish State. One of the main functions of the AIPAC is to keep a close eye on US politics, its elections, and leadership. Most American leaders, particularly those aspiring to be the President, attend AIPAC congregations, and promise unabated support for the State of Israel and that they will stand by it through thick and thin. Things changed after 1967, with the USA backing Israel on almost all its decisions, mainly regarding security measures. Whether this is due to the pressure exerted by pro-Israeli groups, or whether it is USA's own interest in the region is a matter of debate.

A good example of how the US leadership chooses what to say is President Carter's March 1977 statement in which he said that he supported Palestinian human rights, including the "right to a homeland". Before that, Carter acknowledged how his own pro-Zionist beliefs had influenced his Middle East policy.[36] He described the State of Israel as, "a return at last, to the biblical land from which the Jews were driven so many hundreds of years ago...The establishment of the nation of Israel is the fulfilment of biblical prophecy and the very essence of its fulfilment."[37] However, American voters supporting Israel had different plans for Carter. When Carter vacillated over the Israeli settlement programme and proposed the creation of a Palestinian homeland, he alienated the pro-Israeli coalition of Jews and evangelicals who switched their support to Ronald Reagan in the 1980 elections.

Reagan, in return, ushered in not only, arguably, the most pro-Israel administration in US history but also gave several Christian Zionists prominent political posts.[38] He reportedly believed that the USA, like Israel, was the product of a 'divine plan', and identified the USA with Israel as two 'stable and democratic' countries sharing the same Judeo-Christian heritage. A believer in the literal truth of the Bible, Reagan also believed in its prophetic predictions. On at least seven public occasions, he alluded to biblical prophecies about the coming of Armageddon, or the final conflict between good and evil.[39]

Bill Clinton (1993–2000) was more favourable to the secular elements of the Israeli political system. His Israeli ties were with the Labour Party, led by Yitzhak Rabin and Shimon Peres, and not with the conservative Likud Party. Through this alliance, President Clinton embraced the Oslo peace accords, which were opposed by Likud and the Christian Zionists because the accords called for reductions, however modest, in the expansion of Jewish settlements, and asked that Israel withdraw from a significant portion of the Occupied Territories. The Armageddon cry resumed with the ascendancy of George W. Bush to power.

US support for Israel on many occasions is well documented in the discussion of bilateral ties. There have been major incidents wherein the US has abandoned Israel completely, and chosen its own interest ahead of the latter's concerns. Thus, for instance, the powerful 'Israeli Lobby' could do nothing when the USA went ahead and helped Saudi Arabia develop its air force with state of the art equipment. In 1991, during the run up to the Madrid Conference, the issue of loan guarantee also remained very contentious. Again, the Bush administration did not listen to the Yitzhak Shamir (Likud) government in Israel. The USA suspected that the money sent for rehabilitation was used in building settlements and, despite efforts made by the pro-Israeli lobby, the US administration did not move from its stand. The noteworthy point here is that although Shamir thought he could gather the support of American Jews on the issue, they remained divided on the question of backing Israel.

The Iranian nuclear issue made news for quite some time, and Israel's concerns were obvious. No one can forget the image of Netanyahu at the UN, holding an image of Iran's nuclear programme depicting a time bomb. He failed to convince the USA regarding his worries, and the USA went ahead with the nuclear agreement with Iran. Now, Israel is hoping to take up the issue with the new US President. With President Trump calling it a badly negotiated deal, Israel can hope that things can change in its favour.

Meanwhile, Russia's return to the region has brought back the memories of the Cold War, and the USA would want to continue its engagement in the region. It is interesting to note that beyond the USA,

Israel is finding a new partner in Russia. According to the Israeli newspaper *Ha'aretz*, the ties between Israel and Russia have never been better.[40] Disappointed with the USA on the Iran nuclear issue, Prime Minister Netanyahu reportedly hopes that Russia can even help negotiating an understanding with Iran.[41] October 2016 also marked the completion of 25 years since Russia and Israel restored diplomatic relations after the Soviet Union severed them in 1967 following the June War. Israel sees Russia as an important player in the Middle East, particularly after its recent advancements against the ISIS in Syria. Indeed, for Prime Minister Netanyahu (or any future Israeli leader) it is important to create a better understanding with President Vladimir Putin, to reduce the possibility of accidental military clashes in Syria, and improve mutual understanding more broadly in order to maintain balanced ties.[42]

Interestingly, in a bid to ensure that Israel does not get too close to Russia, in September 2016, the USA decided to give the Israeli military US$ 38 billion over the next decade. This has been described by Washington as the biggest package of military assistance in its history. However, under this deal, Israel would not be able to solicit extra money from Capitol Hill. In other conditions placed on the new memorandum of understanding, Israel would no longer be allowed to spend over a quarter of the military aid on home-produced weaponry, and would instead be required to spend the full amount on US arms. Nor would it be able to spend any of the aid on fuel for its armed forces.[43] The future will be decided by how the leadership in both the countries treat each other. With President Trump at the helm of affairs and a pro-settlement David Friedman as the new US Ambassador, Israel must be impatiently waiting for some action.

Conclusion

Israel-US relations are based on pragmatism. The US administration has chosen Israel as its ally and strategic partner after careful deliberations. Indeed, it took them almost two decades to realise the potential of the Jewish State. Since 1967, bilateral relations are going smoothly, with continuous US military and economic aid to Israel. The USA has stood by Israel in all international bodies and supported its case for existence. At the same time, the USA has reminded Israel of the Palestinian people and their national rights. US presidents have sought solutions for the Israel-Egypt and Israel-Palestine conflicts, compelling the Israeli leadership to accept peace plans in lieu of security promises.

At the same time, the USA continues its bonhomie with Arab monarchies in the Gulf region and military dictators in North Africa. In the case of the nuclear deal with the Islamic Republic of Iran, the USA seems to have ignored the concerns raised by Israel. This suggests that US interests in Israel are subject to assessments of US foreign policy makers. The latter take up things that are found useful for the larger interests of their own country, caring little about other 'special things'.

Currently, the Israel-US relationship is at an important juncture. One may say that it has virtually come back from where it began. With Russia announcing the return of its influence in the region by bombing the so-called Islamic State militants in Syria, the USA would not want to give any free movement to one of its biggest adversaries ever. Israel too, receiving fewer favours from the USA, has been looking up to Russia. Indeed, its leaders are travelling to Russia. The fact that Israel has a considerable population of Russian origin makes Israel even more interesting for Russia. The USA would definitely not want Israel to slip through. When it comes to international relations, it is not easy to predict what the future holds. One thing is for sure—we are in for a time where Israel will be at the centre of every equation.

NOTES

1. The pact, laid out in a Memorandum of Understanding, will be worth US$ 38 billion over the course of a decade, an increase of roughly 27 per cent on the money pledged in the last agreement, which was signed in 2007. See also, Green, Emma, 'Why does the United States Give so much Money to Israel?' *The Atlantic*, 15 September 2016, at http://www.theatlantic.com/international/archive/2016/09/united-states-israel-memorandum-of-understanding-military-aid/500192/, last accessed on 28 December 2016.
2. The transcript of John Kerry speech is available at http://time.com/4619064/john-kerrys-speech-israel-transcript/ last accessed on 29 December.
3. Dine, Thomas A., "The Revolution in U.S.-Israel Relations", *Journal of Palestine Studies*, Vol. 15, No. 4, pp. 134–143.
4. Henry, Patrick, "And I Don't Care What It Is: The Tradition-History of a Civil Religion Proof-Text", *The Journal of the American Academy of Religion*, Vol. 49, No. 1, pp. 35–49. In the beginning, "Judeo-Christian" had served only to designate connections between Judaism and Christianity in antiquity. Its first appearance, according to the Supplement to the Oxford English Dictionary, occurred in the Literary Guide in 1899 in which a "Judaeo-Christian 'continuity' theory" postulated the development of Church ritual out of the practices of the Second Temple. Not until some decades later did the term begin to be used to refer to values or beliefs shared by Jews and Christians, that is, to a common western religious outlook. For a detailed discussion on the understanding and evolution of the term 'Judeo-Christian' read, Silk, Mark, 'Notes on the Judeo-Christian Tradition in America', *American Quarterly*, Vol. 36, No. 1, pp. pp. 65–85
5. See, Little, Douglas, 'The Making of a Special Relationship: The United States

and Israel, 1957–68' *International Journal of Middle East Studies*, Vol. 25, No. 4, pp. 563–585.

6. Ibid.
7. Radosh, Allis, and Radosh, Ronald, "The Origins of the US-Israeli Relationship: Truman and the Jewish State", The Washington Institute, Policy Analysis, May 2010, at: http://www.washingtoninstitute.org/policy-analysis/view/the-origins-of-the-u.s.-israeli-relationship-truman-and-the-jewish-state, accessed on December 20 2016.
8. Ibid.
9. Little, Douglas, op. cit.
10. Evron, Yair, *Israel's Nuclear Dilemma*, London: Routledge, 1994, p. 3
11. Speech by Senator John F. Kennedy, Zionists of America Convention, Statler Hilton Hotel, New York, NY, August 1960, at http://www.presidency.ucsb.edu/ws/?pid=74217, accessed on 30 December 2016.
12. Ibid. p. 4
13. Aronson, Shlomo, *Conflict and Bargaining in the Middle East*, Baltimore: Johns Hopkins University Press, 1978, p. 51.
14. Spector, Leonard, *Nuclear Proliferation Today* New York: Vintage Books, 1984, p. 375.
15. Haas, Richard N., "South Asia: Too Late to Remove the Bomb?" *Orbis*, 32, Winter 1988, p. 109.
16. Evron, Yair, op.cit. p. 146.
17. Ibid.
18. Cobban, Helena, "Israel's Nuclear Game: The US Stake", *World Policy Journal*, Vol. 5, No. 3, pp. 415–433; see also, Cohen, Avner, *Israel and the Bomb*, Jerusalem: Schocken Books, 2000.
19. John F. Kennedy Administration, "Memorandum on Implications of U.S. Security Assurances to Israel", available at: http://www.jewishvirtuallibrary. org/jsource/US-Israel/FRUS8_7_63.html, accessed 12 September 2016.
20. The US also provides Israel with some of its most advanced military technology and hardware, and frequently shares highly classified intelligence. No other US ally has consistently enjoyed such benefits. Apart from Israel, US military aid goes to Afghanistan, Egypt, Pakistan, and Nigeria.
21. Coren, Ora, and Feldman, Nadan, "US Aid to Israel Totals US$233.7b Over Six Decades", *Ha'aretz*, 20 March 2013, at http://www.haaretz.com/israel-news/business/u-s-aid-to-israel-totals-233-7b-over-six-decades.premium-1.510592, accessed on September 22, 2016.
22. Ibid.
23. Ibid.
24. Jeremy M. Sharp, "US Foreign Aid to Israel", Congressional Research Service Report, 2015, at https://fas.org/sgp/crs/mideast/RL33222.pdf, accessed on 2 October 2016.
25. Op. cit. Thomas A. Dine, 1986.
26. See Mearsheimer John M., and Walt, Stephen, *The Israeli Lobby and U.S. Foreign Policy*, New York: Farrar, Straus and Giroux, 2007
27. Marsden, Lee, "US-Israel Relations: A Special Friendship" in Dumbrell John and Shafer Axel R. (eds.), *America's Special Relationships: Foreign and Domestic Aspects of Politics and Alliance*, London: Routledge, 2009, p. 91.

28. Cited by Verter, Yossi, "How 9/11 Changed U.S. Policy Toward Israel", in *Ha'aretz*, 9 September 2011, at http://www.haaretz.com/israel-news/how-9-11-changed-u-s-policy-toward-israel-1.383437, accessed 2 January 2017
29. Ibid.
30. Rory McCarthy, "Binyamin Netanyahu tells US: We won't stop east Jerusalem settlement building", *The Guardian*, at https//www.theguardian.com/world/2010/apr/22/binyamin-netanyahu-jerusalem-settlements-building, accessed 15 October 2016.
31. A Conversation with Prime Minister Benjamin Netanyahu, video available at: https://www.americanprogress.org/events/2015/11/03/124907/a-conversation-with-prime-minister-benjamin-netanyahu-2/, accessed 29 September 2016.
32. Ahren, Raphael, "Netanyahu's Unprecedented Snub of Obama Meeting Defies Explanation", *The Times of Israel*, 8 March 2016, at http://www.timesofisrael.com/netanyahus-unprecedented-snub-of-obama-meeting-defies-explanation/, last accessed 12 August 2016.
33. Baker, Peter, "For Obama and Netanyahu, a Final Clash after Years of Conflict", *The New York Times*, 23 December, 2016, at https://www.nytimes.com/2016/12/23/world/middleeast/israel-benjamin-netanyahu-barack-obama.html?_r=0, accessed 3 January 2017.
34. Mearsheimer, John J., and Walt, Stephen M., "The Israeli Lobby and US Foreign Policy", at http://mearsheimer.uchicago.edu/pdfs/A0040.pdf, accessed 23 July 2016.
35. Weiss, Lindsay, *"More than Moral Obligation: The US Israel Commercial Relationship"*, Levelhead Politics, at http://www.lhpolitics.com/single-post/2016/06/06/More-than-Moral-Obligation-The-US-Israel-Commercial-Relationship, accessed 19 October 2016.
36. Carter, Jimmy, *The Blood of Abraham: Insights into the Middle East*, London: Sidgwick and Jackson, 1985, p. 70.
37. Speech by President Jimmy Carter on 1 May 1978, Department of State Bulletin, Vol. 78, No. 2015 (1978).
38. James Watt, a Pentecostal and a strong conservative, joined the cabinet as Secretary of the Interior; antiabortion activist C. Everett Koop became surgeon general; and Robert Billings landed a position in the Department of Education. In the GOP-majority Senate, Richard Halverson—the ministerial dean of Beltway evangelicals—served as chaplain. Morton Blackwell used his evangelical connections to massage relations with the Christian Right during his time as Reagan's liaison with the conservatives. Faith Whittlesey, who took over Blackwell's outreach to religious conservatives, likewise kept out the welcome mat for evangelical leaders. Such contacts no doubt factored into Reagan's decision to declare 1983 the "Year of the Bible" and, that same year, to contribute an article to the antiabortion Human Life Review. See also, Steven P. Miller, "The evangelical presidency: Reagan's dangerous love affair with the Christian right", *Salon*, at http://www.salon.com/2014/05/18/the_evangelical_presidency_reagans_dangerous_love_affair_with_the_christian_right/accessed 12 October 2016.
39. Davidson, Lawrence, "Christian Zionism as a Representation of American

Manifest Destiny", *Critique: Critical Middle Eastern Studies*, Vol. 14, No. 2, pp 157–69.

40. Ravid, Barak, "Netanyahu, Usually Outspoken, Dares Not Criticize Putin", *Ha'aretz*, 7 June 2016, at http://www.haaretz.com/israel-news/.premium-1.723558, accessed on October 10, 2016.
41. Sharkov, Damien, "Why Is Israel's Benjamin Netanyahu Warming to Russia's Vladimir Putin?" *Newsweek*, 6 July 2016, at http://europe.newsweek.com/why-israels-netanyahu-warming-putin-467569?rm=eu, accessed 1 January 2017.
42. Borshchevskaya,Anna,"The Maturing of Israeli-Russian Relations", The Washington Institute, at http://www.washingtoninstitute.org/policy-analysis/view/the-maturing-of-israeli-russian-relations, accessed 29 September 2016.
43. Borger, Julian "US pledges record US$38bn military aid to Israel over next 10 years", *The Guardian*, 13 September 2016 available at: https://www.theguardian.com/world/2016/sep/13/us-israel-aid-38-billion-record-military-assistance, accessed 20 September 2016.

REFERENCES

Ben-Zevi, Abraham, *The Origins of the American-Israeli Alliance: The Jordanian Factor*,New York: Taylor And Francis, 2007.

Evron, Yair, *Israel's Nuclear Dilemma*, London: Taylor and Francis, 1994.

Gilboa, Eytan and Inbar, Efraim (eds.), *US-Israel Relations in a New Era: Issues and Challenges After 9/11*,New York: Taylor And Francis, 2008.

Mearsheimer John J. and Walt, Stephen M., *The Israeli Lobby and US Foreign Policy*, New York: Farrar, Straus and Giroux, 2007.

Reich, Bernard, *Securing the Covenant: United States-Israel Relations After The Cold War*,London: Praeger, 1995.

Ross, Dennis, *Doomed To Succeed: The US-Israel-Relationship from Truman to Obama*, New York: Farrar, Straus and Giroux, 2015.

Sheffer, Gabriel (ed.), *US-Israel Relations at the Crossroads*,London: Francis Cass, 1997

Articles

Clarke, Duncan L., "The Arrow Missile: The United States, Israel and Strategic Cooperation", *Middle East Journal*, Vol. 48, No. 3, pp. 475-491

Dine, Thomas A., "Achievements and Advances in the United States-Israel Relationship", *Journal of Palestine Studies*, Vol. 16, No. 4, pp. 95–106

Gazit, Mordechai, "The Genesis of the US-Israeli Military-Strategic Relationship and the Dimona Issue", *Journal of Contemporary History*, Vol. 35, No. 3, pp. 413–422

Lewis Samuel W., "The United States and Israel: Evolution of an Unwritten Alliance", *Middle East Journal*, Vol. 53, No. 3, Special Issue on Israel, pp. 364–378.

Little, Douglas, "The Making of a Special Relationship: The United States and Israel, 1957-68", *International Journal of Middle East Studies*, Vol. 25, No. 4, pp. 563–585

16

India-Israel Relations: The Influence of Third Parties

Manjari Singh

ABSTRACT

India established diplomatic relations with Israel only in January 1992 even though it had recognised the Jewish State in September 1950. Since the establishment of diplomatic relations, political, economic, cultural, and security relations have been flourishing considerably. Important as they are, this chapter looks at the influence of external players in Indo-Israeli relations, especially after normalisation. Some external factors contributed to the delayed normalisation while others have been facilitating a more rapid progress in the bilateral relations. Looking through the external prism, this chapter examines the influence of foreign powers in inhibiting as well as facilitating Indo-Israeli relations through competition and rivalry.

Background

There have been various reasons and justifications for the four-decades of Indian non-relations with Israel; these range from domestic considerations (Indian Muslim population influenced India to be supportive of the Palestinian cause), Cold War political calculations, or limited commonalities between the two countries. The roots of this policy can be traced to early 1920s when the shared anti-colonial worldview resulted in the Indian nationalists forging a common cause with the Arabs of Palestine. The Congress Party and its leaders, including Mahatma Gandhi and

Jawaharlal Nehru, vociferously advocated a pro-Arab position on Palestine, and this trend continued when Britain—the Mandate power—referred the Palestine issue to the newly-formed United Nations. In May 1947, India was elected to the 11-member United Nations Special Commission on Palestine (UNSCOP), and while a seven-member majority proposed partition of Palestine as the solution, India (supported by Iran and Yugoslavia) proposed a Federal plan for Palestine.

Unfortunately, the Indian plan was rejected by both the contending parties: the Arabs were opposed to Jews being granted even minimal autonomy within an Arab Palestine while the Jews rejected the Indian plan because it offered them civil and religious rights when the majority plan offered them sovereignty and statehood. Hence, rejected by both the parties, the Indian plan was never discussed by the UN. When the partition plan came before the UN General Assembly on 29 November, India joined the Arab and Islamic countries, and opposed it. In May 1949, India also opposed Israel's admission into the UN.

However, after considerable hesitation and internal deliberations, India granted diplomatic recognition to Israel in September 1950. There were sufficient indications that India was prepared for a full-fledged diplomatic relationship with Israel, including a resident mission in Tel Aviv. A promise to this effect was made by Prime Minister Jawaharlal Nehru when senior Israeli diplomat, Walter Eytan, met him in New Delhi in early 1952. Diplomatic exchange did not happen— or rather, happened more than four decades after Nehru's promise. Scholars attribute this to senior Congress leader and Education Minister Maulana Abul Kalam Azad who dissuaded Nehru from establishing diplomatic relations with Israel on the ground that such a move would go against domestic Muslim sentiments in India, and could be used by Pakistan for anti-India propaganda in the Arab world, especially over the Kashmir issue. A formal Indian opposition to normalisation came in November 1956 in the wake of the Israel-led tripartite aggression against Egypt over the Suez crisis and, since then, the-time-is-not-ripe became the standard Indian position vis-à-vis normalisation.

Over the years, India sought to further its interests in the Middle East by flagging its support for the Palestinian cause, and the absence of relations with Israel became integral to India's zero-sum approach to the Arab-Israeli equation. India joined various Arab and Islamic countries in proposing or voting in favour of various resolutions against Israel in the UN, and other international forums such as the Non-aligned Movement. This reached its crescendo in November 1975 when India sponsored and voted in favour of the UN General Assembly Resolution that equated Zionism with racism. Thus, it was clear that only a far reaching transformation of the international system could bring about a change in India's attitude towards Israel.

This came with the end of the Cold War and the disintegration of the Soviet Union as well as the emergence of the USA as the pre-eminent global power. Yasser Arafat's support for Iraqi President Saddam Hussein over the Kuwait crisis considerably weakened the Palestine Liberation Organization (PLO) and the Palestinian factor in inter-Arab relations. Arafat's willingness to attend the Middle East Peace Conference in Madrid in October 1991 also diluted India's reluctance to deal with Israel, especially when there were no bilateral disputes between the two. Under such circumstances, Prime Minister P.V. Narasimha Rao signalled India's willingness to deal with the post-Cold War international climate by breaking with the past and, in January 1992, established full diplomatic relations with Israel. Since then, the bilateral relations have been progressing considerably, and have been a major source of international attention and envy.

How have external players responded and reacted to Indo-Israeli relations since then? For the purpose of clarity, the external players can be divided by regions: Palestine, Iran and Saudi Arabia are the Middle Eastern players; the Southern Asian region comprises of Pakistan and China; and the United States and USSR/Russia are the international players. Some contributed to the absence of normalisation while others facilitated Indo-Israeli relations and, in some cases, one could notice a tacit competition. It would not be incorrect to state that the non-relations before 1992 and the progressing relations since 1992 have been influenced by external players.

The Middle Eastern Region

Palestine

Strictly speaking, Palestine cannot be identified as an external factor; but it is an integral to India's Israel policy. The historical commitments to the Palestinian cause have been a major factor in India's Israel policy. On moral as well as political considerations, Indian nationalists have opposed the idea of a Jewish demand for a national homeland in Palestine. Such a position was partly the result of the limited understanding of Mahatma Gandhi and other Indian leaders about Jewish history and problem. In November 1938, Gandhi made his most widely quoted statement on the subject: 'Palestine belongs to the Arabs in the same sense as England belongs to the English and France to the French.' In the wake of considerable criticisms from Jewish figures and the Nazi Holocaust, in July 1946 Gandhi observed,

> Hitherto I have refrained from saying anything in public regarding the Jew-Arab controversy. I have done so for good reasons. That does not mean any want of interest in the question, but it does mean that I do not consider myself sufficiently equipped with knowledge for the purpose.[1]

Since the early 1930s, Indian nationalists viewed the Palestinian issue as an integral part of the larger anti-imperialist and anti-colonialist struggle. After the partition of the Sub-continent, support for the Palestinians became an important instrument through which India sought to blunt the role of Pakistan, and further its interest in the Arab and Islamic countries of the Middle East. If Pakistan used its Islamic credential, India flagged its 'consistent support' for the Palestinian cause, dating back to the first quarter of the twentieth century. During the Cold War, India lacked adequate economic leverage, and its diplomatic status was dented after the Sino-Indian conflict of 1962. Thus, the Palestinian cause became its primary politico-diplomatic instrument, especially in the Middle East.

Seen in this historic context, normalisation was a considerable shift, and signalled India's willingness to abandon the zero-sum approach towards the Arab-Israeli conflict. New Delhi was prepared to deal with both the parties in furtherance of its interests. During the 1990s, this was marked by India trying to 'balance' its newly found relations with Israel by high-profiled visits by PLO Chairman Yasser Arafat to New Delhi, or through pro-Palestinian statements. This practice has been less frequent, especially after the UPA came to power in 2004.

At the same time, India has not abandoned or diluted its position on some of the core issues pertaining to the Arab-Israeli conflict—such as, Palestinian statehood, settlement, borders, or Jerusalem. The only difference is that India has become more balanced and nuanced in its criticism of Israel, and it no longer blames Israel for all the ills. For long, India continued to support the Arabs and Palestinians in various international forums, especially the UN. There was a marked a shift in July 2015, when India abstained in the United Nations Human Rights Council (UNHRC) over the Gaza crisis. Only a year earlier, India voted with the rest on the 'disproportionate use of force' by Israel, and condemned violence in Gaza[2] without trying to consider rocket attacks carried out by militant Palestinian group Hamas against Israeli civilians.

One observer has commented that

> The Indian government's seemingly schizophrenic attitude to the Israeli pounding of Gaza is a classic case of the head and the heart being seriously misaligned. In its heart, the BJP-led NDA would like to be with Israel, and feels an emotional connect with that beleaguered, but militarily powerful, Jewish state; the head, however, dictates that India's economic interests—oil, Indians working in the Gulf—also need to be protected. Then there is the need to mollify the Muslim minority in India, whose sentiments are the exact opposite of the Modi government's — that is, against Israel.[3]

The Indian government attributed its July 2015 abstention to the resolution's reference of the Rome Statute or the International Criminal Court (ICC) of which India was not a signatory.[4] Though it reiterated that its position vis-à-vis Palestine has not changed, it was the first time since 1992 that India has abstained on a major resolution concerning the Israeli-Palestinian conflict. The move has upset a section of the Indian elite as well as the Palestinian leadership,[5] while Israel expressed its gratitude for the Indian move.

According to former diplomat Rajendra Abhyankar, India's public posture regarding the Palestine issue is unlikely to change.[6] Since the Palestine issue has a strong resonance in domestic politics, India is unlikely to abandon or dilute its support for the Palestinians; but, at the same time, it is likely to be less pronounced than in the past, primarily because of the lessening importance of the Palestinian cause in the inter-Arab relations. Facing strong domestic unrest, most Arab regimes are fighting for their survival, and the Palestinian cause is not their top priority. This will be reflected in India factoring in the Palestinian issue while dealing with Israel.

Iran

Israel has had roller-coaster relations with Iran. Until the Islamic Revolution of 1979, the latter was part of its peripheral diplomacy whereby Israel forged closer relations with non-Arab countries (Iran and Turkey) and groups (Kurds in Iraq and Maronites in Lebanon). In 1950, Iran became the second Islamic country after Turkey to recognise the Jewish State[7] and, under the Shah, Iran shared Israel's animosity towards the Arab world, and even provided large quantities of oil to the Jewish State. This bonhomie abruptly ended following the Islamic revolution, and Iran moved closer to the Palestinians, emerging as the most vociferous opponent of Israel's right to exist. In August 1979, Ayatollah Khomeini declared the fourth Friday of the Islamic holy month of Ramadan as Al-Quds (Jerusalem) Day and, since then Muslim communities around the world have been marking this day through various protest actions, meetings, and commemorations.

Since 1979, Iran has also become a major centre for anti-Semitism, and organises a number of events and competitions commemorating or denying the Holocaust. By supporting various Shia (Hezbollah)[8] and Sunni (Hamas)[9] militant groups, Iran has emerged as the de facto neighbour of Israel. If these were insufficient, a number of non-conventional weapons programmes currently underway are explained within the context of the Iranian rivalry and animosity vis-à-vis Israel. The decade-long controversy over the Iranian nuclear programme has resulted in periodic threats and intimidating statements from Israeli leaders and, for long, the international strategic community has speculated a possible Israeli pre-emptive strike against key nuclear installations in Iran.[10]

Both Israel and Iran are key strategic partners of India: one in the military-security arena, the other for energy security. Therefore, maintaining a balance between the two has been a major challenge facing Indian foreign policy. While Iran has been less interventionist in Indo-Israeli relations, the reverse is not true. India and Israel do not see eye-to-eye on Iran; and Israeli concerns emanate from two closely linked security issues: possible technology leaks and terrorism. During the visit of Prime Minister Ariel Sharon to India in September 2003, Israel raised its concerns over the possible leaking of its technology supplied to India.[11] Prime Minister Atal Behari Vajpayee assured Israel against the possible and unintentional transfer or leakage of Israeli technology to Iran.

Because of its support to various militant groups in the region and their activities, Israel sees Iran as the major player in terrorism; some Israeli leaders even accuse Tehran of being 'nerve centre' of terrorism.[12] On 13 February 2012, a member of the Israeli embassy was attacked in a failed car bomb attack in New Delhi, and this was attributed to Iran-associated entities.[13] Even more than four years later, the culprits were not apprehended let alone convicted. Moreover, because of its energy security concerns vis-à-vis Iran, New Delhi has not paid heed to some of Israel's concerns vis-à-vis Iran.

Even on a direct bilateral level, New Delhi has maintained a studied silence over many anti-Israeli and anti-Semitic remarks by Iranian president Mahmoud Ahmadinejad. In October 2005, responding to one of his statements that Israel should be 'wiped off the map,' an official Indian spokesperson merely reminded reporters that India had recognised Israel 'decades ago', and had diplomatic relations with it. While Israelis see Iran as the epicentre of international terrorism, Indians view the Islamic

Republic as a partner in fighting terrorism, especially in Afghanistan. India and Israel, thus, are not on the same page over Iran.

However, there remains a series of subtexts that reflect a more complicated picture.[14] Thus, despite repeated requests, India has not been accommodative of Israel in its policy towards the Iranian nuclear controversy. Indeed, its voting in the International Atomic Energy Agency and other forums were primarily due to American pressures than Israeli requests. For its part, Iran has been pursuing robust relations with India without unduly worrying about Indo-Israeli relations. This accommodative approach has given a greater leeway to Indo-Iranian relations than Indo-Israeli relations. One could even suggest that India has managed to quarantine Israel while pursuing closer relations, especially energy ties, with Tehran.

Saudi Arabia

The Kingdom of Saudi Arabia does not recognise Israel, and indeed, sent a small military contingent during the first Arab-Israeli war of 1948. Though it did not take an active part in subsequent wars, Saudi politico-strategic fortunes changed after the June 1967 war. The Arab defeat marked the end of the secular pan-Arab nationalism championed by Gamal Abdul Nasser, and ushered in the regional domination of conservative religious forces led by Saudi Arabia. This was consecrated in the first Islamic summit conference held in Rabat in September 1969, and the oil crisis during the October 1973 War added an economic component to the Saudi influence. Since then, the Kingdom has emerged as the most important player in the Persian Gulf region. Its prolonged proximity with the USA acquired a strategic dimension in the wake of the Islamic Revolution in Iran and the resultant alienation of Tehran from the West. Thus, since the late 1960s, Saudi Arabia has led the Arab-Islamic opposition to Israel—and this has been so despite its close energy-linked strategic partnership with the USA.

At the same time, a host of regional developments resulted in Saudi Arabia offering a conditional peace with Israel. These include the Camp David Accords between Egypt and Israel (which were concluded in 1978), Islamic Revolution in Iran in 1979, and the Soviet invasion of Afghanistan later that year. In August 1981, Crown Prince Fahd came out with a peace plan that tacitly accepted Israel's recognition in return for the latter withdrawing to pre-1967 borders, and this became a Fahd plan the following year. Neither side was in position to make the transition necessary for an agreement. And, since then, Saudi Arabia did not go beyond endorsing various international developments towards an Arab-

Israeli peace, including the Madrid Peace Conference and the Oslo process.

The September 11 terror attacks in the USA and their backlash against the Kingdom as well as Islam, resulted in Crown Prince Abdullah unveiling a peace plan by the end of 2001 that subsequently became the Arab Peace Initiative in March 2002. Unlike the earlier one, this proposal offered conditional peace between Israel and the wider Islamic world in return for the former withdrawing to the pre-1967 borders. Though significant, both sides could not overcome mutual suspicions, and hence no progress was made. Moreover, the failure of Saudi efforts to bring about a Hamas-Fatah Palestinian unit through the Mecca Accord in February 2007 signalled the limitations of Saudi diplomacy.

However, the controversy over the Iranian nuclear programme has added a strategic dimension to the Saudi approach towards Israel. A nuclear-armed Iran appeared to be a larger and more immediate threat than Israel and its policies. The willingness of the Obama administration to ignore Saudi (as well as Israeli) concerns over Iran and to conclude the Geneva Nuclear Agreement in 2015, also underscored limitations of Saudi influence in Washington, and this resulted in the Kingdom looking to Israel as a possible partner against Iran. In recent years, there are periodic leaks, reports, and speculations about clandestine contacts between Saudi Arabia and Israel. Even if formal relations are far away, strategic convergence vis-à-vis Iran has brought the two countries closer.

These developments indicate a changing Saudi approach towards the Jewish State. From total rejection, Riyadh has moved towards conditional recognition and possible understanding. Thus, India should be less concerned about Saudi Arabia when dealing with Israel. In the 1950, India's hesitation towards normalisation was partly influenced by concerns over Saudi Arabia placing hurdles before the hajj pilgrimage from India.[15] Moreover, for a while, energy security appeared to have influenced India's non-relations policy. This is no longer the case. Economic progress has strengthened India's diplomatic position. This has been vindicated by three high-level political contacts during the past decade: the visit of King Abdullah as the Chief Guest of India's Republic Day celebrations in 2006, and the visits to Saudi Arabia by Prime Ministers Manmohan Singh in February-March 2010 and Narendra Modi in April 2016. Hence, the Saudi factor in Indo-Israeli relations is not significant—or at least, not in the negative sense of the word.

Southern Asia

Pakistan

The role and influence of Pakistan in India's relations with Israel can be traced to the pre-partition years, especially to the 1930s when the Congress Party and the Muslim League competed for the support of the Indian Muslim population. After the partition of the Sub-continent, this emerged as the Indo-Pakistan competition in the Middle East. Pakistan was one of the two reasons (the other being domestic Muslim population) that Maulana Abul Kalam Azad flagged opposing Nehru's decision to normalise relations with Israel in 1952.[16] He feared that Pakistan might use the relations with Israel to out-manoeuvre India in the Arab world regarding the Kashmir issue. For its part, Pakistan has been presenting itself as the champion of Islamic causes in the Middle East, especially Palestine. In 1947, under the leadership of Pakistan, Arab countries unsuccessfully tried to secure the UN endorsement of the unitary plan for Palestine.

Since then, political competition with Pakistan has resulted in India adopting a virulently anti-Israeli position, especially during periodic outbreak of violence in the Middle East. For example, on 25 May, more than two weeks before the commencement of the June war of 1967, External Affairs Minister M.C. Chagla described Israel as the 'aggressor'. In September 1969, India unsuccessfully sought to attend the first Islamic summit conference organised by King Faisal of Saudi Arabia and King Hasan V of Morocco, in Rabat. Despite these incidents, Pakistan received the support of major Arab and non-Arab countries, such as Saudi Arabia, Egypt, Iran, and Turkey, during its 1965 and 1971 conflicts with India.[17] This trend continued until the end of the Cold War, and India's normalisation of relations with Israel.

From 1992, Pakistan has been having a conflicting impact upon India's relations with Israel. For a while, Islamabad sought to present this as India's betrayal of the Arabs. However, the Madrid conference considerably transformed, at least temporarily, Israel's diplomatic fortunes. A number of prominent countries, such as Russia and China, normalised relations with Israel. In the wake of the Oslo process, a number of Arab countries, such as Morocco and Tunisia, established low level consular relations with Israel. Prominent Arab countries even abandoned tertiary economic boycotts against Israel. In the wake of these developments, there were indications that Pakistan was reconsidering its erstwhile opposition, and some leaders have openly called for a pragmatic approach towards Israel.

One can notice a similar shift in Israel's approach towards India. In the initial years, Israeli leaders were openly endorsing India's position on Kashmir and cross-border terrorism supported by Pakistan. Gradually, such pronouncements became less circumspect, and the Delhi Declaration, issued during the visit of Prime Minister Sharon in September 2003, contained no references to Pakistan.

In recent years, a number of scholars have drawn parallels between the historical journeys and post-state trajectories of Israel and Pakistan.[18] Hence, one should not exclude the possibilities of both countries normalising relations when the time is appropriate. Would Israeli-Pakistan normalisation be accompanied by military-strategic ties? While one should not rule out such a possibility, the probabilities are slim because of their potential impact upon the Indo-Israeli relations. At the same time, as long Sino-Israeli military relations do not resume, the possibilities of Israeli technologies reaching Pakistan via Beijing would be slim.

China

Since the end of the Cold War, the People's Republic of China has emerged as the most serious competitor for India in the global market, and significant rival for political influence in Asia, especially in the Middle East. During the Cold War, both India and China[19] adopted a similar policy towards Israel that was governed by the need to befriend the Arab-Islamic countries. Though couched and expressed through ideological concerns, both sought to befriend the Arab countries through pro-Palestinian positions. The end of bloc politics compelled both China and India to reverse their traditional opposition to Israel. China recognised and normalised relations with Israel on 24 January 1992; India followed suit a few days later.

Their post-normalisation trajectory, however, took a different turn. Under intense American pressure, Israel was forced to abandon its lucrative and strategically important military ties with Beijing. Indeed, long before diplomatic relations were established, China sought and forged military cooperation with Israel—dating back to the late 1970s. Through military diplomacy, Israel sought to contain and overcome China's pro-Arab stance and secure Beijing's recognition and acceptance. Israel was an important provider of security assistance to China, especially when most western powers were reluctant to strengthen its military capabilities in the wake of the Tiananmen affair of 1989. The USA, which imposed various sanctions against China, was tolerant of Israeli military sales to Beijing.

However, the end of the Cold War transformed the American strategic worldview and China emerged as its new threat; this forced the USA to abandon its erstwhile position and to veto Israeli military sales to China. Thus, while post-normalisation saw an exponential growth in Indo-Israeli military ties, the Sino-Israeli military ties nose-divided and, in 2000, Israel was forced to abandon the sale of Phalcon AWACS plans to China.[20] Since then, there are no reports of any major Sino-Israeli cooperation in the military arena.

At the same time, its global status makes China an attractive power for Israel, and both countries are cooperating in a host of sensitive but non-military areas such as high-tech and joint ventures. China has also invested in the Israeli economy, and has been undertaking the railway project that would link Ashdod port with Eilat on the Gulf of Aqaba.[21]

Like India, China is also keen to forge closer military ties with Israel but has been inhibited by the US factor. Because of this handicap, China would be extremely sensitive about any major defence deals between India and Israel, and weapon systems which could be deployed in the border areas against China or along the Himalayas would be keenly watched by China. Its great power status, economic clout, and its close relations with countries such as Iran would make China more attractive for Israel. Thus, while Indo-Israeli political and economic ties would be free of Chinese influence, the same cannot be said about military-security cooperation.

Global Players

Russia

Russia has been maintaining a friendlier relation with Israel—that is, more so than during the Cold War era when the bilateral relations were uneven and rocky. Soviet support was critical when the Palestine issue came before the UN in 1947. The USSR viewed the social Zionists, who were the leading Jewish force in the Mandate for Palestine, as an ally in the otherwise feudal Middle East, and the socialist ideas of the kibbutz and collective farming enabled it to view the Jewish State as a potential ally. Hence, not only did the USSR support the partition plan, it was also the second country after the USA and the first one to grant de jure recognition to Israel on 17 May 1948. Moreover, Israel also became one of the few issues that the East and West agreed upon when the USSR voted in favour of Israel's membership to the UN. Though relations became troublesome during the final years of Joseph Stalin, both resumed their friendliness.

Israel's tilt in favour of the USA following the Korean crisis was accompanied by its concern for the welfare of the Jewish Diaspora when the USSR and its eastern European allies had the largest concentration of the Jews. At the same time, the Czech deal of 1955 with Egypt began the Soviet-Arab partnership that continued until the disintegration of the USSR. Prolonged Soviet supply of arms to the Arab countries, especially to Egypt and Syria, was insufficient to prevent an Arab military defeat in the June war. To reiterate its commitment to the Arabs, on 10 June 1967, the USSR broke off diplomatic relations with Israel; this was followed by a similar move by other members of the Warsaw Treaty Organization, except Romania. Hence, from 1967 and until the re-establishment of relations in October 1991, the USSR remained a marginal player in various peace efforts involving Israel.

Even though Moscow co-hosted the Madrid Conference with the USA, the impending disintegration marginalised the USSR from being an important player in the Middle East. It was only after the emergence of Vladimir Putin in May 2000, and backed by oil and gas wealth, one could notice Russian resurgence in the Middle East. Since then, Moscow has been following a delicate policy towards Israel as well as its adversaries, like Iran and Syria. Moreover, in the late 1980s, Soviet leader Mikhail Gorbachev liberalised the emigration policy that resulted in over three-quarters of a million Jews from the Soviet Union moving to Israel.[22] A significant segment of this population has been active in the Soviet military industry which in turn boosted Israeli capabilities. Above all, over the years, this segment of the population has emerged as major domestic force in favour of Russia. In short, Russia has become Israel's domestic policy, and a strong electoral asset.[23]

Seen in this context, Russia has a mixed impact upon Indo-Israeli relations. One could even say that it is a potential model for India to balance its conflicting interests in the region: for example, Russia has been balancing the Israel-Syria, Israel-Iran, and Iran-Saudi relations. Moreover, some of the Israel's premier military exports items (such as Phalcon) are mounted on Russian platforms, and a degree of cooperation becomes inevitable if India and Israel were to boost their militaryties. While Israel has been exporting a host of hi-tech weapons to India, it cannot compete with Russia, especially in exporting platforms such as aircrafts, ships, and tanks. Hence, one could visualize a tripartite cooperation, namely, Russian platforms enhanced by Israeli technology, radar and avionics, and their supplies to India.

The USA

Historically, the USA has been Israel's political and diplomatic benefactor. It began with active American support in the UN for the partition plan, and President Harry S. Truman's recognition within minutes after the Declaration of Independence. In the initial years, the American support was less pronounced and given in a gingerly manner. In the wake of the Suez crisis of 1956, pressures by President Dwight Eisenhower compelled Israel to unconditionally withdraw from the Sinai Peninsula and the Gaza Strip. It was only after the June war of 1967 and the spectacular military success that the USA began seeing Israel as an asset in the Middle East. The benign American attitude towards Israel's nuclear programme was accompanied by the USA coming to its rescue during the early stages of the October war of 1973 through massive military supplies. Since then, the USA has been providing political and diplomatic support, military supplies and technologies, and strategic commitments towards ensuring Israel's qualitative edge over its adversaries. The USA has been active in various peace initiatives such as the Camp David Accords, Madrid Conference, Oslo Process and the Israel-Jordan Peace Treaty.[24]

In line with this approach, the USA prodded India for a long time to normalise relations with Israel; this began as early as in the 1950s. The USA was one of the factors leading to India's recognition of Israel in 1950. It was no accident that the normalisation of relations were announced on the eve of Prime Minister Rao's departure for New York to attend the summit meeting of the UN Security Council, also attended by President George H. W. Bush. The US role has been periodically flagged to both explain and criticize Indo-Israeli relations since 1992. For example, speaking before a dinner organised by the American Jewish Congress on 9 September 2003, India's National Security Adviser Brajesh Mishra earmarked that 'the three countries have to jointly face the same ugly face of modern-day terrorism'.[25]

This pronouncement at times has been erroneously interpreted as a clarion call for an India-Israel-US alliance. A more logical explanation can be that India wishes to avoid the kind of problems China faced in its post-1992 military relations with Israel. By keeping the US informed and onboard, India wants to ensure that the USA does not exercise its veto over Indo-Israeli military-security relations. Such an insurance policy is essential in the light of the politico-strategic leverage that the USA wields over Israel: besides being its principal arms supplier, the USA has provided technology or funded Israeli research and development. The American ability to intervene and block the Indo-Israeli military partnership is substantial, and by keeping the USA on board, India wishes to prevent an American veto. This strategy has been effective and since 1992—there are no major American impediments aimed at slowing or blocking emerging military ties between India and Israel.

Conclusion

Since the establishment of relations with Israel, India has been under different kinds of pressures from various countries. Some are prepared to endorse and facilitate the furthering of Indo-Israeli bilateral relations; others have reluctantly accepted India's political will, and the desire to follow and pursue an independent course in the furtherance of its interests. A positive attitude of the USA is necessary for the furtherance of Indo-Israeli military ties. Though the geopolitical situations in the Middle East have weakened its importance, the historic legacy and the periodic upsurge of violence means that the Palestine factor would continue to be relevant in India's ability to pursue closer ties with Israel.

NOTES

1. Mohandas Karamchand Gandhi, "Jews and Palestine", *Harijan*, in Gandhi serve Foundation, 21 July 1946, at http://www.gandhiserve.org/e/information/writings_online/articles/gandhi_jews_palestine.htm#Jews;
2. Shubhajit Roy, "India Votes in favour of UNHRC Resolution on Gaza", *The Indian Express*, New Delhi, 24 July 2014, at http://indianexpress.com/article/india/india-others/india-votes-in-favour-of-unhrc-resolution-on-gaza/.
3. R. Jagannathan, "India's Schizophrenic Vote on Gaza: Why We Made a Mistake", *Firstpost*, New Delhi, 24 July 2014, at http://www.firstpost.com/india/indias-schizophrenic-vote-on-gaza-why-we-made-a-mistake-1632351.html.
4. "India Abstains from Voting on Palestine Resolution at Human Rights Council in Geneva", *NDTV*, New Delhi, 4 July 2015, at http://www.ndtv.com/india-news/india-abstains-from-voting-on-palestine-resolution-at-un-human-rights-council-in-geneva-778128;See also, "UN Human Rights Council Adopts Resolution on Palestine, India Abstains", *The Economic Times*, New Delhi, 3 July 2015, at http://articles.economictimes.indiatimes.com/2015-07-03/news/64068214_1_unhrc-india-abstains-resolution.
5. Shubhajit Roy, "UNHRC Vote: Palestine Asks India to Explain Why It Abstained", *The Indian Express*, New Delhi, 9 July 2015, at http://indianexpress.com/article/india/india-others/unhrc-votepalestine-asks-india-to-explain-why-it-abstained/.
6. Rajendra Abhyankar, "The Evolution and Future of India-Israel Relations", *The S. Daniel Abraham Center for International and Regional Studies-Aspen Institute India-The Harold Hartog School of Government and Policy*, Research Paper No.6, March 2012, pp. 10–43.
7. P.R. Kumaraswamy, *Israel Confronts Iran: Rationales, Responses and fallouts*, Institute for Defence Studies and Analysis (IDSA), Monograph No. 8, November 2012, at http://www.idsa.in/system/files/Monograph8.pdf.
8. Ryan Mauro, "Iranian Support for Terrorism", *Clarion Project*, at https://www.clarionproject.org/sites/default/files/Iranian-Support-For-Terrorism.pdf;See also, Omid Townsend, "Hezbollah and Iran: The New Resistance Model and Why It Will Fail", *International Affairs Review*, May 2010, pp. 12-26, at http://www.iar-gwu.org/sites/default/files/articlepdfs/

Townsend%20-%20Hezbollah%20%26%20Iran.pdf,

9. Martin Kramer, "Hamas, Hezbollah and Iran: The Challenges for Israel and the West", The Sydney Papers, *Sydney Institute*, Vol. 18, No. 3-4, 6 June 2006, pp. 19–27, at http://www.martinkramer.org/sandbox/wp-content/uploads/2010/10/HezbollahHamas.pdf.
10. Jonathan Marcus, "How Israel Might Strike at Iran", *BBC*, 27 February 2012, at http://www.bbc.com/news/world-middle-east-17115643; See also, Shai Feldman, Brig. Gen. Shlomo Brom and Shimon Stein, 'What to do about Nuclearizing Iran? The Israeli Debate', *Crown Centre for Middle East Studies*, Brandeis University, No. 59, pp. 1–7, February 2012, at http://www.brandeis.edu/crown/publications/meb/MEB59.pdf.
11. Ibid.
12. Matthew Levitt, 'Iran's Support for terrorism in the Middle East', The Washington Institute Testimony before the U.S. Senate, Committee on Foreign Relations, Subcommittee on Near Eastern and Central Asian Affairs, 25 July 2012, at https://www.washingtoninstitute.org/uploads/Documents/testimony/LevittTestimony20120725.pdf; see also, Raoul Wootliff, "Iran Pledges Thousands of Dollars for Palestinian Terrorists", *The Times of Israel*, 24 February 2016, at http://www.timesofisrael.com/iran-pledges-thousands-of-dollars-for-palestinian-terrorists/.
13. "Blast in Israeli Embassy Car in Delhi, Diplomat Among Four Injured", *NDTV*, New Delhi, 13 February 2012, at http://www.ndtv.com/india-news/blast-in-israeli-embassy-car-in-delhi-diplomat-among-four-injured-569090, see also, Dan Williams, "Israel Blames Iran After Attacks on Embassy Staff", *Reuters*, Jerusalem, 13 February 2012, at http://www.reuters.com/article/us-israel-security-embassies-idUSTRE81C0QZ20120213.
14. P.R. Kumaraswamy, "The Maturation of Indo-Israeli Ties", *Middle East Quarterly*, Spring 2013, Vol. 20, No.2, pp. 42, at http://www.meforum.org/meq/pdfs/3494.pdf.
15. Avatar Singh Bhasin, "India's Foreign Relations-2008", Ministry of External Affairs, Public Diplomacy Division, 2008, at https://www.mea.gov.in/images/pdf/main_2008.pdf. See also, P.R. Kumaraswamy, "Reading the Silence: India and the Arab Spring", The Leonard Davis Institute for International Relations, The Hebrew University of Jerusalem, April 2012, pp. 1–48, at http://davis.huji.ac.il/sites/default/files/davisinst/files/readingthesilence.pdf.
16. Rajendra Abhyankar, "The Evolution and Future of India-Israel Relations", The S. Daniel Abraham Center for International and Regional Studies-Aspen Institute India-The Harold Hartog School of Government and Policy, Research Paper No.6, March 2012, pp. 10–43.
17. Safdar Sial, "Emerging Dynamics in Pakistan-Saudi Relations: An Analysis", *Eurasia Review*, 7 November 2015, at http://www.eurasiareview.com/07112015-emerging-dynamics-in-pakistani-saudi-relations-analysis/. See also, Michael M. Bishku, "In Search of Identity and Security: Pakistan and the Middle East, 1947–77", *Conflict Quarterly*, Summer 1992, pp. 30-51, at https://journals.lib.unb.ca/index.php/JCS/article/viewFile/15047/16116.
18. Rajendra Abhyankar, "The Evolution and Future of India-Israel Relations", The S. Daniel Abraham Center for International and Regional Studies-Aspen Institute

India-The Harold Hartog School of Government and Policy, Research Paper No.6, March 2012, pp. 10–43.

19. Yakov M. Rabkin, "Russia, China and India and the Israel-Palestine Conflict", *Holy Land Studies*, Edinburgh University Press, Vol. 12, No. 1, 2013, pp. 9-24, at http://archives.cerium.ca/IMG/pdf/Three_nuclear_powers_Israel.pdf.
20. Jonathan Adelman, "The Phalcon Sale to China: The Lessons for Israel", Jerusalem Centre for Public Affairs, No. 473, 1 March 2002, at http://www.jcpa.org/jl/vp473.htm.
21. Joshua Levitt, "Israel-China Alliance moves forward with $2 Billion 'Red-Med' Freight Rail Link Alternative to Suez Canal", *The Algemeiner*, 24 March 2014, at https://www.algemeiner.com/2014/03/24/israel-china-alliance-moves-forward-with-2-billion-red-med-freight-rail-link-alternative-to-suez-canal/.
22. Victor Rosenberg (2015), "Refugee Status Soviet Jewish Emigrants to the United States", *Touro Law Review*, Vol. 19, No. 2, at http://digitalcommons.tourolaw.edu/cgi/viewcontent.cgi?article=1563& context= lawreview.
23. Yakov M. Rabkin, "Russia, China and India and the Israel-Palestine Conflict", *Holy Land Studies*, Edinburgh University Press, Vol. 12, No. 1, 2013, pp. 9–24, at http://archives.cerium.ca/IMG/pdf/Three_nuclear_powers_Israel.pdf.
24. "History of Mid-East talks", BBC, 29 July 2013, at http://www.bbc.com/news/world-middle-east-11103745;see also, *European Union and Konrad-Adenauer-Stiftung*, "The Regional Implications of the Establishment of a Palestinian State", at http://www.kas.de/wf/doc/kas_35872-544-2-30.pdf?131030093544.
25. Louise Tillin, "US-Israel-India: Strategic Axis?", *BBC*, 9 Tuesday September, 2003, at http://news.bbc.co.uk/2/hi/south_asia/3092726.stm.

REFERENCES

Agwani, M. S., "The Palestine Conflict in Asian Perspective", *The Transformation of Palestine* (ed.), Ibrahim Abu-Lughod, Evanston, Ill.: Northwestern University Press, 1971, pp. 443–462.

Bhasin, Avatar Singh, *India's Foreign Relations-2008*, New Delhi: Ministry of External Affairs, Public Diplomacy Division, 2008.

Blarel, Nicolas, *The Evolution of India's Israel Policy: Continuity, Change and Compromise since 1922*, New Delhi: Oxford University Press, 2015.

Ganguly, Sumit (ed.), *India's Foreign Policy: Retrospect and Prospect*, New Delhi: Oxford University Press, 2009.

Heptullah, Nejma, *Indo-West Asian Relations: The Nehru Era*, New Delhi: Allied Publishers, 1991.

Kumaraswamy, P.R., *Beyond the Veil: Israel-Pakistan Relations*, Tel Aviv: Jaffee Center for Strategic Studies, Tel Aviv University, 2000.

Kumaraswamy, P.R., *India's Israel Policy*, New York: Columbia University Press, 2010.

PART 6

EGYPT

17

Al-Sisi's Egypt: An Introduction

Sudhir Vyas

Egypt has been facing difficult times ever since former President Hosni Mubarak was forced to step down amidst surging popular optimism and hope in 2011. The Egyptian Armed Forces are today again in firm control, and freedom from political repression in Egypt remains as elusive as ever.

The two studies on Egypt in this book, "The Increasing Control of Armed Forces over Governance: the Deteriorating Security Situation in Egypt" by Colonel Rajeev Agarwal, and "State-Society Ties in Egypt: Recent Developments" by Tanzoom Ahmed, analyse the imperatives and choices before President Abdel Fattah al-Sisi and his responses. President Al-Sisi has become an authoritarian, repressive leader, intolerant of opposition and seeking to rally everyone and every institution behind him. Widespread human rights violations and a crackdown on press freedoms have alienated even that liberal section of Egyptian citizenry who initially supported his takeover.

Admittedly, the challenges before Egypt are formidable. Decades of authoritarian rule have warped and constrained the institutions of democracy and, with its deep societal cleavages and prejudices, a difficult neighbourhood battered by contradictions, uncertainties and relentless terror attacks, Egypt demands enormous political skill in governance. A brief stint under its first democratically elected leader, Mohamed Morsi, on the other hand, was marred by the Moslem Brotherhood's long suppressed ideological over-reach and lack of political capacity. President Al-Sisi's response now is driven by rigid anti-Islamism and counter-terrorism, a hyper-nationalism with the state/military as the primary political and economic actor. An amended Constitution, pushed through in the face of boycotts and protests, curtails Islamic expression and safeguards military dominance as he faces a very serious threat from various extremist Islamist groups, all with the goal of destabilising his government.

Were this not enough, Egypt is in an economic crisis, with the collapse of tourism (which was the primary revenue earner) in the face of extremist terror attacks, raging inflation and unemployment, declining exchange reserves, and lack of investment and entrepreneurship. As he keeps a tight lid on the internal situation, President Al-Sisi's priorities at this point are the critical economic situation and the unrelenting security threat faced by the country.

All through the Sadat and Mubarak years since the Camp David accords of 1978, the USA's partnership with Egypt had been alinchpin of the American role in the region, and it invested billions to reinforce Egypt's stability and relationship with Israel. But, with the democratic upsurges of the Arab Spring, shifting US interests and priorities, and an internal debate that could more closely tie US aid to political and economic reforms, it was clear that Egypt's dependency on US largesse could not no longer be taken for granted.

Egypt hedged its bets in an evolving regional geopolitical realignment as the Russian intervention in West Asia—with the stated objective of fighting Islamic State extremism in the Middle East and West Asia—opened new opportunities. The developing relationship between Russia and Egypt offers fresh options for cooperation, both civilian and military. Political concerns that Egypt may have vis-à-vis Iran have been overshadowed by its single minded focus on fighting ISIS and extremist Islamic terror, and it has shifted positions on Syria to align then more closely with those of Russia and Iran.

With Morsi's ouster in 2013, Saudi Arabia and UAE had extended overt support to the Al-Sisi regime as a bulwark against the Brotherhood, even urging the USA to keep up its military assistance. The Egypt-Saudi dalliance peaked in April 2016 with a strategic partnership announced during King Salman's visit to Cairo. This was appreciated by Tel Aviv too, which saw it as a welcome expression of Sunni-Arab support to keep President Al-Sisi in power and the Brotherhood at bay. However, within six months, upset by the contrary position taken by Egypt at the UN on the Syrian situation, Saudi Arabia backed away from a partnership deal that would have saved Egypt US$ 4 billion annually over five years on its petroleum product imports, seriously ratcheting up financial pressures on the country. The partnership announced in April is floundering: an Egyptian court has since rejected the agreement to transfer two Red Sea islands to Saudi Arabia, in a ruling that could exacerbate bilateral tensions, at least in the short term. Promises of concrete support for the Saudi intervention in Yemen remain unimplemented.

Faced with an economic crisis, Egypt was compelled to conclude a record US$ 12 billion loan with the IMF under stiff austerity conditions. The Egyptian Pound was allowed to float and lose nearly half its exchange value, and an arduous fiscal reform program was put in place. With subsidies reduced, inflation rose to 15 per cent, and high food prices fuelled discontent and fears of a popular backlash. Egypt signed MOUs for oil supplies from alternative sources, including Iraq.

These difficult decisions, however, may be beginning to show some positives. Lured by a cheaper currency, tighter fiscal policies, and backed by the IMF loan, foreign investors have shown renewed trust with substantial inflows, and foreign holdings in Egyptian Treasury options have shown an upward trend, helping to bolster Egypt's Central Bank's reserves. Export competitiveness has improved. But, it is clear that the economy will take time to recover, and the risk of popular unrest remains.

In Egypt's immediate neighbourhood, security concerns are uppermost in President Al-Sisi's agenda. While Syria is relatively peripheral, the civil war in Libya, where Islamist terror groups (including ISIS) have established themselves, represents a real and immediate threat. Egypt has tried to mediate between conflicting Libyan parties seeking a political resolution, but with limited success so far.

In Palestine, President Al-Sisi had initially clamped down on the liberal facilities provided to Hamas at the Gaza border by a sympathetic Morsi government; but has since opened a diplomatic channel with Hamas with some easing of restrictions on trade and movement in return for tighter controls at borders, the handover of ISIS extremists accused of armed attacks on Egyptian territory, and distancing from the Muslim Brotherhood. Israel is understood to be on board with these Egyptian initiatives on the management of the Gaza border for greater stability.

Visiting India in September 2016, President Al-Sisi had emphasised the dangers that extremist terror posed to both countries, and that India and Egypt must work for greater cooperation on terrorism at a "whole new level", as stabilising forces in their respective regions. Under President Al-Sisi, Egypt's positions on counter terrorism have moved much closer to India's, even though its divergent policy stance at the UN on the CCIT remains unchanged so far. And, on Syria, with the shift in Egypt's positions, the two countries are now more congruent. Bilateral relations too have been developing satisfactorily.

2016 has been a difficult year for President Al-Sisi's Egypt. His foreign policy outreach, which seemed so ill considered and fatuous initially albeit under compelling circumstances, has lately displayed a greater degree of maturity and adaptability. Yet, it remains to be seen whether his foreign policy shifts reflects conscious, well thought out, and pragmatic geopolitical strategy or whether it remains tactical and opportunistic.

Initial contacts between Presidents Al-Sisi and President Trump, as he assumed office, also seem to have been positive, with the latter underscoring his commitment to bilateral ties and to fighting extremism, as well as personal support for President Al-Sisi (and the Israeli Prime Minister Netanyahu) as his "strongest allies" in the region. In the evolving global power realignments, there may well be pragmatic and sustainable opportunities and broader options that President Al-Sisi would ignore at his peril.

With its geographical weight, its historical foundations as a nation-state, and an educated population, Egypt has played an important role in past years as a powerbroker and centre of gravity for the region. Today, it has little productive regional role to play. Its institutions weakened, it offers no appealing economic model or soft power to manifest, nor the capacity to extend aid. Its diplomacy is constrained by internal problems, policy instability, and corruption. In fact, apart from battling terror, it just does not have the bandwidth to focus on regional affairs.

It is not clear whether President Al-Sisi's approach is going to work. It remains a state- and military-led strategy to maintain tight internal control and quash any vestige of opposition while it sorts out Egypt's economic and security threats. The armed forces and the vested interests of the Deep State in Egypt draw enough benefits from the domestic status quo for them to resist changes that would threaten their own privileges. But, Egypt has ninety million people and huge youth bulge. It has to focus on a human-development strategy, on the domestic needs and welfare of its own citizens, and develop a political system in which ordinary Egyptians can have a voice. For a military dictator riding a tiger, that will be the real test of success.

18

The Increasing Control of the Armed Forces: The Deteriorating Security Situation in Egypt

Rajeev Agarwal

ABSTRACT

The modern history of Egypt and its military are closely interlinked. The birth of Israel in 1948 and the crushing defeat of Arab Armies in 1948 in the First Arab-Israel war was a vital factor in the downfall of the monarchy in Egypt through a military coup in 1952. Ever since, the military has been an important influence in Egypt, and has exercised power and influence through successive military rulers.[1]

The coup in 1952 installed the first military president, Gamal Abdel-Nasser (1954–1970), who formed an Arab socialist regime in which military officers occupied the most important administrative and economic positions.[2] *Two military presidents succeeded Nasser: Anwar Sadat (1970–1981) and thereafter Hosni Mubarak, who further cemented the prominence of the armed forces in Egypt. Even after the recent revolution in January 2011, it was the Supreme Council of Armed Forces (SCAF) which governed Egypt for 16 months till it paved the way for a democratically elected Muslim Brotherhood led civilian government. And ultimately, it was again the military which removed President Morsi in July 2013, and is now back in the forefront.*

Under President Al-Sisi, there is a growing perception that the Egyptian Armed forces (EAF) are calling the shots, and are back on the centre stage. Any discussion of the military's role in politics, or the authority of the civilian government over the armed forces is taboo. The latest Constitution provides overwhelming powers to the EAF, and empowers the SCAF to approve the appointment of the Defence Minister (who must be a military officer) for a period of two full presidential terms. Coupled with this is a continuing crackdown on Islamist groups and the media as well as the EAF's growing stranglehold over the economy. This has raised fears among the Egyptians of the return of a military dictatorship akin to the Mubarak era, or worse—the return of the 'Deep State', perhaps more repressive than ever.

As regards the economy, the Egyptian Armed Forces (EAF) has traditionally exercised tremendous influence over the Egyptian economy. Ex-generals head the public authorities of power and influence. Even the recent US$9 billion New Suez Canal expansion project was managed entirely under the EAF.

The Internal Security situation, however, is a major concern for Egypt and the EAF. Since the removal of President Morsi, violent attacks have surged throughout the country. Terror groups related to Islamic State (IS) have mushroomed astride Egypt. Ansar Bayt al-Maqdis, operating in the Sinai Peninsula, has pledged allegiance to the Islamic State (IS), and has targeted Egyptian security forces and government establishments with impunity.

Against this context this paper examines the following issues

- *The EAF, its expanding role under President Al-Sisi and the fear of the return of the 'Deep State'.*
- *EAF and the Egyptian economy.*
- *Deteriorating internal security situation: a major challenge.*

The expanding EAF under President Al-Sisi: the Return of the 'Deep State'

The EAF has always enjoyed a pre-eminent role in Egypt ever since the overthrow of King Farouk in 1952. Over the following decades, under successive military presidents, the role got more corporatised, and the EAF found comfort in controlling the strings of Egypt's discourse from the background. However, the January 2011 revolution forced the EAF to come to the forefront, and side with the protesting public to facilitate the ouster of President Mubarak. Even thereafter, it was the SCAF which governed the nation till the first democratically elected Mohammad Morsi was declared President. However, Morsi was ousted in a 'soft coup' on 3rd July 2013, after his attempts to gain sweeping powers[3] through a constitutional declaration[4] in November 2012 which sought to place supreme powers in his hands, and relegate the EAF to the sidelines. Under the threat of being marginalised, the SCAF, under General Al-Sisi, gave President Morsi forty eight hours to set the house in order, or be ousted.[5]

Initially, the ouster of Morsi was welcomed, and the EAF was seen as the ultimate patriots and the nation's saviours, enjoying huge public support.[6] 60 per cent of non-Islamists favoured a temporary return to army rule. However, ever since election of Al-Sisi as the President, and the subsequent overwhelming powers granted to the EAF, there have been concerns and fears of a new kind of repressive regime in Egypt— one that is, perhaps, even worse than experienced under President Mubarak.

EAF and the Overwhelming Constitutional Powers

One of the major developments under President Al-Sisi has been the Constitution, which was passed in December 2013, and was followed by a national referendum on 14–15 January 2014. The new Constitution[7] was approved by an overwhelming majority of 98 per cent[8] of the people. When compared to the 2012 Constitution[9] of the ousted President Morsi, it grants powers beyond scrutiny to the EAF, removing most of the controversial Islamist articles while giving the EAF special status by allowing it to select its own candidate for the job of Defence Minister, and empowering it to bring civilians before military tribunals in certain cases.[10]

The 2014 constitution also gives more decisive powers to the military than previous Constitutions with regard to questions of 'national security', budget matters, and military justice. In doing so, the military 'is no longer treated as part of the executive branch of government but rather a branch unto itself'. Article 234 is especially remarkable, as it stipulates that, for at least two presidential terms, the Minister of Defence should be appointed with the SCAF's approval—perhaps a strong indication that the SCAF was unwilling to subordinate itself to a new political leader, even if that leader were to hail from the military leadership itself.[11]

The 'Deep State'

Professor Nathan Brown at George Washington University states[12] that the idea of the "Deep State" was first used to describe the political structure of Turkey, which has a democratic government, but also a powerful military which steps in to intervene when the leadership veers too far, in its view, towards Islamism. The same notion has been dominant in Egypt wherein the EAF has ruled through a set of well established institutions, controlling the strings from the background. Egypt's 'Deep State' is dominated by the military, but is supported by four other branches: the intelligence services, the police, the judiciary, and the state media, which maintains the staunch support of the military.

Mohammed Nosseir, cautioning people against underestimating the reach of Egyptian 'Deep State' has said,

> The question isn't whether Egypt's 'Deep State' really exists or is a fantasy. The real issue is, just how far-reaching is the Deep State and what is the extent of its influence after the revolution? Egypt's 'Deep State' has managed to shrug off the revolution, getting rid of politicians, activists and even a President.[13]

Another comment on the 'Deep State' reminds us that,

> In a way it was never gone. When Mubarak became untenable, the army let him fall in order to preserve its vested interests. During their short rein, the Muslim Brotherhood and President Mohamed Morsi never managed to penetrate the pillars of the ancient regime, the Ministry of Interior, the judiciary, and the military.[14]

Under President Al-Sisi, the SCAF and the military intelligence have become more powerful than ever before, and have been given a direct role in electoral politics. The direct involvement of the military in politics and its resultant power has raised fears of the possibility of a well established and institutionalised 'Deep State'. There have been changes to the Electoral Law in 2014, and the conduct of parliamentary elections ensured that the majority of those elected to the 2015 Parliament had close connections to the military and the former elites. Under the law, Egyptian parliament had to elect 567 deputies. Of these, 420 were to be elected by an individual candidate system, while 120 were to be elected via a list system, and the remaining 27 appointed by President Al-Sisi. Only the list that wins an absolute majority in each district would receive any seats, thus severely limiting the role and representation of political parties. Favouring the individual system provides greater control to the President over the candidates who need to have the financial means, and perhaps the support of the SCAF, for success.[15]

The appointment of ex-generals of the armed forces and the police in important posts is another example of tight collusion between President Al-Sisi and the EAF. 19 out of 27, or 70 per cent, of the country's provinces are led by a man with the rank of "liwa" (Major-General). Also, on 18 October 2014, General Khaled Abdel-Sallam al-Sadr was appointed Secretary-General of Egypt's parliament, the House of Representatives. He is the first military officer in Egypt's history to serve in this role.[16]

In addition, since the time he assumed office in June 2014 until the first parliamentary session, President Al-Sisi has issued 342 decrees. When the parliament was convened in January 2016, the legislatures were faced with the daunting task of debating and ratifying more than 20 decrees per day to meet the 15-day constitutional deadline.

Crackdown on the Media

The EAF has been consistent and brutal in its crackdown on the media not ready to tow the official line. The crackdown on the Muslim Brotherhood and the shutting down of several Islamist channels immediately after overthrow of President Morsi was followed by the crackdown and arrest of any journalist or media house criticising the government. Mohammad Bader, cameraman for Al-Jazeera, was arrested in July 2013 while covering clashes between the Egyptian security forces and supporters ofthe ousted President Mohamed Morsi. Bader was charged with attempted murder and possessing a weapon. This was followed by the arrest of Abdullah al-Shami in August, again of *Al-Jazeera, for similar reasons. The detention of* four journalists working for the broadcaster Al-Jazeera in the capital, Cairo, in December 2014 evoked international condemnation. The journalists included the TV network's Cairo bureau chief Mohamed Fadel Fahmy, and the former BBC correspondent Peter Greste.[17] The Committee to Protect Journalists has been quoted to state that the number of journalists in detention in Egypt had doubled since 2015: "It's the largest number of detentions since we started documenting arrests in Egypt in 1991," said Sherif Mansour, the Committee's coordinator for the Middle East and North Africa. "The situation ha[s] been going from bad to worse."[18]

In November 2015, the arrest of a prominent advocate of the freedom of expression in Egypt, Hossam Bahgat, was strongly condemned by all, including UN Secretary General Ban Ki-moon who described Bahgat as a "human rights defender." Ban Ki-moon expressed concern that "This is just the latest in a series of detentions of human rights defenders and others that are profoundly worrying."[19]

The continuing crackdown on the media came under severe criticism once again by the UN after the Egyptian security forces stormed the Egypt's Journalist Syndicate office in Cairo on 1 May 2016, and arrested two journalists. A statement released by the UN Human Rights Office of the High Commissioner said: "The worsening crackdown on peaceful protest and dissent in Egypt represents a further setback for an open political environment and a vibrant civil society."[20]

On 14 June 2016, in yet a step to have tighter control over the media, the Egyptian parliament's Media and Culture Committee approved a legislative amendment aimed at granting the President the right to reshuffle the Higher Press Council—the body in charge of naming editors and board chairmen of 'state-owned press organisations.'[21] In its report on Egypt, Freedom House commented on the state of affairs in Egypt stating that "The government harshly restricted dissent and assembly by activists from across the political spectrum during the year. The media were also targeted, with authorities harassing and sometimes jailing journalists who reported on political opposition of any kind".[22]

In its annual report on Egypt for Year 2015–16, Amnesty International also highlights the sustained crackdown by the state on dissent and freedom, stating that,

> The human rights situation continued to deteriorate. The authorities enacted a draconian new anti-terrorism law, and arrested and imprisoned government critics and political opposition leaders and activists. Security forces used excessive force against protesters, refugees, asylum-seekers and migrants. Detainee Courts handed down hundreds of death sentences and lengthy prison sentences after grossly unfair mass trials.[23]

Khalil Al-Anani was quoted in *Al Ahram* stating that the revolution of January 2011 sought to end state oppression, and it is no surprise that it began on the day the State celebrates one of its most repressive agencies, namely the police force. But what has been taking place since 3 July until today is an attempt by the incumbent regime not only to re-manufacture security and political repression—which was institutionalised and systematic throughout Mubarak's era— but also to generate the psychological acceptance of it through creating a public constituency that accepts to coexist with repression.[24]

Even on the eve of the Presidential elections in June 2014, one of the noted observers on the region, Jon B. Alterman commented, "As Egypt faces presidential elections, the future looks less bright and less new than any would have predicted three years ago. The military is clearly back, the economy is in shambles, and political space is constricting."[25] In her thesis titled 'The Role of Military in Political Transitions: Egypt a Case Study', Rozetta Meijer states that the mass demonstrations across Egypt at the beginning of 2011 toppled Mubarak, but left the 'Deep State', of which the military is a part, intact.[26]

Finally, an observation by Ahmed Abd Rabou, an Assistant Professor of Comparative Politics at Cairo University perhaps sums up the state of affairs in Egypt, "Politically, Al-Al-Sisi needs the army. He has no political institution. The army is his only source of political legitimacy. It has become a political group in and of itself." And, at this stage, that's exactly what the EAF wants. They have secured their place as President Al-Sisi's primary constituency.[27] President Al-Sisi has only just obliged.

Thus, the EAF enjoys a tight grip over politics and governance in Egypt. The autocratic style of President Al-Sisi reminds the Egyptian populace of the 'Deep State' and its associated fears. Restrictions on freedom threaten to subjugate the nation into another age of repression and fear. Looking back, while popular demand for reform toppled Hosni Mubarak in 2011, the transition period that followed showed the determination of the remnants of the regime and the 'Deep State' to continue preserving the underlying institutional structures of an entrenched authoritarian system.

The EAF and the Egyptian Economy: A Virtual Stranglehold

Apart from being the largest and amongst the most modern armed forces in the Arab world, the Egyptian armed forces also draw their strength and power from the fact that they have tremendous influence and stakes in the Egyptian economy. Though, not officially declared under the shroud of 'national security', most estimates suggest that the Egyptian military controls huge chunk of the national economy which could range from five to 40 per cent of the national output.[28]

Going back in time, the military's involvement in the economy took root under President Nasser in the 1950's when high-ranking officers were involved in his nationalisation project and the "import substitution industrialisation" model—a model that favours domestic products over foreign alternatives.[29] Economic liberalisation under President Anwar Sadat further increased the involvement. Later, after the 1979 Peace Treaty with Israel, large-scale privatisation took place under Hosni Mubarak when he chose to reassign personnel to newly opened military factories and business ventures. More recently, military-economic ties have grown through programmes that allowed the EAF officers to purchase state assets at heavily discounted rates. As a result of all these steps, the army is heavily involved in construction, including in large infrastructure projects, as well as the manufacture of consumer durables. It is also active in the agricultural sector, tourism, and healthcare services.

Organisations like the Arab Organisation for Industrialisation and National Service Projects Organization (NSPO) have helped the EAF take control over the economy, become self-sufficient, and avoid relying on the private sector for its needs.[30] Documents published by *Wikileaks* quote Minister Sayed Meshal, a former general, stating that Egypt's Ministry of Military Production revenues from the private sector are about 2 billion Egyptian pounds a year (US$ 345 million) and it employs 40,000 civilians.[31] In addition, there are large amounts of land owned by the military in the Nile Delta and on the Red Sea coast. Such property is termed as a "fringe benefit" in exchange for the military ensuring regime stability and security.[32]

The EAF has been largely protective of its commercial ventures, irrespective of the changing regimes. In a press conference in 2012, the Vice Minister of Defence for Financial Affairs and SCAF member, General Mahmud Nasr, pledged to "fight" to protect the armed forces business. He asserted,

> Our money does not belong to the state; it is the sweat of the Ministry of Defence from the revenue of its enterprises. We will not allow the state to intervene in it. We will fight for our economic enterprises and we will not quit this battle.[33]

Under President Al-Sisi, the role and control of the EAF has only expanded. Ex-generals have been given top civilian positions in the state's administrative apparatus and are in control of key sectors.[34] Ex-generals head the public authorities of industrial development, agricultural development, import and export control, maritime transport, railways, sea and Nile ports, and the Suez Canal. Other important positions—the Minister of Transportation, the Chairman of the National Telecommunication Holding Company, and the Chairman of Maritime and Land Transport Holding Company are also occupied by other ex-generals.[35] Commenting on the expanding role of EAF under Al-Sisi, a noted commentator on the region, Joshua Stacher, stated, "We're dealing with a brand-new economy that's now run by 'Military Inc'."[36]

In July 2014, in another favour to military owned businesses, President Al-Sisi issued a Presidential Decree 117/2014 amending the 196/2008 Property Tax Law. The amended law mentioned that hotels, clubs, hospitals, medical centres, and clinics affiliated to the armed forces are exempted from paying taxes.[37] On May 18, 2015, adding to the military's portfolio of economic activities, the Ministry of Military Production issued a decree ordering the establishment of a military company conducting wide-ranging activities in the fields of contracting, construction, and development. The company, named MP for Engineering Projects, Consultancies and General Supplies, shall enjoy financial and administrative independence.[38] Further, on 12 June 2015, President Al-Sisi issued a law which authorised the Ministry of Defence, the Interior Ministry, and the General Intelligence Agency to found security companies which provide protection services to facilities and/or money transport. The law stipulates that the Minister of Interior is the only authority which can issue licenses and revoke them to private security companies.[39]

In December 2015, Al-Sisi issued a decree to amend Law 53/1981 that set out the governing framework of the Armed Forces Land Projects Agency (AFLPA). The amendment allowed the agency to expand its commercial activities and form for-profit corporations, both on its own and jointly with national and international capital sources.[40] Again, in February 2016, President Al-Sisi issued a decree to direct the AFLPA to oversee the construction of two mega-projects to be built on 16,000 acres under military control in New Cairo and Sheikh Zayed City.[41] All these laws/decrees are clearly illustrative of the direction taken by government under Al-Sisi—that is, to expand EAF involvement in Egyptian economy.

Under Al-Sisi, the role of the military companies has expanded from merely being awarded contracts to actually taking over the management of entire projects. Theoretically, this is intended to encourage foreign investment, promising a simpler, more streamlined process for investors. However, according to Shana Marshall, Associate Director and Research Instructor at George Washington University's Institute for Middle East Studies, this ploy is little more than rhetoric; it just centralizes corruption.[42] Add to that, the military's budget—and by extension, its economic fiefdom—is kept secret. EAF-controlled businesses can, therefore, benefit from subsidies that are kept off the books, as well as have more freedom of manoeuvre amid the lack of oversight.[43]

Among the recent economic activities led by the EAF banner, perhaps the most significant has been the US$ 9 billion New Suez Canal expansion.[44] Delivered over an astonishing time line of just over a year, it was seen by President Al-Sisi as one of the public symbols of claiming legitimacy of his military backed government, and a signal to the Egyptian public to retain its faith in the EAF to deliver on all promises. Once again, the project was entirely headed by a military man—Admiral Mohab Mameesh.[45]

There are other recent examples of the further tightening of the virtual stranglehold of the EAF over national economy. In November 2015, President Al-Sisi approved the establishment of a phosphate and fertiliser factory complex, supervised by the military-owned El-Nasr Company for

Intermediate Chemicals.[46] The agricultural mega-project—a new and ambitious plan for the reclamation of 1.5 million feddans of desert land in the area of Sahl Baraka—seeks to expand Egypt's total agricultural land by approximately 20 per cent.[47] With key ministries led by ex-generals leading the project, it once again has a strong military imprint.

Thus, the economy of Egypt is well and truly under the total control of the EAF. With the new Constitution in place, major political rivals sidelined, and more than US$ 12 billion in the form of Gulf aid[48] President Al-Sisi and the EAF has consolidated its hold over the economy and major economic projects. The GDP of the country has improved by 1–2 percent points since President Al-Sisi took over, and the fiscal deficit is down.

GDP Growth in the Period Since President Al-Sisi Took Over

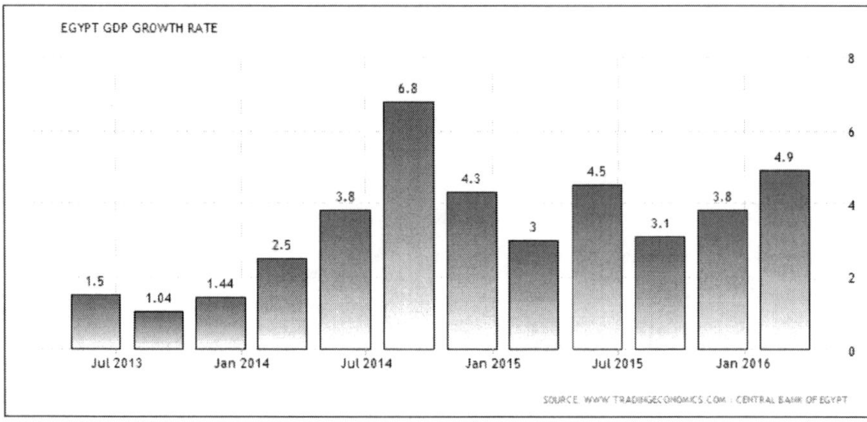

Source: http://www.tradingeconomics.com/egypt/gdp-growth

Some of the macro-economic measures—including cutting down of fuel subsidies—has been appreciated by the IMF and the World Bank.[49] In a latest reprieve to the nation, the IMF approved a US$ 12 billion loan in November 2016. The loan was sanctioned after Egypt raised US$ 6 billion in external financing, and agreed to significant economic changes, including allowing the currency to trade freely as well as reducing energy subsidies.[50] The long term sustainability of these steps is, however, a question mark. In the latest inputs on the Egyptian economy, inflation has risen—up 20 per cent in October 2016; the Egyptian pound is devalued to 18 per US Dollar compared to 8.8 a few months ago; and the country's external debt is above 100 billion US Dollars. However, the EAF and the President are hopeful that they will be able to pull out the Egyptian economy from this crisis.

Inflation in Egypt under President Al-Sisi

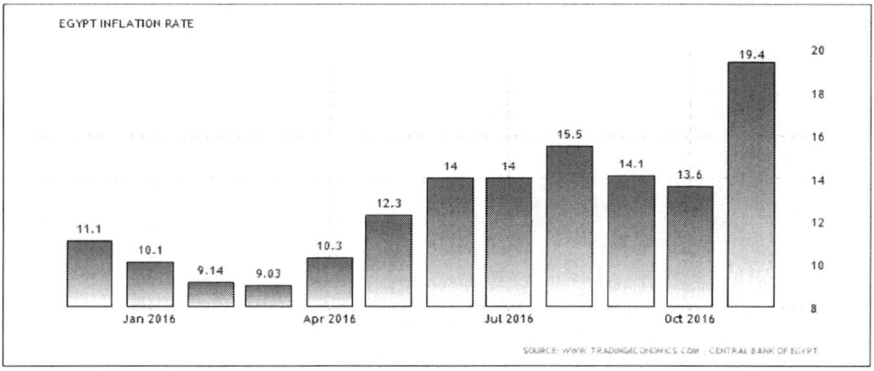

Source: http://www.tradingeconomics.com/egypt/inflation-cpi

The Deteriorating Internal Security Situation: a Major Challenge

While President Al-Sisi has consolidated his hold politically and the EAF has virtual control over the economy, the internal security situation has been a major source of concern for Egypt. The fact that it has deteriorated manifold after the ouster of President Morsi in July 2013 adds to the worry. The area of concern has been primarily the region of Sinai along the Egypt-Israel border. However, since 2014, security threats have expanded to the heartland of Egypt to include regions of Greater Cairo. Militants have exploited the uncertain security situation after the ouster of President Morsi, and have targeted Egyptian security forces and government officials with remarkable consistency and success.

Some of the factors that have led to the ongoing fragile security situation could be attributed to both internal and external developments. The toppling of Libyan dictator Muammar Gadhafi and the steady stream of Libyan weapons flowing to the Sinai, the rise in Iraq and Syria of the Islamic State (IS), and the unrest in Sudan to the South have greatly impacted Egypt. Internally, the freeing of jihadists from Egyptian jails by the transitional government in 2011–12, Morsi's close ties with Hamas in Gaza, and his lenient attitude towards the smuggling of personnel and material between Gaza and Sinai also helped the militants initially. Thereafter, President Al-Sisi administration's crackdown on smuggling with Gaza, and Israel's construction of a border fence turned the local and trans-national groups against the Egyptian state.[51] The crackdown on Islamist groups, especially the Muslim Brotherhood by the Al-Sisi government and the EAF, has only worsened the situation.

As a result, incidents of terrorist attacks in Egypt have been the highest since the 1990s. One of the groups that has taken the lead was (as it was formerly known) *Ansar Beit al-Maqdis*. This emerged as a terrorist organisation in the Sinai following the overthrow of President Hosni Mubarak in 2011 and the crackdown on the Muslim Brotherhood. *Ansar Beit* and other Islamist militant groups initially focused on attacking Egyptian security forces; they have however since expanded to attacking civilians in Cairo itself.[52] Immediately after Morsi was ousted in July 2013, there were nearly 90 terrorist attacks in the Sinai within a month. Less than a month later, on 19 August 2013, terrorists ambushed two mini-buses carrying off-duty policemen in the northern region of Egypt's Sinai Peninsula, killing 25 of them in a brazen daylight attack.[53] In January 2014, Ansar Beit al-Maqdis claimed credit for downing an Egyptian M-117 helicopter in northern Sinai with a surface-to-air weapon, killing five crewmen.

In November 2014, *Ansar Beit al-Maqdis* pledged allegiance to the IS and changed its name to *Wilayat Sinai*—the so-called Sinai Province. This new affiliation was accompanied by a series of lethal and spectacular attacks by the group, targeting police stations, checkpoints, military installations, and tourists on an almost daily basis. During the group's July 2015 "Ramadan offensive", *Wilayat Sinai* simultaneously assaulted fifteen army and police positions in the town of Sheikh Zuwaid, deploying three suicide bombers to target two checkpoints and an officers' club in Al-Arish, killing nearly 70 government forces in a single day. In July 2015, the group targeted an Egyptian warship anchored off the Mediterranean coast,[54] while on 31 October 2015, a Russian airliner carrying 224 passengers crashed into a mountainous area of Egypt's Sinai Peninsula killing all on board—an act again claimed by the militant group named the 'Sinai Province'.[55]

In its report on Egypt's security,[56] the Tahrir Institute for Middle East Policy states that the rate of terrorist attacks—which was around 30 per month throughout 2014, four times the rate of prior years—jumped to an average of over 100 attacks per month by August 2015. While *Ansar-Bayt al-Maqdis* pledged allegiance to the IS, other groups—like *Ajnad Misr* and the Allied Popular Resistance Movement—also emerged, carrying out attacks on the Egyptian mainland, including in Greater Cairo, Fayoum, and Sharqia. The report adds that the political nature of the violence became more evident through the use of social media to spread messages and images of violence. Of the attacks reported from July 2013 to December 2014, 71 per cent of these were carried out against police or military persons or installations. Perhaps, it was a part of this campaign which led to the assassination of Egypt's Chief Prosecutor, Hisham Barakat, in June 2015 in a bomb attack on his car in Cairo.[57] Continuing their attacks on government and military assets, on 1 July 2015, the group simultaneously attacked several police and security installations in the Sinai's Sheiykh Zuweid region, resulting in the deaths of more than 30 soldiers.[58]

The attacks have continued in year 2016 unabated. On January 28, bombing in North Sinai's provincial capital of El-Arish targeted the troops' armoured vehicle killing a colonel and three soldiers.[59] On 21 March, mortar strikes against a police checkpoint near Al-Arish killed 15 policemen including three officers.[60] On 19 May, Egypt-Air Airbus A320 flying from Paris to Cairo crashed into the eastern Mediterranean Sea.[61] The Black Box recording confirmed smoke and internal explosions in the aircraft moments before the plane went down. Although no group claimed responsibility for it, investigations so far have not ruled out a terrorist angle. On July 13, three army conscripts were killed by an improvised explosive device (IED) that targeted their armoured vehicle in the city of Al-Arish, an attack once again orchestrated by the group 'Sinai Province'.[62] Attacks on security forces stepped up in November-December 2016. While 12 army conscripts were killed in an attack on November 24 in the North Sinai city of Al-Arish,[63] six members of security forces were killed when a police checkpoint was bombed on a main road that leads to the Pyramids at Giza.[64] Coupled with attacks on security forces, the minorities, especially Coptic Christians, have also been the target of attacks, with the deadliest attack coming on 11 December 2016 when a bombing at the Main Coptic Cathedral at Cairo killed 25 people, evoking international condemnation.[65]

President Al-Sisi and the EAF have strengthened their campaign against the militants groups, and have also extended the state of emergency in Sinai. President Al-Sisi has also promulgated tighter anti-terrorism laws adopted through a Presidential decree in 2015. The "Terrorist Entities Law," adopted on 24 February 2015, establishes a mechanism for designating organisations or individuals as terrorist entities, a procedure which had previously been ad hoc. On August 15, spurred in part by the assassination of Prosecutor General Barakat, the government issued a sweeping new counter-terrorism law. The law expands the definition of terrorism to encompass acts committed outside of Egypt, and also establishes penalties for those who travel in order to commit acts of terrorism as well as those who support and recruit for them. The law also imposes a steep fine for publishing "false news" that contradicts official government reports on terrorism.[66]

All these measures and a stepped up military campaign against the militant and Islamist groups have met with limited success for the Al-Sisi government. Growing internal dissent due to restrictions on civil society and the crackdown on the Muslim Brotherhood coupled with developments within the neighbouring region, especially in Syria-Iraq-Libya, has restricted the reach and success of EAF over the internal security challenges. As a result, the internal security situation continues to be a lingering threat to the Al-Sisi government.

Conclusion

It was not long ago that Egypt set the agenda for the Arab world. The outbreak of the Arab Spring in 2011, and the swift action within Egypt brought hope to the region. The experiment with the democratically elected government under President Morsi failed to meet public aspirations, and his Islamic agenda was seen as a threat by most. His ouster and the taking over of reins by General Al-Sisi brought hope to people due to his connection with the only institution trusted by people— the EAF. In the following three years, President Al-Sisi has been successful in consolidating his hold over the country while the EAF has slowly and steadily taken virtual control over key issues in the government and the economy. The new Constitution and the recently constituted parliament have made EAF as the primary stakeholder in the country. However, strong arm tactics and crackdown by the EAF have led to increasing internal unrest and dissent within Egyptian society. The fear of the return of the 'Deep State' is clearly noticeable in the common man— especially those who dare to speak their mind, seek equal rights, and freedom of expression.

The EAF's stranglehold over the economy and government has put serious doubts in the minds of regional experts. In an interview to Al Jazeera, Abdullah Al-Arian, Assistant Professor at the Georgetown University, commented that President Al-Sisi has resorted to unprecedented levels of state violence while failing to develop a broad political base to legitimise his rule. Adding to this is Egypt's fragile economic situation, wherein the State's foreign reserves are down by more than half, the value of the Egyptian pound has dropped at unprecedented rates, and tourism, a major source of revenue for Egypt, has been decimated since the coup in July 2013.[67]

Commenting on the state of affairs in Egypt, Maged Mansour has also stated that, contrary to popular belief, there has been an increase in all forms of protests since the military coup, although most of these have been under-reported and crushed. Economically, the regime has mismanaged large projects (like the New Suez Canal) as also the large amounts of Gulf aid, contributing to a spiralling fiscal crisis.[68] In an analysis on the eve of the fifth anniversary of the January 2011 Revolution, Eric Trager too has shared similar concerns on the continuing state of affairs under the EAF dominated governance by President Al-Sisi, stopping short of declaring Egypt as a 'Deep State'.[69]

As Egypt traverses a new phase of history under President Al-Sisi, it would be interesting to see if he and the EAF can survive the shrinking confidence of the people and the gloomy predictions of analysts; or whether they can, once again, win back the confidence of the people, and chart a course for Egypt to regain its primacy and leadership role in the region.

NOTES

1. Rajeev Agarwal, *Egypt's Uneasy Transition: Internal and External Dynamics and Challenges for Indi*a, IDSA Occasional Paper No.35, IDSA, New Delhi, August 2014.
2. Zeinab Abul-Magd, "The Egyptian military in politics and the economy: Recent history and current transition status", *CMI Insight*, October 2013, No 2.
3. "Egypt's President Morsi expands power, defies judiciary with new declaration", Ahram Online, 22 November 2012, at http://english.ahram.org.eg/NewsContent/1/0/58936/Egypt/0/Egypts-President-Morsi-expands-power,-defies-judic.aspx; see also, "Morsy issues new constitutional declaration", *Egypt Independent*, 22 November 2012, at http://www.egyptindependent.com/news/morsy-issues-new-constitutional-declaration.
4. English text of Morsi's Constitutional Declaration, *Ahram Online*, 22 November 2012, at http://english.ahram.org.eg/NewsContent/1/64/58947/Egypt/Politics-/English-text-of-Morsis-Constitutional-Declaration-.aspx.
5. "Egypt's Military Steps In: Issues Ultimatum", *Al Monitor*, 1 July 2013, at http://www.al-monitor.com/pulse/originals/2013/07/egyptian-military-threatens-intervention-following-protests.html#ixzz4Ff9WqL8F.
6. According to a Zogby poll published in June 2013, the army as an institution enjoyed a 94 per cent confidence level; see"After Tahrir: Egyptians Assess Their Government, Their Institutions, and Their Future", Zogbi Research Services June 2013, p. 12, at http://www.zogbyresearchservices.com/blog/2013/11/12/zrs-releases-latest-egypt-poll.
7. Unofficial English translation available at http://www.sis.gov.eg/Newvr/Dustoren001.Pdf
8. "Egypt's new constitution gets 98 per cent 'yes' vote", *Guardian News*, 18 January 2014, at http://www.theguardian.com/world/2014/jan/18/egypt-constitution-yes-votemohamed-morsi
9. "Egypt's constitution 2013 vs. 2012: A comparison", *Al Ahram Online*, at http://english.ahram.org.eg/NewsContent/1/0/88644/Egypt/0/Egypts-constitution—vs—A-comparison.aspx, 12 December 2013, at http://english.ahram.org.eg/NewsContent/1/0/88644/Egypt/0/Egypts-constitution—vs—A-comparison.aspx.

10. Rajeev Agarwal, "Egypt's Uneasy Transition: Internal and External Dynamics and Challenges for India", IDSA Occasional Paper, No.35, IDSA, New Delhi, August 2014.
11. Stephan Roll, "Managing change: how Egypt's military leadership shaped the transformation", *Mediterranean Politics*, 21:1, 23–43, DOI:10.1080/13629395.2015.1081452, http://dx.doi.org/10.1080/13629395.2015.1081452
12. Nathan Brown, "The Deep State: How Egypt's Shadow State Won Out", *Frontline*, 17 September 2013, at http://www.pbs.org/wgbh/pages/frontline/foreign-affairs-defence/egypt-in-crisis/the-deep-state-how-egypts-shadow-state-wonout/
13. Mohammed Nosseir, "The Ugly Truth: Egypt's Deep State", *Daily News Egypt*, 16 November 2013, http://www.dailynewsegypt.com/2013/11/16/the-ugly-truth-egypts-deep-state/
14. Eckart Woertz, "Egypt: return of the deep state", *Open Democracy*, 20 January 2014, at https://www.opendemocracy.net/arab-awakening/eckart-woertz/egypt-return-of-deep-state
15. Egypt Outlook, http://www.westsandsadvisory.com/news/egypt-outlook-2016
16. Tom Stevenson, "Egypt: Land of the Generals", *Middle East Eye*, 07 November 2014, at http://www.middleeasteye.net/in-depth/features/land-generals-1661973598
17. "Egypt crisis: Al-Jazeera journalists arrested in Cairo", *BBC News*, 30 December 2013, at http://www.bbc.com/news/world-middle-east-25546389
18. Amina IsmailandDeclan Walsh, "Egypt Is Intensifying Its Crackdown on Journalists, Rights Group Warns",The *New York Times*,11 December, 2015, at http://www.nytimes.com/2015/12/12/world/middleeast/egypt-intensifying-crackdown-on-journalists-rights-group-says.html?_r=0
19. "Foreign Ministry slams UN condemnation of Hossam Bahgat's arrest", *Mada Masr*, 10 November 2015, at http://www.madamasr.com/en/2015/11/10/news/u/foreign-ministry-slams-un-condemnation-of-hossam-bahgats-arrest/
20. "UN: 'Disproportionate' crackdown on dissent in Egypt", *Al Jazeera News*, 10 May 2016, at http://www.aljazeera.com/news/2016/05/egypt-human-rights-160510054343780.html
21. Gamal Essam El-Din, "Egypt parliament's media committee approves new amendments to press law", *Al Ahram*, 14 June 2016, at http://english.ahram.org.eg/NewsContent/1/64/223014/Egypt/Politics-/Egypt-parliaments-media-committee-%E2%80%8Eapproves-new-am.aspx
22. "Egypt-Freedom in the World 2016", Freedom House, at https://freedomhouse.org/report/freedom-world/2016/egypt
23. "Egypt 2015–16, Annual Report", by Amnesty International, at https://www.amnesty.org/en/countries/middle-east-and-north-africa/egypt/report-egypt/
24. Khalil Al-Anani, The return of the repressive state in Egypt, *Al Ahram*, 11 Jan 2014, http://english.ahram.org.eg/NewsContent/4/0/90488/Opinion/The-return-of-the-repressive-state-in-Egypt.aspx
25. Jon B. Alterman, "A Partnership for Egypt," *Middle East Notes & Comment*,Centre for Strategic & International Studies, 21 May 2014.
26. Rozetta Meijer, "The Role of Military in Political Transitions: Egypt a Case Study",

Master's Thesis, MSc Political Science: Conflict and Cooperation, Leiden University, July 2014

27. Emily Crane Linn, "The Army and its President", *Foreign Policy*, 28 January 2016, http://foreignpolicy.com/2016/01/28/the-army-and-its-president-egypt-Al-Sisi/
28. "Military Commercial Activities, Military Balance 2014", International Institute for Strategic Studies, p. 306
29. Safa Joudeh, "Egypt's Military: Protecting its Sprawling Economic Empire", *Atlantic Council*, January 29, 2014, at http://www.atlanticcouncil.org/blogs/egyptsource/egypts-military-protecting-its-sprawling-economic-empire
30. Rania Rabeaa Elabd, "Will Egyptian parliament cut into the military's profit margin?" *Al Monitor*, 01 April 2016, at http://www.al-monitor.com/pulse/originals/2016/03/egypt-military-economic-empire-Al-Sisi-parliament-limit.html#ixzz47VWHhTCS
31. RESEARCH REQUEST - EGYPT - military's money, *Wikileaks*, Released on April 04, 2013, http://search.wikileaks.org/gifiles/?viewemailid=220683.
32. "Military in Politics", Global Security, at http://www.globalsecurity.org/military/world/egypt/politics-military.htm
33. Wael Gamal, "Al-'Askarai: Mashru'atuna 'Araq Wazarat al-Difa'..wa lan Nasmah li-l-Dawla bi-l-Tadakhkhul Fiha," *Al-Shorouk*, 27 March 2012. Quoted in Zeinab Abul-Magd, "Egypt's Military Business: The Need for Change", 19 November 2015, Middle East Institute, at http://www.mei.edu/content/map/egypt%E2%80%99s-military-business-need-change
34. Zeinab Abul-Magd, "Egypt's Military Business: The Need for Change", 19 November 2015, Middle East Institute, at http://www.mei.edu/content/map/egypt%E2%80%99s-military-business-need-change
35. Ibid.
36. Abigail Hauslohner, "Egypt's military expands its control of the country's economy", *Washington Post*, 16 March 2014, at https://www. washington post.com/world/middle_east/egyptian-military-expands-its-economic-control/2014/03/16/39508b52-a554-11e3-b865-38b254d92063_story.html
37. Doaa Farid, "Al-Sisi amends Property Tax Law to exempt owning EGP 2m in one unit", *Daily News Egypt*, http://www.dailynewsegypt.com/2014/08/20/al-Sisi-amends-property-tax-law-exempt-owning-egp-2m-one-unit/
38. "New military company established with wide mandate", *Mada Masr*, 23 May 2015, at http://www.madamasr.com/news/new-military-company-established-wide-mandate
39. "Al-Sisi issues law authorising Egypt ministries of defence, interior to found security firms", *Al Ahram*, 13 June 2015, at http://english.ahram.org.eg/NewsContent/1/64/135226/Egypt/Politics-/Al-Sisi-issues-law-authorising-Egypt-ministries-of-de.aspx
40. Laila sawaf, "The Armed Forces and Egypt's land", *Mada Masr*, 26 April 2016, at http://www.madamasr.com/sections/economy/armed-forces-and-egypts-land
41. Ibid.
42. Emily Crane Linn, "The Army And Its President", *Foreign Policy*, 28 January 2016, at http://foreignpolicy.com/2016/01/28/the-army-and-its-president-egypt-Al-Sisi/

43. Henry Harding, "Analysis: Egypt's military-economic empire", *Middle East Eye*, 26 March 2016, at http://www.middleeasteye.net/news/analysis-egypts-military-economic-empire-35257665#sthash.aQLi0uyz.dpuf
44. "Egypt launches Suez Canal expansion", *BBC News*, 06 August 2015, at http://www.bbc.com/news/world-middle-east-33800076
45. Emily Crane Linn, "The Army And Its President", *Foreign Policy*, 28 January 2016, at http://foreignpolicy.com/2016/01/28/the-army-and-its-president-egypt-Al-Sisi/
46. Doaa Farid, "Egyptian army's economic empire: Unidentified market share yet high impact", *Daily NewsEgypt*, 07 November 2015, at http://www.dailynewsegypt.com/2015/11/07/egyptian-armys-economic-empire-unidentified-market-share-yet-high-impact
47. "Al-Sisi inaugurates 1st phase of 1.5 million feddan reclamation project", *Mada Masr*, 31 December 2015, at http://www.madamasr.com/news/Al-Sisi-inaugurates-1st-phase-15-million-feddan-reclamation-project
48. Mohsin Khan and Richard Le Baron, "What Will the Gulf's $12 Billion Buy in Egypt?", *Atlantic Council*, 11 July 2015, at http://www.atlanticcouncil.org/blogs/menasource/what-will-the-gulfs-12-billion-buy-in-egypt
49. "One Year On: The Economy under Al-Sisi", *Atlantic Council*, 9 July 2015, at http://www.atlanticcouncil.org/blogs/menasource/one-year-on-the-economy-under-Al-Sisi
50. Diaa Hadid, "Painful Steps Help Egypt Secure $12 Billion I.M.F. Loan", *New York Times*, 11 November 2016, at http://www.nytimes.com/2016/11/12/world/middleeast/egypt-gets-final-imf-approval-for-12-billion-loan.html?_r=0
51. David Schenker, "Security Challenges in Egypt Two Years after Morsi", The Washington Institute for Near East Policy, 16 December 2015
52. "Islamist Militancy in Egypt", Global Conflict Tracker, Council on Foreign Relations, updated 04 August 2016, at http://www.cfr.org/global/global-conflict-tracker/p32137#!/conflict/islamist-militancy-in-egypt
53. "Egypt: police officers killed by militants in Sinai, say officials", *Guardian News*, 19 August 2013, at https://www.theguardian.com/world/2013/aug/19/egypt-police-officers-killed-sinai
54. Erin Cunningham, "Islamic State claims bold strike on an Egyptian navy vessel", *Washington Post*, 16 July 2015, at https://www.washingtonpost.com/world/middle_east/islamic-state-claims-bold-strike-on-an-egyptian-navy-vessel/2015/07/16/5779386a-2bca-11e5-960f-22c4ba982ed4_story.html
55. Yusri Mohammed and Ahmed Mohammed Hassan, "Russian airliner with 224 aboard crashes in Egypt's Sinai, all killed", *Reuters*, 31 October 2015, at http://www.reuters.com/article/us-egypt-crash-idUSKCN0SP06V20151031
56. "Egypt's Rising Security Threat", The Tahrir Institute for Middle East Policy, 2015, at http://timep.org/wp-content/uploads/2015/11/Tahrir_Report_FINAL_WEB.pdf
57. "Egypt prosecutor Hisham Barakat killed in Cairo attack", *BBC News*, 29 June 2015, at http://www.bbc.com/news/world-middle-east-33308518
58. "Egyptian army counters major attack by IS militants in North Sinai; dozens killed", *Ahram Online*, 01 July 2015, at http://english.ahram.org.eg/NewsContent/1/64/134218/Egypt/Politics-/BREAKING-At-least—Egyptian-soldiers-killed-as-mil.aspx

59. "ISIS claims deadly attack on Egyptian soldiers in Sinai", *Al Arabiya News*, 28 January 2016, at http://english.alarabiya.net/en/News/middle-east/2016/01/28/ISIS-claims-deadly-attack-on-Egyptian-soldiers-in-Sinai.html
60. Jason Ditz, "ISIS Mortar Attacks in Egypt's Sinai Kill 15 Police", *Antiwar.com*, 20 March 2016, at http://news.antiwar.com/2016/03/20/isis-mortar-attacks-in-egypts-sinai-kill-15-police/
61. "Egypt Air flight MS804: What we know", *BBC News*, 16 June 2016, at http://www.bbc.com/news/world-middle-east-36330879
62. "Taha Sakr, IED explosion kills 3 army conscripts, injures 12 in Al-Arish", *Daily News Egypt*, 13 July 2016, at http://www.dailynewsegypt.com/2016/07/13/ied-explosion-kills-3-army-conscripts-injures-12-al-arish/
63. "12 conscripts killed in attack on army checkpoint in Al-Arish", *Daily New Egypt*, 26 November 2016, at http://www.dailynewsegypt.com/2016/11/26/12-conscripts-killed-attack-army-checkpoint-al-arish/
64. "Militants claim Cairo blast that killed six police", *Arab News*, 09 December 2016, http://www.arabnews.com/node/1021521/middle-east
65. "Bombing at Egypt's main Coptic Christian cathedral kills 25", *Fox News*, 11 December 2016, at http://www.foxnews.com/world/2016/12/11/blast-at-egypts-main-coptic-christian-cathedral-kills-22-wounds-35.html
66. "Country Reports on Terrorism 2015", Chapter 2, Country Reports: Middle East and North Africa Overview, US Department of State, at http://www.state.gov/j/ct/rls/crt/2015/257517.html
67. "Is Sisi losing his grip on Egypt?", *Al Jazeera*, 28 April 2016, at http://www.aljazeera.com/news/2016/04/sisi-losing-grip-egypt-160426080703098.html
68. Maged Mandour, "Can Sisi stop Egypt's implosion?, Open Democracy, 21 May 2016, at https://www.opendemocracy.net/arab-awakening/maged-mandour/can-sisi-stop-egypt-s-implosion
69. Eric Trager, "Sisi's Fracturing Regime", *Foreign Policy*, 22 January 2016, at http://foreignpolicy.com/2016/01/22/sisis-fracturing-regime/

19

State-Society Ties in Egypt: Recent Developments

Tanzoom Ahmed

ABSTRACT

For many decades now, the Egyptian state has exercised control over society through authoritarian mechanisms, a powerful security apparatus, and a centralized economy. In addition, the government maintains an intricate and close relationship with religious establishments, mainly with the Ulema of the Al Azhar. Post the 2011 Revolution, things have changed drastically for religious institutions, as all political forces have collectively agreed that they should be more independent from the regime. The relations between the State and the religious establishments, while still intertwined, are constantly evolving. The current turmoil in Egypt also shook the decades-old institution of the Muslim Brotherhood. Yet, even as it loses popular appeal, the Brotherhood retains some resonance in Egyptian society and cannot be wiped out through repression.

This chapter attempts to briefly address all the major aspects of the changing relations between state, society, and the forces of political Islam, and the ways in which they influence each other in today's Egypt. Additionally, it attempts to understand the basic politics of the Brotherhood, and the possible lines of evolution of political Islam in Egypt's current pressure cooker atmosphere. The most relevant question now is to see whether President Al-Sisi's inability to cope with the country's challenges and his reliance on external support will spawn a new generation of grievances in Egyptian society, and will these give rise to a new generation of radical Islamists that go beyond the Brotherhood.

Evolving State-society Relations under Nasser, Sadat, and Mubarak

It is well understood that, for decades, the ideological and theoretical underpinnings of the Egyptian state relied heavily on the influence of authoritarian regimes.[1] The origins of Egypt's sixty years of a military-dominated system lie in the ideological and political struggles that followed after the Free Officers deposed the earlier regime.[2] The Egyptian state under Nasser, Sadat, and Mubarak failed to present an appealing narrative to Egyptian society because their understanding of democracy, social justice, and economic change was strikingly different from the existent realities.[3] Scholar Stephen Cook highlights that the lack of vision in the Egyptian leadership led to an unending struggle to understand the nature of Egypt, and raised many questions: Is Egypt a republic or a democracy? What role should Islam, nationalism, and liberalism play in the country's politics and society?[4] Egypt's leaders have constantly failed to address these questions, which ultimately led to the Egyptian Revolution of 2011.[5] Hence, post-1952, the primary features that were retained within the Egyptian State's constitutional and legal framework and influenced its political behaviour were elitism, centralism, and violence.[6]

After the British Protectorate ended, and Egypt gained nominal independence in 1922, the country established a democratic parliamentary system of government on contemporary European lines. However, this democratic period ended with the advent of military rule in 1952. Unfortunately, even the years from 1922–1952 were plagued with political and social instability.[7] The majority party during this period—the Wafd Party—failed to retain power for more than eight years, indicating that the liberal democratic experience was unsuccessful in solving the socio-economic issues of the country.[8]

After 1952, President Nasser and the Free Officers established an authoritarian regime, promulgated a law banning all political parties, and made the Arab Socialist Union the only legitimate political party. In spite of Nasser's charismatic appeal, he failed to institutionalise his ideologies. His regime also faced a number of crises towards the end of the 1960s. Nasser's one-party system, the concentration of power in the hands of elites, and a non-political view of politics as adopted by the ruling elite, led to increasing incidences of nepotism and decreasing political competitiveness. These eventually diminished the regime's credibility.[9]

Soon after Nasser's demise in 1970, his successor President Anwar Sadat tried to regain popular support, and to legitimize his rule by adopting ideas that promoted rule by law, government by institutions, and political freedom. Under Sadat's rule, Egypt witnessed political and economic liberalisation, and experienced a change in political climate. Soon after, the idea of Democracy became increasingly popular, and the system could no longer ignore or suppress the popular voice in support of a more egalitarian system.[10] However, faced with challenges, such as the widespread food riots of 1977, Sadat reverted to a more authoritarian style of governance. Sadat's rule adopted a personalised style that managed to suppress the rise of any political opposition, and ostracized the pro-Nasserites. The final results were the adoption of measures that further truncated the rights of political parties; and additionally, he also banned communists and religious extremists.[11]

After Sadat's assassination in 1981, in an effort to move from an authoritarian to a more democratic regime, President Mubarak achieved a major milestone by releasing political prisoners, and calling for national reconciliation among the separate political factions. In the beginning, Egyptians embraced Mubarak's process of political liberalisation, and he managed to win significant support and goodwill. The parliamentary elections of 1984 were the first elections in the history of Egypt to follow the process of proportional representation in the electoral system in which five political parties contested the elections. However, during this election, Mubarak allowed his government to mobilise the country's bureaucracy to help produce a crushing victory for his ruling NDP party.[12]

It was clear that the regime's tactics and the electoral law favoured the ruling party and restricted the representation of other parties. This move by Mubarak made the Egyptian public question his real intentions towards the democratisation of the country. In 1987, following the Constitutional Court's ruling of the election law being unconstitutional, a second parliamentary election was held. The final results of this election witnessed a 10 per cent rise in the opposition's share of elected seats, while the number of seats held by the ruling party dropped from 87 percent to 77 percent.[13] Although in his speeches Mubarak always emphasised the importance of democracy, the opposition parties continued to complain about election laws and the rigging of votes. After the election of 1987, two other elections were held—one in 1990 and the other in 1995. While the election of 1990 was boycotted by most major political parties, the election of 1995 gave the ruling party of NDP the highest vote share.

The year 2000 witnessed some major developments in the country. First, the Supreme Constitutional Court declared the country's parliament illegitimate; thus, both the elections of 1990 and 1995 were deemed unlawful. This action taken by the Constitutional Court confirmed the opposition's claim of the NDP having used illegal means to win elections. Second, the first parliamentary elections in Egypt, held under full judicial supervision, took place that same year. However, the NDP once again managed to win 87.8 per cent of the seats, and won with an overwhelming majority.[14]

During the early years of Mubarak's regime, political pluralism seemed to flourish to some extent. However, the constant dominance of the political scene by a single party did not help to enhance the regime's legitimacy. Its performance was marked by its inability to solve most of the major developmental issues that plagued Egyptian society. During the latter half of Mubarak's regime, it became clear that the ruling NDP ruled for the sake of power and dominance. This curbed the chances of the real rotation of power and led to stagnation in the political system as well as of developmental opportunities for the country. This led to rising frustration among Egyptians which, clubbed with slow development, increasing political and administrative corruption, and a presidential style of governance led the state becoming more authoritarian in response.[15]

One of the most dramatic outcomes of Egyptian history was the forced departure of President Hosni Mubarak. Egypt after Mubarak went through a complete revamp. The military junta positioned itself as the defender of popular aspirations: it provided the assurance of parliamentary and presidential elections, the restoration of civilian rule, and the drafting of a new constitution.[16]

After Mubarak's three decades long rule, the leader of the Muslim Brotherhood, Mohammed Morsi, narrowly won the June 2012 elections. Although President Morsi had gained popularity prior to the elections, his public support plummeted after his November 2012 Constitutional declaration asserting absolute executive powers in the Presidency. His assertion alienated a substantial part of the Egyptian public, igniting frequent and violent demonstrations that continued for months.[17] Meanwhile, the Egyptian economy further deteriorated, and public opinion increasingly shifted against him. The opposition grew so strong that the bureaucracy stopped obeying the Brotherhood ministries. The police refused to guard the properties of the Brothers and, in some extreme cases, uniformed policemen were seen supporting anti-Morsi protestors on the street. The Muslim Brotherhood underestimated and misinterpreted the depth of the crisis, and refused to come up with a concrete political solution. Instead, the Brotherhood mobilised its cadres to defend Morsi's regime, and indicated the use of violence if necessary. This led to clashes between the Brotherhood and the opposition, and the killing of many of the Brothers. This led to complete chaos, and provided the opportunity to General Abdul Fattah al-Sisi—Egypt's Defence Minister— to remove President Morsi from power.[18]

State-Society Relations under President Abdul Fattah al-Sisi

The manner in which Abdul Fattah al-Sisi removed Morsi from power has had serious consequences for Egypt's democratic prospects, and has locked the military in an aggressive battle with the Brotherhood.[19] The current regime is not only looking at repressing the Brotherhood but also at suppressing any form of opposition activity, including criticism by the press, youth movements, and non-Islamist opposition.

According to the Middle-East scholar Marina Ottaway (the Woodrow Wilson International Centre), President Al-Sisi has explicitly chosen to revert back to the authoritarian style of governing, and argues that the country cannot afford the luxury of democracy as yet. He believes that the two current priorities for the country are to restore security and to rebuild a strong Egyptian state. In order to achieve these two priorities, citizens must sacrifice their own interests.[20] In President Al-Sisi's style of governance, military support is the key to assert the authoritarian model; it frees the regime from the compulsion of gaining support of civil society institutions, political parties, and voters.[21]

President Al-Sisi's economic model—which is yet to be completely developed—also heavily depends on the military. Two elements of the economic model have clearly emerged: President Al-Sisi wants robust and quick economic growth to restore Egypt's position as a regional power. He believes that this robust economic growth can only be achieved by establishing large projects under military supervision.[22] Although he acknowledges the contribution of the private sector in building the economy, most of his policies are geared towards a military-led process of economic development.

The Future of the State-society Relations

After analyzing Egypt's past regimes and examining current President Al-Sisi's style of governance, it is clear that although there have been a few concrete attempts to democratise the country's political system, successive Egyptian regimes have invariably reverted back to the age old authoritarian style of governance. This has been due to various extrinsic and intrinsic factors. One of the major factors has been the obvious unwillingness to promote and continue with any kind of real democratic systems. Additionally, the State's relationship with various local and civil society institutions has been to obtain their endorsement of the State's oppressive policies; indeed, most times these institutions have been used as a liaison to disseminate the State's ideologies within the public.

In the last decade, Egypt has witnessed three forms of collective protest movements: the movement for change mainly to fight corruption; the movement demanding higher wages and improved working conditions; and a social media movement by the young populace to debate and discuss important political issues.[23] A few years ago, many scholars predicted that these movements could become a catalyst of democratisation; however today—five years after the Egyptian revolution of 2011—Egypt still has a long way to go. Perhaps the more pertinent question that is often debated is whether democracy is the best way of governance in Egypt. President Al-Sisi has repeatedly pointed out that, considering the current economic and social turmoil, Egypt cannot afford the luxury of a democracy. And yet, in the past three years President Al-Sisi has not been able to effectively address the political and economic issues of the country.

The State's reliance on the external support of the USA, Saudi Arabia, and Israel further curtails civil and political alternatives. The country currently receives aid of about US$ 1.3 billion from the USA, and close to US$ 13 billion from Saudi Arabia. Such reliance on external supplements only leads to greater dependency and negligence in developing Egypt's own internal institutions.

Relations between the State and the University of Al-Azhar

Since its inception in 973 AD, Al-Azhar has been Egypt's most respected institution of Islamic studies, and has acted as a liaison between the state and society for many decades. However, Al-Azhar has had a troubled relationship with the country's leaders, as it struggled to gain greater autonomy and continuously challenged the government's increasing hold as well as its oppressive policies. By the early 1990s, the Al-Azhar establishment began to adopt increasingly bold ways to oppose the strategies of the government of the day, and challenged its policies on many sensitive issues, such as population control and censorship.[24] The Islamist movement from 1992 to 1997 gave Al-Azhar an edge over the Mubarak government by capitalising on government-Islamist tensions, and offered to defend it from radical Islamist critics in return for major concessions as well as the acceptance of moderate Islamic policies in governance.[25]

Since the reign of Muhammad Ali (1805–48) until the last three or four regimes, Egypt has experienced increasing state control over its religious establishments. Muhammad Ali was the first ruler to strategically challenge the power of religious institutions in Egypt. In his efforts to build a modern state and break away from the shackles of the old Ottoman Empire, Muhammad Ali reorganised land ownership, and nationalised 600,000 feddans (approx. 623,000 acres) of *waqf* land. The latter had earlier financed mosques and other religious institutions as well as supported the economic base of the Ulema. Muhammad Ali's action shattered the autonomy of the Ulema, and made the establishment dependent on the state's financial institutions.[26] Al-Azhar faced another significant setback with the establishment of Muhammad Ali's secular school system for physicians, lawyers, engineers, and bureaucrats. The graduates from secular institutions took up most of the jobs, which left Al-Azhar graduates with little or no opportunities.[27]

The regimes that succeeded Muhammad Ali's rule gained further control of the institution of Al-Azhar, and reorganised laws in 1896, 1911, and 1930 to gain stronger control. Reorganisation centralised the institution's administration which encouraged easy control by the government. Simultaneously, the centralised powers also benefitted interests within Al-Azhar, as this reorganisation vested greater powers in the hands of the Shaykh of Al-Azhar. The existence of common interests between the government and influential players within the Al-Azhar hierarchy explains why some Al-Azhar Shaykhs were motivated to collaborate with the government despite its increasing imposition of regulation on religious organisations.[28]

When Gamal Abdel Nasser assumed power, he recognised the importance of maintaining a decisive say over the University of Al-Azhar, and continued with his ambitious attempts to secure an important position in the decision making process of the institution. President Nasser's implementation of the 1961 laws radically reorganised the establishment, and brought it under the formal jurisdiction of the Ministry of Endowments. The 1961 law also allowed the Egyptian President and the Minister of Endowments to formally appoint the Shaykh of Al-Azhar. Moreover, the Al-Azhar High Council was mandated to appoint three government chosen experts within the university's management. In addition, President Nasser's government also gained administrative control over thousands of mosques by nationalising *waqf* land. There was further control on the preachers at state-owned mosques to control extremist ideologies. When President Sadat came to power, he established a network of district offices charged with appointing Imams and monitoring their actions to screen for any radical religious or political sympathies.[29]

After President Mubarak took over, one of the most significant developments was the appointment of the pro-government Muhammad Sayyid Tantawi as the new Shaykh of Al-Azhar. Although Tantawi had huge support from the progressive section of the Ulema, the conservative side was highly sceptical of his appointment.[30] After the death of Tantawi, Al-Tayyib was made the Shaykh of Al-Azhar. However, this drew even more criticism as he held a position in the Policies Committee of the National Democratic Party, an organisation headed by Gamal Mubarak, President Mubarak's son.[31]

However, despite the Egyptian state's efforts at maintaining strong control over religious institutions as well as using strong screening methods to prevent the growth of radical religious and political ideologies, these have both backfired. The rise of Radical Islam in Egypt was a consequence of the State's continuous efforts to dominate institutions. Apart from understanding the historical State-Al-Azhar relations, it is important to analyze the evolution of Al-Azhar itself post the Egyptian Revolution of 2011, and understand the various possible scenarios which could evolve in the future.

Post-revolution Al-Azhar

During the Egyptian Revolution of 2011, Al-Azhar's different campuses stayed away from the revolution. In fact, politics inside the campuses waned, and there were only sporadic demonstrations over religious and political matters. However, many academicians and students participated in demonstrations outside the campuses. The Shaykh himself had discouraged agitations and bloodshed; but at the same time, he also refused to sanction the government's harsh actions against the activists. This left him vulnerable and exposed to criticism when the revolution succeeded.[32]

Although Al-Azhar had little impact on the revolution, the revolution had a significant effect on the institution. It was not long before the revolutionary wave reached the campuses of Al-Azhar, with the new trend of activism seeing demonstrations by employees and students. Opposition dominated networks of scholars sprang back to life again; many students and faculty members participated in demonstrations both in and outside campuses. In an attempt to reiterate his position, the Shaykh began to entertain some unlikely guests—such as the leaders of the Muslim Brotherhood, Khalid Mishal of Hamas, and televangelist Amr Khalid.[33] The University authorities portrayed these visits not as an attempt to recalibrate its position in politics but as a symbol of its prestige that attracted such visitors to willingly come to the university to give speeches and lectures.

In recent years, there have been a lot of contradictory theories discussing the role of Al-Azhar. However, there is a clear consensus that the institution deserves respect, support, and greater independence. Nathan J. Brown's paper "Post-Revolutionary Al-Azhar" outlines three distinct yet contrasting versions of Al-Azhar's role. The first is "the *Shaykh's Wasatiyya*": this concept comes directly from the Shaykh's office that reinforces the institution as an epitome of learning and heir to an intellectual strain of Islamic thoughts. The concept of *Wasatiyya* establishes that the intellectual traditions of Islam are centuries old, and it is the responsibility of the institution to render the Islamic teachings helpful to modern day Egyptians by interpreting them in ways applicable to contemporary conditions. In the heart of *Wasatiyya* lies the approach that divine interpretations were given to humans for their own interests. The *Wasatiyya* approach contrasts with the extreme Salafi approach that relies on the literal meaning of Islamic texts.[34]

The second version arises from "Liberals and the al-Azhar document". Liberals and leftist intellectuals who are concerned about growing Islamist political forces have an equivocal attitude towards Al-Azhar. On the one hand, Al-Azhar played a significant role in promoting Islamic political and social movements; on the other hand, its role in cultural censorship, the general conservatism of both the institutions and ranks of Al-Azhar's scholars of Salafi, militant, and obscurantist thinking, create doubts. However, the concept of *Wasatiyya* does placate some of the liberal's rising concerns.[35]

The third is the concept of "militant traditionalists". This view calls for the independence of the institution in a much more forceful manner. This concept was made public by Gamal Qutb, the former head of Al-Azhar's Islamic Research wing. He and his supporters argue that problems of state dominance over Al-Azhar began during the British era (much before Nasser's rule) when they divided the institution's role among various bodies to prevent the rising of any potential opposition. This camp's proposal is to restore all fiscal, financial, and administrative autonomy in the hands of the institution, and also to fold the role of *Dar-El-Ifta* and the Ministry of Religious Affairs within the institution. However, most opponents of the concept argue that Al-Azhar has no intentions of becoming like the Vatican.[36] The concept of the militant traditionalists also finds resonance with the Brotherhood, and the movement does regard them with substantial sympathy. However, the position of the Brotherhood is ambiguous as it is currently caught in other impulses, and has other priorities to handle.

While it is difficult to predict the absolute direction of the state's relationship with the Islamic Institution of Al-Azhar considering the on-going problems with Radical Islamist ideologies, the concept of *Wasatiyya* might find some resonance with global moderate Islamic communities. Recently, President Fattah Al-Sisi called on Al-Azhar's scholars to push back against the Islamic extremist discourse. However, President Al-Sisi's critics argue that the current crackdown on freedom of speech and dissent (resulting in thousands of opponents in prison) in itself encourages the spread of radical Islam within the country. It has become apparent that the society and the institutions such as Al-Azhar are sceptical of President Al-Sisi's decisions which will breed further disagreement.

The State and the Brotherhood

The Muslim Brotherhood is the world's largest, oldest, and most influential Sunni Islamist group. The organisation was founded in March 1928 by Hassan al-Banna as a religious, political and social movement. Originally a school teacher, Hassan al-Banna believed in implementing Islamic Sharia law in all aspects of life. The Brotherhood's ideologies were mainly based on the ideas of Hasan al-Banna and the influential Islamist theorist, Syed Qutb. The Brotherhood's first teacher, Hasan al-Banna concentrated on reinforcing the Sharia laws in Islam, and emphasised that Islam is not just a religion but a way of life. Syed Qutb, a renowned Islamist theorist, also had a deep impact on the Brotherhood's ideologies. Qutb believed that the materialistic ethos of the West had so deeply penetrated Muslims in countries like Egypt that they were no longer Islamic in character. He said that the rulers had seized the legislative powers that only belong to God, and that thereby they had precipitated *Jahiliyya* or "ignorance" of the divine mandate.[37] Qutb's popularity came as no surprise—he was the first theorist to systematically establish Islam as a culturally authentic, programmatic ideology at odds with the various political orders dominating the Muslim world.[38]

What Lies Within the Brotherhood?

The Muslim Brotherhood is the only Islamist organisation to have survived eight decades. The reasons for its survival has been many, including a systematic and well organised approach for recruiting, cultivating, and training Brothers while forging the ideologies of the Brotherhood in a deep seated manner. The Brothers who occupied higher positions within the hierarchy of the organisation made serious efforts to incubate the ideologies of the group in a highly insulated environment.

Hazem Kandil's book *Inside the Brotherhood* talks about every intricately designed step that the Brothers have adopted to protect and safeguard their organisation. The process of recruitment starts at a relatively tender age through observation of young students in mosques and religious schools. Gradually, the more religiously inclined and less inquisitive students are chosen, and the ideologies of the Brotherhood are cultivated in them. Within the Brotherhood, there is no room for dissent; Brothers are encouraged not to question and argue but to simply devote most of their time to studying religious texts. Brothers are also given access to a library of books written by people they approve of; outside sources—even newspapers—are discouraged. Kandil mentions a number of instances when Brothers have purged members who have debated or questioned their ideologies. Some senior Brothers have gone as far as to blatantly lie about any opposing group or person by calling them fugitives and criminals, and cooking up false stories about them. In a few cases, junior members have tried to validate the information given to them by the senior Brothers, only to find that the information given was untrue.[39]

In spite of its many flaws, the Brotherhood has managed to survive because of its strong fundamentals and systematically laid foundations. The defining pillars of the Brotherhood are: comprehension; loyalty; action; jihad; sacrifice; obedience; perseverance; devotion; brotherhood; and trust. These have gained popular support in Egyptian society which has been suppressed for decades. Additionally, the senior members of the Brotherhood comprise of a number of wealthy Egyptian elite who donate huge sums of money, mainly as a membership fee, to run the organisation. Also, these are individuals who are socially and politically influential, and have succeeded to tilt the laws in their favour.

While the Brotherhood's insulated environment has helped them to preserve and protect the ideologies of Hasan al-Banna and Sayyid Qutb, at the same time this format has also backfired as it has prevented it from gaining the skills needed to sustain it politically. The Brotherhood's curriculum, and the structures of learning and the way of imbibing knowledge, are restricted to religious texts as well as to studying theories and interpretations made by their own founding preachers. Such methods curtail their knowledge of other subjects such as economics and the political sciences. Many younger generations of Brothers have raised the idea of encouraging a more holistic form of learning so as to build a stronger base to help them compete as a major political opposition party. However, the older Brothers—the decision makers—have discouraged this, and have been closed to the idea of any reformation within the organisation. Although, Mohammad Morsi, an engineer by profession, managed to become the President of Egypt, the myopic vision of the senior Brothers did result in his ouster, thus marking one of the greatest failures of the Brotherhood.

The Muslim Brotherhood and the Future of Political Islam

Following the removal of President Mohamed Morsi on 3 July 2013, there was a dramatic change of fortunes of the Muslim Brotherhood. The change was so intense, and the crackdown on the regime was so aggressive that many analysts began to question if this violent series of events against the Brotherhood marked the end of Political Islam in Egypt. The situation worsened as the Brotherhood lacked a coherent strategy, their response to Al-Sisi's crackdown being highly volatile and chaotic. As a matter of fact, the Brotherhood now faces a massive challenge of completely transforming its organisation, and addressing the popular demands of an inclusive, egalitarian, and pluralistic political space.[40] After the failure of the Brotherhood to establish a progressive and inclusive political model during the one and a half year entrusted to them, it remains unclear whether they will be able to make any changes in the near future. There are also other factors—such as the State's policies towards them, the internal consistency of the current regime, and the regional situation—that will have an impact on the future of Islamist groups in Egypt.[41]

Professor Ashraf El Sharif (American University, Cairo) predicts five possible scenarios and outlines their implications for Egyptian society.

- Al-Sisi's administration remains dedicated to eradicating the Muslim Brotherhood, and the Brotherhood itself faces a crunch of resources. Most likely, the Brotherhood will continue facing a ruthless crackdown, which will lead to the arrest of its members, frozen assets, and violent clashes.
- Some new protests may erupt which will rattle the regime, and the Brotherhood returns to power.
- The regime and the Islamists negotiate a return to Mubarak's political formula of the limited political inclusion of the Brotherhood with certain regime-determined rules.
- The Brotherhood splits into two factions: Moderates who are open to reforming the internal policies of the Brotherhood, and the Hardliners who consider current policies as ideologically incorrect and over compromising.
- The Brotherhood understands its own internal shortcomings, withdraws from any political activity, and focuses on reinventing its ideologies.[42]

It is uncertain which of scenarios is most likely to happen as the regime is committed to the complete eradication of the Islamists; on the other hand, the Islamists are struggling for a triumphant comeback. President Al-Sisi must understand that the Brotherhood has proved to be more resilient than it initially appeared to be. Hence, their total eradication seems unlikely. Additionally, President Al-Sisi has been unable to efficiently fix the economic issues of the nation, making him vulnerable to increasing criticism and public frustration.

Conclusion

State-Society relationships in Egypt have always been complex. Ever since its Pharaonic past, there has been a tendency of Egyptian rulers to maintain an autocratic regime—or at least constantly revert to an autocratic form. Although there have been attempts to democratise and create a more pluralistic model of governance (for instance, by President Mubarak), the efforts were not very concrete. Serious internal issues of poor governance, an externally dependent, over-centralised and sluggish economy, poverty, and corruption have also added to the weakening of society-state relations. Democracy has not always been considered as an efficient way to deal with the economic issues of the country. Post the Egyptian Revolution of 2011, President Morsi did have an opportunity to build on an equal and diverse society; but the internal issues plaguing the Brotherhood could not effectively address the issues of the country at large. The coming of Fattah al-Sisi to power was accompanied by its own set of challenges. His regime is looking at implementing a more military styled economic and political model.

The regime has also overseen a violent crackdown of the members of the Brotherhood by arresting, executing, and freezing their assets. This exhibits the intolerance of the regime to any form of opposition. President Al-Sisi's policies have also led to a much stricter censorship of the press and the required reiteration that democracy is a luxury that the country cannot afford. These policies are leading to further frustration in Egyptian society which is fighting for change that is modern, inclusive, and pluralistic. Although democracy comes with its own set of challenges and may not be the most ideal form of governance, there should be an attempt to design a model that balances the state-society relationship in a better way, and does not tilt the power equation so as to become a one sided affair. Civil society institutions also need to be nurtured, and the voices of the public need platforms to express themselves. Only then will a robust civil society be ensured. While this seems highly unlikely under the current regime, it might be a good way to begin with a more inclusive state-society relation.

The relation between the State and the highly regarded institution of Islamic Studies of Al-Azhar also remains unpredictable yet interesting. Al-Azhar may not be the Vatican of the Islamic world, but it still has substantial control of the Sunni Islamic population. While the Shaykh of Al-Azhar has publicly expressed his support towards supporting moderate Islamic ideologies, he is split between the various extremist ideologies that rise from within the institution itself. By centralising power in the hands of the Shaykh, the State has constantly attempted to subtly maintain its dominance over the institution. Therefore, even as the Ulema and the Shaykh of al-Azhar demand the complete autonomy and independence of the institution, under President Al-Sisi's rule it appears more and more unlikely.

The Brotherhood, which still has popular support of the Egyptian public, but faces a violent crackdown by the current regime, may or may not be able to return to its earlier status. However, given President Al-Sisi's politically short-sighted regime, the Brotherhood does stand a chance to come back to power. For this to happen, the Brotherhood needs to rethink its strategies and revamp its internal policies.

Additionally, President Al-Sisi has been relying on the external support of the USA, Saudi Arabia, and Israel for complete and unquestioning support. Such policies may only encourage President Al-Sisi to further adopt the path of the repression of political dissent and the control of institutions that can absorb and manage such dissent—like the parliament, the judiciary, the universities, or civil society. President Al-Sisi will look at strengthening his capacity to selectively offer economic placebos in order to find support. This may help create a semblance of stability, but for this he will need to rely on external support even more. Since, he has no political support base of his own other than the Deep State, President Al-Sisi will play to the tune of the highest donor even if it means going against popular opinion in his own country. Such actions might lend an opportunity for the rise of an opposition and an increasing support for a new reformed Brotherhood.

The moment one of the members of the Muslim Brotherhood was elected to be the President of Egypt, the organisation went from being a pariah to becoming the political powerhouse of the nation. However, this victory was short-lived; and the organisation has once again been sidelined. Hence, there is a possibility that the Brotherhood could adopt more violent ways to revert to power. Also, the current government has further provoked the group by declaring it a terrorist organisation. In its current state, there is a possibility that a faction of the larger movement radicalizes, and adds to regional instability. It is important to understand that, in the past, despite its illegal status, the Brotherhood was always allowed to carry on its civic actions. A major part of the Egyptian population relied on the social service provisions made by the Brotherhood. However, with the current government banning the organisation and freezing its funds, this may push the organisation against a wall and change its attitude towards use of violence.

Another perspective argues that President Al-Sisi's harsh crackdown of the Brotherhood is a deliberate attempt to push its members towards radicalisation, which will eventually justify the government's actions towards the Brotherhood. Also, the Brotherhood with more radical approach might lose some of its more moderate members and supporters. In spite of the growing Western perceptions that the Brotherhood may become more violent in the near future, and the current government's efforts to criminalise the movement, Muslim Brotherhood members have not resorted to any violence so far. This might emphasise its commitment to peaceful means and highlight its opposition towards political violence. Whether the movement will become more frustrated with using peaceful ways and begin to act in collusion with other radical actors and violent forces to ensure its survival is something that only time will tell. On the other hand. President Al-Sisi's regime is backing ultra Islamist conservative parties, such as the party of Al-Nour, to further suppress the re-emergence of the Brotherhood.

In a future scenario, if the Brotherhood does become more radical, the reaction of Egyptian society will be noteworthy. Since Egyptian urban society is not normally inclined towards violent or extremist means, there is a possibility that the Brotherhood's popularity will wane, giving a greater advantage to President Al-Sisi's government. However, many experts argue that President Al-Sisi does not have a grip on Egyptian society, and this is one of the root causes behind the current unfortunate state of the country. While it is a fact that street protests have died down due to the anti-protest law which was passed in November 2013, popular unrest has not completely stopped; the protest of April 2016 was a reminder that there is still a possibility of people coming out in the streets out of frustration with the current regime.

In the Egyptian and foreign media—both within Egypt and abroad—President Al-Sisi has been facing increasing criticism because of the faltering Egyptian economy and the rise in cases of police abuse. On 18

October 2016, the *Daily News Egypt* carried a story about the shooting of a non-commissioned police officer. The same news piece reported that random shootings by police forces have been on the rise since 2015, and have resulted in the deaths of civilians. In April 2016, Al-Jazeera interviewed three Egypt experts on the kind of support that President Al-Sisi and his policies have been receiving. The article reiterates that his regime has been damaged by its own actions—such as the wheat import crisis and the incompetency showed by the regime in investigating the Russian metro jet bombing. Such incidents have all led to dwindling support for President Al-Sisi's policies.

President Al-Sisi seems to be failing to understand that popular protest can become a threat to his own government as well. He does not appear to have learned from the past—that even after a 30 years rule, when President Mubarak lost the ability to manipulate the polity and serve the interests of each player in the government, he was quickly removed. Ever since President Al-Sisi's rise to power, it has been constantly predicted that the regime will soon see its end. Moreover, Egypt's poor economic situation has added to his problems. Tourism, which was a primary source of revenue for the nation, has been drastically affected since the coup with the worsening security situation. The current government has no concrete plan or answers to the growing economic and political issues of the country. As problems continue to plague Egyptian society, political stability remains a mirage—giving rise to some legitimate questions about whether this pattern of changing regimes is causing irretrievable scathing political and economic damage to the country, and about what it would take to break this invidious cycle.

NOTES

1. Hassan, H.A., "State versus society in Egypt: Consolidating democracy or upgrading autocracy", *African Journal of Political Science and International Relations*, 4(9), December 2010, pp. 319–329, at www.academicjournals.org/ajpsir.
2. Cook, S.A., *The Struggle for Egypt: From Nasser to Tahrir Square*, New York: Oxford University Press, 2013.
3. Ibid., pp. 1–12.
4. Ibid., pp. 1–12.
5. Ibid., pp. 1–12.
6. Sherif, A. E., "Egypt's Post-Mubarak Predicament", January 2014, Carnegie Endowment for International Peace, p. 5.
7. Hassan, H.A., "State versus Society in Egypt: Consolidating Democracy or Upgrading Autocracy", *African Journal of Political Science and International Relations*, 4(9), December 2010, pp. 319-329, at www.academicjournals.org/ajpsir.
8. Ibid.

9. Hassan, H.A., "State versus Society in Egypt: Consolidating Democracy or Upgrading Autocracy", *African Journal of Political Science and International Relations*, 4(9), December 2010, pp. 319–329, at www.academicjournals.org/ajpsir.
10. Ibid. pp. 320.
11. Ibid. pp. 321.
12. Ibid. pp. 321.
13. Ibid. pp. 321.
14. Hassan, H.A., "State versus Society in Egypt: Consolidating Democracy or Upgrading Autocracy", *African Journal of Political Science and International Relations*, 4(9), December 2010, pp. 319–329, at www.academicjournals.org/ajpsir.
15. Ibid. pp. 319–329
16. Brown, N.J., "Post-Revolutionary Al-Azhar", September 2011, Carnegie Endowment for International Peace, at CarnegieEndowment.org/pubs.
17. Trager, E., "Egypt Two Years After Morsi", The Washington Institute, Washington DC, 20 May 2015, at http://www.washingtoninstitute.org/policy-analysis/view/egypt-two-years-after-morsi, accessed 17 May 2017,
18. Ibid.
19. Ibid.
20. Ottaway, M., "Al-Sisi's Egypt: The Military Moves on the Economy", *Occasional Paper Series*, June 2015, Middle East Program, Wilson Centre, at [https://www.wilsoncenter.org/sites/default/files/alsisi_egypt_military_moves_ on_economy_0.pdf]
21. Ibid., p. 6.
22. Ibid., p. 6.
23. Hassan, H. A., "State versus society in Egypt: Consolidating democracy or upgrading autocracy", *African Journal of Political Science and International Relations*, 4(9), December 2010, pp. 319–329, at www.academicjournals.org/ajpsir.
24. Moustafa, T., "Conflict and Cooperation between the State and Religious Institutions in Contemporary Egypt", *International Journal for Middle East Studies*, Vol. 32, 2000, retrieved from JSTOR.
25. Ibid., p. 4.
26. Ibid., p. 4.
27. Ibid., p. 5.
28. Ibid., p. 5.
29. Moustafa, T., "Conflict and Cooperation between the State and Religious Institutions in Contemporary Egypt", *International Journal for Middle East Studies*, Vol. 32, 2000, retrieved from JSTOR.
30. Ibid., p. 2.
31. Brown, N. J., "Post-Revolutionary Al-Azhar", September 2011, Carnegie Endowment for International Peace, at CarnegieEndowment.org/pubs.
32. Ibid., p. 10.
33. Brown, N.J., "Post-Revolutionary Al-Azhar", September 2011, Carnegie Endowment for International Peace, at CarnegieEndowment.org/pubs.
34. Ibid., p.10.
35. Ibid., p. 4.
36. Ibid., p. 10.
37. Calvert, J., *Sayyid Qutb and the Origins of Radical Islam*, New York: Oxford University Press, 2013

38. Ibid. p. 3.
39. Kandil, H., *Inside the Brotherhood*, Malden, MA: Polity Press, 2015.
40. Sherif, A.E., "The Muslim Brotherhood and the Future of Political Islam in Egypt", October 2014, Carnegie Endowment for International Peace, at CarnegieEndowment.org/pubs.
41. Ibid. p. 3
42. Sherif, A.E., "The Muslim Brotherhood and the Future of Political Islam in Egypt", October 2014, Carnegie Endowment for International Peace, at CarnegieEndowment.org/pubs

REFERENCES

Books

Brown, N. J., *Peasant Politics in Modern Egypt: The Struggle against the State*, Yale University Press, 1990.

Calvert, J., *Sayyid Qutb and the Origins of Radical Islam*, New York: Oxford University Press, 2013.

Cook, S. A., *The Struggle for Egypt: From Nasser to Tahrir Square*, New York: Oxford University Press, 2013.

Fahmy, N. S., *The Politics of Egypt: State-Society Relationship*, New York: Routledge, 2008.

Kandil, H., *Inside the Brotherhood*, Malden, MA: Polity Press, 2015.

Journals

Brown, N. J., "Post-Revolutionary Al-Azhar", Carnegie Endowment for International Peace, September 2011, at CarnegieEndowment.org/pubs

Hassan, H. A., "State versus society in Egypt: Consolidating democracy or upgrading autocracy", *African Journal of Political Science and International Relations*, 4(9), December 2010, pp. 319–329, atwww.academicjournals.org/ajpsir.

Moustafa, T., "Conflict and Cooperation between the State and Religious Institutions in Contemporary Egypt", *International Journal for Middle East Studies*, 32, 2000, retrieved from JSTOR.

Ottaway, M., "Al-Sisi's Egypt: The Military Moves on the Economy", Occasional Paper Series, June 2015, Middle East Program, Wilson Centre, retrieved from Wilson Centre [https://www.wilsoncenter.org/sites/default/files/alsisi_egypt_military_moves_on_economy_0.pdf].

Sherif, A.E., "The Muslim Brotherhood and the Future of Political Islam in Egypt", October 2014, Carnegie Endowment for International Peace, at CarnegieEndowment.org/pubs

Sherif, A.E., "Egypt's Post-Mubarak Predicament", Carnegie Endowment for International Peace, January 2014

Trager, E., "Egypt Two Years after Morsi", The Washington Institute, Washington DC, 20 May 2015, retrieved 17 May 2017, from http://www.washingtoninstitute.org/policy-analysis/view/egypt-two-years-after-morsi,

PART 7

SYRIA-IRAQ

20

The Civil War in Syria: A Regional Battleground—An Introduction

V.P. Haran

Be it war or peace, Syria has always been in the midst of developments in West Asia through the centuries. The civil war raging in Syria since March 2011 is one it could have done without. My presence in Damascus from January 2009 to December 2012 gave me a close ringside view of Syria, both before and after the outbreak of unrest.

When unrest broke out in the North African countries in December 2010/January 2011, Syria was relatively peaceful. There was no discernible disaffection towards the regime. President Assad was a popular leader. Also, there were no serious internal problems—political, economic or social—that indicated the likelihood of popular upheaval. The reasons for the unrest in Syria lie in its external policies: its closeness to Russia and Iran did not go down well with the West and the Gulf countries; its role as a conduit for Iranian weapons to Hezbollah (which were seen as posing a threat to Israel's security) was a matter of serious concern to the West; and the Gulf States saw Syria as completing the Shia arc encircling them, despite Assad reaching out to them. 'The Arab Spring' was seen as an opportunity by external forces to get rid of an inconvenient leader and regime.

There was clear evidence of foreign involvement in the outbreak of violence from the first week itself, if not in the Daraa demonstration of 18 March 2011. The outbreak could not have happened all of a sudden. Sophisticated weapons, communication equipment, and cash were freely available to those who were willing to rise up against the regime. Some days later, the rebels started getting real time intelligence inputs. Though it was clear that these were reaching the extremists, the external sponsors chose to look the other way. To compound the problem, some external players actively facilitated movement of extremist elements to Syria. It is this indifference or callousness that has resulted in the Islamic State and the *Jabhat al Nusra* (now renamed *Jabhat Fateh al Sham*) developing deep roots in the region.

These terrorist forces, many of whom are not Syrians, have no interest in the welfare of the people of Syria, and are now posing critical challenges in the region and beyond. IS wants to set up an Islamic state in the region. The way the IS cadres have entrenched themselves in Al Bab, and are fiercely resisting the capture of the town by Turkish forces and some sections of Syrian opposition is an indication of how difficult it is going to be to overcome them. When operations in Mosul to flush out the IS are completed, Syria—particularly the eastern part—will face renewed challenges from the IS. A monster genie has been given birth; the struggle now is how to put the genie back in the bottle.

There was no credible political opposition in Syria, thanks to the domination of the political space by the Baathists for over 40 years. Many external attempts over the last 6 years to bring together the fractured opposition and to identify a credible and acceptable leader have not borne fruit. Attempts by the regime to reach out to the opposition in the initial stages of the conflict were rebuffed by the opposition under pressure from abroad. The role of external forces was actively aided by some sections of the media which took upon itself, with missionary zeal, the project to overthrow the current regime. The result of all this is the untold and seemingly endless suffering of the people of Syria.

It is easy to say that peace is the need of the hour. Given the sectarian animosities that the conflict has engendered, it will take a very long time for the wounds to heal. There is need for restraint all around. The ceasefire worked out in December 2016 should be given a chance to succeed. External involvement should be limited to addressing the problems posed by the terrorists who are not part of the ceasefire agreement. In any case, assistance in any form to terrorist forces should stop. The IS problem is likely to bedevil the region for a long time. The chances of ceasefire bringing about all round peace are not bright as the IS and *Jabat Fateh al*

Sham are not part of it. Further, in many cases, the armed opposition has not yet forsaken violence but has only been allowed to move to areas not under government Control; from here they can continue to indulge in violent activities in areas under government control. Some of them are even likely to gravitate towards the IS.

However, there are some positive developments which give one a ray of hope, faint though it is. The first is the UNSC Resolution 2336, welcoming the efforts of Russia and Turkey to end the violence in Syria and to start a political process. This indicates the support of the major players to the process. But, some questions remain. First, will this lead to the major players cutting off assistance to extremist forces? The second is the willingness of the Government to accept into the mainstream those from the opposition who are willing to give up arms and, equally importantly, the willingness of many sections of the opposition to respond positively to the offer of the Government. On the negative side, there is the challenge posed by the IS and the *Jabhat Fateh al Sham*. To compound matters, the aspirations of the Kurds in Syria for autonomy (if not complete independence), have been kindled by their being enlisted by the USA to fight the IS. This is understandably causing concern to Turkey, and will have wider repercussions in the region in due course. In the process of addressing the IS problem, no doubt another major problem is getting created.

21

The Civil War in Syria: A Regional Battleground

Tsupokyemla

ABSTRACT

The matrix of the Syrian Civil War remains multifaceted and multilayered. The initial congruence of interests for regime change in Syria by the USA, Britain, Saudi Arabia, Qatar, and Turkey has lost its salience with the radical turn of events in the past five years of conflict which continues till today. The unprecedented preponderance of the so-called Islamic State in the region has changed the overall dynamics of its geopolitical landscape. The threat of the Salafist and the Jabhat al-Nusra Front taking over the reins of Syria has decelerated the move by the USA for regime change. On the other hand, Turkey's preoccupation with the Kurdish issue has aggravated with the Kurds consecrated strangely by Bashar Al-Asad to establish a "federal territory" in Northern Syria. This has intensified Turkey's call for regime change.

The US-Saudi-Iran polemics has set off a different trajectory. The breakthrough in the Iranian Nuclear deal and the lifting of sanctions has brought the US and Iran relatively closer, making Saudi Arabia insecure and jittery and a rapprochement between Saudi and Iran more elusive. In another spectrum, the Geneva peace plan is not promising and strikes continue despite the ceasefire. Turkey and the Gulf-led Saudi Arabia are more determined to create a military counterweight against the Russian-Iran-Hezbollah axis. Concomitantly, Russia, Iran and Hezbollah have overwhelmingly made their military presence felt in Syria, though Iran denies any combat role in Syria. Both sides of the party have been consistently violating Security Council resolution 2268. Interestingly, the tentative cessation of hostilities between the USA and Russia, with each toning down their otherwise harsh language, has triggered curiosity that they might have zeroed down to some sort of win-win situation at Syria's expense.

This chapter attempts to study whether an establishment of a "credible, inclusive and non-sectarian" government in Damascus is feasible in the context of the intricate domestic and regional scenario. It also tries to analyse the competing political and geostrategic interests among the various external powers played out in the ever changing geopolitical spectrum of the Syrian conflict.

Introduction

Ever since Syria attained independence in 1946, it has been thrown into the throes of conflicts both internal and external. Syria became a local theatre of the Cold War and a place where Arab states vehemently "struggle(d) for Syria".[1] In March 2011, what began as a peaceful uprising for democratic reforms, social justice, and free political participation, has convoluted into a battleground wherein local, regional, and global powers have once again converged to struggle over Syria.

The strategic location in which Syria is placed undoubtedly attracts outsiders. Albert Hourani and Raymond Hinnebusch believe that Syria's geography has always been shaped by her historical fate.[2] The Westphalian notion of the nation-state, which was forcibly and reluctantly thrust upon Syria and on the rest of the present Levant countries by the Mandate Powers, also sowed the seeds of discord among the diverse communities. Coupled with this, the ruling Sunni elite behaved like political autocrats. The process of state-building in the early years of Syrian statehood was not distributive and inclusive by nature. The strong resistance by Syrians to the distribution of political power and harsh repressive rules amongst Syria's "mosaic" society—both social and economic—led to the reinforcement of acute economic differentiation and distinct ethnic and sectarian polarisation. A great centre-periphery cleavage divided the dominant Sunni Muslim elite in the cities. They controlled the state and much of societal wealth, with the masses of peasantry and tribesman in their patriarchal communities, including a variety of minority communities, being ranged along the periphery.[3] The coming to power of Hafiz Al-Assad in 1970 stabilised the country that had been wrecked by multiple coups. He scuttled the power of the Sunni clergy through "calculated decompression" strategy.[4] This strategy was patrimonial and Leninist in nature; it followed populist and statist governance which amounted to a tacit contract between "dictators and different constituencies, whereby the latter acquiesce to constraints on their political participation and liberties in exchange for economic security.[5]

Close affiliation with the Sunni clerical establishment would have helped mitigate the frustration and distress of the marginalised Sunni religious establishment. However the regime "displayed a striking lack of interest in the development of the religious bureaucracy, preferring a strictly security focused approach aimed at reducing the influence of clerics over the administration...they preferred to support loyal, but privately funded clerical networks."[6] Thus, the popularly titled "stable, safe"[7] regime had dissident voices and, as Hama Batatu rightly anticipated, led to a revival of the spirit of revolt which no repression, however brutal, can extinguish."[8] This showed its early signs in June 1979, resulting in the 1982 Hama massacre which got aggravated further with the onset of the Arab Spring, thereafter, and then "distinctively turning into a Sunni 'awakening'".[9]

The schism in Syrian society is predominantly economic, although it is compounded by a rigid political structure. According to Safadi, Munro, and Ziadeh,

> [the] Syria's economy suffers from deep-rooted structural weaknesses and a business environment plagued by bureaucratic red tape, governance weaknesses, and a lack of corporate transparency.[10]

In 2005, David Lesch put a straw in the wind by saying that "it would be a recipe for social unrest if unemployment which was rising between 20 percent and 25 percent [of labour force] were to continue unabated".[11]

Hafiz Al-Assad had no "strategic vision for Syria's economic transformation. Reform was always piecemeal and driven by need of the moment rather than long-term planning."[12] Bashar Al-Assad attempted to correct his father's economic policy by propounding and implementing "social market economy"[13] which, however, led to a zigzag approach. The ad-hoc liberalisation was not effective. As part of the neo-liberalisation drive, the regime dismantled all state farms and handed them over to private hands. This process of neo-liberalisation benefitted the privileged elite, primarily in Damascus and Aleppo. By contrast, rural communities had state support withdrawn and subsidies lifted, leading to significant rural discontent and rural-to-urban migration. The slum villages on the outskirts of urban areas absorbed much of the rural migration; they ended up housing nearly a third of Syria's population and became centres of anti-regime activity in 2011.[14]

Internal Sectarian Discord

Syria's population is diverse, and encompasses a wide variety of religious, ethnic, and linguistic groups. This diverse tactfully balanced composition under "autocratic secularism" gradually dissipated after the Syrian uprising, and gave rise to sectarian conflicts. Over the years, the civil war has sharply demarcated the Sunni Arabs and the Alawite Shiites. Though not all Sunnis are with the opposition rebels, they comprise the majority, and are backed by the Sunni states of Saudi Arabia, Qatar, Jordan, and Turkey. The heterogeneous population consisting of various religious and ethnic minorities are caught between the regime and the opposition rebels. The religious and ethnic identities have become increasingly politicized through the course of the conflict as they have faced mounting pressure to take sides. This has left the religious minorities with a dilemma over whom to support to ensure survival.

Sunnis comprise about 72 percent—mostly of Arabs, Kurdish, and Turkoman ethnicities—of the country's 22. 85 million population.[15] The Alawites, the predominant Shiite group to which Bashar Al-Assad belongs, represent 11 percent of the Syrian population, and they are usually presented as strong supporters of Al-Assad. However, not all Alawites have backed the regime through the conflict. Tens of thousands of Alawite men have been forced into military service for the regime, and died in the conflict.[16] Moreover, they are wary of the vicious nature of ISIS and the al-Nusra Front (Al-Qaeda's Syria affiliate, now the Jabhat Fateh *al* Sham) who view the minorities—Druze, Ismailis, and Christians—as heretics, thus leaving them with little option.

The Assad regime, dominated mainly by Alawites, has notoriously pounded the rebel-held areas with impunity; the latest one is in Atareb, west of Aleppo. The Druze in the south (loyal to the regime) clashed with the neighbouring Sunni districts who are allied with the rebel opposition groups, and who are also fighting the Islamic state. Christians of various denominations in Syria support the Assad regime under which they have long enjoyed religious freedom, and had their ethnic rights protected. However, the fear of revenge attacks by opposition rebels has caught them in the crossfire. With the conflict ever growing worse and the fear of being disavowed in the event of a Sunni resurgence, the Christians are opting to emigrate to the West. In the southern Syrian province of Sweida, where most of Syria's 500,000 Druze live, the loyalties of the Druze to the Assad regime have become increasingly strained.

Regionalisation of the Syrian Crisis

In March 2011, discontent among the masses was ripe. There was high rate of unemployment in the rural sector; the social safety net had diminished; there was a wide social gap between the rich and the poor; and the ineffective promises of Bashar al-Assad[17] frustrated the masses. By the time populist measures were announced, the patience of the public had withered.[18] The first flaw of Assad was that he totally blamed the Islamists and *jihadists* for playing a hand in the uprising, and portrayed it as a foreign-inspired conspiracy. Though this was true to some extent, it was not the sole factor. Skirmishes along the Israel-Syrian border were also reported, which appear to have been done on purpose to divert attention from the uprising.[19] Rather than rectifying the system's flaws and resorting to open dialogue, Al-Assad's repressive force compelled the people to resort to violence, and aggravated the situation by giving it a sectarian colour and leading to the greater involvement of external players.

On the other hand, the fragmented and dysfunctional nature of the Syrian opposition made ISIS grow. The disparate political groups, exiled opposition figures, and grass root coalitions were unable to agree on how to overthrow President Bashar al-Assad. The Syrian National Coalition—once recognised as the "sole legitimate representative of the Syrian people"—could not present a credible alternative to the Assad government. The Syrian National Council (SNC) has become a sort of a rag tag, leaderless organisation that had no definite vision and plan.[20] Disillusioned with the SNC and Free Syrian Army (FSA)—another Syrian opposition group founded by defectors from the Syrian armed forces—the moderate opposition groups who were still on the fringes started getting attracted to more radical *jihadi* and conservative *Salafi* groups.[21]

Turkey, Saudi Arabia, and Qatar, who were to become the staunchest foes of Al-Assad, did not initially voice out for regime change. The hesitancy with which the regional community acted toward the regime of Bashar Al-Assad was mainly due to the unrest in the neighbouring countries. Post-Saddam Iraq was teetering on the brink of collapse; Libya was embroiled in a mosaic of turf wars; and civil unrest was rife in Bahrain, Egypt, Tunisia, and Yemen. The "democratising effect" of the Arab Spring prevented the regional states from responding in a measured and calculated manner. However, the internal conflict eventually metastasized into a regional conflagration. By April 2011, Saudi Arabia, Qatar, and Turkey started providing the rebels with arms and other military support. Iran came all out in support of Syria. Although Iran initially denied any combat role in Syria, in the eventual course of events, it admitted (in May 2014) that the Islamic Revolutionary Guards Corps-Quds Force (IRGC-QF) was present in Syria to provide advice and economic assistance.[22] It was also reported that Iran was shipping weapons and personnel to Syria via Iraq.[23]

Given the historical animosity between Iran and Saudi Arabia—characterised by religious-ideological antagonism, competing political and geostrategic interests, and the ongoing competition for regional hegemony—Iran's "meddling" in the region is perceived by Saudi Arabia as a serious threat to its security. The involvement of Iran led some of the Gulf States—prominently Saudi Arabia and Qatar—to accelerate the sectarian nature of the Syrian conflict as also fuel the sectarian stand-off across the region.[24] Saudis as well as citizens of other Gulf States, were increasingly accused of channelling money to radical groups in the war. Saudi Arabia has been financing the main opposition parties—but not Jabhat Fateh *al*-Sham and the ISIS whom it has labelled as terrorist entities in March 2014.[25] While officials denied it, there are, however, suspicions of Qatar tacitly supporting groups such as Jabhat Fateh al-Sham, and other radical groups.

From the Saudi perspective, Iran's ambitions and its military capabilities might be used to further Iranian influence over the Organisation of the Petroleum Exporting Countries (OPEC) and over the Shiite minority population in the Saudi kingdom.[26] The phrase "Shiite Crescent"—used first by King Abdullah of Jordan way back in 2004 and who accused Iran of regional expansionism—has certainly hit the psyche of the Sunni ruled monarchies after the way events have unfolded in the region. The fall of Saddam Hussein in Iraq paved the way for Iran to become Iraq's new patron. Iraq's fight against Al-Qaeda in Iraq (AQI) and Syria's against ISIS has brought the two nations together to fight a common enemy. Nouri al-Maliki, the then Prime Minister of Iraq, defended his stand by saying that "the most dangerous thing" would be a rebel military victory because it would lead to "a civil war in Lebanon, divisions in Jordan, and a sectarian war in Iraq."[27] Despite the withdrawal of Syria from Lebanon in 2005 (following the assassination of former Prime Minister Rafiq Hariri), the predominant presence of Shiite Hezbollah in Lebanon continues to give Iran a foothold in Lebanon. In October 2016, Lebanon choosing Iran-backed politician Michel Aoun as President speaks of Iran's growing influence in Lebanon.

The Houthi rebels' takeover in Yemen in 2014 was seen to have an Iranian hand, and Saudi Arabia considers the Houthis as nothing more than an Iranian proxy.[28] Comments made by Iranian politicians have reinforced such perceptions in Abu Dhabi and Riyadh. For instance, after Sanaa was captured by the Houthis, a member of the Iranian parliament said that Iran now governed in four Arab capitals: Beirut, Damascus, Baghdad, and Sanaa. Thus, Saudi Arabia's overriding priority is to stem Iran's influence in Syria and Yemen, for which the Kingdom is trying to balance its difficult relations with the Muslim Brotherhood, as the Islah party in Yemen which it supports has a significant number of Brotherhood leaders.[29]

In addition, the breakthrough in the Iranian Nuclear deal in 2015 is also seen as an improvement in US-Iranian relations. This has been understood as meaning Shiite forces will gain a stronger footing in the region. Questions have been raised in Saudi Arabia about the US commitment to the region, despite repeated assurances from Washington. The deepest fear is that the USA may be seeking to build a new relationship with Iran at the expense of Saudi Arabia.[30] This has led Saudi Arabia to look to Israel as an ally. However, in the context of the Syrian crisis, Israel has largely turned a blind eye to Russian activities on their border. A former Israeli ambassador to Moscow, Zvi Magen, has commented, "Israel made clear to him [Putin] that we have no real problem with Assad, just with Iran and Hezbollah, and that message was understood."[31] Along with three Sunni countries, Bahrain, UAE and Sudan, Saudi Arabia severed relations with Iran over attacks on the Saudi embassy in Tehran following the execution of Shiite cleric, Nimr al-Nimr, by Saudi Arabia in January 2016. The scope for rapprochement between Iran and Saudi Arabia appears to have narrowed even further.

Concomitantly, there is a growing ideological battle within the Sunni bloc on their version of political Islam. Saudi Arabia and the UAE view the Muslim brotherhood as an "enemy", and have labelled its followers as terrorists in March 2014—although after the Houthi rebellion in 2014, Saudi Arabia seems to be warming up its relations with some sections of the Muslim Brotherhood.[32] On the other hand, Sunni states like Turkey and Qatar are sympathetic towards the Muslim Brotherhood and, as a result, this is disrupting their co-ordinated efforts to fight against their common enemy—Al-Assad. Saudi Arabia is reserved in funding radical rebels as it is increasingly alarmed at the possibility that by funding fighters abroad, it might be also fuelling the growth of extremist and radical groups—such as ISIS—who regard them as "un-Islamic." The fear of a new generation of *mujahideen* returning home and perpetrating terrorist attacks in the Saudi Kingdom and across the Gulf has finally come about, with triple bombings in Riyadh during Ramadan (5 July 2016). Therefore, the rise of ISIS has added another threat, making the Saudi-Iran relations even more complex.[33]

Syria is also ensnared in an intricate regional web of competition and confrontation with Turkey as well as Kurdish groups seeking greater autonomy from both the Arab and Turkish governments. However, the alliance of cooperation and confrontation that existed amongst the parties before the uprising has taken a sharp twist. Once a close ally of Al-Assad, Turkey has become one of the most vocal countries for ousting him.[34] From the very beginning of the crisis, Turkey has provided a base for the operations as well as a safe zone for defectors and opposition groups. In retaliation, Al-Assad manipulated the Kurdish issue which was a bone of contention between Turkey and Al-Assad for a long time.[35] The Democratic Union Party (PYD)—the Kurdistan Workers' Party (PKK) offshoot in Syria—was allowed to operate freely, recruit new fighters for its campaign against the Syrian armed opposition, and undertake a pseudo-governmental role in the Kurdish regions of Syria. In return, the PYD used its influence on Syrian Kurds to prevent their participation in the uprising.[36] Al-Assad's policy of going soft with the PYD was one of the decisive factors that made Turkey categorically demand Al-Assad to step down. However, Turkey was reluctant to join the US-led multinational coalition against ISIS, and refused to tighten its borders.

The rise of ISIS appeared fortuitous for Turkey initially, and fitted into Erdogan's"neo-ottoman" scheme of consolidating Turkey's position in the region by weakening the dominance of Shiite rule in Syria and Iraq, and also by containing the rise of Kurdish forces. Therefore, it followed an "open door policy" wherein borders were left porous to allow jihadi fighters and arms to enter Syria through Turkey. One consequence of this position was a surge of more than two million refugees into Turkey, and the security problems that stemmed from arms and fighters massing around the border area. The killing of 32 people in Suruc on July 2015 by an ISIS suicide bomber became the last straw. This prompted Turkey to fight ISIS.[37]

This policy shift is most clearly manifest in decisions made with respect to domestic and international policies. On the domestic front, Turkish police have initiated a series of large-scale raids, and enforced security and border controls. Externally, Turkey relented by agreeing to US requests to use the Incirlik Air Base in southern Turkey to send fighter jets and armed drones to fight ISIS. However, it is worth mentioning here that the Turkish air force has conducted far more strikes on PKK than on ISIS, leading to the annulment of the ceasefire brokered in 2013 between the PKK and Turkey. Indeed, the inevitable choice of shifting its policies has landed Turkey in a complex web. Domestically, security is under threat, schisms amongst the citizens have crept in with President Erdogan's radical Islamic measures, shaking its very foundation.[38]

Thus, at the time of writing, President Erdogan is at the receiving end.

What Turkey had desired out of the Syrian crisis has boomeranged. Bashar Al-Assad is still in power and gaining in strength, whereas Turkey has become a hotspot for the ISIS for terror attacks. It has also become a home for more than two million Syrian refugees; PYG forces continue to grow more resilient, receiving assistance from the West in its fight against ISIS; and Turkey's international posture as a strategic ally of the US in the region[39] has, once again, entered troubled waters over the issue of the extradition of Fethullah Gulen who, Turkey alleges, masterminded the coup attempt against Bashar Al-Assad on 15 July 2016.

The Internationalisation of the Syrian Crisis

The extensive involvement of external powers in Syria is changing the political spectrum of the conflict immensely. The call for democratic change in Syria by the citizens has long passed its age. The two conflicting parties—the US-led coalition forces and Russia led pro Assad forces, with the ISIS as the common enemy—has transformed the Syrian crisis into a matrix of wars. The US-led coalition forces' approach towards the Syrian crisis has evolved through three stages over the last five years. In the first stage, their response to the Syrian uprising before ISIS came on the scene was alarmingly non-committal and hesitant. Italy was the first European country to condemn the violent oppression of the Al-Assad regime, and recalled its Ambassador. It took almost six months for the international community to react and also condemn the regime. On the other hand, since October 2011, Russia gave political support to Al-Assad, earning the condemnation of the world community. So far, Russia has vetoed six times, and China has vetoed five times, on the Syria-themed resolution proposed by the UN Security Council.

Syria is a long-term strategic ally of Russia. Strategically, the Syrian port city of Tartous is Moscow's last naval facility in the Mediterranean, and was recently upgraded by Russian technicians, indicating Moscow's long term intention of maintaining access to the port. Syria's geo-strategic centrality in the region gives Moscow some diplomatic leverage. With her growing appetite for energy, China has been enlarging her footprint in the West Asian region. Trade between China and Syria has seen significant growth: by 2010 China had become Syria's third largest importer.[40] With the initiatives of One Belt One Road and the Silk Road, it is important for China to have a stable Syria. Unrest in the region would adversely affect the trade and the economy.

The Sino-Russian refusal to join the US-led coalition forces in Syria was also because of what happened in Libya in 2011. The two countries abstained on the UNSC Resolution 1973 to establish a no-fly zone over Libya, intended as a protective measure to safeguard civilian lives. It was, however, used to their advantage by the USA, France, Britain, and other interested parties to bring down Libyan dictator Muammar Gaddafi instead. Thus, the Kremlin perceives the West's attempts to remove Al-Assad more as a way of weakening Iran than of helping the Syrian people to bring about a regime change. In contrast to the Libyan case—in which the international response was largely unanimous in its fight against the Libyan regime[41]—coalition forces were not fully determined for the total condemnation and direct action against the Bashar Al-Assad regime. Relatively less condemnation and insignificant assistance came from the international community—more was needed to turn the tide to the opposition's advantage. This led Khaled Khoja, President of the Syrian National Coalition, to say that the West is giving only "cardboard support".

However, Russia has undertaken a bombing campaign against ISIS strongholds in the country. It has also decided to provide humanitarian aid.[42] For varying reasons, Western policies have been hesitant, cautious, and limited in their involvement. While, Western governments have been providing humanitarian assistance, they were have been more restrained about giving game changing arms and military support to the opposition forces. They have ruled out direct military intervention other than to secure Syrian chemical and biological weapons. And, when it became clear that the regime has deployed them, they have provided only 'non-lethal' support. When the purported "red line" was crossed, the Obama Administration was reluctant to act—although British, French, Israeli, and US intelligence agencies all acknowledged that small quantities of the nerve gas Sarin had been used against civilians in Khan al-Assal (near Aleppo) in 2013. Who used the gasis still shrouded in mystery; but the rare show of "prudence" by the USA is noteworthy. Apparently, in the first stage, "confusion" seems to be the word that befits the response of international actors to the Syrian crisis.

President Obama's four-point plan to "degrade and ultimately destroy" ISIS remains unfulfilled.[43] The unprecedented success of the ISIS in Syria led to the Obama administration to enunciate the policy of differentiating between moderate and radical factions among the Syrian rebels in the second stage. David Cameron famously claimed that there are 70,000 armed moderates, but there appear to be disparate groups of gunmen fighting for a tribe, clan, a village or for whoever will pay them.[44] By March 2013, Raqqa became the first provincial Syrian city to fall in the hands of the ISIS. Simultaneously, the forces of Bashar Al-Assad—backed by Russia and his Iranian allies—were also gaining ground. Division 30, also known as the New Syrian Forces (created by the USA and trained by Pentagon) was reportedly said to have given allegiance to ISIS at Albu Kamal on the Syria-Iraq border in June 2014.[45] Division 30 was effectively a propaganda tool to portray that there are secular rebels in Syria to fight the Al-Assad regime. But as has been observed, "There is simply no real separation between 'moderate' rebel groups and hardline Salafists allied with Al-Qaeda." The US, despite four years of vetting the rebel groups, is yet to find a credible dependable ally in Syria. The dilemma amongst the powers is that there is no viable alternative after Assad exits. The fight against Assad and fight against ISIS have intricately got intertwined, and it has become quite a Gordian knot to unravel. Mehmet Seyfettin Erol, Director of Gazi University's Strategic Research Centre in Ankara, told Al Arabiya English that, "The entry of Russia into the battleground has opened the door for other powers to intervene in the region."[46]

Added to this is the growing assertion of Russia's foreign policy and its aggressive polices in the Central Asian Region, particularly in Ukraine. This has made the US-led coalition forces uneasy, hindering them in finding a durable solution to the Syrian crisis. European policies have also been incoherent as EU member-states are not unanimous on the degree of arming the rebels, and have not agreed on the question of military intervention, thus sending confused and confusing signals.[47]

In particular, France has stood firm for the removal of Syrian President Bashar Al-Assad from the very start. In November 2012, it became the first Western country to recognise the SNC as "unique representative", and initiated talks on lifting the European arms embargo so as to provide weapons to "moderate" rebels. France also facilitated the marginalisation of the country in the international effort to end the conflict, especially after the Russian-American meeting in June 2012 in Geneva, and the announcement of further talks about the "Geneva II" conference in which France did not take part. A common EU stance is needed; and for this, French cooperation is a must.

The disclosure by retired Lieutenant General, Michael Flynn, former head of the Defence Intelligence Agency (DIA), given to *Al Jazeera*'s Mehdi Hasan, unfolds a different narrative. It confirms earlier suspicions that Washington was monitoring *jihadist* groups emerging as opposition in Syria, and it was a "wilful Washington decision" not to interfere with the rise of anti-government *jihadist* groups in Syria, backing a secret 2012 memo predicting their [salafist] rise.[48] Thus, the US-led coalition forces' "supposed" effort to stamp out ISIS must also be taken with a pinch of salt.

However, the co-ordinated large scale terror attacks in Europe and America since 2015 have reinforced the fight against the ISIS, entering the third stage of response. In December 2014, the US Central Command set up Combined Joint Task Force-Operation Inherent Resolve (CJTF–OIR), to coordinate military efforts against ISIS. Those who have conducted airstrikes in Syria include the USA, Australia, Bahrain, Canada, France, the Netherlands, Jordan, Saudi Arabia, Turkey, the United Arab Emirates, and the UK.[49] The Islamic countries under the aegis of Saudi Arabia formed 34-state military coalition to fight terrorism. Syrian Democratic Forces (SDF)—formed in October 2015, dominated by the powerful Kurdish People's Protection Units (YPG) but also includes an Arab contingent—has been steadily growing to around 50,000 fighters. It entered Manbij which was under ISIS since 2014. Turkey backed the Free Syrian Army (FSA) and the USA backed SDF are in military assault against each other in Manbij and Al Bab as Turkey does not want Kurdish autonomy in Northern Syria, though their declared goal is to fight ISIS.

Despite the reinforcement, Russia and the USA carry out separate campaigns of airstrikes against the Islamic State, and US officials have complained that many of Russia's strikes are aimed at groups fighting Al-Assad, including US-backed rebels. Similar accusations are volleyed by Russia and the Al-Assad regime towards the US-led coalition forces.[50] Reportedly, there is an interagency squabble between the CIA and the Pentagon over the support to rebels in Aleppo.[51]

At the time of writing, the Russians have taken a lead of sorts in Syria, bombing strategic targets of the ISIS while, at the same time, supporting the Al-Assad regime and protecting its own assets in the country. The Russian military has told *CNN* that their air force chooses and pinpoints targets on their own, with no input from the Syrian military.[52] They were also instrumental in negotiating a deal with the Al-Assad regime earlier with regard to the removal of its chemical weapons, as mentioned earlier.

In fact, the conflict has brought back Russia into the diplomatic and security game in West Asia. The EU, France, and Germany have changed their rigid stance from "first remove Assad" to cooperation to fight against the ISIS in the backdrop of marathon terror attacks in Europe.[53] The French President has already called for rapprochement between Russia and the USA to fight the ISIS.[54] It appears that President Putin is likely to have a more receptive global audience. Turkey has apologised for the downing of a Russian war plane in November 2015 which restored their relationship, and the mature stance taken by both the countries after the assassination of the Russian envoy to Turkey, Andrey Karlov, in 19 December 2016 in not blaming the other surely does indicate that Russia is determined to win the fight in coordination with Turkey. Germany, Austria, and Spain are now in support of Russia in the fight against ISIS.

The ISIS matrix had evolved to an extent that it has increasingly put the international players and the Arab states in a dilemma. The UN Security Council which has unanimously adopted a resolution calling for a ceasefire and the establishment of a "credible, inclusive and non-sectarian" government in Damascus. This, however, remains elusive. From the very start, there was no political will in the parties concerned to resolve the conflict. After the UN plan was adopted, the then Turkish Prime Minister, Ahmet Davutoglu, blasted the peace proposal, saying it "lacks realistic perspective," and refused to allow the Kurds at the negotiating table. The Syrian government says any truce does not apply to "terrorists"—a label it has used to describe ISIS and opposition rebels. The government also believes that it reserves the right to retaliate against attacks. Thus, the three rounds of Geneva peace talks initiated since 2012 have not resulted in any positive developments. The resignation of Mohammad Alloush (the chief peace negotiator of Syria's mainstream opposition) in May 2016 has brought the "cessation of hostilities" to a grinding halt. The UN-backed parties have not set a date for the resumption of peace talks after the High Negotiations Committee (HNC) suspended its participation over the intensifying of regime air strikes.

India and the Syrian Crisis

India's approach to the conflict in Syria has ranged from being a bystander to that of muted support for Bashar al-Assad's government, as it is shows India continuing its five decades old cordial relations with the Syrian regime. India believes that the Syrians should be left alone to sort their problems out through negotiations, and that externally imposed 'regime change' is not acceptable. However, security threats to India emanating from the growing tentacles of ISIS in Syria, and the spillover effect of the turmoil on the Gulf region threatens the wellbeing of nearly 7 million Indian migrant workers. Ever since the conflict started, there has been an array of visits to India of Syrian government officials, culminating in the visit of the Deputy Prime Minister and Foreign Minister, Walid Mohi Edine al Muallem, in January 2016. This speaks of the expectations of a potential Indian role in diplomatic solutions, given its growing sway with all the countries involved in the conflict and cease fire negotiations. India participated in the Geneva IItalks to deliberate on Syria's future. India has been steadfast in its assistance to Syria. India was sending medicines worth

US$1 million to Syria. Syria is the only country in West Asia where India has extended a "line of credit". The visit of the Minister of State for External Affairs, M. J. Akbar, to Syria in August 2016 and his meeting with President Al-Assad indicates India's growing willingness to engage with the ruling dispensation, and to explore opportunities beyond the Gulf. Cooperation in counter-terrorism and reconstruction are the two notable areas that were addressed in the meeting, which would be in sync with India's growing aspiration for more clout in the international arena.

Conclusion

Syria is in the doldrums, and outside powers are aggravating the situation. The matrix of this conflict has turned multifaceted and multilayered, making the situation more complex. It has become an international problem that threatens to rip apart the 1916 Sykes-Picot arrangement, created one hundred years ago. The massive influx of refugees to the neighbouring countries like Turkey, Jordan, Lebanon, and Iraq as well as to Europe has already started creating ripples in the international order. The Syrian Kurds sense an opportunity to achieve their dream of acquiring "Kurdistan", considering the PYG's predominant role in its fight against ISIS. However, an escalated demand for Kurdish statehood might put Al-Assad in a tight spot in the coming days, and any move towards independence may bring on the wrath of Turkey. The present ISIS stronghold in the northern and eastern parts of Syria and its dream of establishing a caliphate looks grim, with almost all the entry points choked by the Al-Assad and Russian forces.

However, with the break-up of the social fabric, the destruction of homes, the loss of lives and livelihood, there building of a Syrian nation-state will be an arduous task.

A rapprochement between Iran and Saudi Arabia is essential to bring about stability in the region and restoring Syrian order. However, but much of it also lies with the US diplomacy. However, with the current diplomatic snag between the two countries and the committed efforts of the USA to keep the two countries at loggerheads, the prospect for reconciliation looks grim.[55] Though the declassified report released in July 2016 did not point to the direct involvement Saudi Arabia royals in the 9/11 incident, the USA still has a card for politicking.

The military intervention by Russia, which has given a new lease of life to the Al-Assad regime in its fight against opposition forces and ISIS, has changed the political dynamics and calculations of all the stakeholders. Syria has, once again, become the "the centre piece of Soviet Middle East policy",[56] and appears that it will remain so in the foreseeable future. On the other hand, the attempts of US-led coalition forces to destroy the ISIS have set off major reverberations in the internal security of their own respective countries.

ISIS has certainly polarised communities, turning them one against another. Patrick Calvar, head of the French Direction Générale de la Sécurité Interieure, recently warned that his country was "on the brink of a civil war between rightwing and Islamist extremists".[57] Since November 2015, France is under a state of emergency, and is likely to continue with it after the July 2016 massacre in Nice. Turkey has escaped a military coup and has also declared state of emergency. The UK's decision to exit from the EU cannot be mulled over without considering the refugee factor—a direct outcome of the Syrian crisis. The prognosis of the crisis is grim—unless the world community invests collective and sincere efforts in finding a durable solution. The balkanisation of Syria would be a major disaster in the already fragmented region. In other words, Henry Kissinger's statement, "There can be no peace without Syria," stands true even today.

NOTES

1. Seale, Patrick, *The Struggle for Syria: A Study of Post-War Arab Politics, 1945-1958*, London: Oxford University Press, 1965.
2. Hourani, Albert, "Even if there were no Syrian people, a Syrian problem would still exist. Syria owes its political importance less to the qualities of its population than to its geographical position", in *Syria and Lebanon: A Political Essay*, London: Oxford University Press, 1946, p. 6.
3. Hinnebusch, Raymond, *Syria: Revolution from Above*, London: Routledge, 2002, p. 12.
4. This term was used by Raymond A. Hinnebusch in his article, "Calculated Decompression as a Substitute for Democratisation in Syria", in Bahgat Korany (ed.), *Political Liberalization and Democratization in the Arab World: Comparative Experiences*, Boulder, Co., Lynn Reinner Press, 1998, pp. 238–239.
5. Raj M. Desai, Anders Olofsgard, and Tarik M. Yousef, "The Logic of Authoritarian Bargains," *Economics and Politics*, Vol. 21, No.1, March 2009, p.93.
6. Pierret, Thomas, *Religion and State in Syria: The Sunni Ulama from Coup to Revolution*, Cambridge University Press, 2013, p.19, p.64.
7. Danaher, Paul, *The New Middle East: The World after the Arab Spring*, London: Bloomsbury Publishing, 2013, p. 370
8. Hannaa Batatu, "Syria's Muslim Brethren", *Middle East Research and Information Project*, Vol. 110, 1982, p.20
9. Lefevre, Raphael, *Ashes of Hama: The Muslim Brotherhood in Hama*, Oxford University Press, 2013, p. 186. Also, Hama was one of the major epicentres of the uprisings.
10. Raed, Safadi, Laura Munri, and Radwan Ziadeh, "Syria: The Underpinnings of

Autocracy: Conflict, Oil and the Curtailment of Economic Freedom", in Ibrahim Elbadawi and Samir Makdisi (eds.), *Democracy in the Arab World: Explaining the Deficit*, London: Routledge, 2011, p. 146.

11. Lesch, David W., *The New Lion of Damascus: Bashar al-Assad and Modern Syria*, London: Yale University Press, 2005, p.222.
12. Perthes, Volker, "The Political Economy of the Syrian Succession," *Survival*, Vol. 43, No.1, 2001, p.143.
13. The 10th Conference of the Arab Baath Socialist Party (June, 2005) officially adopted the Social Market Economy that, in principle, combines a market with social protections.
14. Tsupokyemla, and Kohli, Neha, "The Syrian Uprising and the Rise of ISIS," in Muni, S.D. and Chadha, Vivek (eds.), *Asian Strategic Review*, IDSA, Pentagon Press, New Delhi, 2016, p. 146.
15. See, https://en.wikipedia.org/wiki/Demographics_of_Syria
16. Sam Dagher, "Syria's Alawites: The People behind Assad," *Wall Street Journal*, June 25, 2015.
17. Bashar's first inauguration speech stressed the need for "a comprehensive development strategy providing a specific framework for steps and measures to be taken to achieve this strategy." However, there has been no clear roadmap towards economic liberalisation and the building of a liberal market economy.
18. Emergency law was lifted, an election was announced, wages were raised, etc.
19. Lesch, David W., *Syria: The Fall of the House of Assad*, London: Yale University Press, 2012, p.135.
20. In November 2012, the US Secretary of State, Hilary Clinton, dismissed the group saying, "the bloc could no longer be viewed as the possible leader of the opposition" at http://www.voanews.com/a/brahimi-seeks-chinese-support-for-syria-solution/1536429.html
21. The US-backed rebel faction Harakat Hazzm disbanded; its members joined extremist groups, such as the Nusra Front, the Al-Qaeda offshoot in Syria. Some of the men joined a group called the Levant Front, a coalition of rebel militias that also has ties to the Al-Qaeda. See, http://www.ibtimes.com/four-years-later-free-syrian-army-has-collapsed-1847116
22. Interview with IRGC 'Commander Mohammad-Ali Aziz Jafari', *ISNA*, 16 September 2012. More details are available at http://www.businessinsider.com/iran-syria-2014-5?IR=T
23. Louis Charbonneau, Exclusive: Western report—Iran ships arms, personnel to Syria via Iraq, *Reuters*, 19 September 2012. at http://www.reuters.com/article/us-syria-crisis-iran-iraq-idUSBRE88I17B20120919
24. For more on this theme, see Hokayem, Emile, "Iran, the Gulf States and the Syrian civil war", in *Middle Eastern Security the US pivot and the rise of ISIS*, International Institute for Strategic Studies, 2014
25. Boghardt, Lori Plotkin, "Saudi Funding of ISIS," Washington Institute, *Policywatch* 2275, 23 June 2014, at www.washingtoninstitute.org/policy-analysis/view/saudifunding-of-isis.
26. Nasr, Vali, "When the Shiites rise",*Foreign Affairs*, LXXXV, Vol. 4, 2006, p.59.
27. http://www.businessinsider.in/It-Looks-Like-Iraq-Has-Joined-Assads-Side-In-The-Syrian-War/articleshow/21292112.cms

28. The Houthi rebels expelled President Abd Rabbo Mansour Hadi in February 2015. The Saudi-led Arab coalition has been engaged in a war against the Houthis since late March with the aiming of restoring Hadi's legitimacy.
29. The former Saudi King Abdullah desires to get rid of President Bashar al-Assad and containing the role of Hezbollah in Lebanon. In state department cable released by *Wikileaks*, he professed his desire to "cut off the head of the snake" —meaning Iran
30. Sailer, Matthias, "Changed Priorities in the Gulf: Saudi Arabia and the Emirates Rethink their Relationship with Egypt," Stiftung Wissenschaft und Politik German Institute for International and Security Affairs.
31. http://www.economist.com/news/middle-east-and-africa/21669563-though-opposite-sides-syrian-conflict-binyamin-netanyahu-and-vladimir-putin-agree
32. http://www.aljazeera.com/news/2015/07/saudi-arabia-warming-muslim-brotherhood-150727121500912.html
33. The fact that Riyadh pulled out of the anti-Brotherhood block should, above all, be interpreted as an attempt to forge a broad alliance of Sunni states and transnational actors against Shiite Iran, in a less and less favourable regional and international environment.
34. By July 2011, Turkey was totally involved in the Syrian crisis. It hosted the Syrian National Council (SNC); sheltered the Free Syrian Army (FSA), and over 300,000 Syrian refugees who fled Assad's violent crackdown.
35. Regionally, Syria had been a key component of Turkey's ruling Justice and Development Party's (AKP) "zero problems with neighbours" policy. Domestically, the engagement with the Syrian regime ensured Syrian cooperation on Turkey's three-decade fight against the Kurdistan Workers' Party (PKK). However, the uprising led the Syrian government to secure the support from the Kurdish constituencies. Concessions were announced, citizenship were given to 250,000 Kurds, and the Kurdish New Year (Nawrooz) was declared a national holiday.
36. http://www.mideasti.org/content/kurdish-dimension-turkeys-syria-policy
37. For almost two years Turkey and ISIS avoided fighting. Soner Cagaptay, Director of the Turkish Research Program at The Washington Institute, terms it as the "Cold War." On 24 August 2015, Turkey finally formally agreed to join US-led coalition against ISIS.
38. Refer to the June 2016 attack in Istanbul airport by ISIS and the 15 July 2016 abortive military coup against President Erdogan. Though it is still early to ascertain whether it was 'staged' by President Erdogan as some sources claim, it does imply that there are serious problems gripping the nation.
39. Kinzer, Stephen, *Reset: Iran, Turkey and America's Future*, New York: Times Books, Henry Holt and Company, 2010.
40. http://edition.cnn.com/2012/02/05/world/meast/syria-china-russia-relations/
41. Only Algeria and Syria opposed the Arab League resolution that called on the United Nations for a no-fly zone over Libya.
42. "Russia to Focus on 'Humanitarian Ops' in Syria," *Sky News*, 15 January 2016, at http:///news,sky.com/story/1623383/russia-to-focus-on-humanitarian-ops-in-syria

43. This plan includes air strikes against ISIS targets, increased support to local forces on the ground, the continuation of counter terrorism efforts to prevent future attacks, and humanitarian assistance to non-combatants in the region.
44. http://www.independent.co.uk/news/world/middle-east/syria-civil-war-bringing-conflict-to-an-international-level-is-helping-to-hold-the-ceasefire-a6933081.html
45. http://www.infowars.com/isis-and-al-nusra-merge-on-syria-iraq-border/
46. https://english.alarabiya.net/en/perspective/analysis/2016/02/17/Military-moves-Turkey-and-Saudi-Arabia-close-ranks-on-Syria-.html
47. Asseburg, Muriel, "Syria's Civil War: Geopolitical Implications and Scenarios", German Institute for International and Security Affairs (SWP), Berlin. http://www.iemed.org/observatori-es/arees-danalisi/arxius-adjunts/anuari/iemed-2013/Asseburg%20Syria%20Geopolitical%20Implications%20EN.pdf
48. The document, declassified through the Freedom of Information Act (FOIA), analysed the situation in Syria in the summer of 2012 and predicted the following: "if the situation unravels, there is the possibility of establishing a declared or undeclared Salafist principality in eastern Syria...and this is exactly what the supporting powers to the opposition want, in order to isolate the Syrian regime." https://www.rt.com/usa/312050-dia-flynn-islamic-state/
49. "Airstrikes hit ISIL Terrorists in Syria, Iraq", *U.S. Department of Defence*, 30 September 2015.https://www.defense.gov/News/Article/Article/621107/airstrikes-hit-isil-terrorists-in-syria-iraq
50. Russian Foreign Minister, Sergey Lavrov, called into question the effectiveness of the US-led coalition against Islamic State (IS).
51. According to one Pentagon official, the rebels in Aleppo are fighting the Bashar Al-Assad regime whereas their objective is to destroy the ISIS. According to PNP magazine, he stated that the concerned colleagues from within the US-led coalition turned to him. They informed him that the US-military did not give clearances to their fighter pilots even though they clearly located and identified Islamic State positions. See, https://southfront.org/syria-germany-leaving-the-ranks-of-the-us-alliance-against-russia/
52. http://edition.cnn.com/2016/05/09/middleeast/russia-military-syria/
53. Since 2012, France is number one in the targeted list: the Bataclan theatre massacre; the assault on the offices of the French satirical magazine *Charlie Hebdo*; killing 12 in the name of Al-Qaeda in the Arabian Peninsula (AQAP); and targeted soldiers and the Jewish community. Then there were the 2015 November's ISIS-organised strike at a concert hall, bars, and a football stadium. Finally, there was the recent attack on Bastille Day at Nice.
54. William E. Pomeranz, "Does Paris Open Door for Russia", at https://www.wilsoncenter.org/article/does-paris-open-door-for-putin
55. http://english.alarabiya.net/en/News/middle-east/2016/06/28/White-House-tells-Iran-to-stop-funding-Hezbollah.html
56. The US Department of Defence in 1985 termed Syria "the centre piece of Soviet Middle East policy."
57. https://www.theguardian.com/world/2016/jul/15/why-does-france-keep-getting-attacked

REFERENCES

Danaher, Paul, *The New Middle East: The World after the Arab Spring*, London: Bloomsbury Publishing, 2013.

Hinnebusch, Raymond, *Syria: Revolution from Above*, London: Routledge, 2002.

Lefevre, Raphael, *Ashes of Hama: The Muslim Brotherhood in Hama*, Oxford University Press, 2013.

Lesch, David W., *The New Lion of Damascus: Bashar al-Assad and Modern Syria*, London: Yale University Press, 2005.

Seale, Patrick, *The Struggle for Syria: A Study of Post-War Arab Politics, 1945–1958* London: Oxford University Press, 1965.

Pierret, Thomas, *Religion and State in Syria: The Sunni Ulama from Coup to Revolution*, Cambridge University Press, 2013.

22

Islamic State in Iraq and Syria: Causes and Consequences— An Introduction

A.R. Ghanashyam

In the aftermath of two devastating World Wars, if there is a single security issue that has increasingly engaged the attention of the global community in the later decades of the twentieth century and thereafter, it is terrorism. The Palestinian and Sri Lankan outfits have localised individual narratives of their own. However, the Al-Qaida, its successors, affiliates and franchisees trace their origins to a more global context in which the West is pitted against the East. The Islamic State of Iraq and Syria (ISIS, or in short IS) started as Al-Qaida in Iraq (AQI) a decade and a half ago. The USA invaded Iraq in 2003 to neutralise President Saddam Hussein. The Soldiers of the defeated Iraqi Army abandoned by the USA, and several disgruntled Sunni elements persecuted by the Iraqi regime of the Shiite leader Nouri Al-Maliki, form the core of the IS. Thus, the outfit has the requisite military training and capacity to mount precision attacks on soft as well as hard targets.

In the last couple of years, IS has come into prominence despite being disowned in February 2014 by Al-Qaida, once its mentor. At its peak, operating from two headquarters—Mosul in Iraq and Raqqa in Syria—IS is believed to have held sway over a third of the geographies of Iraq and Syria, with an annual revenue estimated at nearly US$ 3 billion from oil and gas, taxation and extortions. UN estimates that over 3 million Iraqis have been internally displaced because of the conflict and warns that the battle for Mosul could spark a mass exodus of another million. The UN also adds that over 4.8 mil Syrians have fled abroad to escape the fighting in Syria, reaching Turkey, Lebanon and Jordan. A growing number tried to make it up to Europe in 2015.

By virtue of concerted opposition attacks, the influence of IS appears to be waning in Iraq and Syria. The British Broadcasting Corporation (BBC) estimates that, in January 2015, IS controlled an area of 90,800 sq km, administering around 10 million people. In July 2016, the numbers have declined to 68,300 sq km, and 6 million people. IS has moved towards Libya, and is now known to have its presence in 18 countries as per the US based National Counter Terrorism Centre. IS's revenues have rapidly dwindled, and it is believed that it is finding it difficult to finance its operations with impunity as before. They may not be able to take on the might of the opposition for long. But their resort to suicide lone wolf attacks indicates their global reach even if they are dismantled in Iraq and Syria.

The question we need to dwell upon is how insulated is India from IS. Traditionally, Muslims in India have remained uninfluenced by the *Jihadi* rhetoric as is evident from their total lack of interest on possible overtures of IS, and others of its ilk, to take part in *jihadi* activities. They have scrupulously remained on the side of constitutional and democratic ways in addressing and redressing their problems. Be that as it may, we must take note of the fact that IS has already reached Pakistan and Bangladesh in our neighbourhood. Further, while its physical and financial bearings may have taken a beating, the digital and ideological moorings of the IS are invisible and formidable. The lone wolfs have changed the profile of a *jihadi* who was once influenced by poverty, unemployment, and ideology to a new persona: that of a person coming from a middle and upper middle class background with a better education, but with perceptions of injustice. Technology has enabled IS to digitally expand itself to a global outreach. There is need for awareness on these facts among the stake holders in India, including the government and the governed, when we address issues relating to IS terrorism.

23

The Islamic State: Origins, Evolution and Consequences

Alvite Singh Ningthoujam

ABSTRACT

Of West Asian origin, the Islamic State of Iraq and Syria (ISIS) has emerged as one of the most organised terrorist organisations in recent times. Its roots can be traced to 2004, the year when Al-Qaeda in Iraq (AQI) was formed. However, due to internal discords (primarily for leadership and dominance in Syria and Iraq), the AQI got fragmented, and its faction—ISIS—went on to become the world's most-dreaded terror organisations since 2013. The unique characteristic of this outfit was its possession of swathes of territories in Syria and Iraq as well as huge financial wealth during its heyday. From an estimated value of US$1.9 billion in 2014, ISIS's finance was dropped to US$870 million in 2016.[1]

This chapter addresses the evolution of ISIS and its global expansion in a short duration. It also examines the steps taken by international powers due to which the outfit is losing ground in its core areas in Syria and Iraq, and facing defeat both territorially and financially in these two countries. The chapter also highlights briefly how the influence of ISIS has penetrated into India. Finally, after its decline in West Asia, the likely direction in which the organisation is heading is also discussed.

The Origin

The dreaded terror phenomenon called the Islamic State of Iraq and Syria (ISIS), which has spread its influence over large swathes of West Asia, has become a major concern not only for the countries of the region but the world over. As it has been understood, the primary motive behind the inception of this Sunni militant outfit was to establish a Caliphate, or an Islamic state, to be governed by rigid Islamic laws. During late July 2014, Abu Bakr al-Baghdadi declared himself the new Caliph of this group. Ibrahim Awwad Ibrahim Ali al-Badri al-Samarrai, the real name of the self-appointed Caliph, studied in the Islamic University of Baghdad, and obtained a degree in Islamic Studies.[2] Since his taking over of the terror organisation, he is referred to as Caliph Ibrahim by his followers. It is understood from this name—which means 'succession' in Arabic—that the ultimate ambition of the leader is to establish the mentioned state globally. However, this is now becoming more of a crumbling dream.

The Islamic State of Iraq and Syria was earlier a part of the Al-Qaeda in Iraq (AQI), the group that was formed in 2004 when the US-led coalition forces tried to establish control in Iraq after the toppling of Saddam Hussein's Ba'athist regime. The fighters in the ranks of the ISIS were mainly composed of soldiers who had earlier served in the said regime, and were known for their extremely brutal campaigns, mainly to spark off sectarian clashes against the Shia community, particularly in war-ravaged Iraq. But their leader, Abu Musab al-Zarqawi, was replaced by Abu Ayyub al-Masri as the former was killed in a US airstrike in October 2006. The newly inducted leader then changed the outfit's name to Islamic State in Iraq (ISI), and appointed Abu Omar al-Baghdadi as the leader.

Similar to al-Zarqawi's fate, this leadership lasted only for a few years and, as result, from April 2010 onwards, the onus of running ISI fell on Abu Bakr al-Baghdadi. It was he who finally gave it the name Islamic State in Iraq and the Levant (ISIL) or ISIS. Abu Bakr al-Baghdadi declared ISIL in early 2013, after the absorption of the Al-Qaeda backed militant group in Syria known as Jabhat al-Nusra or Al-Nusra Front,[3] which is now renamed as Jabhat Ftah al-Sham (Conquest of Syria Front). Consequently, Abu Bakr al-Baghdadi's announcement of this merger led to the development of rifts between Al-Nusra and ISIS, resulting in them going their separate ways since 3 February 2014. The extreme brutalities of the ISIS towards the local civilian populations ran contrary to Al-Qaeda's mission to unite all Muslim across the region, and this difference became one of the most important factors for the eventual divorce between them.

Although their core ideology remains mostly the same, ISIS and Al-Qaeda have adopted different strategies and operational tactics. ISIS coerces local populations while advertising to a global audience. It has created local governance. It has also targeted potential recruits around the world, with propaganda in dozens of languages weighing in on issues unique to Muslim communities in France, Russia, or elsewhere. However, ISIS's message is a zero-sum game: you are either with ISIS, or you are an infidel. It has been prepared to act ruthlessly against those who do not share its hard-line worldview. Its tactics are coercive. In the end, it tends to act unilaterally.

In contrast, al-Qaeda groups have focused more on local populations and local flashpoints. Al-Qaeda co-opts; it seeks local buy-ins that makes the movement sustainable in the long term. Al-Qaeda has positioned itself as an actor on a higher moral ground by building alliances with local militias and limiting collateral damage in an incredibly brutal civil war. Al-Qaeda's long-term objective is the same as the Islamic State's: to reform society and govern it under a strict interpretation of the Sharia. However, they differ in methodology and timelines.[4]

There is now a competition for dominance between these two groups, although global attention has tilted towards the ISIS with its ever expanding activities—physically and ideologically—not only in West Asia but also in Europe, North America, Central America, South and Southeast Asia. These two organisations are playing on each other by closely monitoring each one's achievements and failures. The ISIS has been branding itself as being more successful, and illustrates this in the form of capturing more territories, recruiting more local and foreign fighters, and importantly, acquiring large financial wealth. In the words of Michael Weiss and Hassan Hassan, the author of *ISIS: Inside the Army of Terror*,

> Inside Iraq, the dynamics and nature of ISIS changed as well. Al-Baghdadi had earnestly taken up [the] PR gambit inaugurated by al-Zarqawi, and then expanded by al-Masri and the first al-Baghdadi, and further Iraqized ISIS, outfitting its upper echelons with former Saddamists. By incorporating al-Nursra's lower and middle cadres, al-Baghdadi thus found himself once again commanding a more internationalised terror army, one that spanned the Levant and Mesopotamia. Thus, by renouncing al-Qaeda, al-Baghdadi actually returned ISIS to a version of its earliest incarnation in Iraq.[5]

As for Al-Qaeda, its activities and influence are noticeably downgraded since the past few years, after being clouded over by ISIS. However, one cannot afford to underestimate as yet the potential of this major terror organisation.

Right from the time of its inception, ISIS had followed stringent behavioural norms and strategies. This made it starkly different from other militant organisations operating in the region. Its brutality first came to notice when the fighters started massacring their rivals, but attracted global attention after they executed thousands of Iraqi soldiers and 100 odd Syrian troops during mid-2014. Their extreme intolerance to external interventions in various West Asian crises, particularly in Iraq and Syria, has been signified by the killings of foreign nationals, including aid workers and journalists. Its adherence to strict Islamic punishments is noticeable in the form of floggings; imposing bans on smoking and music; and enforcing other social restrictions, which are deemed as un-Islamic. Notwithstanding the differences, Al-Qaeda and ISIS will continue to exploit the presence of disillusioned youths and disaffected groups wherever possible. They will play their roles continuously in undermining the existence of modern-day state systems in West Asia and in other parts of the world. Their rivalries and competition do "not weaken the jihadist threat; it widens its scope".[6]

Due to ISIS's ambition to establish a Caliphate, thousands of foreign fighters of all profiles and backgrounds, from over 100 countries, have flocked to Syria and Iraq to fight in the ranks of the organisation. During its peak period, particularly between 2014 and mid-2015, the number is estimated at being 30,000.[7] A majority of these fighters came from Tunisia, Jordan, and Saudi Arabia. During the early days, the Syrian humanitarian crisis and the establishment of an Islamic state in a particular territory, etc. were some of the radicalising and recruiting factors. Alongside this, family problems; societal pressures; the search for identity; acceptance and purpose; and peer pressures are some of the attributing factors for the rising rate of radicalisation amongst the youth. This makes them vulnerable to the recruitment activities conducted by ISIS. Many of such youth have travelled to Syria and Iraq voluntarily. However, a sense of marginalisation and depravation are not the sole reasons for their drift towards religious extremism. In some cases, adventurism and mercenary desires are other attributed factors which resulted in departures for Iraq and Syria and joining ISIS.

A systematic recruitment pattern is another trait which has enabled this ISIS to recruit fighters, and this is being carried out by using some of the latest social media applications, particularly Twitter,[8] Skype, Kik, Facebook, and other popular platforms. Beyond this, publications in the vernacular languages, including Russian, Turkish, and Malay, also help in pushing ISIS propaganda into a particular region. While *Dabiq* used to be a popular English propaganda magazine, a new publication—*Rumiyah*—is propagating the extremist ideology and activities of ISIS. Furthermore, since the beginning, ISIS has been using narratives such as 'Islam is in danger', and that 'Muslims are severely oppressed and marginalised' to fuel the process of radicalisation, ultimately leading to recruitment. In other words, "grievances, jihad, and martyrdom" are the "recurring narratives".[9]

Another dimension of global concern is ISIS' sources of funding. One of the most important sources has been the kidnap-for-ransom tactic, with foreign workers often being the prime targets. There are also reports of funds being transferred to ISIS by Persian Gulf countries, such as Kuwait, Qatar, Turkey, and Saudi Arabia.[10] This was allegedly done through Kuwait, with the tacit approval of the regimes in the mentioned countries.[11] However, some of the studies conducted on this aspect of funding have mentioned the lack of "hard evidence" of donations from the mentioned countries, particularly for the period 2014–2016, in contrast to the "limited donations" to the predecessors of ISIS which does have some evidence, during the 2000s.[12]

However, along the journey, ISIS has exploited various other means to garner financial support. During the initial days, it could gather a large sum of money out of petty crimes and bank robberies. After capturing Mosul's Central Bank, ISIS reportedly looted 500 billion Iraqi dinars, approximately US$ 425 million and, with a total fund worth approximately US$ 2 billion (in 2014), it was considered "the world's richest terrorist group".[13] Another breakthrough happened when ISIS captured large oil fields in Syria and Iraq.[14] The oil seized from these fields was sold at a discounted price, which was estimated at US$25 to US$60 a barrel, as against the market price of US$ 100 then, and the total profits from such sales was over US$ 3 million a day.[15] Turkey, Jordan, Iraqi Kurdistan, and the rebels in Syria were suspected to be the recipients of oil sold by ISIS in the black market.[16] However, due to the military campaigns of the coalition forces in Syria and Iraq, ISIS significantly began to lose these natural resources. Moreover, most of the illegal trade routes were destroyed by the security forces. This has resulted in the decline of its financial wealth, and by 2016, it has dropped to approximately US$ 870 million (annual revenue).[17] Under the current circumstances, this decline will become more acute, and ISIS will find it extremely difficult to rebuild its financial stability to the level it was a couple of years ago.

Evolution: ISIS's Territorial Expansion

From the word 'state', it is evident that the ISIS carries an objective to establish a well-defined Islamic state which will be governed by strict Sharia law. In order to meet this goal, since the beginning of 2014, the organisation has fought unrelentingly to capture as much territory as it could. Such efforts have led to the takeover of some of Iraq's and Syria's cities, such as Tikrit, Fallujah, Mosul, Ramadi, Raqqa, Palmyra, along with other towns and villages. In other words, by the time the self-appointed Caliph made his first public appearance on 4 July 2014, ISIS had already taken control of territories "stretching from al-Bab in Syria's Aleppo governorate to Suleiman Bek in Iraq's Salah ad Din province, over 400 miles away".[18] Unlike Al-Qaeda, ISIS "requires territory to remain legitimate and a top-down structure to rule it".[19] This is one of the traits which has lifted it to global prominence, unlike other organisations which are operating today.

The territorial conquests of 2014, followed by unfolding events in West Asia during early 2015 wherein ISIS militants captured two strategically and historically important places have indicated its vigour to consolidate, control, and expand its territories. The fall of the city of Ramadi, the capital of Anbar Province in Iraq, on 17 May, and the historic city of Palmyra in Syria on 20 May (both in 2015) happened amidst efforts to destroy this Sunni militant group. The victory came contrary to the claim by American officials that the ISIS was on the defensive in Iraq. By capturing these cities with very well-planned tactics, the organisation demonstrated its capability to operate on multiple fronts, and carry out effective offensive operations.

The breakneck speed at which the cities were captured has raised several questions about the fighting capabilities of the security forces of Iraq as well as of US-led coalition airstrikes. The lack of strategy, as mentioned by President Barack Obama in August 2014 vis-à-vis the fight against ISIS in Syria, had become more visible as there seemed to be no stoppage to the terror organisation's forward movement. ISIS' success in Ramadi was particularly a setback in America's effort inside Iraq. The American forces fought bitterly with the Islamist militants during 2005 and 2006 to take this city from their control. However, this city became a prized possession for ISIS. Moreover, the "Anbar Province [also] holds painful historical import for the United States as the place where nearly 1,300 marines and soldiers died after the American-led invasion of 2003."[20] Therefore, this episode has become quite galling for the Americans.

The ISIS takeover of Ramadi did not come without major resistance. It happened after a continuous battle between ISIS militants and the Iraqi Security (ISF). The campaign to take control of cities began in Ramadi and nearby places (such as Fallujah) during late December 2013. While the ISF had the upper hand over Ramadi, Fallujah fell into the hands of the extremists. Since then, Ramadi became the prime target for the ISIS, and the group had been eyeing it for months. It started making strategic moves in the surrounding areas as early as December 2014. The manner in which Ramadi fell was similar Mosul's capture by the ISIS in June 2014, except that there were no coalition bombings in the case of the latter. The forces of the government had to flee from their posts, abandon their weapons and vehicles after the militants began with intensified attacks. These included suicide bombings by explosives-laden cars as well as artillery shelling. In the words of one, "Ramadi finally cracked when struck with a hammer blow—namely, twenty-eight suicide car bombs in three days, including at least six massive fifteen-ton armed truck bombs on single attack."[21] The triumph over the state forces— despite the military back-up of the Western powers—highlights the extent of the strength of this organisation.

Even before the takeover of Ramadi sunk in, the ISIS, in a quick succession, captured the historic city of Palmyra in Syria. This victory came after the forces loyal to the Syrian President Bashar al-Assad lost out to the ISIS militants in a seven-day siege. The immediate concern out of this unfolding was fear of the possible destruction of the city's magnificent historical ruins. Once a Silk Route hub and presently one of the most important cultural centres of the ancient world, Palmyra is known for its several well-preserved ruins from antiquity, including the famous Temple of Bell whose construction dates back to the first century.

Since the beginning of 2015, ISIS started to bulldoze its way through many invaluable cultural heritage sites of Syria and Iraq. It vehemently opposes the preservation of historical ruins as it feels that these glorify idolatry. Besides destroying archaeological sites, ISIS has even burned 1,500 historical manuscripts. ISIS attacks are anti-humanity in nature: "[they] threaten to upend millennia of coexistence in the Middle East."[22] The destruction of these antiquities should not be seen as sporadic events but as are part of a systematic campaign taken up by the organisation to uproot "humanity's cultural legacy."[23] However, at the same time, many of the artefacts have been reportedly sold by ISIS on the black market in European cities to raise funds for the organisation. This was one of the many ways in which the entire financial system of ISIS has been managed. In late September 2014, the UNESCO warned about the imminent danger Iraq's cultural heritage would face should the ISIS manage to capture it. However, this was not the first time lootings took place in Iraq: Iraqi heritage had already suffered blows following the toppling of the Hussein regime in 2003. The recurrence of these incidents and the failure to protect thousand-year-old artefacts/monuments reflect the lackadaisical attitude of both Iraq and the international powers that are striving to bring stability in the region.

Crises in the Caliphate: Territorial Shrinkage

While territorial annexations increased ISIS's credibility as an organisation that remained committed to building an Islamic state, over a period of time, this dream has started to fade. For an organisation like ISIS, which swears by its ambition to establish a global Caliphate, the loss of territory is definitely a setback. The coalition military campaign led by the USA since September 2014 began to keep a check on the forward movements of ISIS, particularly in Iraq. Despite several gaps in the overall strategy, the counter-offensive measures have paid off well in Syria also. During 2015 and early 2016, ISIS started to lose its grip in some of the areas it controlled in both these countries. Before its decisive victory (in Ramadi in May 2015), Iraqi forces, in coordination with tribal forces and locals, recaptured the strategic city of Tikrit in April. With this triumph, efforts to free Mosul from the clutch of the group had begun. In November 2015, coordination between Kurdish Peshmerga fighters and the Yazidis resulted in regaining full control of Sinjar in Iraq, and parts of a road which served as a link with Syria.[24] This restricted the movements of the fighters between Iraq and Syria, curbed the smuggling of weapons, and caused financial strain. In a quick succession, a US-led coalition campaign liberated Ramadi in late December 2015. Since then, ISIS did not made any significant progress in its attempts to occupy more territories though it continues to carry out attacks.

Similarly, ISIS territories inside Syria have begun to shrink although its so-called headquarters at Raqqa is still under its control. From early 2015, Syrian Kurds, who are fighting against the ISIS militias, have made concerted efforts to take back the border down of Tal Abyad in Syria, which is close to the Turkish border. This was a strategic asset as ISIS fighters used it to cross into Turkey; Tal Abyad has also served as a supply conduit for Raqqa. The Kurdish Popular Protection Units (YPG), backed by US air strikes, has assisted in the liberation campaign. Along with the loss of territories, the financial system of the ISIS was severely affected in both the countries. This is increasingly causing rifts amongst the fighters. Amidst these developments, Turkey has remained extremely concerned about the rising capabilities of the Syrian Kurds along its borders as they have been demanding a separate entity for themselves. As observed by an American defence expert,

> the situation in Syria is not dissimilar to what is occurring in Iraq: Kurdish territorial successes in expelling ISIS safe havens are emboldening Kurdish nationalist groups and stirring ethnic tensions...But their successes will...stir deep concerns across the border in Turkey.[25]

The divergence of interests is the reason why external players, including Turkey and the USA, do not see eye-to-eye on combating ISIS, or any other organisations. This mainly pertains to the Syrian crisis where a few countries do not want to see the back of Bashar al-Assad, while others support the establishment of a new government without him.

In 2015, ISIS territory (in Syria and Iraq) shrunk from 90,000 sq km to 78,000 sq km—a net loss of 14 per cent. Data released in early October 2015 mentioned that there was a decline from 78,000 sq km to 65,000 sq km in the first nine months of this year.[26] The commencement of Russian air strikes from 30 September 2015 has also contributed to the cornering of ISIS in Syria. The Russian intervention enabled Al-Assad's forces and its allies to push out ISIS from Palmyra during late March 2015. After Russian President Vladimir Putin announced the drawdown of troops from Syria on 14 March 2016, the Russian military campaigns shifted its targets towards Palmyra and the nearby areas, resulting into the breakthrough. This has reignited the debate over Russia's potential return to West Asia as a major player. While Russia's military prowess has been exhibited, it is yet to be seen how far Moscow's political clout will help in resolving the Syrian crisis. This still looks shaky as other players, including the USA, are not on the same page over the issue of political transition.

As ISIS upholds the centrality of establishing an Islamic state, the continuous shrinking of territories under its direct governance has become a serious drawback. It was the territorial expansion since mid-June 2014 which made ISIS unique as compared to other contemporary terror organisations. Even its parent-organisation, Al-Qaeda, could not keep defined territories (despite its enormous network) of such magnitude since its inception in the late 1980s. The idea of having a Caliphate with administrative units, currency, social services as well as judicial, educational, and banking systems has attracted like-minded terror organisations, supporters and sympathisers from different corners of the world. When the territorial control starts crumbling, the ambition of raising such an entity diminishes.

Despite the gradual retreats from Iraq and Syria, ISIS has still managed to keep certain areas intact. Its leadership continues to make strategic decisions, and give orders vis-à-vis operations for the region and beyond. Moreover, the physical and logistical capabilities to conduct attacks have not been fully contained or destroyed. Another worrisome factor is the potential of chemical and biological attacks. This terror outfit was reportedly responsible for an attack involving mustard gas.[27] After an alleged use of such lethal weapons against the Kurdish forces in August

2015,[28] the European Parliament and US intelligence have warned of the possibility of such attacks, particularly in Europe. A serious debate on this issue was kick-started after the 13 November Paris attack.[29] The profiles of the foreign recruits of ISIS are mostly with educational and professional experiences on technical subjects such as physics, chemistry, and computer science; this is another reason to be concerned.

As ISIS started to lose ground, it has begun to export its terror activities abroad. There have been several attacks either directly linked to ISIS or inspired by it. Some of the major incidents have taken place between late 2014 and March 2016 in France, Yemen, Tunisia, Turkey, Belgium, Kuwait, Saudi Arabia, Lebanon, Bangladesh, Afghanistan, Australia, Libya, Indonesia, and Egypt.[30] The carnage, particularly in Paris[31] and Brussels, are clear manifestations of ISIS's rising ability to strike overseas targets with meticulous planning. They also signify a level of proficiency. Further attacks cannot be ruled out as there are already vast Islamist networks with access to weapons systems, financial assistance, and returnees with battlefield experiences. This is also applicable to the South and Southeast Asian context from where fighters have moved towards West Asia, and disaffected groups and local terror outfits are looking for the right moment to strike. Thus, they are going to be a major challenge to the counter-terrorism measures of countries which have already witnessed either ISIS-directed or ISIS-inspired attacks.

Another challenge is the issue of controlling the territories re-captured from ISIS. Owing to the highly sectarian nature of the conflict, and the involvement of various factions with different objectives, there should be clear-cut policies of how to integrate and govern. It will be undesirable to witness an emergence of new fighting between different groups wherever ISIS has not been completely uprooted.

Merely liberating territories alone will not break the backbone of ISIS; but fighting its extremely pernicious ideology should be helpful in the long run. However, the reality is that there are still no effective counter-narratives or de-radicalisation programmes that could prevent impressionable youths from blowing themselves up in the name of a holy war. The present-day radicalisation process, particularly in Europe, is a suitable example. ISIS has gone transnational in its campaigns. Tackling these eminent problems is going to be a major challenge in the foreseeable future.

Financial and Internal Discords

From being considered the world's wealthiest terror organisation in 2014,

ISIS now faces financial constraints. In mid-2015, its overall monthly revenue in the territories under its control in Syria and Iraq was estimated at US$ 80 million; but these plummeted to US$ 56 million in March 2016. This has come about with the destruction of several oil fields by air campaigns conducted by the US-led coalition as well as by the coordinated efforts of Russia and its allies. A direct impact is being felt by ISIS fighters, and the organisation is struggling to maintain its military infrastructures. Moreover, the oil trade has become more difficult due to the recapture of strategic cities (in Syria and Iraq) which were once used as routes for illegal trade, the movement of fighters, and smuggling (particularly along the Turkish border). Earlier, a significant amount of oil was reportedly marketed within Iraq as well as in ISIS-controlled and rebel-held territories in northern Syria.[32] Beyond the borders, Turkey has been identified as an alleged buyer of such oil. The air strikes have resulted in the destruction of almost 30 per cent of the organisation's oil infrastructures.[33] Indeed by the end of 2016, the annual revenue of ISIS dropped to US$ 970 million.[34]

With the decline in the oil trade, ISIS has shifted to imposing different forms of taxes on the population. The *jizyah* or taxation from the non-Muslims (particularly Christians) is an example. It has been collecting monetary fines from people who are unable to answer correctly questions related to the holy Quran, or anyone found violating the Sharia law.[35] Some of the prime sources of the revenue of ISIS include extortion, kidnapping, the smuggling of arms and drugs as well as private funding. It also levies heavy taxes on people's income, and collects fees for the use of basic facilities such as water, electricity, and cellular mobile services.

Considering the growing crises, ISIS will no doubt make unrelenting efforts to retain those territories which are still under its governance. This will help it in serving strategic purposes such as generating funds from the remaining oil they still possess, continue running the extortion business, and keep training foreign fighters. Without recapturing all the territories, efforts to cut all the financial lifelines will be a huge challenge for the allies involved in the fight against the organisation.

Another fund-related problem is the slashing of the salaries of ISIS fighters in Syria and Iraq by almost 50 per cent. While is its unclear as to how much every fighter was paid during the organisation's heyday, the reduced monthly salary for Syrian fighters is estimated at US$ 200, and US$ 400 for the foreign fighters.[36] The perception that outsiders are paid higher—on the ground that they have left behind comfortable lives in their respective countries—has triggered serious the "ire and resentments of local ISIS members."[37] Such an anomaly has given rise to internal discord amongst the fighters. Foreign recruits have been blamed by the locals for the fall of territories due to their incompetence, and there are complaints pertaining to their disregard for the local culture, traditions, and tribal structures.[38] The former rationale fits well with the assumption that the fighters, mainly from India, Pakistan, Bangladesh and Africa, are inferior and "expendable" as compared to their Arabs and Western counterparts.[39] Moreover, there is also the belief that the estrangement is caused due to the dominating nature of the foreign recruits over the local fighters. An amalgamation of these factors is leading to serious internal chaos within the group. As a result of the rising rift between the local and the foreign fighters, there has been a decline in the influx of foreign recruits. From an average influx of about 1,500—2,000 fighters every monthly till recently, the current speculated number is between 200 and 500.[40] This has been a major setback for ISIS which once boasted about its ability to recruit thousands of fighters from across the globe.

These challenges within Iraq and Syria are apparently leading to the expansion of activities elsewhere, and now ISIS is adopting new strategies or tactics. Increasing ISIS-connected activities in North Africa, Europe, Afghanistan, Bangladesh, and Southeast Asia are the manifestations of this. Some foreign recruits are likely to start moving towards other places where ISIS has established links. The attackers in Paris and Brussels were once in Syria where they received training. There is likely to be recurrences of similar assaults, particularly in other parts of Europe. This is also primarily due to the reason that there are already Islamist networks many European countries capable of providing logistical support for carrying out attacks. With their back-up and financing, Paris/Brussels-like carnage will not remain an impossible task. As estimated by an American terror-financing analyst, the total cost of the Brussels attack was between US$ 10,000 and US$ 15,000 only which, according to him, is "cheap."[41] Orders for further attacks need not come from the leadership in Syria but can be executed by the returnees or local outfits which have been heavily influenced by ISIS. The continuous evolution of extremism or jihadism will sustain these radical elements, whether the Sunni outfit is destroyed or not.

India and ISIS

While India continues to face threats from terror organisations—the Lashkar-e-Taiba (LeT), Jaish-e-Mohammed (JeM), and Hizbul Mujahideen—it is also concerned with the rise of ISIS. Initially, India's main concern was the safety of the migrant workers who are in the Persian Gulf countries. The West Asian region alone gave India remittances worth US$

35 billion during 2014–2015. As a result, it is a very important region in terms of economic reasons. The deterioration of the security and political order in West Asia is watched by New Delhi with much concern. In the light of this, the manner in which ISIS has spread its influence worldwide is taken seriously by India like any other country elsewhere.[42]

India was always been more worried about its citizens residing in West Asia; indeed it hardly thought that ISIS influence would penetrate into the country.[43] However, this perception was short lived as it has made several ISIS-connected arrests. The initial complacency of the Indian establishment was because an insignificant number of Indian Muslims joined the organisation in Syria or Iraq, and there has been no attack conducted by it. Many were under the impression that Muslims in India are well integrated into mainstream society, and are not affected by extremist ideology. Because of this belief, many in the country do not view ISIS as a major threat while there are others who remain wary, particularly considering the its export of terror and ideology. The departure of four Muslim youths from Kalyan in Maharashtra to Iraq in July 2014 received some attention; but it did not trigger an immediate concern in India.

However, the situation changed after one of the youths returned to India after serving briefly in the so-called "Caliphate" and during interrogation, exposed certain previously unknown facts, some of which included the role of the social media in radicalisation and recruitment, the presence of insiders within the country who make the necessary arrangements for travel, and most importantly, the nexus that exists between Indians in the country and abroad, particularly in the Persian Gulf countries. These are some characteristics of the workings of ISIS which have been noticed in other countries too.

Over a period of time, ISIS-connected activities in India have escalated, and are no longer dormant. Security agencies—mainly the National Intelligence Agency (NIA), Anti-Terrorist Squad (ATS), and state police—have arrested over 50 ISIS supporters/sympathisers between late 2015 and mid-2016.[44] This dispels the myth that Indian Muslims are immune to the lure of ISIS propaganda or that only a few youths joining it hardly makes any difference. Geographical distance is not a barrier which prevents radicalised persons from travelling to be in the caliphate. Despite a strict surveillance being put into place in India under difficult circumstances, instances of radicalisation and recruitment have been discovered. This is causing great concern to the government, the security agencies, and the civil society. This is taking place at this crucial stage when ISIS's end is being predicted repeatedly by various strategists and analysts who are looking at the current scenarios in Syria and Iraq. Thus, while it is losing ground in Syria, Iraq, and Libya, the successful penetration of its influence in other countries is sustaining its profile as an organisation which the international community has to continuously fight against. It should be acknowledged that ISIS has been transformed from a mere physical entity that could be toppled militarily to an idea which is getting harder to counter. It is the latter phenomenon which is currently being seen in India.

While the threats from ISIS need not be either exaggerated or underplayed, the authorities in India and its citizens should at least be aware of the fact that the country is under the radar of people who are highly influenced by this organisation. This is where the threats from the radicalised youths hold substance. Regardless of how many radicalised people were absorbed as well as the 22-minutue video clip released in May 2016 by ISIS with a specific focus on India and South Asia,[45] it is true that radicalised Muslim youth are either allegedly travelling to Syria or are planning operations by remaining in the country. ISIS has tried to invoke anti-state sentiments by referring to the "violence against Muslims in many places, including Mumbai, Gujarat, Assam and Moradabad."[46] There are reports of 21 youths from Kerala who have gone missing, with a few allegedly joining ISIS. Moreover, the arrests in Hyderabad by the NIA are an indication of the developments which have taken place in India. These impressionable youths had access to weapons systems, possessed lethal explosive-related chemicals, and received financial assistance from their handlers, both in India and abroad.[47]

Although the terror plots by these radicalised people in India were foiled, the above-mentioned ISIS-connected developments are worrisome. The phenomenon of radicalisation of youths in different Indian states should be monitored closely, and be dealt with accordingly. In this context, a robust coordination between civil society and security establishments is crucial. Incitement to violence in person, or through social media tools by influential leaders, or ideologues in the country needs to be countered ideologically.

As ISIS influence has already penetrated India, it is the duty of civilian society, alongside security apparatus, to put up a commendable job in tackling the menace. There are constant efforts from the Ministry of Home Affairs (MHA)—in coordination with state police—not just to nab terror-linked people but also to prevent departures of such elements to the conflict-ridden West Asian countries (Syria/Iraq). These security authorities are also roping in families and peer groups while fighting the problem of radicalisation. It is because of this, the Indian Home Minister emphasised the strength of "India's traditions and values". A constant monitoring of suspicious youths and their activities is in place. Moreover, as this phenomenon is predominantly seen in Muslim society, several religious leaders, Non-government organisations (NGOs), and civilian organisations from the community itself are coming out in the public and condemning the atrocities committed by outfits like ISIS in the name of religion. Notwithstanding these positive arrangements, the challenges ahead are still enormous as it is not only a fight against individuals or a terror group but also against an ideology which has spread far and wide.

Likely Consequences

The ongoing coalition military operations in Syria and Iraq are putting tremendous pressure on ISIS fighters. However, there are also a couple of parallel activities taking place beyond West Asia which need to be considered. The first is the return-journeys of well-trained foreign fighters back to their native countries. The second comprises the rise of lone-actor/ wolf attacks, both in the USA and Europe. This particular phenomenon is raising many security concerns.

Earlier, terrorism comprised of coordinated attacks by existing organisations which had developed the wherewithal to inflict damage. However, this has changed with the induction of unknown lone wolves whose actions are difficult to detect and deter. A vast majority of attacks in the Western world have either been carried out by ISIS operatives or by the lone wolves who have drawn inspiration from the organisation. Activities by these individuals have gone in favour of this outfit which continuously attempts to spread its tentacles all over the world.

With the significant decline in the influx of fighters into Iraq and Syria, a pertinent question has arisen: is the "terrorism threat ... actually easing or just morphing into a more dangerous new phase"?[48] This is where the relevance of the returnees comes into the picture as a new phase may be in the offing. There is the possibility of the returnees teaming up with those who have been radicalised but who have not had an opportunity to travel abroad. In other words, the return journeys are likely to exacerbate the problem of violent extremism domestically.

The concerns emanating out of such reversal will be serious not only in countries such as Tunisia, Saudi Arabia, Russia, Turkey, and Jordan (from where highest numbers of foreign fighters joined ISIS)[49] but also in Europe, and as far as Australia. The problem is not only from people departing for Syria/Iraq anymore; it emanates more from the threats emerging from those who are fleeing the strongholds of ISIS. While it has to be acknowledged that not all the returning foreign fighters will want to continue fighting or "form the next generation of global jihadists";[50] however, the presence of even a small fraction with such inclinations should not be taken lightly. Some of them are still convinced "of the righteousness of their cause". This is mostly applicable in the European context, where there is an exponential rise of radicalisation. A study conducted by the Sydney-based Lowy Institute points out that "the future foreign fighter cohort in Syria and Iraq [can be divided] into four categories". These include "...those who choose to remain in Syria and Iraq; those who leave in order to continue violent jihad in another theatre, either at home or elsewhere; those who seek to return to their country of origin; and those who go to a third country of refuge".[51]

Being concerned with the surge in attacks, European and American security officials have expressed concerns about the likely fallout of the military defeats of ISIS. The risk is acute in Europe which has faced a few brazen attacks. For instance, French Prime Minister Manuel Valls (2014–2016) mentioned that there are "nearly 700 jihadists who are either French or live in France are in Iraq and Syria at the moment", and "their return represents an additional threat to our national security... it's going to be a long fight".[52] Moreover, news of ISIS-connected lone-wolf activities and similarly terrifying incidents has been widely reported from Belgium, Germany, and the USA since the last few months. While some of these turned out to be ISIS-directed/inspired, there have been cases when the organisation's connections with the perpetrators were tenuous. Tellingly, a dreaded concoction of mental-health illness, an increase in violence streaks, and religion-based radicalisation are on the upswing, resulting in acts of terror. Lone-wolf attacks are gradually instilling fear amongst civilians. This is more so because of the nature of their target audience, and the locations in which terror attacks are perpetrated such as theatres, pubs, malls, train stations, airports, etc. Between inspired individuals who act alone and those terrorist operatives acting at the orders of leaders from Syria or Iraq, there are also individuals who "operate somewhere between the two extremes".[53] And, as ISIS has heralded many of these attacker its 'soldiers', a copious amount of investigation is required to get to the bottom of the matter and challenge this narrative. However, their presence is increasingly becoming a serious menace for counterterrorism agencies.

Conclusion

The international community cannot afford to remain complacent by merely looking at the decline of ISIS in West Asia. The society in the region is extremely divided on the lines of ethnicity and sect. This Sunni-terror group has further deepened the issue of sectarianism in this part of the world. The unresolved Syrian crisis is also likely to exacerbate the problem in the region. In Iraq, too, the future is still very uncertain as a unity between Shia and Sunni seems apparently impossible. Even if ISIS is eliminated, there is no clarity about who would rule the evicted territories, and this problem will be exacerbated due to the involvement of the Kurds, the Turks, and the Iranians in the fight against the organisation in both these West Asian countries. Each one of these players, undoubtedly, has their own interests.

Moreover, as ISIS is losing ground, it is likely to turn to insurgency in its core areas in West Asia while its fleeing fighters are likely to conduct sporadic attacks in their native countries. The latter scenario is a matter of grave concern, given the rising phenomenon of home grown extremism and radicalisation in different countries. The undetectable nature of these radicalised lots will remain a major security challenge. In the wake of threats coming from radicalised individuals, returnees, and terrorist operatives, there is need for higher security vigilance and enhanced coordination between the agencies of different countries. One should be cognizant of the fact that the threats are fast changing from direct attacks to that of ISIS-inspired ones and they are rapidly spreading. As the foreign fighters go home, they will carry the terror ideology along with them.

Finally, alongside military measures, there is urgent need to counter ISIS's pernicious ideology which has already been received favourably by several terror outfits and individuals in different corners of the world. In the light of this, a comprehensive counter-narrative to tackle radicalisation should be implemented which, otherwise, is dreadfully lacking at the moment.

NOTES

1. Heiber, Stefan, Nerumann, Peter R., Holland-McCown and Basra, Rajan, "Caliphate in Decline: An Estimate of Islamic State's Financial Fortunes", The International Center for the Study of Radicalisation and Political Violence, 17 February 2017, p. 3.
2. Cockburn, Patrick, "Who are ISIS? The Rise of the Islamic State in Iraq and the Levant", *The Independent*, 16 June 2014.
3. For a brief introduction to the Al-Nusra Front, see "Al Nusra Front", *Mapping Militant Organizations*, 24 July 2014, Stanford University, at http://web.stanford.edu/group/mappingmilitants/cgi-bin/groups/view/493, accessed 18 September 2016.
4. Wright, Berger, et al., *The Jihadi Threat: ISIS, Al-Qaeda and Beyond*, Washington

DC: Woodrow Wilson Centre, United States Institute of Peace, December 2016/ January 2017, p. 7.

5. Weiss, Michael and Hassan, Hassan, *ISIS: Inside the Army of Terror,* New York: Regan Arts, 2015, p. 186.
6. Ibid. p. 8.
7. "Foreign Fighters: An Updated Assessment of the Flow of Foreign Fighters into Syria and Iraq", The Soufan Group,December 2015, p. 5.
8. Berger, J.M. and Morgan, Jonathan, "The ISIS Twitter Census: Defining and describing the population of ISIS supporters on Twitter", *I* Paper, No. 20, Brookings, 20 March 2015.
9. Torok, Robyn, "ISIS and the Institution of Online Terrorist Recruitment", Middle East Institute, 29 January 2015, at http://www.mei.edu/content/map/isis-and-institution-online-terrorist-recruitment?print=, accessed 7 January 2017.
10. Levitt, Mathew, "Terrorist Financing and the Islamic State", The Washington Institute for Near East Policy, 13 November 2014.
11. Rogin, Josh, "America's Allies are funding ISIS", The Daily Beast,14 June 2014, at http://www.thedailybeast.com/articles/2014/06/14/america-s-allies-are-funding-isis.html, accessed 23 December 2016.
12. Heiber, Stefan, Nerumann, Peter R., Holland-McCown and Basra, Rajan, "Caliphate in Decline: An Estimate of Islamic State's Financial Fortunes", The International Center for the Study of Radicalisation and Political Violence, 17 February 2017, p. 8. See also, Boghardt, Lori Plotkin, "Saudi Funding of ISIS", The Washington Institute for Near East Policy, *Policy Watch* No. 2275, 23 June 2014.
13. McCoy, Terrence, "ISIS just stole $425 million, Iraqi governor says, and became the 'world's richest terror group", *The Washington Post,* 12 June 2014, at http://www.washingtonpost.com/news/morning-mix/wp/2014/06/12/isis-just-stole-425-million-and-became-the-worlds-richest-terrorist-group/ , accessed 23 December 2016.
14. Lock, Helen, "How ISIS became the wealthiest terror group in history", *The Independent,* 15 September 2014, at http://www.independent.co.uk/news/world/middle-east/how-isis-became-the-wealthiest-terror-group-in-history-9732750.html, accessed 23 December 2016.
15. Ibid.
16. Al-Khatteeb, Luay, and Gordts, Eline, "How ISIS Uses Oil to Fund Terror", *Brookings,*27 September 2014, at https://www.brookings.edu/on-the-record/how-isis-uses-oil-to-fund-terror/. See also, 'Is Turkey Really Benefitting from Oil Trade With ISIS?', at http://time.com/4132346/turkey-isis-oil/, accessed 23 December 2016.
17. Heiber, Nerumann, Holland-McCown and Basra, 'Caliphate in Decline: An Estimate of Islamic State's Financial Fortunes', op cit., p. 5.
18. Lister, Charles, "Profiling the Islamic State", Brookings Doha Center Analysis Paper, No. 13, November, 2014, p. 4.
19. Wood, Graeme, "What ISIS Really Wants", *The Atlantic,* March 2016, at https://www.theatlantic.com/magazine/archive/2015/03/what-isis-really-wants/384980/, accessed 18 January 2017
20. Arango, Tim, "Key Iraqi City Falls to ISIS as Last of Security Forces Flee", *The*

New York Times, 17 May 2015, at http://www.nytimes.com/2015/05/18/world/middleeast/isis-ramadi-iraq.html

21. Ibid.
22. "Isis fighters destroy ancient artefacts at Mosul museum", *The Guardian,* 26 February 2015, at http://www.theguardian.com/world/2015/feb/26/isis-fighters-destroy-ancient-artefacts-mosul-museum-iraq, accessed 15 August 2017.
23. Velozo, Thiago and Vento, Lucas, "ISIS is Destroying Priceless Artefacts. Here's How to Stop Them", *The Diplomat,* 17 March 2015, at http://thediplomat.com/2015/03/isis-is-destroying-priceless-artifacts-heres-how-to-stop-them/, accessed 20 September 2016
24. Pecanha, Sergio and Watkins, Derek, "'ISIS' Territory Shrank in Syria and Iraq This Year", *The New York Times,* 22 December 2015
25. Nour Malas et al., "U.S. Allies in Syria Cut Islamic State Supply Line", *Wall Street Journal,* 16 June 2015.
26. 'ISIS has lost quarter of its territory', *Daily Mail,* 9 October 2016.
27. "At least 72 dead in suspected chemical attack in Syria", *Fox News,* 5 April 2017.
28. "Tests show Isis used mustard gas in Iraq, says diplomat at chemical watchdog", *The Guardian,* 16 February 2016.
29. For further discussions, see "ISIL/ Da'esh and 'non-conventional' weapons of terror", Briefing,European Parliament, December 2015, at http://www.europarl.europa.eu/thinktank/en/document.html?reference=EPRS_BRI(2015)572806 See also, Bar-Yaacov, Naomi, "What if Isis launches a chemical attack in Europe?" *The Guardian,* 27 November 2015.
30. For detailed information, see Yourish, Karen, et al., "Where ISIS has Directed and Inspired Attacks around the World", *The New York Times,* 22 March 2016.
31. Ningthoujam, Alvite Singh, "Paris is Both a Lesson and A Message", *Tehelka,* Issue 28, Vol. 12, pp. 38–39.
32. Solomon, Erika, et al., "Inside Isis Inc: The Journey of a barrel of oil", *Financial Times,* 29 February 2016. On Turkey, see Phillips, David L., "Research Paper: Turkey-ISIS Oil Trade", *The Huffington Post,* 15 December 2015.
33. Faucon, Benoit, and Coker, Margaret, "The Rise and Fall of Islamic State's Oil Tycoon", *The Wall Street Journal,* 24 April 2016.
34. Heiber, Nerumann, Holland-McCown and Basra, "Caliphate in Decline: An Estimate of Islamic State's Financial Fortunes", op. cit., p. 5.
35. "ISIS is struggling to fund its war machine", *CNN Money,*21 April 2016.
36. "Islamic State to halve fighters' salaries as cost of waging terror starts to bite", *The Guardian,* 20 January 2016.
37. Nelson, Brad and Sulaiman, Yohanes, "How Internal Division could Shatter ISIS", *TheNational Interest,*8 April 2016.
38. Bradley, Matt, "Rift Grows in Islamic State between Foreign, Local Fighters", *Wall Street Journal,*25 March 2016.
39. "ISIS Considers Indian Recruits Inferior to Arabs, Treats Them as Cannon Fodder", *NDTV Report,* 23 November 2015.
40. Strobel, Warren, and Stewart, Phill, "US military softens claims on drop in Islamic State's foreign fighters", *Reuters,*28 April 2016.
41. "US Military Campaign Takes Toll on ISIS' Cash Flow", *The New York Times,* 12 April 2016.

42. Ningthoujam, Alvite Singh, "Rising Presence of Daesh in India", Articles,Vivekananda International Foundation, 1 August 2016.
43. Ningthoujam, Alvite Singh, "Islamic State of Iraq and Its South Asian Connection: An Indian Perspective", Occasional Paper,Vivekananda International Foundation, November 2014.
44. "54 ISIS supporters arrested: Govt", *The Times of India*, 26 July 2016.
45. "Islamic States releases video allegedly showing Indian jihadists fighting in Syria", *The Indian Express*, 20 May 2016.
46. "Coming to avenge Babri, Kashmir, Gujarat, Muzaffarnagar: ISIS video", *The Indian Express*, 21 May 2016.
47. "Explosives links Hyderabad to Paris and Brussels", *The Times of India*, 1 July 2016.
48. Witte, Griff, et al., "Flow of foreign fighters plummets as Islamic States loses its edge", *The Washington Post*,9 September 2016.
49. "Foreign Fighters: An Updated Assessment of the Flow of Foreign Fighters into Syria and Iraq", The Soufan Group,December 2015,
50. Burke, Liz, "Returned Jihadists: The horror that comes after Islamic State", News.com.au,28 September 2016.
51. Khalil, Lydia, and Shanahan, Rodger, *Foreign Fighters in Syria and Iraq: The Day After*, Analysis, Lowy Institute, September 2016, p. 7.
52. "Ticking Time Bomb of Foreign ISIS Fighters Returning Home", *NDTV*, 9 September 2016.
53. Levitt, Mathew, *The New York Bomber was not a Lone Wolf*, The Washington Institute for Near East Policy,21 September 2016, at http://www.washingtoninstitute.org/policy-analysis/view/the-new-york-bomber-was-not-a-lone-wolf

The Mentors

Ambassador A.R. Ghanashyam has a Post Graduate degree in Physics and Business Management. After working in the Oil & Gas and Shipping industries for six years, he spent three and a half decades in the Indian diplomatic corps in Syria, Nepal, Pakistan, Belgium, United States, and Africa. He has been the Indian Envoy to eight countries including Angola and Nigeria. He has also overseen Indian bilateral relations with countries in South Asia, the Gulf, and Africa. He has also worked on Climate Change in the Ministry of External Affairs. He now advises Indian and foreign entities and speaks on international economics and foreign policy issues.

Dr. Javed Ahmed Khan is Professor and Officiating Director atthe Centre for West Asian Studies in Jamia Millia Islamia, (Central University) in New Delhi. He is currently engaged in teaching and research in the finance and economy of West Asian countries. His publications include *India and West Asia: Emerging Markets in the Liberalisation Era* (1999); *India's Energy Security and the Arabian Gulf* (2005); and *Islamic Banking in India: Scope and Challenges* (edited 2003). He has also been the editor of the bi-monthly *Islamic Economics Bulletin* (1991–2003). His areas of academic interest include Indo-Arab economic and energy relations, modern Arab economies, and Islamic banking and finance in West Asia.

Ambassador Ranjit Gupta has spent 39 years in the Indian Foreign Service. During his first posting in Cairo, though only a Third Secretary probationer, he was hand picked by the National Liberation Front of South Yemen to be their Advisor for their independence talks with the British in Geneva in November 1967. When the entire world believed that the Royalists would overthrow the Republican regime in Yemen in the winter of 1967/68, he—still a Third Secretary persuaded his influential Ambassador, Apasahab Pant, that the Republican regime would not fall. Consequently, in January 1968, he was deputed to Sana'a as the Prime Minister's Special

Envoy to express India's support for the beseiged Republican regime in Yemen. During his career, he has served as Third Secretary in Cairo; the Deputy Chief of Mission in Jeddah (the first non-Muslim Foreign Service officer to be posted to Saudi Arabia); and as the last Head of the undivided West Asia and North Africa Division dealing with Arab countries and Israel. Amongst his subsequent six Head of Mission postings, he served as India's Ambassador in Yemen and Oman.

Ambassador Sanjay Singh is an alumnus of Delhi University, from where obtained a Masters degree in Physics. He joined the Indian Foreign Service in 1976, and has served in Indian Missions in Mexico, Germany, Ghana, France, and Vietnam, as well as in the Ministry of External Affairs, New Delhi on various assignments. He served as Joint Secretary and Additional Secretary in the Gulf Division (from March 2005 to March 2009); was Ambassador to Iran during 2009–2011; and was Secretary (East) from March 2011 and till April 2013, when he retired. Since then, he has been following developments in West Asia and India's relations with the region closely. He has also been participating in numerous activities related to the study of West Asia.

Ambassador Sudhir Vyas retired in 2013 as Secretary in the Ministry of External Affairs, Government of India after over 36 years in the Indian Foreign Service. Born on 24 September 1953, Ambassador Vyas graduated with a B.Tech degree in Engineering from the Indian Institute of Technology in Kanpur (1975), and was selected to join the Indian Foreign Service in 1977. After serving in Indian Missions in Nepal, Algeria, Egypt, and at the Permanent Mission of India to the UN in New York, he was posted as Deputy High Commissioner in Pakistan (1999–2003), and Tanzania. He served as Ambassador of India to the UAE (2003–2005); to Bhutan (2005–2009); and to Germany (2009–2011). He has held various positions in the Ministry of External Affairs in New Delhi, including as Head of Division Level dealing with SAARC and India's northern neighbours. He has also held Secretary-level positions dealing with India's bilateral relationships with Europe, Canada, Africa, and Latin America, with a focus on India's Economic Relations.

Ambassador Talmiz Ahmad joined the Indian Foreign Service in 1974. He served as India's Ambassador to Saudi Arabia (2000–03; 2010–11); to Oman (2003–04), and the UAE (2007–10). He was also Additional Secretary for International Cooperation in the Ministry of Petroleum and Natural Gas in 2004–06. He has published three books: *Reform in the Arab World: External Influences and Regional Debates* (2005), *Children of Abraham at War:*

the Clash of Messianic Militarisms (2010), and *The Islamist Challenge in West Asia: Doctrinal and Political Competitions after the Arab Spring*(2013).He writes and lectures frequently on Political Islam, the Politics of West Asia, and Energy Security issues.

Dr. Meena Singh Roy is currently a Research Fellow and Coordinator West Asia Centre at the Institute for Defence Studies and Analysis (IDSA), New Delhi, India. She was previously a senior research scholar in the Department of African Studies, University of Delhi. She has been associated with Institute of Commonwealth Studies and the School of Oriental & African Studies (London) for research work. She also has been a Visiting Research Fellow at the German Institute of Global and Area Studies; at the Institute of Asian Studies (GIGA); and at the Begin-Sadat Centre for Strategic Studies Israel. She has been involved in net assessment reports on Central Asia. She has authored many national and international publications.

Professor P.R. Kumaraswamy teaches the Contemporary Middle East in Jawaharlal Nehru University, New Delhi, and is the author of *India's Israel Policy* (Columbia University Press, 2010) and the *Historical Dictionary of the Arab-Israeli conflict* (Scarecrow Press, 2015). He is also the Honorary Director of Middle East Institute, New Delhi. He is available at www.mei.org.in

Ambassador V.P. Haran is a former diplomat. He was Ambassador to Syria (2009–2012) and Bhutan (2013–2014]. He has served in Moscow, Kabul, Colombo, Brussels, Geneva and Kathmandu. He has extensive experience in neighbourhood diplomacy and international trade issues, and was in West Asia when the Arab Spring set in. He was in Syria when the troubles unfolded in that country. His interests include international affairs and trade. He has contributed occasional articles to reputed journals.

The Contributors

Dr. Adil Rasheed is a Research Fellow at the Institute for Defence Studies and Analyses (IDSA). Earlier, he was Senior Research Fellow at the United Service Institution of India. He has served at the Abu Dhabi-based Emirates Centre for Strategic Studies and Research for eight years (2006–2014). He was also Editor (Newsdesk) and political commentator of the Dubai-based daily newspaper *Khaleej Times* from 2000 to 2005. He is the author of a book titled *ISIS: Race to Armageddon* (2015).

Dr. Alvite Singh Ningthoujam is a Senior Research Associate at Vivekananda International Foundation, New Delhi, India, and looks after Middle Eastern security dynamics, international terrorism—the Islamic State of Iraq and Syria (ISIS) in particular. He has also focused on Israel's arms exports, Indo-Israel/Iranian relations, and Israeli-Southeast Asian ties. Before submitting his Ph.D thesis in July 2016 to Jawaharlal Nehru University (JNU), he also served as a Fellow at the Begin-Sadat (BESA) Centre for Strategic Studies, Bar-Ilan University, Israel (2010–2011). His articles have been published in the *Jerusalem Post*, *Asia Times*, *The National Interest*, *The Diplomat*, *Indian Defence Review*, *RUSI News Brief*, *World Focus*, *Unmanned Flying Machines*, and the *Daily Pioneer*. He also writes for the International Strategic and Security Studies Program (ISSSP-India), and the International Institute for Counter-Terrorism, Israel.

Ashiya Parveen is a Ph.D student at the School of International Studies, Jawaharlal Nehru University, New Delhi. She did her M.Phil from the Academy of International Studies, Jamia Millia Islamia, New Delhi. Her areas of research include the History and Politics of West Asia, the Arab Uprisings, Global Media, Egypt, and Yemen.

Colonel Rajeev Agarwal was commissioned into the Regiment of Artillery of the Indian army in June 1990, and has had varied operational and service experience for over 26 years. He has commanded his Regiment on the Line of Control in Jammu and Kashmir. He has been Director Military Intelligence at the Army HQ, and a military observer with the United Nations in DRC. He has held Research Fellowship at IDSA, New Delhi, and holds a Master's degree in Defence and Strategic Studies from Madras University. His published works include "Security in the Gulf Region: India's Concerns, Vulnerabilities, Interests and Engagement Options", in Rumel Dahiya (ed.) *Developments in the Gulf Region: Prospects and Challenges For India in the Next Two Decades* (2013); "'Arab Spring' and Democracy: Possibility or an Elusive Idea", *Indian Foreign Affairs Journal*, Vol. 8, No.4 (2013); "Turkey and its Quest for Leadership Role in the West Asian Region, IDSA Monograph Series No.32 (2014); "US Pivot to the Asia Pacific: Impact and Implications for West Asia" (Co-authored), in S.D. Muni and Vivek Chadha (eds.) *Asian Strategic Review 2014: US Pivot and Asian Security* (2014); "Threat of Israel's Regional Isolation and Imperatives for the Future", IDSA Occasional Paper No. 34 (2014); "Egypt's Uneasy Transition: Internal and External Dynamics and Challenges for India", IDSA Occasional Paper No. 35 (2014); "Afghanistan Post-2014: Can India Emerge as a Key 'Security Collaborator'?" in S.D. Muni and Vivek Chadha (eds.) *Asian Strategic Review 2015: US Pivot and Asian Security* (2015); "Gulf Security Architecture and the GCC: Time to Shed Past Baggage and Start Anew", in P.K. Pradhan (ed.) *Geopolitical Shifts in West Asia: Trends and Implications* (2016).

Dipanwita Chakravortty is a doctoral candidate in the Centre of West Asian Studies, Jawaharlal Nehru University. Her thesis is on "The Gender Debates in the Israel Defence Forces." She is a recipient of the Israeli Government Scholarship 2015–2016 under which she was located in the Ben-Gurion University as a Research Fellow in the Conflict Management and Resolution Program. She has written various articles/chapters on India-Yemen relations, the conflict in Yemen, and on Elections in the Middle East.

Dr. Moinuddin Ahmad is a New Delhi-based journalist and researcher, currently working as the News Editor of Indiatimes.com. Previously, he has worked in different editorial positions with *The Statesman*. He has an M.Phil and Ph.D in West Asian studies, focusing on Israeli politics and political groups. His areas of interest include Israeli studies, the Jewish Diaspora, Muslim political groups, comparative religion, and anthropology.

Dr. Muddassir Quamar is an Associate Fellow at the Institute for Defence Studies and Analyses (IDSA), New Delhi. He obtained a Ph.D degree in Middle East studies from Jawaharlal Nehru University, New Delhi (2016). His research interests include contemporary Gulf societies, Political Islam, and Indo-Gulf relations. In 2014–15, he was a visiting fellow in the King Faisal Centre for Research and Islamic Studies, Riyadh. He has published research papers in reputed national and international journals, and contributes opinion pieces for many India-based websites. He also serves as an Associate Editor of the *Contemporary Review of the Middle East* (Sage, India).

Manjari Singh is a doctoral candidate at the Centre for West Asian Studies in Jawaharlal Nehru University, New Delhi, and is also a Ryoichi Sasakawa Young Leaders Fellowship Fund (SYLFF) fellow. Her areas of interest are Development Studies, Sustainable Development, and Environment Studies.

Neha Kohli is Associate Editor, *Journal of Defence Studies*, published by the Institute for Defence Studies and Analyses (IDSA), New Delhi. She has a Bachelors' degree in Journalism from Delhi University; a Masters degree in International Relations; and an MPhil degree in West Asian Studies from Jawaharlal Nehru University, New Delhi. She has worked in the print media as well as in academic publishing prior to her present position.

S. Samuel C. Rajiv is Associate Fellow, Institute for Defence Studies and Analyses (IDSA), New Delhi. His recent publications include *Iran Sanctions and India: Navigating the Consequences* (IDSA, July 2016) and *Indian Responses to Israel's Gaza Operations* (BESA, May 2016). He was awarded the IDSA President's Award for Excellence in 2014 and 2013 for the best articles published during the year in a refereed journal. These were "Politicised Safeguards: Iran-IAEA Contentions, Drivers, Policy Implications" (in *Strategic Analysis*, September 2014), and "In Pursuit of a Chimera: Nuclear Imbroglio between Sanctions and Engagement" (in *Strategic Analysis*, November 2012). He is concurrently pursuing his Ph.D in the Centre for West Asian Studies (CWAS), Jawaharlal Nehru University, New Delhi.

Dr. Sameena Hameed is Assistant Professor in the Gulf Studies Programme, Centre for West Asian Studies, School of International Studies, Jawaharlal Nehru University, New Delhi. Her areas of specialisation include the West Asian Economy and India's economic relations with West Asia as well as Energy Security issues. She has been a member of a MEA constituted 'Select Group on Gulf and West Asia '. She was also the member of Indian team for "The India-GCC Strategic Partnership", jointly organised by Gulf Research Council, Dubai, and the Public Diplomacy Division, MEA, New Delhi. She has also been the member of the Indian delegations in the first, second, third, and fourth interactions during the Indo-Saudi Dialogue in New Delhi and Riyadh.

Shafat Yousuf is currently pursuing an MPhil in the Centre for West Asian Studies, Jamia Millia Islamia, New Delhi. He has an M.A. degree in Political Science from the University of Hyderabad (HCU), and a B.A. (Hons.) degree in German Studies from Jawaharlal Nehru University (JNU), New Delhi. His is currently working on Iran's ideological apparatus as well as its defence and foreign policies. His M.A. dissertation was on *Wilayat al-Faqih*. He has presented papers in different seminars and workshops, including one on Iran's nuclear policy at a workshop in Middle Eastern Studies Research Network (MESnet), University of Exeter (UK).

Tanzoom Ahmed is a Research Associate at Delhi Policy Group. She holds a Master's degree in Public Policy from George Mason University, Washington DC (USA). Her special focus was on International Governance and Institutions. She has a Bachelor's degree in English Literature from the Clarion University of Pennsylvania. She has worked as the Political and Economic Officer at the Consulate General of Singapore, Mumbai. She also headed the membership team at a Mumbai based foreign policy think tank named Gateway House. She has also interned with several organisations, including the Study of Terrorism and Responses to Terrorism (START), University of Maryland; the National Women's Law Centre in Washington DC; and the Entrepreneur Magazine (Network 18) in New Delhi. She is an US State Department Alumni and a Fulbright Fellow.

Dr. Tsupokyemla is a research scholar in the Centre for West Asian Studies, School of International Studies, Jawaharlal Nehru University, New Delhi. Her doctoral research is on Syria's role in Lebanon (1976–1989). She is currently working as a Documentation Officer in the Gulf Studies Programme, Jawaharlal Nehru University. Her research interests include the politics and foreign policies of Syria and Lebanon, as well as identity politics, ethnic conflicts, and conflict resolution in West Asia.

Index